The Cambridge Companion to Electronic Music

Musicians are always quick to adopt and explore new technologies.
The fast-paced changes wrought by electrification, from the
microphone via the analogue synthesiser to the laptop computer,
have led to a wide diversity of new musical styles and techniques.
Electronic music has grown to a broad field of investigation, taking in
historical movements such as musique concrète and elektronische
musik, and contemporary trends such as electronic dance music and
electronica. A fascinating array of composers and inventors have
contributed to a diverse set of technologies, practices and music. This
book brings together some novel threads through this scene, from
the viewpoint of researchers at the forefront of the sonic explorations
empowered by electronic technology. The chapters provide accessible
and insightful overviews of core topic areas and uncover some
hitherto less publicised corners of worldwide movements. Recent
areas of intense activity such as audiovisuals, live electronic music,
interactivity and network music are actively promoted.

The Cambridge Companion to

Electronic Music

. . . .

EDITED BY
Nick Collins and Julio d'Escriván

CAMBRIDGE
UNIVERSITY PRESS
Qm 154706335

CAMBRIDGE UNIVERSITY PRESS
Cambridge, New York, Melbourne, Madrid, Cape Town, Singapore, São Paulo, Delhi

Cambridge University Press
The Edinburgh Building, Cambridge CB2 8RU, UK

Published in the United States of America by Cambridge University Press, New York

www.cambridge.org
Information on this title: www.cambridge.org/9780521688659

© Cambridge University Press 2007

First published 2007

Printed in the United Kingdom at the University Press, Cambridge

A catalogue record for this publication is available from the British Library

ISBN 978-0-521-86861-7 hardback
ISBN 978-0-521-68865-9 paperback

Contents

Part III • Analysis and synthesis

Illustrations and figures

Notes on contributors

Amy Alexander is Assistant Professor of Visual Arts at the University of California, San Diego. Her artwork spans the fields of digital media art and audiovisual performance and has been presented on the Internet, in clubs and on the street, as well as in festivals and museums. Her projects include *The Multi-Cultural Recycler* (1996), *theBot* (2000), *CueJack* (2001), *CyberSpaceLand* (2003), *Scream* (2005) and *SVEN: Surveillance Video Entertainment Network* (2006). She is also a co-founder of the Runme.org software art repository and is active in curating and writing about software art.

Natasha Barrett (UK 1972) works as a freelance composer and performer of acousmatic and live electroacoustic music. Her compositional output consists of works for instruments and live electronics, sound installations, dance, theatre, and animation projects, but all energy stems from her acousmatic approach to sound and its spatio-musical potential. Barrett's projects are frequently commissioned from international organisations and her work has received awards in many of the prominent electroacoustic music competitions. In 2006 she received the Nordic Council Music Prize. Since completing her doctoral composition studies in London (1998) she has lived in Oslo, Norway. For more information: http://www.notam02.no/~natashab

Nick Collins (1975) is a lecturer in computer music at the University of Sussex, and has indulged in both mathematics and instrumental composition in the past. His interests run the gamut of topics in electronic music, but particular specialisms include algorithmic composition, live electronica, machine listening and interactive music systems. He occasionally tours the world as the non-Swedish half of the Swedish audiovisual laptop duo klipp av.

Nicolas Collins studied composition with Alvin Lucier, worked for many years with David Tudor, and has collaborated with soloists and ensembles around the world. He lived most of the 1990s in Europe, where he was Visiting Artistic Director of Stichting STEIM (Amsterdam), and a DAAD composer-in-residence in Berlin. He is a Professor in the Department of Sound at the School of the Art Institute of Chicago, and Editor-in-Chief of the Leonardo Music Journal. Recent recordings are available on PlateLunch, Periplum and Apestaartje. His book, *Handmade Electronic Music – The Art of Hardware Hacking*, was published by Routledge in 2006.

Julio d'Escriván is a composer who uses music technology, both for concert music, and in its applications to the moving image. He has twice won prizes at the International Electroacoustic Music Competition of Bourges, France. His electroacoustic music has been recorded, broadcast and performed in Europe and the Americas. He has worked extensively in music for TV advertising, documentaries and film with some incursions into new media. He is a senior lecturer in music at Anglia Ruskin University, Cambridge.

Karlheinz Essl was born in 1960 in Vienna. Austrian composer, improviser and performer. He studied composition with Friedrich Čerha and musicology at the University of Vienna (doctorate 1989, with a thesis on Anton Webern). Besides writing experimental instrumental music, he performs on his own computer-based electronic instrument, develops algorithmic composition software and creates generative sound and video environments. From 1990–4 he was composer-in-residence at the Darmstadt summer courses, and from 1992–3 he worked as a commissioned composer at IRCAM/Paris. In the period 1995–2006 he taught 'algorithmic composition' at the Bruckner-University in Linz. In 2007 he will become professor of composition at the University of Music and Performing Arts in Vienna.

Andrew Hugill (1957) is Director of the Institute Of Creative Technologies (IOCT) at De Montfort University, Leicester. Between 1976 and 1980, he studied composition with Roger Marsh at the University of Keele. After university he earned a living as a music copyist and as musical assistant at the Opéras de Lyon and Paris. Hugill's compositions have been performed and broadcast worldwide. *Symphony for Cornwall* (1999) used the internet in a ground-breaking way. Hugill's research is wide ranging and includes 'pataphysics, which is rooted in French literature. He is an Associate Researcher of the Université de Paris, Sorbonne, and his 2006 CD and booklet entitled *'Pataphysics* has received rave reviews in almost every European language.

Sergi Jordà (1961), digital luthier (*FMOL, reacTable . . .*) and improviser, likes to invent new digital musical instruments without forgetting to make music with them. His music has been released on various labels and compilations (Hazard Records, SGAE, MIT Press . . .), he has composed for different instrumental setups (including a brass band) and for films, but he prefers the immediacy and volatility of free improvisation. During the 1990s, he worked extensively in performances and installations in collaboration with other artists (La Fura dels Baus, Marcel.lí Antúnez . . .). He holds a Ph.D. in digital communication and is a researcher of the Music Technology Group of the Pompeu Fabra University, where he teaches computer music, audio programming, HCI and interactive media arts. He has written many articles and two books, and has given workshops, lectured and performed though Europe, Asia and America.

Julian Rohrhuber is a German artist and theorist, working in the fields of cultural theory, philosophy and media art. His art projects include installations and performances, film sound tracks, a system for interactive sound programming, and various collaborative and network art pieces. He currently works in a research project at the University of Cologne, and at the Academy of Media Arts Cologne, where he teaches algorithmic acoustics and works on art theory, programming and philosophy.

Margaret Anne Schedel is a composer and cellist specialising in the creation and performance of ferociously interactive media. While working towards a DMA in music composition at the University of Cincinnati, her thesis, an interactive multimedia opera, *A King Listens*, premiered at the Cincinnati Contemporary Arts Center. She is working towards a certificate in Deep Listening and serves as the musical director for Kinesthetech Sense. Margaret sits on the boards of the BEAM Foundation, the EMF Institute, the ICMA, NWEAMO, Organised Sound, and the Women's Audio Mission. Usually found in the San Francisco bay area, she runs workshops for Making Things.

Stefania Serafin is currently associate professor in sound modelling at Aalborg University in Copenhagen. She holds a Ph.D. in Computer Based Music Theory and Acoustics from CCRMA, Stanford University, and a Master in Acoustics, Signal Processing and Computer Science from IRCAM in Paris. She has been visiting researcher at Cambridge University, Stanford University and KTH in Stockholm, and visiting professor at the University of Virginia. Stefania has published her research on sound synthesis by physical models in the *Computer Music Journal,* the *Journal of New Music Research, Organised Sound,* and *IEEE Transactions of Speech and Audio Processing,* and she presents regularly at the International Computer Music Conference (ICMC), New Interfaces for Musical Expression (NIME), Digital Audio Effects (DAFX), and musical acoustics conferences.

Petri Toiviainen is a professor of music at the University of Jyväskylä, Finland, with a specialisation in music cognition. He has published numerous articles on computational modelling of music perception and cognition. Currently his research focuses on computational music analysis, music and movement, and modelling of musical emotions. He is the head of the Finnish Centre of Excellence in Interdisciplinary Music Research, located at the Universities of Jyväskylä and Helsinki.

Ge Wang received his B.Sc. in computer science from Duke University in 2000 and is a Ph.D. candidate studying with Perry Cook in Computer Science at Princeton University. Ge conducts research in computer music languages, interactive systems for sound synthesis/analysis and musical composition/performance, visualisation of sound, interface design, new performance ensembles (e.g. the Princeton Laptop Orchestra), live coding, and methodologies for education in computer science, computer music, and new media. Ge also composes and performs via various electroacoustic and computer-mediated means.

Acknowledgements

So begins a round of thanks to many individuals, and most especially, those we've inevitably forgotten to mention. The editors wish to thank all of the contributors to this book who've put up with our requests and editing. Without the chapter authors and the artists who have kindly provided statements, there would hardly be any book to have the honour of editing!

We also have to say a big thank you specifically to Vicki Cooper, Becky Jones, Helen Waterhouse, Jo Breeze, Michael Downes and all others associated with the production of the book at Cambridge University Press.

For external reviews of chapters we very much appreciate the time and effort of Robert Rowe, Chris Brown, Fredrik Olofsson, Bill Hsu, Alberto de Campo, Bob Gluck, Brian Kane, John Hawks, Michael Scroggins, Curtis Roads and Jøran Rudi. Additional proofreading and comments were provided by a number of the chapter authors.

For assistance with obtaining artists' statements, many thanks to Terumi Narushima, Joana Seguro, Daniel Klemm, Sharen Norden, Kathinka Pasveer, and of course to the various chapter authors, friends and enemies who themselves suggested people and helped us to get in contact with them.

Karlheinz Essl wishes to thank Florian Cramer (Rotterdam) for his attendance to discuss the history of algorithmic thinking in philosophy and literature and Jennifer Walshe (Berlin/New York) for proofreading the manuscript.

Meg Schedel owes a debt of gratitude to her proofreading parents, Rita and Charles Schedel.

Julian Rohrhuber appreciates the immensely useful advice from, and acknowledges the inspirations of, his colleagues. He'd like to thank Anthony Moore, Alberto de Campo, Renate Wieser, Chris Brown, Julio d'Escriván and Nick Collins for their generous interest in his article. He'd also like to express gratitude to Kurd Alsleben, Antje Eske, Jin Hyun Kim, Hannes Hölzl, Alex McLean, Frank Wörler, Guy van Belle, Georg Hajdu, Maarten Bullynck and many others, who pointed out numerous interesting aspects of networks and network art.

Ge Wang wishes to extend hearty thanks to Perry Cook for his teaching and insights on the history of programming and music, to Ananya Misra for providing invaluable feedback from beginning to end, to Mark Ballora for his excellent online history of computer music, to Max Mathews for information and perspective, and to Rebecca Fiebrink, Spencer Salazar and Matt Hoffman for their support.

Nick Collins thanks everyone who suffered any editorial attention from him, and acknowledges with great respect and warmth his collaborators and colleagues in the field. He particularly welcomes the support and essential input of his co-editor. He also wishes to extend a special thank you to the third person.

Julio d'Escriván wishes to thank Julian Rohrhuber for his review and suggestions. Also a special thanks to his co-editor, for roping him into this wonderful project and for his invaluable constructive criticism. A warm thanks to Sue Guilmurray from the university library at ARU, Cambridge. And . . . very especially he wishes to acknowledge the love, patience and support of Milly, Isa, Mari, Emi and Ana throughout this project.

Chronology

1928	Fritz Fleumer invents the magnetic tape recorder in Germany
	Maurice Martenot invents the *Ondes Martenot*
1929	Friedrich Trautwein invents the *Trautonium*
1931	First electroacoustic montage is created by the sound department of Paramount Studios in Hollywood, for the film *Jekyll and Hyde*
1932	In Oskar Fischinger's film, *Tönende Ornamente* (Ornament Sound), the soundtrack is created by drawing directly onto the optical soundtrack
1933	The theremin is used by composer Max Steiner to expand the timbral palette of the orchestra in the film *King Kong*
1936	Varèse publishes his manifesto *The Liberation of Sound*
1937	John Cage delivers his lecture *The Future of Music: CREDO*
1938	Orson Welles' *War of the Worlds* radio play successfully deceives its audience into believing a Martian invasion is taking place
1939	Cage begins working with live electronic sound in his piece *Imaginary Landscape No. 1*
1944	Egyptian-born Halim El-Dabh experiments by electronically processing recordings made with a wire recorder, a medium that predated tape
1946	*The Schillinger System of Musical Composition* is published posthumously
	Raymond Scott writes the patent disclosure for the 'orchestra machine'
1948	At the French National Radio-Television (RTF), Pierre Schaeffer experiments with mixing pre-recorded sources on various turntables and creates *Etude aux Chemins de Fer*. The RTF studios host the Groupe de Recherches Musicales (GRM)
	Claude Elwood Shannon publishes *A Mathematical Theory of Communication*
1951	Pierre Schaeffer and Pierre Henry compose *Symphonie pour un homme seule*, a landmark in musique concrète
	The Studio für Elektronische Musik at West German National Radio (WDR) is founded
	Percy Grainger invents the *Kangaroo Pouch Machine*
	The Columbia Tape Music Center, in New York, is started by Luenning and Ussachevsky. It would later become the Columbia–Princeton Electronic Music Center in 1959
	Louis and Bebe Barron compose *Heavenly Menagerie* in their studio, months before the more famous Cologne Studio is established
	Bernard Herrmann uses theremins as main instruments with the film orchestra in his score for *The Day the Earth Stood Still*
	Schaeffer investigates spatialisation with the *potentiomètre d'espace*
1952	Schaeffer publishes a syntax for musique concrète in the treatise *Esquisse d'un solfège concrète*
	Cage composes *Williams Mix*; the realisation takes a team of tape splicers (in reality, Louis and Bebe Barron) many months

1953	In Milan, the Studio di Fonologia is established. In Tokyo the Electronic Music Studio for Japan Radio (NHK) is opened
	Herbert Eimert composes *Struktur 8*
1950–4	Varèse composes *Déserts*, which combines an ensemble of live instrumentalists with tape
1955–9	Lejaren Hiller and Leonard Isaacson experiment with using a mainframe computer to algorithmically generate musical scores, composing the *Illiac Suite* for string quartet in 1957
1955	Iannis Xenakis publishes *The Crisis of Serial Music*, critiquing integral serialism on psychological and statistical grounds
1956	Louis and Bebe Barron create the first purely electronic film score for *Forbidden Planet*
	In The Netherlands, the Center for Electronic Music is established within the Philips Research Laboratory
	The BBC Radiophonic Workshop is founded
	Stockhausen's *Gesang der Jünglinge* combines concrète and elektronische
	Xenakis completes the first granular study – *Analogue B*
1957	In Warsaw, the Studio Experimentalne is established at Polish National Radio
	The Bell Telephone Laboratories host the first digital music experiments: Max Mathews programs the first sounds ever generated by a digital computer and creates *MUSIC 1*, the earliest programming environment for sound synthesis
1958	Xenakis designs the Philips Pavilion at the Brussels World's Fair for which Varèse composes *Poème électronique*; Xenakis also provides *Concrèt PH* for the interludes between shows
	In Santiago de Chile, the Laboratorio de Acústica is used for the earliest electronic music work done in South America
	Scott invents and begins development of the Electronium, an algorithmic composing machine without a musical keyboard
	In Toronto, the University of Toronto Electronic Music Studio is founded
1958–60	Stockhausen works on *Kontakte*
1960	Andreij Markowski creates, at the Experimental Studio in Warsaw, electronic music and sound design for *The Silent Star*, directed by Kurt Maetzig
	Raymond Scott composes a completely electronic soundtrack for the *Vicks: Medicated Cough Drops* commercial
1961	The Norsk Rikskringkasting (NRK) in Oslo allows its studios to be used for the earliest experiments in electronic music in Norway
	Kelly and Lochbaum design an algorithm to simulate the human vocal tract
	James Tenney creates the plunderphonic tape piece *Collage #1 (Blue Suede)*, sampling and manipulating a famous Elvis track

1962	In Buenos Aires, the Laboratorio de Música Electrónica associated to the Instituto Torcuato di Tella is founded; in Ghent, Belgium, the Institut vor Psychoakoestiek en Elektronische Muziek; in East Berlin, the Experimentalstudio für Kunstliche Klang und Gerauscherzeugung, Laboratorium für Akustisch-Musikalische Grenzprobleme
1963	Gottfried Michael Koenig's *Projekt 1* program is devised, for automatic aleatoric serial composition
1964	Stockhausen composes *Mikrophonie I* for amplified and processed tam-tam
	Jean-Claude Risset visits Bell Labs for the first time and uses MUSIC IV to investigate the timbre of trumpets
1965	Steve Reich creates his first phase piece: *It's Gonna Rain*
	Alvin Lucier creates his *Music for Solo Performer*, the first live electronics piece to use amplified alpha brainwaves
1967	In Gordon Mumma's composition *Hornpipe* (1967) an analogue device analyses and amplifies the resonances of the hall in which a performer is playing the French horn, thus predating interactive machine-listening systems
	John Chowning discovers Frequency Modulation sound synthesis
1968	MUSIC V becomes the first computer music programming system to be implemented in FORTRAN
	Tudor composes the first of his *Rainforest* pieces, featuring a multitude of objects acting as loudspeakers dangling directly from their cables
	Raymond Scott invents the first 'drum machine', *Bandito the bongo artist*
	Jean-Claude Risset creates a catalogue of computer-generated sounds at Bell Labs including guidelines to synthesise different musical instruments using MUSIC V; Risset also composes *Computer Suite from Little Boy*, utilising auditory illusions
	Wendy Carlos's *Switched-On Bach* achieves popular success, promoting Robert Moog's modular synthesisers
	Lee Scratch Perry sets up his Upsetter record label – the Jamaican sound system and studio scene is a fertile backdrop for the development of dub and the remix
1969	Max Mathews builds the GROOVE synthesiser, being the first to connect a computer to an analogue synthesiser
	First performance of Lejaren Hiller and John Cage's *HPSCHD*, for massed audiovisual forces
	Luc Ferrari's *music promenade* manipulated field recording
1970	Pierre Boulez founds the Institut de Recherche et Coordination Acoustique/Musique (IRCAM)
1970–2	François Bayle's *L'expérience acoustique*

1971   Richard Teitelbaum's piece *Alpha Bean Lima Brain* involves the
transmission of brain waves by telephone to control jumping beans
    Walter Carlos creates the electronically instrumental score for
A Clockwork Orange by Stanley Kubrick
    Hiller and Ruiz develop the first computer simulations by physical
models, of instrumental sounds
    John Chowning describes techniques for the computer simulation
of moving sound sources that are based on the Doppler effect as well
as reverberation effects
    Tonto's Expanding Head Band release the psychedelic and
progressive *Zero Time*, composed with the expanded Series III Moog
synthesiser

1972   Salvatore Martirano builds the *SalMar Construction*, a realtime
generative electronic music instrument.
    F. Richard Moore, Gareth Loy, and others at the Computer Audio
Research Laboratory (CARL) at University of California at San Diego
develop and distribute an open-source, portable system for signal
processing and music synthesis, called the *CARL* System, modelled
after *UNIX*
    Eduard Artemiev produces the electronic score for *Solaris* by
Andrei Tarkovsky
    Pong by Atari becomes a mass gaming phenomenon

1973   The Composers inside Electronics collective is formed

1974   Paul De Marinis builds *Parrot Pleaser*, an automatic music
composing circuit intended to be played by a bird
    Curtis Roads writes a program with MUSIC V implementing
granular synthesis
    François Bayle establishes the Acousmonium loudspeaker
orchestra
    DJ Kool Herc is experimenting with turntable mixing at parties in
the Bronx

1974–9   Laurie Spiegel develops the *VAMPIRE* (Video And Music Program
for Interactive Realtime Exploration/Experimentation) system

1975   Michel Waisvisz unleashes the Cracklebox synthesiser
    John Appleton produces the prototype for the Synclavier

1976   Denis Smalley writes *Darkness After Time's Colours*

1977   *The League of Automatic Composers* is founded by Jim Horton, John
Bischoff and Rich Gold.
    Ben Burtt coins the term 'sound designer' to reflect his
contribution to the film *Star Wars*

1978   Atari releases the Atari Video Music audio-visualiser
    Brian Eno creates the ambient music installation *Music for Airports*
    Kraftwerk create their *The Man-Machine* album, touring with
robotic mannequins

1988	Miller Puckette publishes his paper *The Patcher*; at IRCAM he develops this visual patching system into an interactive computer music programming environment called *Max*
1989	Public Enemy's album *Fear of a Black Planet* demonstrates the power of their sampled hiphop production allied to strong political messages
	John Oswald releases the *Plunderphonic* EP and is later forced to 'recant', destroying all remaining copies, by the litigious music industry
1990	Max (later Max/MSP) is released commercially, becoming available to non-academic musicians
1991	Nic Collins creates the piece *Broken Light* by hardware hacking CD players
	Common Lisp Music (or CLM), a sound synthesis language is written by Bill Schottstaedt at Stanford University
1992	Reed Ghazala starts publishing articles on 'Circuit Bending' in the journal Experimental Musical Instruments
1993	Björk's *Debut* is the first example of her many collaborations with electronic dance music producers
1994	Autechre's *anti-EP* (particularly the third track, 'Flutter') is designed not to repeat in such a way as to confound recent anti-rave legislation
1995	The *Synthesis Toolkit* (STK), a collection of building blocks for realtime sound synthesis and physical modelling, for the C++ programming language, is authored by Perry Cook and Gary Scavone
1996	James McCartney develops *SuperCollider*, an environment and programming language for realtime audio synthesis
	Miller Puckette releases *Pure Data*, a freeware program with a similar environment to Max/MSP
1997	Coldcut release *Let Us Play*, an extended CD including the live AV sampling demo *Timber*
	Maurice Methot and Hector LaPlante start streaming algorithmic music live on the internet with *The Algorithmic Stream*
	Introduction of the *Open Sound Control* (OSC) network music connectivity protocol
	Ryoji Ikeda releases $+/-$
1998	Atau Tanaka and Kaspar Toeplitz install *Global String*, uniting space with cyberspace
	The gameboy *Nanoloop* sequencer is created by Oliver Wittchow
	Chris Watson releases *Outside the circle of fire*
2000	Tabletop tangible musical controllers such as *SmallFish* and *Jam-O-Drum* begin to develop; they would be followed by others such as the *reacTable* and the *Audiopad*
	Radiohead's *Kid A* openly assimilates electronica influences
2000–3000	Jem Finer's *LongPlayer* installation intends to run for a thousand years
2001	Chris Chafe's *Network Harp* uses network latency for sound synthesis

Introduction

NICK COLLINS AND JULIO D'ESCRIVÁN

Electronic music is the mainstream. From musique concrète to audiovisual sampling, from elektronische musik to minimal techno, from the Telharmonium to the laptop, electrical technology[1] has facilitated more than a century of original music, spawning a multitude of new styles, instruments and methods. Fruitful crossovers with other media and arts have allowed it to reach new audiences and to become an accomplice in many forms of expression. It appears ubiquitous, from mobile phones, television and podcasts to the art gallery and other unorthodox performance spaces. In many ways, electronic music is now so well accepted and integrated into contemporary practice that it is transparent to the observer. Yet on the periphery of musical exploration it remains highly visible – from sonic art, to live electronics, to new advances in computational music.

Whilst electronic music would not restrict itself to computer-mediated art, much current work in this area is related to computational applications and the boom in accessibility of home computers. The last sixty years have seen a move from rare electronic music studios to the ubiquity of bedroom studios. As if the thought experiment about Shakespearian monkeys has come true, millions of composers are at large exploring a multiplicity of software and devices in the pursuit of their own musical worlds. The entry cost of an electronic music hobby is no longer the hard graft of acoustic instrument practice, but a simple willingness to explore musical outputs within predominantly visual software paradigms. The influence of computers in compositional techniques, sound analysis and processing, performance interfaces and concert practice is astounding.

Yet the mass of software and hardware recording and performing tools are resting on a wonderful heritage. The essential musical tools of the twentieth century have often been proclaimed to be microphones and loudspeakers.[2] In this era, the mass availability of electronic music-making tools is such that to create musical items is a daily occurrence: from composing ring tones on a mobile phone, to selecting and adding sound media to visual presentations and video, through to creating sophisticated works of expressive value that incorporate original sound processes.[3] Whilst not all musicians care to delve into the background and latest developments in this field, living with the common manifestations of the technology without critical complaint or luxury, for the curious reader, this companion should deliver access to a powerful territory of inspiration and excitement.

A rich history underlies electronic music, full of radical inventors, pioneering composers and daring innovators. Modern-day musicians indiscriminately employing the technology might only know Karlheinz Stockhausen as a face on the cover of *Sgt. Pepper's Lonely Hearts Club Band*, Raymond Scott from incidental music in Warner Bros cartoons, and not know the contribution of Lee Scratch Perry to the history of remixing and dub. However, the worldwide success of electronic dance music and other electronica has raised the profile of the pioneers of electronic music and increased our curiosity about the foundations of this subject area. And as new experimental music inevitably proves itself in time (or dissolves from view) the cutting-edge research of today will inform new musical movements of the future.

Given such a vibrant tableau, this book can only attempt to survey and analyse a proportion of the developments and innovations. We have gathered here what we hope is an exciting collection of perspectives on electronic music. We have tried to encourage novel approaches to the more well-trodden topics, taking in the distant history and origins of electronic music, the relation of computers to music, and highlighting fascinating figures such as Halim el-Dabh, Laurie Spiegel and Gottfried Michael Koenig. We have also commissioned chapters on some less widely represented themes from the research front. Topics vary from virtual and artificial musicians, through audiovisual and crossmedia practice, to aspects of interactivity, music psychology and network music. Whilst there may be some overlap with familiar notions and history of electronic music, we have tried to avoid duplicating the content that can be found in already well-known books (a representative sample of which are included at the end of this introduction).

Indeed, in this manically communicating world the target is moving quickly. For instance, the proliferation of dialects and idioms is nowhere more publicised than in electronic dance music, where new genres are promoted each week in a desperate bid to put space between producers and their rivals for economic advantage. This rapidity of advance may eventually make writing any book impinging on contemporary topics an exponentially difficult task.

Rapidity is also fun however; there is no need to be bored or uninspired, look at all the activity! Far more recordings are released each year than you could ever listen to in multiple lifetimes. And look at the fads and fashions of devices: vocoded vocals, Roland x0x's, Max/MSP with nato, Max/MSP with jitter, Minimoogs, mainframes, a Kim-1 or Amiga.[4] We could profitably hold a moratorium on the technological head charge and just experiment with what we have; you could spend another lifetime exploring all the freeware and shareware music programs available from the World Wide Web.

To guide us in our coverage of the subject, the contributors to this book range widely, across a number of generations of academics, writers and composers, from many locations in the world. An international flavour befits the current age of mass participation and mass communication, and we hope to see a truly global accessibility and a globally intensive exploration of electronic music in the future. In alliance with such an aspiration, we have gathered a series of artists' statements, showcasing diversity across many styles of electronic music. Whilst it remains true that many accounts and explorations of electronic music have involved European and American artists, the wider world has not been idle, even if the media coverage and technological apparatus have not always been of the same order.

We have also deliberately engaged with media beyond sound alone. Though the acousmatic is covered on its own terms, we have also reserved two chapters for audiovisual art. This is not just because such practice is an exciting area of contemporary activity, but because its history is interleaved with that of electronic music; indeed, early experiments with optical sound-tracks predate magnetic tape. We have also pursued an active approach to live electronic music, as opposed to fixed recordings; the latter medium remains an area where traditional Western classical music might (however misguidedly) claim superiority over electronic experimentation. We wish to show how much interesting work has been undertaken to confront the possibilities of electronic music for concert use, and honestly appraise the issues involved in the union of machines and musicians.

It seems pertinent at this point to confront one division in contemporary musical life which is the subject of much discussion (and stress to some): the polarity of electroacoustic (caricatured as serious academic art music) and electronica (as popular electronic music,[5] but also including many forms of experimental electronic music). In reality, various continua stretch between these forms. Perhaps there is a certain amount of posturing going on for economic and artistic reasons; this can lead to a certain sociological resistance to new states of play in musical affairs. Electronic music is joyfully accessible to anyone with a computer of even limited power – an instrument today as intuitive to some as the electric guitar was to previous generations. For others, it can be threatening that those lacking formal training still produce fascinating electronic music; yet many successful practitioners learn as they go.

What does this mean in practical terms? Well, perhaps we should relax a bit, but what you'll find in this book is some mingling of electronica and electroacoustic in a bid to defuse some of the dangerous divisionism. That's also why Kevin Blechdom's statement is next to Karlheinz Stockhausen's.[6]

In truth, we hope to reconcile the electroacoustic and electronica worlds. We may show that electroacoustic composition is nothing but 'academic' if it doesn't acknowledge what is happening in the popular ambitus, and that electronica is inconsequential and disposable if it doesn't learn from the history of electronic creativity.[7]

This book is structured in three parts, covering the history, practice and foundations of electronic music. These divisions are not meant to be overly prescriptive, for chapter authors discussing practices or foundational themes will also delve into the history, and vice versa. Whilst we hope that these chapters will be accessible to a reader previously unfamiliar with electronic music, the authors have not shied from making original assertions and bringing in subjects of controversy and contemporary research.

We've provided a chronology which draws together many events mentioned in this book.[8] It is particular to this book; like any history, it is just one view amongst many. And in a field that actively develops at the pace of electronic music, that engages with a great plurality of techniques and approaches, and indeed, isn't adverse to the odd algorithmic game, readers are encouraged to find their own personal tapestries of works and experiments. Part of the charm of this area is that it is very much alive and continually transforming, and the most fascinating works may be yet to come; indeed, from readers of this book!

Further reading

Chadabe, J. (1997) *Electric Sound: The Past and Promise of Electronic Music.* New Jersey: Prentice-Hall

Cox, C. and Warner, D. (eds.) (2004) *Audio Culture: Readings in Modern Music.* New York: Continuum

Dodge, C., Jerse, T. A. (1997) *Computer Music Synthesis, Composition, and Performance* (2nd edition). New York: Schirmer Books

Holmes, T. (2002) *Electronic and Experimental Music.* New York: Routledge

Manning, P. (2004) *Electronic and Computer Music.* Oxford: Oxford University Press

Prendergast, M. (2003) *The Ambient Century.* London: Bloomsbury

Roads, C. (1996) *The Computer Music Tutorial.* Cambridge, MA: MIT Press

Shapiro, P. (ed.) (2000) *Modulations: A History of Electronic Music: Throbbing Words on Sound.* New York: Caipirinha Productions Inc. / Distributed Art Publishers Inc.

PART I

Electronic music in context

1 The origins of electronic music

ANDREW HUGILL

Classical visions

> We have also sound-houses, where we practise and demonstrate all sounds
> and their generation. We have harmony which you have not, of
> quarter-sounds and lesser slides of sounds. Divers instruments of music
> likewise to you unknown, some sweeter than any you have; with bells and
> rings that are dainty and sweet. We represent small sounds as great and
> deep, likewise great sounds extenuate and sharp; we make divers tremblings
> and warblings of sounds, which in their original are entire. We represent
> and imitate all articulate sounds and letters, and the voices and notes of
> beasts and birds. We have certain helps which, set to the ear, do further the
> hearing greatly; we have also divers strange and artificial echoes, reflecting
> the voice many times, and, as it were, tossing it; and some that give back the
> voice louder than it came, some shriller and some deeper; yea, some
> rendering the voice, differing in the letters or articulate sound from that
> they receive. We have all means to convey sounds in trunks and pipes, in
> strange lines and distances. Francis Bacon, *The New Atlantis* (1626)[1]

The origins of electronic music lie in the creative imagination. The technologies that are used to make electronic music are a realisation of the
human urge to originate, record and manipulate sound. Although the term
electronic music refers specifically to music made using electronic devices
and, by extension, to certain mechanical devices powered by electricity, the
musical possibilities that these technologies have opened up are a recur-
ring theme in literature, art, engineering and philosophy. But it was not
until the turn of the twentieth century, when electronic and electromechanical instruments started to become a physical reality, that certain forward-
looking musicians began to turn to the new possibilities already imagined by
others.

Francis Bacon's celebrated description of a modern sound studio is one
of many examples of such a creative imagination. *The New Atlantis*, written
in 1624 and published in 1626, was a utopian tale of mariners in the south-
eastern seas who were shipwrecked upon an island containing a model civil-
isation, in which science and spirituality found union. The 'sound-houses'
passage is one of a series of descriptions, given by the island's governor, of
its various knowledge resources and houses of learning.

Bacon was familiar with some of the most experimental technologies of his time, including those devised by Salomon de Caus (1576–1626), a Frenchman who moved to England in 1612, to work as a garden designer and engineer specialising in hydraulics. De Caus created steam engines, fountains and many water-driven musical instruments including a player-piano, mechanical songbirds and various organs.

Bacon himself wrote an essay 'On Gardens', but the description of imaginary technologies of music in the 'sound-houses' text goes much further than merely reproducing the contemporary mechanical devices used in garden displays. It seems to express a desire to expand musical language beyond the familiar pitch-based system of Western instrumental music, to incorporate sound processing, novel timbres, microtonal tunings, amplification, recording, spatialisation – in short, every technique known to electronic music.

Bacon's frame of reference was as much classical as contemporary. The majority of his work and thought arose from a rejection of the received wisdom of the period, founded upon Plato and Aristotle, and an enthusiastic reappraisal of the pre-Socratic philosophers, such as Epicurus (341–270 BC), Democritus (460–370 BC) and Thales (*c.* 635–543 BC). These philosophers developed a theory of matter. Thales argued for an underlying unity based on the idea that the world was made from water. Democritus developed this idea to suggest that all matter is made from imperishable indivisible elements called atoms, which are surrounded by a void, and have various characteristics (size, shape, mass, etc) whose complex interactions give rise to physical reality. Epicurus in turn refined Democritus by theorising that the atoms are in continuous state of parallel motion from an absolute high to an absolute low. Every so often, one atom inexplicably makes a slight swerve (the *clinamen*) in its path, creating a chain reaction of collisions, which give rise to matter. The theories of these 'atomist' philosophers seem largely to have come from their imaginations, but there was at least *some* experimental basis for their ideas. Thales, for example, wrote that amber rubbed with animal fur could lift straw and feathers, and Democritus observed fire to conclude that motion is inherent to atomic particles.

Bacon was not the only sixteenth/seventeenth-century scientist interested in these ideas. In 1600, William Gilbert published *De Magnete, Magneticisque Corporibus, et de Magno Magnete Tellure* (On the Magnet and Magnetic Bodies, and on That Great Magnet the Earth) which contains the first discussion of an 'electric force'. This was static electricity, and Gilbert made explicit reference to the pre-Socratic philosophers' discovery of the attractiveness of rubbed amber. The word 'elektron' is Greek for 'amber', and the Latin word 'electricus' means 'produced from amber by friction'.

Some of the elements required for 'electronic' music already existed at this time.

Music theory in the sixteenth century was in the grip of a debate about tuning systems. Writers such as Nicola Vicentino (1511–c. 1576) were defending just intonation against the steady rise of compromised tuning systems such as meantone and equal temperament. The adoption of these latter systems enabled both musical instruments and, ultimately, published music notation, to be disseminated across Europe. The central importance given to pitch and hence harmony in music theory led to a musical practice which ignored most of the sound-based concepts described in Bacon's text.

Vicentino's *L'antica musica ridotta alla moderna prattica* (ancient music adapted to modern practice), published in Rome in 1555, outlined his interpretation of the music theories of Pythagoras (569–475 BC), Aristoxenus (fourth century BC), Ptolemy (c. 90–168 AD) and Boethius (c. 480–525 AD). Vicentino himself built a number of instruments, such as the *archicembalo*, a keyboard with thirty-six keys to the octave, designed to play the Greek *genera* (diatonic, chromatic, enharmonic) derived from Pythagoras's discovery of a *harmonic series* made up of whole-number ratios subdividing a vibrating string or other body.

Other theorists, however, were less interested in the refinements of such 'just' intonations than in the development of a musical language that was reproducible and standardised, with an accompanying notation system that similarly privileged pitch. The meantone tuning system[2] deliberately detuned certain intervals (particularly fifths) in order to achieve the maximum number of 'pure' thirds. Equal temperament systematically detuned all the fifths in order to achieve a 'cycle' that is both effective and practical. This solution is still the dominant western musical tuning system today.

The source of all these theories of tuning, Pythagoras, was also the leader of an elitist cult, which was divided into an inner circle called the *mathematikoi* and an outer circle called the *akousmatikoi*, or 'listeners'.[3] The latter were obliged to listen to the master from behind a curtain, a practice which has given its name to present-day *acousmatic* music in which the original source of the sound is not visually apparent, the immediate source being the loudspeakers which are apparent. Where acousmatic music explores a 'sound-houses' model, by manipulating and processing sound, the instrumental tradition, on the other hand, uses a pitch-centred model, and ultimately abandons Pythagoras in favour of the pragmatic distortion of nature that is equal temperament. It is only as electronic technologies have become available that the music envisaged by Bacon (and perhaps Pythagoras too) has become a reality. However, the absence of these technologies in the intervening years did not eliminate the urge to create this kind of music.[4]

Automata

The eighteenth century saw a surge of interest in mechanical musical devices such as carillons, music-boxes and mechanical organs of various types. The most celebrated engineer was Jacques Vaucanson (1709–82), whose machines took on a life of their own by mimicking natural and biological functions. His life-size flute-player (1738) blew, breathed and played twelve different melodies so convincingly like a human being that it surpassed previous mechanical devices. This *automaton*, or self-operating machine, started to resemble a robot in its simulation of human action. Vaucanson's most celebrated automaton was a duck, which moved its wings, legs and body, quacked and, most amazingly, both ate food and dabbled in the water. Vaucanson was keen to reveal the inner workings of the duck, showing the 'digestive' tubing through which the food passed, the throat, and so on.

Vaucanson had numerous imitators, and the general spirit of mechanical and scientific experiment at that time was contagious. New musical instruments were also created with varying amounts of automation, and there was even an electronic instrument: the *claveçin électrique*, built in Paris in 1761 by Jean-Baptiste Delaborde, which used statically charged clappers to ring bells, controlled by a harpsichord keyboard. The fascination with automata was also pursued in contemporary philosophy, most notably in the writings of Julien de La Mettrie (1709–51). In *L'homme machine* (Man a Machine) (1748), La Mettrie developed his ultra-materialist, atheistic vision of man as a machine made from a single universal substance. In doing so, he set himself against the prevailing Cartesian idea that mind and body are separate and occasioned the wrath of many of his contemporaries. Not that this bothered him: he cheerfully asserted the idea that we only have one life and it is our duty to enjoy ourselves as much as possible while we are alive. He duly lived fast and died young.

As the interest in automata grew, so did the concept of an artificial intelligence (although that phrase was not itself used at the time). The most celebrated example of this was a hoax, but the fact that people were fooled gave rise to a large amount of imaginative fiction that predicted, amongst other things, electronic music. Once again, the creative imagination (in this case the literary imagination) anticipated developments which musicians themselves ignored.

The hoax in question was a turban-wearing chess-playing automaton popularly known as 'The Turk'. It was created in 1769 by Baron Wolfgang von Kempelen, and its most famous exploit was to beat Napoleon Bonaparte at chess. Von Kempelen passed on 'The Turk' to Johann Maelzel (1772–1838), who was developing a reputation as an inventor and showman. Among

Maelzel's inventions was the Maelzel Metronome (after which the 'MM' marking at the beginning of musical scores is named) which was adopted by Ludwig van Beethoven. Maelzel also created a musical machine called a 'panharmonicon', for which Beethoven wrote his piece *Wellington's Victory*.[5] Maelzel toured 'The Turk' widely and created a sensation wherever he went. In the 1830s it visited America, where Edgar Allan Poe finally exposed the truth in an essay entitled 'Maelzel's Chess-Player', published in the *Southern Literary Journal* in 1836. The truth was that 'The Turk' concealed a human chess-player, a deception which finds echoes today. When the world chess champion, Garry Kasparov, was first beaten by the IBM computer 'Deep Blue' in 1997, he had no hesitation in calling foul, claiming that one crucial move had in fact been made by a human being. The rest of the match (which Kasparov lost) was played in an atmosphere of rancour, secrecy, accusation and counter-accusation, and 'Deep Blue' was immediately mothballed at the end.

The literary imagination

The first major writer to be inspired by such automata to apply their capabilities to music was E. T. A. Hoffmann (1776–1822). In his story 'Automata' (1814), after a lengthy description of 'The Turk', and a concert by musical automata, the main characters fall to debating the musical possibilities of as yet only imaginary technologies.

> Now, in the case of instruments of the keyboard class a great deal might be done. There is a wide field open in that direction to clever mechanical people, much as has been accomplished already; particularly in instruments of the pianoforte genus. But it would be the task of a really advanced system of the 'mechanics of music' to observe closely, study minutely, and discover carefully that class of sounds which belong, most purely and strictly, to Nature herself, to obtain a knowledge of the tones which dwell in substances of every description, and then to take this mysterious music and enclose it in some sort of instrument, where it should be subject to man's will, and give itself forth at his touch. All the attempts to evoke music from metal or glass cylinders, glass threads, slips of glass, or pieces of marble; or to cause strings to vibrate or sound in ways unlike the ordinary ways, are to me interesting in the highest degree . . . according to my theory, musical sound would be the nearer to perfection the more closely it approximated such of the mysterious tones of nature as are not wholly dissociated from this earth.

In 1831, Honoré de Balzac (1799–1850) wrote a story called 'Gambara', about an eccentric composer who devises a fantastic instrument called the 'panharmonicon' (clearly inspired by Maelzel), which sets out to explore the relationship between all sounds, thoughts and emotions. As he says:

> Composers work with substances of which they know nothing. Why should a brass and a wooden instrument – a bassoon and horn – have so little identity of tone, when they act on the same matter, the constituent gases of the air? Their differences proceed from some displacement of those constituents, from the way they act on the elements which are their affinity and which they return, modified by some occult and unknown process. If we knew what the process was, science and art would both be gainers. Whatever extends science enhances art.

The result of Gambara's efforts is that he is dismissed as a madman. The music he creates is judged to be too far ahead of its time, too incomprehensible, by his audience.

At almost the same time as Balzac's story was published, Ada Byron, Lady Lovelace (1815–52) met Charles Babbage at Cambridge. Babbage had partially built a calculating machine, or 'Difference Engine', and was planning a more sophisticated 'Analytical Engine'. This was an early model for a programmable computer, and Ada Byron immediately recognised the potential for the 'universality' of the device. Writing in 'The Sketch of the Analytical Engine' of 1843, she describes all aspects of Babbage's machine, including this passage about its musical application:

> Again, it might act upon other things besides number, were objects found whose mutual fundamental relations could be expressed by those of the abstract science of operations, and which should be also susceptible of adaptations to the action of the operating notation and mechanism of the engine . . . Supposing for instance, that the fundamental relations of pitched sounds in the science of harmony and of musical composition were susceptible of such expression and adaptations, the engine might compose elaborate and scientific pieces of music of any degree of complexity or extent.

Ada Byron passionately advocated Babbage's concept, although a working machine was never completed, thanks partly to her early death. She may nevertheless be regarded as the first computer programmer. Her writings, although scientifically and technically grounded, display the same tendency to Romantic vision as those of her own father, the poet Lord Byron.

The combination of science with fiction is a theme in the work of E. T. A. Hoffmann, Balzac and Mary Shelley, who created perhaps the most sophisticated fantasy of an artificial life in *Frankenstein* (1816). The monster, it will be recalled, is awakened by electricity by using a lightning-rod. This was undoubtedly inspired by the discoveries of Benjamin Franklin, himself a musical inventor,[6] who first flew a kite designed to conduct electricity in 1750. As the nineteenth century developed, so such fantastic stories proliferated, mixing scientific discoveries with pure imagination to create forerunners of what would eventually be called 'science fiction'.

Some mystical and visionary writings of the nineteenth century also contain descriptions of musical possibilities enabled by new technologies that prefigure electronic music. A typical example occurs in the novel *A Crystal Age* (1887) by W. H. Hudson (1841–1922), in which seven highly polished brass globes hover in the air, driven by an unknown power and emitting sound until the air is 'palpitating with strange exquisite harmony'. Even more extraordinary is the following extract from Edward Bellamy's (1850–98) novel *Looking Backward* (1888). The hero, Julian West, awakens in Boston in the year 2000, after more than a century of sleep, to find the world changed beyond recognition and with most of the social problems of his time resolved. In describing the world of the future he outlines numerous imaginary technologies, including the following description of a music system. It is Julian West's hostess, Edith, who is speaking:

> 'There is nothing in the least mysterious about the music, as you seem to imagine. It is not made by faeries or genii, but by good, honest, and exceedingly clever human hands. We have simply carried the idea of labor-saving by cooperation into our musical service as into everything else. There are a number of music rooms in the city, perfectly adapted acoustically to the different sorts of music. These halls are connected by telephone with all the houses of the city whose people may care to pay the small fee, and there are none, you may be sure, who do not. The corps of musicians attached to each hall is so large that, although no individual performer, or group of performers, has more than a brief part, each day's program lasts through the twenty-four hours. There are on that card for today, as you will see if you observe closely, distinct programs of four of these concerts, each of a different order of music from the others, being now simultaneously performed, and any one of the four pieces now going on that you prefer, you can hear by merely pressing the button which will connect your house wire with the hall where it is being rendered. The programs are so coordinated that the pieces at any one time simultaneously proceeding in the different halls usually offer a choice, not only between instrumental and vocal, and between different sorts of instruments, but also between different motives from grave to gay, so that all tastes and moods can be suited.'

This not only seems to realise Bacon's description of 'sounds in trunks and pipes', but is also a highly prophetic description of a radio broadcast network, or even of download culture.[7] However, there are also some parallels between Bellamy's imaginary technologies and contemporary inventions. In 1876, Elisha Gray had created a 'Musical Telegraph' which transmitted single note oscillations along wires. In 1898, Valdemar Poulson patented a magnetic 'Telegraphone', which could both record and play back sound and, in 1897, Thaddeus Cahill patented the *Art of and Apparatus for Generating and Distributing Music Electronically*. This idea of a telegraph-based music distribution system led to the construction of the first really influential electronic musical instrument. Cahill's *Dynamophone* or *Telharmonium* appeared in 1906, weighing about two hundred tons and measuring about eighteen metres in length.[8] It used 145 modified dynamos with geared shafts and associated inductors to produce alternating currents of different audio frequencies.

Sound recording

In his classic essay 'The Work of Art in the Age of Mechanical Reproduction' (1936), Walter Benjamin makes the following argument about the effect on art of the technologies of reproduction, including sound recording: 'for the first time in world history, mechanical reproduction emancipates the work of art from its parasitical dependence on ritual. To an ever greater degree the work of art reproduced becomes the work of art designed for reproducibility.' The 'ritual' to which he refers is the performance, a unique set of circumstances under which an individual or a group experiences a work of art.

The beginnings of this fundamental change in the way music is experienced and consumed lie in the later part of the nineteenth century, although some purely mechanical recording devices, such as the musical box and the player-piano, existed earlier. One such device worth noting was the *phonautograph*, invented in 1857 by Leon Scott. This recorded a sound through a vibrating membrane attached to a pen which drew a line resembling the waveform. This could only record, however, and could not reproduce the original sound.

The earliest microphones were, strictly speaking, the telephone transmitter devices invented by Elisha Gray and Alexander Graham Bell, but Emile Berliner is usually credited with the invention of the first true microphone in 1877. However, when Thomas Edison invented the carbon microphone later in the same year, his was the first to become commercially available. Edison also invented the phonograph in 1877, although a Frenchman, Charles Cros, came up with the same idea independently and slightly earlier. The phonograph used a similar principle to the phonautograph, except that the pen drew grooves into a relatively soft material (wax, tin foil or lead). These grooves could then be retraced by a needle and amplified mechanically. It was not long before this system was mass produced. In 1887, Emile Berliner patented a phonographic system using flat discs rather than cylinders, called the gramophone.

Loudspeakers were invented independently by Ernst Werner von Siemens in 1877, and Sir Oliver Lodge, who patented the design of the modern moving-coil loudspeaker in 1898. These, combined with both the electromechanical and magnetic systems described above, evolved rapidly. By the early 1930s, electrical recordings would become a viable medium thanks to the invention of magnetic tape recording in 1928 by Fritz Fleumer in Germany.

The impact of recorded and reproducible sound on music in general was, of course, enormous. However, it was some time before composers and musicians began to realise the creative potential of this new medium. With a few exceptions, such as Ottorino Respighi's inclusion of a phonograph (playing birdsong) in his orchestral composition *Pini di Roma* (Pines of Rome) in 1924, these technologies were used purely for the reproduction of live sounds or musical performances. The systematic exploration of tape music had to wait until the early 1950s, when Pierre Schaeffer began his experiments.

Early 'electronic' music

'Electronic' music therefore began with the invention of new electronic instruments, even though they were normally seen as novelties or curiosities. A good example, and probably the first truly electronic instrument, was the *Singing Arc*, invented by William Duddell in 1899, which used the sounds emitted by carbon arc lamps (the precursors of the electric light bulb). It was some time before electronic instruments would come to be included alongside their acoustic counterparts but, even so, Western music was already beginning to evolve to a point at which such new means of expression would be required. Composers were exploring musical material in a variety of different ways, and some of these started to focus upon the sonic and timbral properties that the pitch-centred notation system had marginalised.

One such example was the third of the *Fünf Orchesterstücke* (Five Orchestral Pieces) Op. 16, composed in 1909 by Arnold Schoenberg. This movement, entitled 'Farben' (Colours), had neither melodic contour nor harmonic direction, but rather featured a fairly static sound-mass built from a single chord which changed timbre, or colouration. The skill of the orchestration emphasised the acoustic and tonal properties of the instrumental combinations and the work is quite startling in its anticipation of 'spectral' music. However, this was not a direction that Schoenberg pursued in his subsequent work, preferring to continue to overturn the orthodoxies of the tonal system instead.

The first leading composer who seems to have realised the potential for an entirely new musical language that could also use the new technologies was Ferruccio Busoni, who wrote in his *Sketch for a New Aesthetic of Music* (1907):

> We have divided the octave into twelve equidistant degrees because we had to manage somehow, and have constructed our instruments in such a way that we can never get in above or below or between them. Keyboard instruments, in particular, have so thoroughly schooled our ears that we are no longer capable of hearing anything else – incapable of hearing except through this impure medium. Yet Nature created an infinite gradation – *infinite!* Who still knows it nowadays? . . . While busied with this essay I received from America direct and authentic intelligence which solves the problem in a simple manner. I refer to an invention by Dr. Thaddeus Cahill. He has constructed an apparatus that makes it possible to transform an electric current into a fixed and mathematically exact number of vibrations. As pitch depends on the number of vibrations, and the apparatus may be 'set' on any number desired, the infinite gradation of the octave may be accomplished by merely moving a lever corresponding to the pointer of a quadrant.

Although Busoni's own compositions did not themselves explore these new avenues, his visionary ideas and his teaching inspired others to do so. In 1908, Gabrielle Buffet, having graduated from the Schola Cantorum, went to Germany to join her fellow student Edgard Varèse. Both of them were so fascinated with the *Sketch for a New Aesthetic of Music* that they actually tried to build machines to realise Busoni's ideas. Buffet noted in her essay *Music of Today*: 'With the help of and through improvements to these sound-machines, an objective reconstitution of the life of sound could be possible. We would be discovering sound-forms independently of musical conventions.'[9]

Sound in art

At the same time that Buffet and her contemporaries were becoming excited by the new musical possibilities being opened up by technological innovations, a number of leading painters were developing an abstract art that drew heavily on music. The 'Blue Rider' group, Der Blaue Reiter, included Arnold Schoenberg and Wassily Kandinsky (1866–1944), who began to paint 'Improvisations' and 'Compositions' during the years immediately preceding the First World War. Kandinsky was inspired by Theosophy and other spiritual ideas to create work that aspired to the condition of music. He also experienced synaesthesia, in which the senses become confused, by 'hearing' specific sounds when seeing certain colours or shapes (yellow as the note C played on a trumpet, for example). Many other artists and composers explored these ideas: for example, Alexander Skryabin (1872–1915) whose *Prometheus: The Poem of Fire* (1910) included a part for 'light organ', which was intended to bathe the concert hall in colour from electric lights corresponding to the changing tonality of the music.

In June 1912, Buffet and her husband, Francis Picabia, accompanied the artist Marcel Duchamp and the poet Guillaume Apollinaire to a performance of *Impressions d'Afrique* (Impressions of Africa) at the Théâtre Antoine, Paris. This was a staged version of a novel by Raymond Roussel, in which various bizarre machines and musical instruments were powered by (amongst other things): a thermo-sensitive chemical called Bexium; drops of heavy water let fall by a large worm; extended vocal techniques; resonating pulmonary braid; and lightning. All four artists, in their different ways, were inspired by this performance, and went on to become leading figures in Dada, the absurdist movement which arose in 1916/17 (initially in Zurich) out of disgust at the First World War. According to Hugo Ball, the Dada cabaret included African music, a balalaika orchestra, and Dada music by composers such as Erwin Schulhoff. However, for electronic music, a far more significant innovation was 'sound poetry'.[10]

The experimental use of the human voice to use phonetic (rather than semantic) sounds as poetry was probably pioneered by Hugo Ball sometime before 1915: 'I created a new species of verse, "verse without words," or sound poems . . . I recited the following: gadji beri bimba glandridi lauli lonni cadori . . .'[11]

However, there was a close correspondence between Dada and the Italian Futurists, led by F. T. Marinetti, who in 1914 published *Zang Tumb Tumb*, a sound-poetic attempt to convey the noises of battle[12] using typography and 'free words'.

It was this daring and iconoclastic text that inspired Luigi Russolo to write his manifesto *L'arte dei rumori* (The Art of Noises) in 1913, and to build *intonarumori* ('intoners' or 'noise machines') with which to perform Futurist music. *The Art of Noises* is an important text in the history of electronic music, because it is the first attempt seriously to categorise all sounds and, indeed, to treat them as potential music. In a crucial passage, Russolo wrote:

> Every manifestation of our life is accompanied by noise. The noise, therefore, is familiar to our ear, and has the power to conjure up life itself. Sound, alien to our life, always musical and a thing unto itself, an occasional but unnecessary element, has become to our ears what an overfamiliar face is to our eyes. Noise, however, reaching us in a confused and irregular way from the irregular confusion of our life, never entirely reveals itself to us, and keeps innumerable surprises in reserve. We are therefore certain that by

selecting, coordinating and dominating all noises we will enrich men with a new and unexpected sensual pleasure.

Although it is characteristic of noise to recall us brutally to real life, the art of noise must not limit itself to imitative reproduction. It will achieve its most emotive power in the acoustic enjoyment, in its own right, that the artist's inspiration will extract from combined noises.

Here are the 6 families of noises of the Futurist orchestra which we will soon set in motion mechanically:

1.	2.	3.	4.	5.	6.
Rumbles:	Whistles:	Whispers:	Screeches:	Noises obtained by percussion:	Voices of animals and men:
Roars	Hisses	Murmurs	Creaks	Metal	Shouts
Explosions	Snorts	Mumbles	Rustles	Wood	Screams
Crashes		Grumbles	Buzzes	Skin	Groans
Splashes		Gurgles	Crackles	Stone	Shrieks
Booms			Scrapes	Terracotta	Howls
				Etc.	Laughs
					Wheezes
					Sobs

In this inventory we have encapsulated the most characteristic of the fundamental noises; the others are merely the associations and combinations of these.

The *intonarumori* included percussion, but also a range of machine-like instruments deriving from the categories above. Russolo even devised a graphic notation for scoring his noise music, and achieved notoriety in 1914 after performances in Milan and London. After the war the *intonarumori* were recorded in combination with classical orchestras, but none of the original instruments survives today.

The spirit of Dada and Futurism permeated through to mainstream concert music. In 1917, Erik Satie included the 'Futurist' sounds of sirens, starting pistols, typewriter and a foghorn in his ballet *Parade* (although he did so only at the request of the poet Jean Cocteau), and in 1924 Georges Antheil created his *Ballet mécanique*, which included electric bells, air-plane propellers and a siren in its orchestra of multiple percussion, pianos and player-pianos. Electronic instruments such as the *Theremin*, invented by Professor Lev Termen (Leon Theremin) *c*. 1919–20; the *Trautonium*, invented by Friedrich Trautwein *c*. 1929; and the *Ondes Martenot*, invented in 1928 by Maurice Martenot, also began to appear regularly in concerts around this time.

Electronic music

The inclusion of electronic sounds in conventional music does not in itself amount to the origins of an electronic *music*, as distinct from any other kind

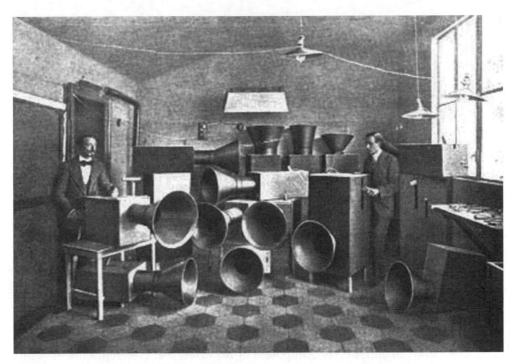

Figure 1.1 Russolo's *intonarumori*

of music. Electronic music is a synthesis of many different aspects of what has already been described: the array of loudspeakers, or acousmatic situation; the creation of new electronic instruments; the exploration of novel tunings and timbres; the use of recording and reproduction technologies; the relationship between science, mathematics and music. Certain compositional techniques which are features of electronic music have their roots in much earlier music. To take one example, algorithmic composition, which uses a strict set of rules to compose music, can be traced back through voice-leading counterpoint to the metrical procedures of certain types of late medieval music. Electronic music has, thanks largely to digital technologies, been able to make algorithms that are more complex and more diverse, by including chance and extreme determinism, artificial intelligence and generative processes.

In 1937, the composer John Cage delivered a highly prophetic lecture in Seattle, entitled 'The Future of Music – Credo':

I BELIEVE THAT THE USE OF NOISE
Wherever we are, what we hear is mostly noise. When we ignore it, it
disturbs us. When we listen to it, we find it fascinating. The sound of a truck
at 50 m.p.h. Static between the stations. Rain. We want to capture and
control these sounds, to use them, not as sound effects, but as musical

instruments. Every film studio has a library of 'sound effects' recorded on film. With a film phonograph it is now possible to control the amplitude and frequency of any one of these sounds and to give to it rhythms within or beyond the reach of anyone's imagination. Given four film phonographs, we can compose and perform a quartet for explosive motor, wind, heartbeat, and landslide.

TO MAKE MUSIC

If this word, music, is sacred and reserved for eighteenth- and nineteenth-century instruments, we can substitute a more meaningful term: organization of sound.

WILL CONTINUE AND INCREASE UNTIL WE REACH A MUSIC PRODUCED THROUGH THE AID OF ELECTRICAL INSTRUMENTS

[. . .]

The special property of electrical instruments will be to provide complete control of the overtone structure of tones (as opposed to noises) and to make these tones available in any frequency, amplitude, and duration.[13]

Cage was here expressing a commonly held aspiration amongst avant-garde musicians and composers at the time, derived to a great extent from Russolo's manifesto. The composer Edgard Varèse was even replacing the word 'music' with the phrase 'organised sound'. However, during the early years of the twentieth century, the musical spirit that would ultimately form into 'electronic music' found itself stultified and frustrated by the limitations of both the technology and the conventions of the day. This is probably best exemplified by examining the careers of two visionary composers: Percy Grainger (1882–1961) and the aforementioned Varèse (1883–1965).

In the early 1890s the Australian, Grainger, had begun to dream of new technologies for music. He described a mechanically operated music desk that would do away with the need for a conductor, and first outlined his concept of 'Free Music', characterised by continuously gliding tones and an absence of regular rhythm. Grainger experimented with random composition in *Random Round* (1912) and wrote for highly unusual instrumental combinations, despite his successful career as a pianist and 'light music' composer. It was nevertheless many years before Grainger was able to build his own machines to perform the Free Music. A typical example is the *Kangaroo Pouch Machine* of 1948, which is essentially the controller of a collection of solovoxes (or theremins). Here, undulating pitch-control graphs and tone-strength controllers are made from paper wrapped around a revolving 'feeder' turret and passing through a metal cage to an 'eater' turret. These control eight oscillators, connected by electrical wires, which play the Free Music.

By the time Grainger was able to build his machines, there were probably technologies in existence which would have made the realisation of Free

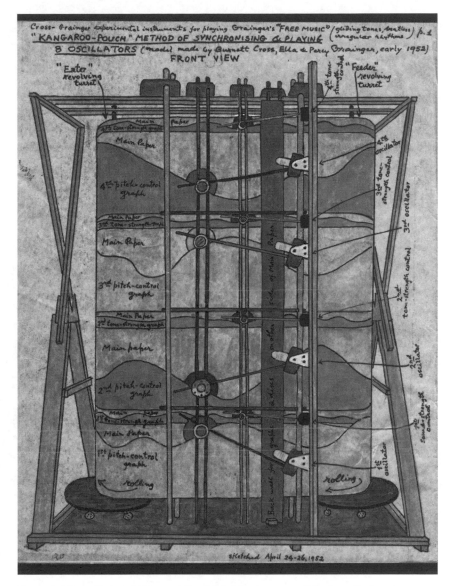

Figure 1.2 Percy Grainger's Kangaroo Pouch Machine (courtesy of The Percy Grainger Society/Estate)

Music more straightforward (although less delightfully idiosyncratic), but his determination to hear this electronic music in the way he had first imagined it was evidently the driving-force behind his persistence. The recordings that exist of these fleeting sonic experiments are rough, but repeated listening reveals a clear musical concept at work.

Varèse similarly spent the majority of his life dreaming of a day when the technologies available to him would be capable of realising his musical

Figure 1.3 Le Corbusier, Iannis Xenakis, Edgard Varèse: Philips Pavilion, 1958

ideas. As he remarked, bitterly: 'in music we composers are forced to use instruments that have not changed for two centuries.' In his manifesto 'The Liberation of Sound', published in 1936, he wrote:

> The raw material of music is sound. That is what the 'reverent approach' has made people forget – even composers. Today when science is equipped to help the composer realize what was never before possible . . . the composer continues to be obsessed by traditions which are nothing but the limitations of his predecessors . . .
>
> As far back as the twenties, I decided to call my music 'organized sound' and myself, not a musician, but 'a worker in rhythms, frequencies, and intensities.' Indeed, to stubbornly conditioned ears, anything new in music

has always been called noise. But after all what is music but organized noises? And a composer, like all artists, is an organizer of disparate elements . . .

The electronic medium is adding an unbelievable variety of new timbres to our musical store, but most important of all, it has freed music from the tempered system, which has prevented music from keeping pace with the other arts and with science. Composers are now able, as never before, to satisfy the dictates of that inner ear of the imagination. They are also lucky so far in not being hampered by aesthetic codification – at least not yet! But I am afraid it will not be long before some musical mortician begins embalming electronic music in rules.

With such passionate, even Romantic, views, it is no surprise that Varèse encountered constant obstacles to his musical expression. He composed only a handful of works, and he experienced rejection both by the general public and his professional colleagues (including Schoenberg). His attempts to convince Bell Laboratories to allow him to research electronic music during the 1920s and 1930s failed. It was only during his seventies that the musical world and the technological world caught up with Varèse. He composed *Déserts* for orchestra and tape in 1950–4, supported by Pierre Schaeffer who provided facilities at the Radiodiffusion-Télévision Française (RTF) studios, where he was working on musique concrète.

Finally, in 1958, Varèse was invited by the architect Le Corbusier to create *Poème électronique* for the Philips Pavilion at the 1958 World's Fair. This was essentially a sound installation, which used four hundred loudspeakers to create a walk-through sonic experience that combined synthesised and recorded and processed sounds. It is also in many ways the realisation of Bacon's 'sound-house'. This classic work remains highly influential today: a high point in the early development of electronic music. What Varèse's career demonstrates, however, is that the *origins* of electronic music lie much further back than this work, in the creative imagination of the artist.

2 Electronic music and the studio

MARGARET SCHEDEL

In 1996 Yuko Nexus6, a composer and lecturer based in Nagoya, Japan, coined the term *kotatsutop music* to describe the current state of electronic music in Japan. One can find kotatsu, low tables, covered by blankets with a heater underneath, in almost every Japanese household. Nexus6 implied that the tools for making electronic music were just as ubiquitous as this piece of common household furniture: 'Those days when synthesisers and computers were the prized possessions of a limited number of universities and other institutions are over, and instead, these items can be found cluttering the tops of kotatsu in small boarding houses in these same areas' (Nexus6 1998). It should come as no surprise that the face of electronic music has changed dramatically since the 1940s, but the field has changed spectacularly even within the past ten years. My laptop is more powerful today than the fastest computers I had access to ten years ago, and I can store more data on a portable drive no bigger than my finger than I ever could on the hard drives in the studios where I worked fifteen years ago. Technology is no longer a limiting factor for most musicians, but what does this mean for the field as a whole? What are the implications of being able to create electronic music at a local café? Given the portability of recording and production technology, how will electronic music reflect local and even transient cultures? Does the ease of production imply a healthy democratisation of the aesthetic of electronic music or perhaps its corruption? How does the liquidation of the studio change the process of composition and production? How does kotatsutop music differ aesthetically, sociologically and conceptually from the music created at major electronic music centres?

To answer these questions I interviewed electroacoustic musicians of many different ages, nationalities and experiences. Some names, such as Max Mathews and Pauline Oliveros will be familiar to readers who have even a passing acquaintance with the field of electronic music; others, such as Takuro Mizuta Lippit (aka DJ Sniff) and Mara Helmuth will be familiar to only a few. It may be tempting to give more credence to the words of the 'elder statespeople', but I ask the reader to try to think about *what* people have said about the past, present and future of electronic music, rather than focusing on *who* has said it. This chapter is an attempt to provide an inclusive overview of electronic music studios from around the world.

History

> I came to the studio to make noises speak, I stumbled onto music.
>
> Pierre Schaeffer (1998)

Pierre Schaeffer is generally acknowledged as the first composer to create music with pre-recorded media: his sound collage *Etude aux Chemins de Fer* (1948) has a prominent place in most histories of electronic and computer music. These same histories tend to concentrate on the studios of Europe and North America, and indeed most electronic music studios are concentrated in these two continents. Yet this is most likely due to reporting bias, for the most dominant nations tend to control history. While researching this chapter I was determined to overcome this prejudice, and interview people from all areas of the world. I was pleased to discover that important work has been happening in every corner of the globe for many decades. I know composers from many different countries, but I wasn't so aware of the rich international history of electronic music outside Europe and America. During the year in which I was writing this chapter, more attention has been brought to the diverse history of electronic music. Bob Gluck published interviews with several electroacoustic composers from outside North America and Europe for the Electronic Music Foundation Institute's website, and at the 2006 International Computer Music Conference, Larry Polansky (USA) chaired a panel with Erdem Helvacioglu (Turkey), Rodrigo Sigal (Mexico), and Shlomo Dubnov (Israel). They discussed electronic and computer music beyond Europe and North America, exploring 'the breadth and depth of creative expression in the field throughout the regions where its history has not been fully documented' (Polansky 2006, p. 154).

Composers of electronic music in many parts of the world have operated in relative obscurity for years. Often, performance opportunities in countries outside Europe and North America have been limited and resources tight. Wider international knowledge of their work has at times been limited to those with whom they studied, such as in Utrecht and New York City.[1] At times, composers, such as Egyptian-born Halim El-Dabh, discovered new technologies on their own. His experiments, in 1944, electronically processing recordings made with a wire recorder, a medium that predated tape, may be counted among the first works for pre-recorded media:

> [I] emphasised the harmonics of the sound by removing the fundamental tones and changing the reverberation and echo by recording in a space with movable walls . . . some of this using voltage controlled devices. It was not easy to do . . . [I] didn't think of it as electronic music, but just as an experience . . . [I] called the piece *Ta'abir al-Zaar*.[2]

A portion of this piece has been released as *Wire Recorder Piece,* and is now available on CD (ElDabh 2001). El Dabh experimented with sound artistically in his own time with equipment he borrowed from the Middle East Radio while Schaeffer worked in a environment focused on research which was funded by the Radiodiffusion-Télévision Française (RTF). In the second half of the twentieth century much of the electronic music research and composition was done in highly specialised research studios similar to the RTF; in the twenty-first century most composers have high quality artistic studios at their homes with no corporate interest dictating research directions.

Technology and aesthetics

> Technology precedes artistic invention . . . first came the electric guitar and
> then came rock and roll.   John Adams (1997)

The history of electronic music is tied inexorably to advances in technology. The character of electronic music changes much more quickly than traditional Western classical music because the rapid pace of technological advances influences the aesthetics of any given decade. We have gone through an incredible number of phases, riding on the technology which has become much more powerful with each passing year.[3] Beyond these generational differences, each traditionally professional studio had its own signature sound which came not only from the equipment itself – GRM had handmade phonogenes, Columbia had the RCA synthesiser – but also from 'the operational characteristics of a particular studio [which] exert a considerable influence on the range and type of compositional operations which may be satisfactorily executed. A proliferation of studios equipped with identical synths dictates a single design philosophy to all potential users' (Manning 1985, p. 152).

Aesthetic differences in compositional techniques also dictate a philosophy to studio users. The classic example of this division is of course the ideological schism in the 1950s between GRM's Parisian musique concrète and WDR's elektronische musik from Cologne (Harrison 1989). Composers produced musique concrète by recording and manipulating sampled sound, while elektronische musik practitioners favored the total control of synthesis using sine waves.

In addition to creating a wholly new aesthetic, technology can also augment or influence a practice which is already in place; Kwaito, most often defined as South African hip-hop, uses sequencers, drum machines and samplers to create a distinct style of music which is still based on a symmetrical timeline pattern – additive structures with a base of fast elementary pulse units. Kwaito producers use a computer to create complex rhythmic structures which reference the past. Even though they are not creating a new aesthetic, Kwaito musicians are still influenced by their new tools: most local productions, even in traditional styles, now use drum machines for reasons of expedience but also to give the music a 'contemporary edge'. Alas, they are often programmed in very blunt ways, both rhythmically and sonically, whereas most rhythms played by African musicians contain a great amount of subtlety and irregularity, arising from idiosyncrasies in phrasing that might vary from place to place, or due to personal style, historical precedence, or even deliberate imprecision in its execution (Ligeti 2007).

If the tools musicians use influence the music they make, what happens when an attempt at standardisation occurs? With Stockhausen's help, Japan's first studio, Nippon Houso Kyokai (NHK), was modelled on his space in Cologne (Shimazu 1994, p. 102). It should come as no surprise that the music coming out of Japan was much more similar to German music, than the geographically closer Korean electronic music. Korea historically never had a major studio, but Sung Ho Hwang believes that this limitation helped Koreans develop as idiomatic composers.[4] While Stockhausen was a proponent of studio standardisation (Stockhausen 2004, p. 377), there is even less homogeny in studio design today than in 1958. In the United States, there was a similar desire to create a standard studio: SUNY Stony Brook and the Jerusalem Academy of Music in Israel built studios modelled on Columbia–Princeton Electronic Music Center.[5] Both schools have since upgraded to different systems.

Today almost every studio has a unique combination of equipment, which should lead to different sounds, but to my ear it seems there is more similarity in the music from different studios today than there was in the past. Perhaps this is a consequence of the information age – ideas are transmitted instantaneously across the Internet, and software is much easier to duplicate than hardware. Thus composers from different parts of the world have many of the same tools at their disposal. Another result of the propagation of home studios is that fewer composers are travelling to use professional studios. Barry Truax misses the days when composers would come to Simon Fraser University to use his facilities; he hopes the custom-built AudioBox, a computer-controlled system for diffusion, will be an incentive for composers to visit again.[6] The AudioBox is a 16×16 matrix mixer produced by Richmond Sound Design, used in combination with ABControl software by Chris Rolfe. Pieces mastered at Simon Fraser using the AudioBox have a unique sound, although it is not timbral; rather the distinction comes from the swiftly moving surround sound experience.

Unlike Berio's now defunct RAI studios (Manning 1985, p. 81) and the analogue synth room at the Institute of Sonology,[7] which were filled with

custom-made audio equipment, most studios in the later half of the twentieth century contained a mixture of commercial machines joined together by
a giant patch bay and mixer. The trend is now swinging away from commercial hardware and software and back towards custom-built as people seek to
give their sound a unique quality; the challenge now is to create things other
people can't.[8] Instead of simply being filled 'with equipment that was built
for other purposes' (Stockhausen 2004, p. 377), studios are once again 'seen
as both a school of musical thought and a laboratory' (LaBelle 2006, p. 26).
It remains to be seen if studios will be able to retain a cohesive aesthetic
within this renewed pioneering spirit of do-it-yourself electronics.

Accessibility: cost, size and speed

> The dynamaphone [Telharmonium] weighed two hundred tons, was over
> sixty feet in length and cost two hundred thousand dollars.
>
> Peter Manning (1985)

The barriers to electronic music have dropped significantly in the past twenty
years; cost, size and speed are the three main factors in this revolution.
In contrast to the 1897 dynamaphone, Pauline Oliveros's favourite new
piece of equipment is a portable audio recorder[9] which weighs 0.0001 tons
(including a memory card and batteries), is 9.1 centimetres long and costs
four hundred dollars (Nakamura 2006). It is obvious from these numbers
that the exponential growth of microprocessors has changed the landscape
of electronic music radically (Manning 1985, p. 155). The total number of
people working in the field is staggering when compared to the 1960s, when
maybe a few hundred people were involved; there are now millions alone
with access to the music editing software that comes pre-installed on Apple
computers.

> While producing highly virtuosic music, early electronic music composers
> were nevertheless constrained to construct their pieces via painstaking
> tape-manipulation techniques; cutting and splicing tiny sections of recorded
> electronic material. Expensive and enormous electronic equipment was
> confined to well-funded research centers and radio stations . . . fast forward
> to the early 1990s. A technologically adept generation raised on home
> computer and video games begins to explore the equipment at its
> disposal . . . in their own bedrooms and basements they begin to
> recapitulate the experiments and discoveries of early electronic music.
>
> (Cox and Warner 2004, p. 366)

It wasn't just difficult to gain access to electronic music equipment in
the early decades of electronic music, it also took a tremendous amount

of time. Musicians using analogue equipment had to spend untold hours physically grappling with tape and razor blades. Those using the earliest digital tools suffered from delays ranging from overnight to several days between creating a program and hearing the resultant music. A trip across the city was sometimes necessary to complete a work because the digital to analogue converters were only found in a few locations, while computers were more plentiful (Manning 1985, p. 240). Now laptops are so fast that there is virtually no delay between composing and hearing the result, so powerful that most musicians do not use their full capacity, and priced so low that it is not uncommon for musicians, even in developing countries, to own several machines.[10]

The tipping point in the accessibility of digital music technology came in 1983 with the release of the Yamaha DX-7, a programmable digital music synthesiser. Takayuki Rai believes: 'It was a revolution in the digital music world . . . starting up computer music studios and keeping them became much cheaper and we didn't need to rely on the huge subsidy from the government any more.'[11] The minimum cost of the previous generation of machines capable of music synthesis, the general purpose PDP-11 computing system, was a hundred thousand dollars; only schools and research institutions could afford them. Yamaha priced the DX-7 at an attractive 'two thousand dollars – a fifty-fold difference – and the number of people and institutions doing digital work increased almost overnight'.[12] The DX-7 wasn't just an inexpensive synthesiser; its programmability made the possibilities of music creation quite interesting.[13] Yamaha most likely sold 160,000 of these synthesisers between 1983 and 1988 (Kolb 2002), permanently changing the world of electronic music and democratising access to sound synthesis equipment.

Sound technologies are more than just tools for the creation of music; they are social artefacts. The human ear on Alexander Graham Bell's phonautograph 'marked the collision of acoustics, physiology, otology, the pedagogy of the deaf, the state's relation to the poor, and Western Union's research agenda' (Stern 2003, p. 338). For years, electronic musicians have been influenced by the competing agendas of audio research, commercial profit, government programs and artistic expression. For poorer countries, such as Mexico, where there has never been a governmental investment in electronic music, falling equipment prices have meant that the government can now help to fund studios. The new Center for Music and Sonic Art in Morelia, Mexico is funded half by the federal government and half by the local government,[14] hopefully creating a lasting socio-political musical entity.

It is very easy to explain the explosive growth in computer music by tracing the falling costs of tools, but the culture of 'how-to-do-it' has gradually spread as electronic musicians have learned to share information and software more efficiently.[15] For example, the Center for New Music and Audio Technologies at the University of California at Berkeley recommends that all students purchase a laptop and also provides them with site licences for software.[16] Today, even in Mexico, all students have their own laptops, even though most of them have to run open source software, or cracked copies of commercial software.[17] At Rensselaer Polytechnic Institute all students are required to have their own laptop, 'liberating them from the tyranny of having to sign up to use a studio'.[18]

Electronic musicians now have unfettered access to most of their tools, and they can access information on the World Wide Web, from their home, the studio and even their local café. Before he started working at STEIM, Takuro Mizuta Lippit had never even spent time in a professional studio; he learned everything from the internet, and he freely admits that about eighty per cent of the code he uses is written by someone else.[19] This kind of self-education would have been unheard of even ten years ago. The internet is more than a repository for code; it has allowed for many other possibilities including the download of audio, the study of history, and the creation virtual communities.[20] Over the past decade the internet has helped spawn a new movement in digital music. It is not academically based, and for the most part the composers involved are self-taught (Cascone 2004, p. 392).

Does this accessibility have its own cost? In the early days of electronic music, composers had to have a true commitment to their craft; they had to plan out what they wanted to do with the limited time available to them, and program their machines carefully so time wouldn't be wasted tracking down bugs. Today's environment is much more immediate: when I program in Max/MSP I can listen to the results instantaneously and adjust parameters or debug on the fly. Do the astonishing capabilities of today's realtime performance systems result in our losing a certain gravitas with effortless editing? R. Luke Dubois thinks the ease of creation has an impact on the quality of his work; therefore, he deliberately creates projects which have to 'render', forcing him to think through his process completely before programming.[21] Although many of the people I interviewed expressed some nostalgia for the old way of 'having to think before you create', no one thought the rewards of deliberation outweighed the advances in computer technology.

The democratisation of tools extends to all areas of music production; the composer can be his/her own 'copyist, proofreader, conductor and orchestra . . . this is the most staggering breakthrough in the art of music since the invention of counterpoint' (Russcol 1972, p. xvii). The invention may be staggering, but the world of experts has been replaced by the world of technology, creating a desultory effect on much music.[22] Rather than taking pieces to an expert to be mastered, musicians do it themselves because they have access to the technology. Most of the musicians I interviewed believe that this ease of construction has led to a decided increase in the percentage of poor pieces with electronics, but because the number of people writing for electronics has increased, the actual number of good pieces has increased. Paul Berg put it best: 'In the past when you only had one hundred people working in the field, maybe five pieces a year were interesting. Now you have ten thousand people working in the field, and out of those works between fifty and one hundred pieces are interesting.'[23] Despite having to listen to more bad music, no one misses the days of fighting for studio time, long waits and unreliable equipment. Pauline Oliveros was the only person interviewed to miss equipment – specifically the warmth and ruggedness of tube amplifiers – but she also regrets that there are now more conformity enforcers than innovators.[24] Paul Berg concurs: 'Before there was a sense of excitement and discovery, now everyone has pre-conceived ideas about electronic music. I enjoyed the field before there were definitions.'[25] As composers in modern computer culture we are working with technology which is approximately fifty years old, is still in its infancy and primitive in its own right,[26] yet some are already trumpeting its demise:

> Back in the 'old days', the electronic technology used in music was quite primitive, yet the range of music that was attempted was staggering, and a freewheeling spirit of adventure was prevalent. Today, we have computers with technical capabilities inconceivable at the time of Varèse and the early works of Cage and Stockhausen. Yet as the technical capabilities have expanded, the range of musical possibilities which are being explored has become increasingly restricted.
>
> (Ostertag 2001)

I believe 'academic electronic music' is on the verge of a second upheaval. A revolution is brewing, a revolution based not on technical innovations but on aesthetic growth. As people from all different cultures, experiences and aesthetics gain access to music technology, the field will be compelled to accept the influences of music outside the Western canon. Academic electronic music initially grew out of the European avant-garde, serialism and algorithmic composition. Today electronic music is ubiquitous and the internet-educated music technologists are making inroads into the academy; J. Anthony Allen notes that 'many composers at conferences . . . present a tape piece that is extremely abstract and avoids even a hint of a beat. During a post-concert discussion over a few drinks, they offer a copy of their techno album, referring to it as their "real music"' (Allen 2005, p. 9). As these young composers begin to assume positions of power within established studios, they will instigate a change in the restrictive definition of academic electronic music.

Studios

> We have also sound-houses, where we practise and demonstrate all sounds,
> and their generation.
> Francis Bacon (1626)

As early as the 1600s there was a desire to create a space dedicated to sound in all its forms. In 1937, John Cage called for 'centers of experimental music [to] be established . . . where the new materials, oscillators, turntables, generators, means for amplifying small sounds, film phonographs etc. will be available for use' (Cage 2004, pp. 26–7). Many electronic musicians saw the need for specialised studio spaces, yet few dared to dream that those spaces could one day be found inside every home. Max Mathews was one of the few visionaries to foresee the day when each home has its own computer, enabling music as a means of self-expression to be accessible to all (Mathews 1969, p. 16). 'The latest generation of computers and software has now made it easy for the musician to record, create, produce and edit music alone in his or her own studio' (Assche, Ranciere and Diederichson 2004, p. 8). With the advent of home studios, what is the purpose of the public studio today?

The advantages of having a home studio are numerous: primarily, it liberates the composer, promoting flexibility and freedom of self-expression. In South Africa, especially, the affordability of computers and open source software has had a strong impact in less advantaged communities, allowing home studios to flourish.[27] The difference between working at a public studio and a private home is huge: 'instead of eking out every last bit of energy to stay alive in the studio late at night, bringing in snacks and coffee and taking naps on several chairs lined up, [musicians] can now do most of their work at home, with tea, food and rests anytime needed.'[28] Most home studios resemble the earliest recording studios as musicians use any available space with 'crude soundproofing and physical separation [to] optimise the room to the needs of the tympanic machine and ensure the unity and distinctness of the sound event being produced' (Stern 2003, p. 236).

As home studios become ever more complex, the role of the public studio must change. The institutions must switch from being providers of computers to being providers of ideas and intelligent criticism about electroacoustic music.[29] A notable exception is the Institute of Sonology where the mission statement has remained the same. Their intent was never to provide equipment, rather they have always created an environment to explore programmed music, make noise at the sound level, and use waveforms and concepts as control structures.[30] Most other studios have had to reinvent themselves, as they try to reverse the exodus of musicians who own their own tools. Today's studio managers see their spaces as a kind of ultimate plug-in. Professional studios have been redesigned for multi-channel work,[31] and offer rigorously tested environments with engineered acoustics as extensions to the home studio.[32] The SARC studios in Belfast, Ireland have a Sonic Laboratory which provides a unique space for cutting-edge initiatives in the creation and delivery of music and audio within a purpose-built, variable acoustic space. Most home studios will never have room for extreme sound diffusion, anechoic experiments, or a large recording stage. The public studio remains viable largely by virtue of its size.

Stanford University actively encourages its users to merge the home and public studio by creating the same work environment at the home and at school. Fernando Lopez-Lezcano created a software suite called Planet CCRMA which is installed on every Stanford studio machine, and ideally on the home computer of every user of the studio as well. Users become familiar with the software on their own time, and can use the programs to their fullest extent at the university.[33] Interestingly, in Korea electronic music practitioners have not had to address the dichotomy between home and professional studio, because they 'did not have any important computer music studio at the Universities or Laboratories which focused on musical composition and technical research, since none of the associations recognised the necessity to support computer music'.[34] Electronic music in Korea has always been created in home studios; institutions are only slowly beginning to support the field. The Korean University of Arts and Hanyang University now have studios and degrees in computer music. Seong-Ah Shin finds it is difficult to encourage her students to use the school's studio because they are more comfortable at home.[35]

The auditory field produced through technicised listening becomes a kind of personal space (Stern 2003, p. 158). People have always had a strong connection to the studios in which they work; spending hundreds of hours a year in a space creating works of artistic expression cements a relationship which goes far beyond the technological resources available; over ten years later, I can still draw a detailed diagram of the studio at my undergraduate school. Although I have always had a strong connection to my studio space, I never felt entirely comfortable composing in a room where my time was limited, where I couldn't leave a mess of papers and sketches laid out on the floor, or even leave the EQ settings on the mixing board set for a particular piece. As soon as it was feasible I started my own home studio. Before entering a doctoral programme in composition I was able to use the dining room in my apartment as my main studio because I had amassed enough personal equipment. Having a space of my own definitely enabled me to do better work. Mara Helmuth also has a home studio that gives her 'a peaceful and natural-feeling workspace without distractions, allowing the spiritual element of composition to come forth'.[36]

Most people interviewed for this article consider their home studio to be their main studio; the large public studios serve to augment these private spaces. In America we can see this as returning to our roots. Unlike the early European studios which were funded by radio stations and audio companies, both the Columbia–Princeton Electronic Music Center and the Mills Tape Music Center started in living rooms as groups of people with an interest in working with electronics pooled their resources. Institutional funding came only after the proven popularity and success of these ventures.

Community

> All music, any organisation of sounds is then a tool for the creation or consolidation of community.
>
> Jacques Attali (2004)

The studio is much more than a collection of equipment; the members of a studio form a special personal bond. The studio offers a place for people to share ideas, to collaborate on projects, and criticise one another's work. I believe Max Mathews was being reductionist when he said 'the role of an electronic music center is to tell people that electronic music exists',[37] but it seems that today, more than ever, the main attraction of a studio is the community which surrounds it. After a trip to the University of Virginia, Brad Garton, director of the Columbia Computer Music Center (CMC) wrote:

> Essentially, we've all had to redefine the purpose of our studios over the past decade, moving from a situation where the purpose was obvious (i.e. only few people had computers at home that could do computer music easily) to one where that obvious purpose has totally disappeared. So then you look beyond that and ask 'what *can* a studio provide that people don't have at home?' In our case (and University of Virginia), we've set up a lot of hardware-hacking workbenches; a lot of the Computer Music Center users are becoming involved in building installations, circuit-bending, performance interfaces, etc. I know others who are providing good spaces for critical listening, performance rehearsals, collaborative meeting-places, etc. But all this also points to a deeper rationale for studios – there was a period before we created the hardware-hacking spaces where the scene at the CMC was at a low ebb. Now the energy and 'vibe' of the place is at a high again, and it made me aware and appreciative (again) of the social role that a studio can play. I think this is almost more important than the specific services being provided – a context can truly make the work happen.[38]

Everyone interviewed for this article eventually mentioned community as a necessary aspect to a studio. John Chowning said at one point he realised that not being in proximity to engineers was a real handicap. Paul Berg misses the time when everyone at the Institute of Sonology would stop working for a 10:30 communal coffee break. Today, studios' communities are strong, but they tend to be centred around the internet rather than personal contact. Chowning misses the immediacy of the early years at Stanford before they installed an audio switch; if one person was testing out a sound for a piece everyone in the building would hear it. During this time Xavier Rodet made a quick advancement in his vocal synthesis program Chant after he heard some of Chowning's sounds and incorporated the idea of random periodic vibrato into his own program. This never could have happened if an audio switch had routed the sound just to Chowning's workstation. Of course awful/loud/hurtful sounds came through the speakers as well, but this communal listening created a close-knit social structure. Today, Pauline Oliveros uses sound to create a community in a similar way, albeit virtually; her students are required to post all of their work to a public site, and they are actively encouraged to manipulate the sounds made by others.

In my experience, the internet communities which spring up around an electronic music centre are usually more robust than those formed by user groups. Even though the digital computer brings strangers closer together (Johnson 1999, p. 39), it seems that in-person connections, however brief or tenuous, define a group. This observation may not hold true in other fields, because those participating in the process of making music, whether individually or together are involved in the fundamentally social process of human being itself (Filmer 2004, p. 97). Music, technology and community have successfully collided in Jamaica where over the past forty years reggae sound systems (three speaker stacks in a triangular configuration pointing inward) 'have become institutions on par with the local churches and football teams . . . the current Dance-Hall Reggae is so named because it could only be heard on the sound systems in open-air dance halls' (Henriques 2004, p. 445). Music technology leads to an aesthetic which leads to a community: the 'need for advice, microphones, speakers, quiet spaces and audiences continues to draw us together'.[39]

Personal performance

> To each his own bubble, that is the law today.   Jean Baudrillard (1988)

As home computers become more powerful, it is not just audio professionals who have their own home studios: almost every family has a machine capable of editing audio at home. The interest in music in the home began long before the age of the computers, with home audio systems. Some composers created works to explore the performance possibilities of living room hi-fi sets. The recorded version of *HPSCHD* by John Cage and Lejaren Hiller contained instructions for the listener to control the settings of a stereo during playback (Manning 1985, p. 242), incorporating the listener into the performance of the piece. In 1966 Glenn Gould saw the home becoming an idealised listening space.

> The listener is able to indulge performances through electronic modifications with which he endows the listening experience, imposes his own personality upon the work and his relation to it, from an artistic to an environmental experience. Dial twiddling in its limited way is an interpretive act. Forty years ago the listener had the option of flicking a switch inscribed 'on' and 'off' and with an up-to-date machine, modifying the volume just a bit. Today, the variety of controls made available to him requires analytical judgment. And these controls are but primitive regulatory devices compared to these participational possibilities which the listener will enjoy once current laboratory techniques have been appropriated by home playback devices . . . permit[ting] him to create his own ideal performance. (Gould 2004, p. 122)

Today it isn't the home stereo system which allows novice musicians to manipulate music, it is the home computer with free audio software such as Garage Band, Audacity and Soundhack.

In 2005 Nine Inch Nails released *The Hand that Feeds* in Garage Band format, which allows users to remix the song using the same digital tracks produced by the band (Mac Minute 2006). Markus Popp of Oval has gone a step further suggesting 'a model for one possible alternative approach to audio productivity in contemporary electronic music, along the lines of music-as-software' (Inglis 2002). *Ovalprocess* is both software and an album; it hands over control of the audio to the audience under very controlled circumstances (Toop 2004, p. 246). In a more academic vein, Christopher Bailey has created a piece called *Sand*, a twenty-five minute long acousmatic composition with a listener interface. It can be experienced as a complete piece of music, listened to from beginning to end, or explored at one's own pace, examining and taking apart its sonic events, in any order one wishes (Bailey 2004, p. 243). The basic home computer is an incredibly sophisticated machine, which gives even a casual user a home studio where (s)he can experiment with sound.

Conclusion

> Considered as a social process, sound reproduction has irreducible social and spatial components. Without studios, and without other social placements of microphones in performative frames that were always real spaces, there was no independent reproducibility of sound. The studio in particular implies a configuration of bodies and sounds in space, a particular ordering of practices and attitudes. Its significance is at once technical, social and spatial. The studio becomes a way of doing things, and a social frame for reproducibility. Jonathan Stern (2003)

Today's electronic music studio is a metaphor,[40] a conceptual transfer involving the withdrawal of schema from an initial literal application, into a new application effecting a different definition (Goodman 1979). Electronic music centres used to be highly specialised literal spaces where a few lucky individuals could work on rare and expensive equipment. Today, through technological advances and an effort of philosophical transformation, a studio can be a laptop sitting on a kotatsu in Japan, it can be a Kwaito community in South Africa, it can be a portable audio recorder in a park in Mexico, a reggae dance-hall in Jamaica, a family home in the suburbs, or even a virtual studio created by a suite of software. The studio is no longer defined by its contents; rather it has become a context created by the user.

3 Live electronic music

NICOLAS COLLINS

It is perhaps a general human habit to view the technological and the organic as opposites. It is certainly the case that the phrase 'live electronic music' strikes many a music fan as oxymoronic. Isn't the purpose of electronics to do things for us so we don't have to do them 'live' ourselves? To record, perfect and play back performances so we can listen while cycling stationarily? To facilitate the creation of inhumanly intricate compositions that spew themselves out of speakers at the touch of a button, instead of all that messy sliding about on strings? While there is no question that composers of tape music and computer music (and a fair number of pop music producers as well) have employed electronics to exactly these ends, electronic technology has another, and possibly more profound power: enabling new and volatile connections. Don't think Edison, think Alexander Graham Bell. Since the 1930s (well before the advent of tape) composers have been using this property of electronics to produce not just new sounds but fundamentally new approaches to organising the sonic world.

Pre-history

Electronic music has its pre-history in the age of steam. In 1897 Thaddeus Cahill patented the Telharmonium, a machine that weighed in at over two hundred tons and resembled a power station more than a musical instrument. It generated sine tones with dynamos, played from an organ-like keyboard. Cahill understood that electricity could provide not only sound but a means of distribution as well: the Telharmonium's sounds were carried over the telephone lines that were beginning to be laid in major cities, intended for playback through speaker systems in restaurants, hotel lobbies and homes of the rich. Cahill envisaged a subscription-based music service, not unlike that of the Muzak corporation thirty-seven years later, but unlike pre-recorded Muzak, the Telharmonium was an instrument that had to be played to be heard.[1]

Better known today is the eponymous electronic instrument of the Russian inventor Leon Theremin, created in 1920. Theremin rejected traditional instrumental interfaces such as keyboards, frets or fingerholes, and introduced the first 'free air' gestural controller. The Theremin was played by moving one's hands in the proximity of two antennas (one controlled pitch, the other affected volume), effectively incorporating the player's body mass into the circuitry. Popularised by a number of charismatic performers (most notably Clara Rockmore), the instrument became the physical embodiment of futuristic sound: in film soundtracks it evoked psychosis and flying saucers, and in pop songs it shifted from ghoulish to groovy (it is the signature instrument in the Beach Boy's 'Good Vibrations'). Though marketed as an instrument that could be played by anyone, it proved to be extremely difficult to play *well* – a fact that limited its popular use.[2]

The Theremin established the paradox of, as well as the paradigm for, the 'Electronic Instrument': it looked and sounded modern, but somehow lacked the legitimacy and substance of more conventional instruments. Other early electronic instruments such as the Ondes Martenot (1928) and the Trautonium (1928) were similarly incorporated into a few works of chamber and orchestral music by some composers of note, and played evocative roles in film soundtracks, but it wasn't until Laurence Hammond's development of the electric organ that bears his name in 1935 that an electronic instrument was generally accepted by the musical public, and it did so by making inroads into broadly popular, rather than elitist, genres – it might be electronic, but it was a workhorse equally adept at playing Hindemith, hymns, polkas and jazz.

These early electronic instruments were just that: they made new sounds but did nothing to change the nature of musical composition or performance. 'Tape Music', which didn't arise until some fifty years after the Telharmonium, did represent a fundamental rupture with older modes of composition, but its roots lay in the film tradition of pre-scripted editing and montage, rather than in live performance. [3] Tape Music embodied a kind of high Modernist desire for extending composerly control and independence. But, beginning in the late 1930s quirky composers began using electronic tools to exploit serendipity on the stage as well.

John Cage

The most radical musical use of electronic technology did not rely on specialised instruments such as the Theremin, but on the rapidly expanding realm of consumer flotsam that characterised mid-twentieth-century America. John Cage established himself early in his career as an innovator not only of musical forms but of instrumental resources as well. In 1939, after several years of writing for ensembles of homemade percussion instruments, he began working with live electronic sound in *Imaginary Landscape No. 1* (1939), scored for piano, a large Chinese cymbal and two turntables equipped with records of test tones. Cage asked the performers to manipulate the pitch and rhythm of the tones by changing turntable speed, spinning the platter by hand, and dropping and lifting the needle. Though vehemently uninterested in pop music, Cage can be credited with inventing the Disc Jockey as a stage performer.

Cage scored his piece for a common household appliance, though a Theremin might have produced a similar sound. It was a statement of circumstances (Cage could not afford a Theremin) but also of principle:

> Most inventors of electrical instruments have attempted to imitate eighteenth- and nineteenth-century instruments, just as early automobile designers copied the carriage. The Novachord and the Solovox are examples of this desire to imitate the past rather than construct the future. When Theremin provided an instrument with genuinely new possibilities, Thereministes did their utmost to make the instrument sound like some old instrument, giving it a sickeningly sweet vibrato, and performing upon it, with difficulty, masterpieces from the past . . . Thereministes act as censors, giving the public those sounds they think the public will like.
>
> (from the 'Credo' of 1937, reproduced in Cage (1966), pp. 3–4)

Cage's ambition, by contrast, was to give audiences the world and allow them to pick and choose.

A decade later Cage turned his attention to another commonplace appliance with *Imaginary Landscape No. 4* (1951) for twelve radios. In keeping with his growing interest in indeterminacy, the score meticulously notates movements of the tuning and volume controls, but does not pretend to govern the actual sound material received and heard in any given performance. The result elegantly demonstrates the difference between *chance*, as Cage would have it – setting up a fixed compositional structure that forces one to listen to unpredictable sound – and *improvisation*, where the performer is free to choose sounds on the basis of personal preference. Cage never stopped writing for more conventional instruments (he once explained to me, 'If I don't write for these virtuosos they'll have to play music by even worse composers'[4]), but he explored electronic resources extensively in the 1950s and 60s. The very instability of the electronics of the time, and the unpredictable output of his re-purposed appliances, made technology a critical partner in his experiments in indeterminacy.

Cage turned again to the record player in *Cartridge Music* (1960), but this time stripped the pickup out of the tone arm and asked performers to DJ *without* records. The stylus is replaced with anything small enough to fit in its socket – a spring, a twig, a guitar string, a broom straw, a pipe cleaner, etc. When amplified, these unassuming objects produce sounds of astonishing complexity and richness: tiny objects emit low marimba-like tones, and simple springs evoke the reverberation of a church. In keeping with the novelty of the instruments employed in the piece, Cage forwent a fixed score in favor of a 'kit' of transparent overlays – a wiggly dotted line, amoeba-like blobs, dots, circles and a clock face – with which the performers assemble their individual parts. The graphics specify the distribution of actions over the course of a performance – when and how to play or change an object, adjust the volume or tone control, etc. The piece can be of any duration, for any number of players, using any kind of objects to produce sound through the cartridges. Given that playing a phonograph cartridge requires no traditional musical skill, interpreting the score presupposes no musical literacy, thus matching a radically new instrument to a correspondingly innovative approach to scoring.

With the significant role of chance in arranging the overlays in *Cartridge Music*, performers sometimes find themselves carrying out absurd instructions: futilely twiddling something in a cartridge when the volume is completely off, or raising the level so high that shrieking feedback obliterates everything else. But as Cage blithely advises in the score, 'all events, ordinarily thought to be undesirable, such as feed-back, humming, howling, etc., are to be accepted' (Cage 1960). Cage's acceptance of electronic accident was a sign of things to come. Feedback became the ur-sound of chance: it erupted whenever composers hooked up sound systems without the benefit of technicians; it opened The Beatles' 'I Feel Fine' with a 'pwwwwaaaaooooi-iiiinnnnnnnggggggggg' in 1964, and then went on to become a defining element in rock music from Hendrix to Lordi. In the tightly proscribed world of pop it became the bad-boy way to insert the irresponsible and unpredictable. Cheap, loud and only somewhat controllable, it possessed a seemingly wilful independence that, in the 1960s, echoed the spirit of the times. But it wasn't just noise, it had *content* – feedback traced in sound the movement of a microphone or speaker, and it revealed the resonant frequencies of rooms, musical instruments, mouths, culverts and barrels. For many composers influenced by Cage, such as those in the Sonic Arts Union, feedback also suggested a *method*, a way of organising or controlling sounds, and served as the first step onto the electronic stage.

Sonic Arts Union

In the mid-1960s, even as European tape music and serialism were flourishing, at least in academic circles, Cage – arguably the most inventive composer of the twentieth century – was still performing for tiny audiences in lofts, chapels and armories. Cage may have had little institutional support, but his pragmatic approach to technology, combined with his desire to re-infuse music with risk, was profoundly influential on younger American composers. In 1966 Robert Ashley, David Behrman, Alvin Lucier and Gordon Mumma formed the Sonic Arts Union for the performance of their own compositions, most of which used live electronics in a distinctly post-Cagean mode.

Behrman's 1966 composition, *Wave Train*, exemplifies the legacy of *Cartridge Music*'s repurposing of commonplace technology, amplification of small sounds, and incorporation of feedback. Loose guitar pickups are placed on the strings of a grand piano and connected to guitar amps under the soundboard, which are turned up to the point of feedback. The result is a loud mix of guitar-like feedback, amplified piano, and percussive rattling as the pickups bounce on the strings. The pitch material can be nudged (if not actually controlled) by moving the pickups to different strings, and the audience is drawn into this cock-eyed cause-and-effect as they watch arms messing about inside the piano and hear the unpredictable results. Behrman also built his own electronic circuits, favouring arrays of multiple copies of relatively simple circuits that combined to form surprisingly complex textures. By 1974 he had constructed an extraordinary homemade synthesiser with dozens of oscillators, a rudimentary sequencer and pitch-detecting circuits. Stepping through a series of lush chords in response to pitches played on a cello, *Cello With Melody Driven Electronics* (1975) was a harbinger of the interactive computer music of the next decade. For the cellist and audience alike it was utterly unexpected to hear electronic sounds react so directly to acoustic ones in an era when a fixed tape was the default method for adding electronics to a solo instrumental composition.

Even before David Behrman, Gordon Mumma was one of the first American composers to build his own musical circuits, designing sophisticated analogue computers that produced and processed sound in reaction to input from acoustic sources and electronic controls. In *Hornpipe* (1967) a player 'rings' the performance space with a French horn, seeking out the strong resonant frequencies of the room (much like finding the best notes to sing in the shower), while filters in Mumma's homemade 'Cybersonic Console' zero in on these pitches, and gradually increase in gain and resonance until they start to oscillate, spilling feedback-like shrieks through the sound system. Unlike more traditional electronic instruments such as Theremins or oscillators, Mumma's circuits produced no sound of their own – without the French horn and the architecture to complete the network, the Console was mute.

Ashley's work with the Sonic Arts Union was a mix of theatre, spoken word and electronics. The performer in *The Wolfman* (1964) controls very loud feedback by shaping his mouth in front of a microphone to form a series of acoustic resonators that force the feedback to shift to different pitches. In the 1972 piece *In Sara, Mencken, Christ and Beethoven There Were Men And Women*, Ashley recites an epic poem by John Barton Wolgamot which purports to list the names of all the important people in the history of the world. Via a complex patch on a Moog synthesiser (programmed by composer Paul De Marinis) that responds to the inflection of Ashley's voice, the composer attempts to translate into electronic sound the very formal, somewhat fugue-like structure of the poem.

For Lucier electronics were a tool for articulating acoustic phenomena, and sometimes social ones as well. In *Vespers* (1969) blindfolded performers carry 'Sondols': flashlight-sized devices, designed as navigational aids for the blind, which emit sharp clicks in emulation of the sonar mechanism of bats. By listening to the returning echoes as they 'sweep' the performance space with the Sondols, the performers attempt to gauge the size of the room and detect and avoid obstacles as they echolocate their way across the space. The audience hears the acoustic traces of this (literally) pedestrian task, a sort of stippled sonic portrait of the architecture. Once upon a time a composer's responsibility had ended with the manuscript paper, and the player's with the bell or belly of the instrument; anything that happened after sound left the instrument was down to the architecture, and beyond the control of composer or musician. But in *Vespers* Lucier usurps the architect by attempting to compose the very movement of soundwaves in space. In his best-known work, *I am sitting in a room* (1969) Lucier records his voice, then plays it back through speakers, and re-records it in the same room through the microphone; he plays back this second recording, and again records it through the microphone; he plays back and re-records this third recording, as before; over and over he repeats the process, twenty or more times. With each generation the words become less intelligible as the acoustic properties of the room emphasise certain pitches at the expense of others until all sense of language is lost in a string of undulating tones. Where *Vespers* renders in sound an image of the concert space itself, *I am sitting in a room*, like a seventeenth-century Dutch portrait of a contented citizen surrounded by his prized possessions, brings into public space an acoustic picture not merely of a different room, but of man in his private world.

Living with tape

Lucier's piece demonstrated for the audience how tape could be used to parse a gradual process and reveal the detail in its stages, rather than simply presenting the final product. In the 1960s tape – the essential tool of studio-based music from Stockhausen to the Standells – was reinvented as a performance instrument. Tape delay systems were used by a number of composers to create realtime counterpoint from live performance. Two reel-to-reel tape decks would be set side by side on a table; a reel of tape would be placed on the leftmost machine and threaded past the heads to a take-up reel on the second machine; the first deck would be set to record and the second to play back; as the tape moved from one deck to the other, sounds recorded on the first would be heard from the second at a delay corresponding to the distance between the machines and the tape speed (a fifteen-inch separation between decks running at seven and a half inches per second yields a delay of two seconds; a fifteen-foot gap would produce a delay of twenty-four seconds).

In works such as *I of IV* (1966) Pauline Oliveros built up thick abstract textures from simple oscillator tones that panned back and forth, reverberated, and accumulated in layers as they fed back from the playback deck to the record deck (Oliveros 1984, pp. 36–46). The delay feedback retained and extended every adjustment made to the oscillators, and having to put up with the consequences of her actions for several minutes put Oliveros in a contemplative state – her tape delay pieces are characterised by small changes over long periods of time. Terry Riley used a similar two-deck delay to provide accompaniment to improvisation on soprano saxophone and electric organ in pieces such as *Poppy Nogood and the Phantom Band* (1969) and *Rainbow in Curved Air* (1970). Riley's work was highly melodic in comparison to Oliveros, and he used the delay accumulation to build up canonical counterpoint that favoured modal playing. For both composers the delay system served initially as a novel performance instrument, but had greater long-term significance as a *listening* tool: the sustained textures, drones and modal, just-intoned harmonies led both Riley and Oliveros into deeper investigation of non-Western music and culture. In the 1970s Riley began many years of serious study of North Indian singing, which greatly influenced his own compositional style. By the 1990s Oliveros had fused her electronic work, her background as an accordionist, and her interest in meditation into her 'Deep Listening' music project, which relies on both computer programs and unusually reverberant acoustic spaces (such as underground reservoirs, caves, etc.) to replicate and extend the effects of her original delay system.

In 1965 Steve Reich began experimenting with a simple and elegant idea: when two identical tape loops of speech were played on two decks running at slightly different speeds, unusual sound patterns would emerge from the interaction of the loops as they slipped out of phase, moving from perfect synchronisation, through flanging-style filtering effects, to distinct rhythmic counterpoint. He created two studio compositions based on this effect (*It's Gonna Rain*, 1965, and *Come Out*, 1966), after which he looked for ways to achieve similar effects with conventional instruments (as a composer his primary interest lay in live performance, not tape composition). In *Violin Phase* (1967), Reich retained the tape loop, but added an instrumental part. In preparation, the violinist records a ten-note, twelve-beat figure that is cut into a tape loop. As this loop plays back, the violinist doubles the part, initially in perfect sync, then – after increasing his speed by a tiny amount – gradually slipping out of phase with the loop until, after five minutes, the violin is four beats ahead of the recording. A second loop, four bars out of phase with the first (and in sync with the violin) is faded up, and the violinist spends a few minutes mimicking the 'chalk talk' – the inner voices that appear as a result of the interaction between the two loops, which Reich likened to optical illusions such as those in the work of M. C. Escher. The violinist repeats the slippage process against the second, and later a third, loop. With *Piano Phase* (1967), for two pianos, Reich abandoned tape entirely and moved on to techniques whereby players could produce 'phase music' without recourse to electronics. As with Oliveros and Riley, experimenting with tape had revealed musical vistas that extended beyond the technology. Today Reich is one of the most visible American composers of large-scale multimedia operas, but artefacts of the tape loops can still be heard in his current works.

Gavin Bryars took a droll approach to phase music in his 1971 composition, *1, 2, 1-2-3-4*: each musician in a small ensemble was given a cassette player, a pair of headphones, and a cassette of the same piece of music. After starting tape playback on cue, the musicians mimic their respective parts on the tape as best they can. Given the inconsistencies in speed between the various machines and the impossibility of all the tapes starting in perfect synchronisation, the musicians gradually drift apart, producing phase patterns similar to those in Reich's work, but with a few critical differences: the source music is often in an 'easy listening' style, and the instruments are somewhat out of tune with one another because of the vagaries in the cassette playback speed, puncturing the potential for pomposity implicit in any avant-garde enterprise, and embracing the idea that *chance* can produce both Zen and slapstick.

Composing inside electronics

The beauty of the tape recorder, as demonstrated in Bryars' piece, is that it can be found and played by anyone. But as Mumma and Behrman had shown, there was something to be gained from getting inside actual circuitry. Just how much could be gained became evident in the career of David Tudor. Tudor started out as a virtuoso pianist of the avant-garde, premiering compositions so technically demanding they were deemed 'impossible' to play, such as Pierre Boulez's *Deuxième Sonate pour Piano*. By the early 1950s Tudor was serving as pianist for the Merce Cunningham Dance Company (whose approach to movement closely paralleled the work of its musical director, John Cage), and assisting in the realisation of Cage's own electronic pieces. Over the next ten years Tudor gradually abandoned the piano and emerged as the first virtuoso of electronic performance – he treated a phonograph cartridge or electronic circuit with the same seriousness of intent and dextrous musicality as he had the piano. Tudor underwent a two-part metamorphosis: from pianist to electronic performer, and then, in the mid-1960s, from performer to composer in his own right. Expanding on Cage's exploration of 'found' technology, Tudor embarked on the arduous process of acquiring enough knowledge of circuit design to construct his own new instruments. He believed that new, object-specific, intrinsically *electronic*, musical material and forms would emerge as each instrument took shape: 'I try to find out what's there – not to make it do what I want, but to release what's there. The object should teach you what it wants to hear' (Schonfeld 1972). This clearly stated ethos of music *implicit* in technology served as a paradigm for much American electronic music of the 1970s.

Beginning in 1968, Tudor composed a series of pieces under the title *Rainforest*, which culminated in *Rainforest IV*, a work developed at a workshop in Chocurua, NH, in 1973. The principle underlying *Rainforest* is that of sounds played through transducers fastened to solid objects, which filter, resonate and otherwise transform the sounds; the processed sounds are directly radiated by the transduced objects, which serve as 'sculptural speakers'; contact mikes on the objects pick up the vibrating surfaces of the objects, and these micro-sounds are mixed and heard through ordinary loudspeakers around the space. *Rainforest* exists in a twilight zone between a concert and an installation: the players sit at tables mixing sounds sent out to a maze of twittering objects, through which the audience is free to wander. With an open-form score that encouraged experimentation in the design of both sound generators and resonated objects, the piece was a creative catalyst for a number of young composers, who subsequently formed a loose collective ensemble called 'Composers Inside Electronics'. Over the next twenty-eight years this group served as a laboratory for artist-designed circuitry and electronic performance, presenting dozens of installations of *Rainforest IV* worldwide, as well as performances of works by individual members of the ensemble.[5]

Tudor, along with other 'first generation' composer-engineers, had had to confront the baffling world of transistors in order to build their instruments, but by the early 1970s Integrated Circuits (ICs) had transformed the landscape of electronic design. ICs grouped transistors and other components into affordable, Lego-like functional modules that contained ninety per cent of a functional circuit – a circuit, moreover, designed by someone who really knew what he was doing. The remaining ten per cent could be filled in by non-engineers swapping notes and browsing hobbyist magazines. A musical community formed around this exchange of information. In addition to the 'Composers Inside Electronics', it included students of David Behrman and Robert Ashley at Mills College in Oakland, CA; of Alvin Lucier at Wesleyan University in Middletown, CT; of Serge Tcherepnin at California Institute of the Arts in Valencia, CA; and others scattered throughout the USA and, more thinly, Europe.[6]

Some participants were naïfs or muddlers who designed beautiful, odd-ball circuits out of ignorance and good luck. Ralph Jones encapsulated this spirit in *Star Networks* (1978), which asks performers to build circuits on stage according to a configuration that forces almost any selection of components into unpredictable but charming oscillation, neatly bypassing any need for a theoretical understanding of electronics on the player's part. In defiance of the conventional wisdom of using oscilloscopes and other test equipment as a visual aid to the design process, in *Star Networks* the instruments are designed by ear alone, and the audience follows every step of the process by ear as well. Other composers proved sublimely talented, if idiosyncratic, designers: Paul De Marinis included bits of vegetables as electrical components so his circuits would undergo a natural ageing process (*CKT*, 1974); incorporated sensors that responded to a person's electronic field (*Pygmy Gamelan*, 1973); and built 'algorithmic' music composing circuits that anticipated later trends in computer music (*Great Masters of Melody*, 1975), one of which was intended to be played by a bird (*Parrot Pleaser*, 1974).

While the American electronic music scene of the 1970s was characterised by a homespun, but rhapsodic, high-tech ethos that embraced seat-of-the-pants performance, in Europe a well-established state-funded tradition of collaboration between composers and technicians perpetuated the production of meticulously crafted tape music in studios. Live performance with homemade music circuitry erupted in odd pockets nonetheless. Andy Guhl and Norbert Möslang formed the Swiss duo 'Voice Crack' in 1972, and over the next thirty years honed their skills at 'cracking' everyday electronics, which included circuits for extracting sound from blinking lights, radio-controlled cars, radio interference, and obsolete Dictaphones. Dutch composer Michel Waisvisz developed a series of synthesisers played by direct contact between skin and circuit board, culminating in the battery-powered, paperback-size, highly portable 'Cracklebox' in 1975. The tactile quality of these gizmos made them extremely expressive, often dramatic performance instruments, which Waisvisz used primarily in improvisational and theatrical situations.[7]

The rise of the computer

The exact moment when 'circuits' grew into 'computers' is hard to pinpoint: composer-designers like Mumma had been building what were essentially analogue computers for sound since 1960, and the same digital ICs that went into 1970s computers were being used in discrete musical circuits at the same time. Music had been produced on massive mainframe computers (those room-sized things with flashing lights and spinning reels) as early as 1949, but this music was made to be recorded directly onto tape in academic computing centres (Dornbusch 2005; McCartney 1999, pp. 163–4). The machines themselves were not seen on stage until the advent of affordable, portable microcomputers in the late 1970s. Cajoled by the visionary Bay Area artist Jim Horton, a handful of musicians invested in the Kim-1 – a single A4-sized circuit board that looked like nothing so much as an autoharp with a calculator glued on. There was no high-level software available, so every action had to be programmed in machine language, the very low-level instructions that the Central Processor Unit must execute to accomplish anything from adding two numbers to emitting a beep. It could be an arduous, counterintuitive, headache-inducing process, but it offered one great advantage over soldering circuits: it was easier to correct a mistake by re-programming than by re-soldering.

Moreover, even computers as crude as the Kim-1 had memory (one kilobyte of RAM!) and could execute sequential logical operations. These features enabled the creation of instruments that could make ad hoc decisions based on past incidents, a feature of particular interest to composers drawn to the quixotic unpredictability of live performance. Rather than just give more control to the composer, computers extended Tudor-esque electronics: a clever programmer could add attributes of the performer to the hybrid of instrument and score that had come to exemplify circuit-based instruments.[8] Over the next decade Apple, Commodore, Atari, Radio Shack and other companies introduced machines whose increasing sophistication and expanding software base gradually reduced the angst of programming. Homemade circuits by and large faded into anachronism.

Despite the musical potential of computers, however, the ASCII keyboard (even when augmented by the introduction of the Macintosh mouse in 1984) was essentially a typing tool, and a poor performance interface compared to Cage's cartridge or Waisvisz's Cracklebox. In 1983 MIDI (Music Instrument Digital Interface) was introduced as a digital protocol for interconnecting synthesisers, which made it possible to connect a basic organ-like keyboard to a computer, but for some musicians even this was not expressive enough. Considerable energy was spent on the design of novel 'alternative controllers' starting from the late 1980s, most notably at STEIM in Amsterdam.[9] In 1987, for Australian musician Jon Rose's 'Space Violin', STEIM engineers attached an ultrasonic distance measuring device and a hair-pressure sensor to his bow. Wired up to a tiny computer, the system translates the movement of the bow – whether rolling across the strings or fencing with Paganini's demons (as was Rose's occasional wont) – into electronic accompaniment to Rose's acoustic improvisation. This remora of an instrument frees Rose from ever having to touch a computer keyboard, and instead extracts extra musical expression not only from the ordinary gestures of playing the violin, but from a new vocabulary of movement across the concert stage.

From 1991–4, STEIM, together with freelance designer Bert Bongers, helped Laetitia Sonami build various versions of her 'Lady's Glove', an eveningwear take on a virtual reality controller. In her text-centred performances, Sonami uses the glove to translate hand gestures into computer-generated accompaniment for her storytelling. In my own 'trombone-propelled electronics' (begun in 1988) I coupled the slide of an old trombone to part of a computer mouse, attached a small keypad to the slide, affixed a compact loudspeaker to the mouthpiece, and connected the whole thing to a homemade digital signal processor. The slide acts as an overgrown mouse: by pressing buttons on the keypad as I move the slide I can adjust various sound parameters in a program that samples and transforms sounds 'on the fly'; these sounds play back through the speaker and come out of the bell of the trombone – they can be acoustically filtered by moving the slide or using a mute, or bounced off surfaces in the room by aiming the trombone. I wanted a computer instrument with a self-contained acoustic quality that would blend well with other more traditional instruments, for use in both composed work (such as *Tobabo Fonio*, 1988, based on processing Peruvian brass band music) and improvised settings (such as the forty-two short duets on my 1989 CD, *100 of the World's Most Beautiful Melodies*).

Working in the real world

In the 1980s, almost half a century after Cage put the first DJ on the stage, the turntable finally achieved broad cultural recognition as a performance instrument. In the hands of musicians as different as Grandmaster Flash and Christian Marclay, it became the most visible – and occasionally the most overtly virtuosic – electronic instrument of the 1980s and 90s. Building on techniques used by club and radio DJs during the Disco era, and by Jamaican toasting DJs such as Kool Herc, Flash (Joseph Saddler) invented, perfected or popularised several of the turntable techniques that formed the core of 'hip-hop' DJ practice, including scratching and back-cueing for rhythmic emphasis, and cutting between two copies of the same record to extend passages (he installed a switch in his mixer to facilitate rapid cross-fading).[10] In the early 1980s Marclay established his reputation as the premier 'Downtown' DJ through his work with John Zorn and other improvising musicians. Marclay favoured a more abstract, less rhythmically driven style, as befitted the looser music of the downtown scene, often performing with four or more turntables ('hip-hop' DJs typically worked with two), using stickers to force records to skip in repetitive loops, drilling off-centre spindle holes that wobbled the pitch of the record, and collaging together pie-like slices from several records to create thumping musical sequences. The notion of 'playing' records actively rather than passively finally came into its own. Recently, younger DJs such as France's Erik M have merged the Marclay and Flash traditions by combining extended, experimental technique with a strong pop sensibility; and for sheer virtuosity it's hard to beat 'turntablism' as practised by the Invisible Scratch Pickles, a Bay Area turntable quartet. In 1999 it was widely reported that turntable sales exceeded those of electric guitars,[11] although most turntable playing these days is used to create a seamless, beat-matched sequence of tracks, with the occasional discreet scratched accent on top – less about performance per se than replaying the music of others.

Searching for life after vinyl, and intrigued by the possibility of corrupting the new and supposedly 'perfect' medium of the Compact Disc, Yasunao Tone began 'wounding' CDs in 1984 with the skilful application of Sellotape. When played back, Tone's CDs fulfill a Cagean dream of an indeterminate record: the output is a torrent of glitches and micro-fragments of the original recording, and while |<< and >>| can be used to encourage the laser to move to different parts of the CD, the damaged CDs often display a wilful disrespect for direct control. Several of my own compositions also depend upon misbehaving CDs, but for pieces such as *Broken Light* (1991) and *Still Lives* (1993) I modified the CD players, rather than the CDs themselves. Hacks to the circuitry allow performers to draw out recordings (typically of early baroque music) into a sequence of slightly irregular, glitch-accented skipping loops, against which they play their acoustic instruments. The musicians familiarise themselves with the original recordings and their scores, but can never be sure exactly where the next loop will land, which lends a certain tension to the performances.[12]

Some composers chose to engage the messy physicality of the real, analogue world in ways antithetical to the innate precision and often cubicle-constricted countenance of the computer. In one of the sweatiest pieces of electronic music ever composed, *Speaker Swinging* (1982), Canadian Gordon Monahan's three performers whirl blaring speakers around their heads. The viscerally three-dimensional Doppler-shifting tornado of sound emanating from three glistening spandex-clad youths has no equivalent

Figure 3.1 Live performance of *Speaker Swinging* at the Music Gallery, Toronto, 1987. Time exposure shows several revolutions of the speakers with light bulbs attached. Speaker Swingers are (clockwise from top left) Bruce Mau, John Oswald, Sandor Ajzenstat. Gordon Monahan at the sound controls (photo by Dwight Siegner)

in the digital domain. For *Mini-Fan Music* (1992), German sound artists Jens Brand and Waldo Riedl placed handheld fans next to a dozen string instruments strewn around the performance space; the fan blades strum the strings until the batteries run down (typically three to four hours with cheap batteries), the droning sound field slowly changing as the fans slip along the floor and lose speed. In *Humbucket* (1990) Dan Farkas connects a guitar cord to a chain of two dozen guitar effect pedals (bought at Brooklyn stoop sales), and plays the hum of his thumb on the end of the jack as he stomps on their switches, building up layers of distortion, echo, wah-wah, equalisation and myriad other effects.

Circuit bending

Underlying all this stomping and swinging and strumming remains the circuit – the thing that makes Electronic Music electronic. And while the geniuses in Silicon Valley and China have made circuits ever more beautiful and mysterious, sealed with stickers that sternly warn 'no user serviceable parts inside', there are those who see these things not as finished products but as raw material. Reed Ghazala started publishing articles on what he dubbed 'Circuit Bending' in the influential (if quasi-underground) journal, *Experimental Musical Instruments* in 1992.[13] Ghazala incited readers to transform inexpensive found electronics, such as toys and cheap keyboards, by connecting wires between various points on the circuit board at random, until one either induced an interesting new noise or the toy blew up. Circuit Bending tries hard to preserve the innocent enthusiasm of accidental discovery, and discourages spoiling the process with theoretical understanding. It emerged as the perfect antidote to the deterministic world of computers, which had come to dominate all aspects of music production, replacing manuscript paper, tape recorders, mixers, effect boxes and instruments. Circuit Bending is also a truly international movement, with active practitioners on every continent, thanks largely to the use of the World Wide Web as a forum for the open sharing of information.[14]

Phil Archer is representative of the emerging generation of benders, who effortlessly combine bent circuits with Tudor-era contact mike technology and even sophisticated computer programming. Archer did a 'classic' bend to his Yamaha PSS-380 keyboard: exposing the circuit-board, placing the inverted instrument on the performer's lap, and making arbitrary connections between components on the board in live performance. As he writes:

> These connections induce tones, bursts of noise and corrupted 'auto-accompaniment' sequences from the device which are unpredictable in their details but generally 'steerable' overall with practice. The precision and control afforded by the standard keyboard interface is eschewed in favour of direct contact with the circuit, and the performer is continually forced to rethink and re-evaluate their relationship with the instrument in light of the sonic results.[15]

The future present

The first years of the new millennium have seen the rise of grassroots movements in electronic music as diverse as Circuit Bending (with its emphasis on wilful damage to found circuitry) and Phonography (the gentle art of recording interesting acoustic environments) – movements that often blur the distinction between pop and avant-garde, and between music and reportage. More and more art – video, sculpture, film, web art – now incorporates sound, which is no longer the exclusive material of music. The 'Dorkbot' movement ('People doing strange things with electricity') has united hackers in the analogue and digital domains of visual and sonic art.

Their monthly meetings in cities around the globe are occasions for musicians, artists and tinkerers to share their work – performances, installations, videos, web sites, or pure research – all presented to a live audience. Multimedia artists Tali Hinkis and Kyle Lapidus (known collectively as LoVid) perform and create interactive installations with bent and homemade video systems, building graphic synthesis circuits into soft sculpture and bar tables. Nintendo and other game systems have become hacking targets of artists such as the Beige collective (Cory Arcangel, Joe Breuckman, Joe Bonn and Paul Davis) – their unauthorised cartridges, requiring active engagement by the player, take performance off the public stage and into the private space of the home. With over a century of electronic history behind them, some younger artists are creating wonderful hybrids of modern and 'ancient' technology. Lorin Edwin Parker recently built a steam-powered synthesiser: he coupled a small steam engine to an electric motor and wired the motor terminals to a speaker; when the motor spins it produces electric sound much the way the Telharmonium did 120 years ago.

And to state the obvious, the World Wide Web has become an invaluable resource for music. Peer-to-peer file exchange has made self-publishing and self-promotion affordable to anyone and, to the chagrin of major labels, greatly increased the public's access to a wide range of recordings. Web sites and e-mail have replaced the inefficient samizdat-style hand-to-hand exchange of information that characterised the first wave of composer-designers, and have facilitated the rapid, global, free dissemination of answers. The Web has also become a venue for the performance of music beyond that of bar-hopping avatars. Sergi Jorda and others have developed software that allows people anywhere in the world to collaborate on group composition and improvisation. In *Global String* (1998) Atau Tanaka and Kaspar Toeplitz stretch several yards of heavy string across a room in each of two cities. Vibration sensors and computers link the strings to each other through the Web. Visitors to either site can pluck the real string in their real space; a computer calculates the pitch and overtones of the enormous virtual string connecting them through cyberspace and plays this sound through speakers in each location.

But the very non-corporeality of the Web has served to highlight the significance of actual physical performance. Rather that disappearing in an onslaught of software, circuits handled by hand continue to insinuate themselves into the fabric of music-making – sometimes it's still nice to reach out, touch a sound, and be surprised. As composer-performer-bender Sarah Washington says, echoing David Tudor from four decades earlier, 'I am an improvising musician . . . the choice of sounds is down to the circuit – whatever it comes up with is fine by me.'[16]

Further reading

Brewster, Bill and Broughton, Frank (1999) *Last Night a DJ Saved My Life – the History of the Disc Jockey*. New York: Grove Press

Cage, John (1966) *Silence*. Cambridge, MA: MIT Press

Chadabe, Joel (1997) *Electric Sound – The Past and Promise of Electronic Music*. Upper Saddle River, NJ: Prentice Hall

Collins, Nicolas (2006) *Handmade Electronic Music – The Art of Hardware Hacking*. New York: Routledge

Collins, Nicolas (ed.) *Leonardo Music Journal*. Cambridge, MA: MIT Press

Duckworth, William (1995) *Talking Music*. New York: Schirmer Books

Ghazala, Reed (2005) *Circuit Bending: Build Your Own Alien Instruments*. New York: Wiley Publications

Holmes, Thom (2002) *Electronic and Experimental Music* (2nd edition). New York: Routledge

Johnson, Tom (1989) *The Voice of New Music – New York City 1972–1982* (a collection of articles originally published in *The Village Voice*). Eindhoven, The Netherlands: Het Apollohuis

Lucier, Alvin (1995) *Reflections/Reflexionen*. Cologne, Germany: MusikTexte

Nyman, Michael (1974) *Experimental Music – Cage and Beyond*. New York: Schirmer Books

Oliveros, Pauline (1984) *Software For People*. Baltimore, MD: Smith Publications

Toop, David (2004) *Haunted Weather – Music, Silence and Memory*. London: Serpent's Tail

4 A history of programming and music

GE WANG

The computer has long been considered an extremely attractive tool for creating and manipulating sound. Its precision, possibilities for new timbres and potential for fantastical automation make it a compelling platform for experimenting with and making music – but only to the extent that we can actually tell a computer what to do, and how to do it.[1]

A *program* is a sequence of instructions for a computer. A *programming language* is a collection of syntactic and semantic rules for specifying these instructions, and eventually for providing the translation from human-written programs to the corresponding instructions computers carry out. In the history of computing, many interfaces have been designed to instruct computers, but none has been as fundamental (or perhaps as enduring) as programming languages. Unlike most other classes of human–computer interfaces, programming languages don't directly perform any specific task (such as word processing or video editing), but instead allow us to build software that might perform almost any custom function. The programming language acts as a mediator between human intention and the corresponding bits and instructions that make sense to a computer. It is the most general and yet the most intimate and precise tool for instructing computers.

Programs exist on many levels, ranging from *assembler* code (extremely low level) to high-level scripting languages that often embody more human-readable structures, such as those resembling spoken languages or graphical representation of familiar objects. *Domain-specific languages* retain general programmability while providing additional abstractions tailored to the domain (e.g. sound synthesis). This chapter provides a historical perspective on the evolution of programming and music. We examine early programming tools for sound, from the rise of domain-specific languages for computer music, such as Csound and Max/MSP, to more recent developments such as SuperCollider and ChucK. We'll discuss how these programming tools have influenced the way composers have worked with computers.

Through all this, one thing to keep in mind is that while computers are wonderful tools, they can also be wonderfully stupid. Computers are inflexible and demand precision and exactness from the programmer. They don't know to inform us even of our most obvious mistakes (unless someone has told the computer precisely what to look for). Furthermore, since we must formulate our intentions in terms of the syntax of the underlying language, musical ideas are not always straightforward to translate into code. On the bright side, programming allows us to explore sounds and musical processes otherwise unavailable or impossible to create. If you haven't programmed before, creating programs to make music can be one of the best ways to learn programming: the feedback can be immediate (at least on our modern systems) and programming is learned on the side – naturally (as a tool) rather than as an end in itself. For beginning or seasoned programmers alike, we highly recommend seeking out and playing with the various music languages and environments available. Have fun with it!

Early eras: before computers

The idea of programming computational automata to make music can be traced back to as early as 1843. Ada Lovelace, while working with Charles Babbage, wrote about the applications of the theoretical 'Analytical Engine', the successor to Babbage's famous 'Difference Engine'. The original Difference Engine was chiefly a 'calculating machine' whereas the Analytic Engine (which was never built) was to contain mechanisms for decision and looping, both fundamental to true programmability. Lady Lovelace rightly viewed the Analytical Engine as a general-purpose computer, suited for 'developping [sic] and tabulating any function whatever ... the engine [is] the material expression of any indefinite function of any degree of generality and complexity.' Her musical foresight was discussed in chapter 1.

Lady Lovelace's predictions were made more than a hundred years before the first computer-generated sound. But semi-programmable music-making machines appeared in various forms before the realisation of a practical computer. For example, the *player-piano*, popularised in the early twentieth century, is an augmented piano that 'plays itself' according to rolls of paper (called *piano rolls*) with perforations representing the patterns to be played. These interchangeable piano rolls can be seen as simple programs that explicitly specify musical scores, and as Henry Cowell advised, and such composers as Percy Grainger and Conlon Nancarrow enacted, could be used by composers to take advantage of their special capabilities.

As electronic music evolved, analogue synthesisers gained popularity (commercially, around the 1960s). They supported interconnecting and interchangeable sound processing modules. There is a certain level of programmability involved, and this block-based paradigm influenced the later design of digital synthesis systems. Those readers new to this concept might simply imagine connecting equipment together, be it a guitar to an effects pedal for processing, or a white noise generator to a filter for (subtractive) synthesis; there are sophisticated softwares that emulate this type of hardware modular system (also see chapter 11 for more on the sound synthesis aspects).

As we step into the digital age, we divide our discussion into three overlapping eras of programming and programming systems for music. They loosely follow a chronological order, but more importantly each age embodies common themes in how programmers and composers *interact* with the computer to make sound. Furthermore, we should keep a few overall trends in mind. One crucial trend in this context is that as computers increased in computational power and storage, programming languages tended to become increasingly high-level, abstracting more details of the underlying system. This, as we shall see, greatly impacted the evolution of how we program music.

The computer age (part I): early languages and the rise of MUSIC-N

Our first era of computer-based music programming systems paralleled the age of *mainframes* (the first generations of 'modern' computers in use from 1950 to the late 1970s) and the beginning of personal *workstations* (mid-1970s). The mainframes were gigantic, often taking up rooms or even entire floors. Early models had no monitors or screens, programs had to be submitted via punch cards, and the results delivered as printouts. Computing resources were severely constrained. It was difficult even to gain access to a mainframe – they were not commodity items and were centralised and available mostly at academic and research institutions (in 1957 the hourly cost to access a mainframe was $200!). Furthermore, the computational speed of these early computers were many orders of magnitude (factors of millions or more) slower than today's machines and were greatly limited in memory (e.g. 192 kilobytes in 1957 compared to gigabytes today). However, the mainframes were the pioneering computers and the people who used them made the most of their comparatively meagre resources. Programs were carefully designed and tuned to yield the highest efficiency.

The early algorithmic composition experiments were conducted with mainframes, and only sought to produce a symbolic score (just as a list of characters rather than any neat notation), certainly without synthesised realisation. In one project, Martin Klein and Douglas Bolitho used the Datatron computer to create popular songs after formalising their own rules from an analysis of recent chart hits – the song *Push Button Bertha* (1956) (with tacked on lyrics by Jack Owens) is jokingly attributed to the Datatron computer itself.[2] Sound generation on these machines became a practical reality with the advent of the first *digital-to-analogue converters* (or DACs), which converted digital audio samples (essentially sequences of numbers) that were generated via computation, to time-varying analogue voltages, which can be amplified to drive loudspeakers or be recorded to persistent media (e.g. magnetic tape).

MUSIC I (and II, III, . . .)

The earliest programming environment for sound synthesis, called *MUSIC,* appeared in 1957, developed by Max Mathews at AT&T Bell Laboratories. It was not quite a full programming language as we might think of one today. Not only were MUSIC (or *MUSIC I,* as it was later referred to) and its early descendants the first music programming languages widely adopted by researchers and composers, they also introduced several key concepts and ideas which still directly influence languages and systems today.

MUSIC I and its direct descendants (typically referred to as *MUSIC-N languages*), at their core, provided a model for specifying sound synthesis modules, their connections and time-varying control (Mathews 1969). This model eventually gave rise, in *MUSIC III,* to the concept of *unit generators,* or *UGens* for short. UGens are atomic, often predefined, building blocks for generating or processing audio signals. In addition to audio input and/or output, a UGen may support a number of *control inputs* that control parameters associated with the Ugen.

An example of a UGen is an *oscillator,* which outputs a periodic waveform (e.g. a sinusoid) at a particular fundamental frequency. Such an oscillator might include control inputs that dictate the frequency and phase of the signal being generated. Other examples of UGens include *filters, panners,* and *envelope generators.* The latter, when triggered, produce amplitude contours over time. If we multiply the output of a *sine wave oscillator* with that of an envelope generator, we can produce a third audio signal: a sine wave with time-varying amplitude. In connecting these unit generators in an ordered manner, we create a so-called *instrument* or *patch* (the term comes from analogue synthesisers that may be configured by connecting components using patch cables), which determines the audible qualities (e.g. *timbre*) of a sound. In MUSIC-N parlance, a collection of *instruments* is an *orchestra.* In order to use the *orchestra* to create music, a programmer could craft a different type of input that contained time-stamped note sequences or control signal changes, called a *score.* The relationship: the *orchestra* determines *how sounds are generated,* whereas the *score* dictates (to the orchestra) what to play and when. These two ideas – the unit generator, and the notion of an orchestra versus a score as programs – have been highly influential to the design of music programming systems and, in turn, to how computer music is programmed today.

In those early days, the programming languages themselves were implemented as low-level assembly instructions (essentially human-readable machine code), which effectively coupled a language to the particular hardware platform it was implemented on. As new generations of machines (invariably each with a different set of assembly instructions) were introduced, new languages or at least new implementations had to be created for each architecture. After creating MUSIC I, Max Mathews soon created *MUSIC II* (for the IBM 740), *MUSIC III* in 1959 (for the IBM 7094), and *MUSIC IV* (also for the 7094, but recoded in a new assembly language). Bell Labs shared its source code with computer music researchers at Princeton University – which at the time also housed a 7094 – and many of the additions to MUSIC IV were later released by Godfrey Winham and Hubert Howe as *MUSIC IV-B*.

Around the same time, John Chowning, then a graduate student at Stanford University, travelled to Bell Labs to meet Max Mathews, who gave Chowning a copy of MUSIC IV. *Copy* in this instance meant a box containing about three thousand punch cards, along with a note saying 'Good luck!'. John Chowning and colleagues were able to get MUSIC IV running on a computer that shared the same storage with a second computer that performed the digital-to-analogue conversion. In doing so, they created one of the world's earliest *integrated computer music systems*. Several years later, Chowning, Andy Moorer, and their colleagues completed a rewrite of MUSIC IV, called *MUSIC 10* (named after the PDP-10 computer on which it ran), as well as a program called *SCORE* (which generated note lists for MUSIC 10).

It is worthwhile to pause here and reflect how composers had to work with computers during this period. The composer/programmer would design their software (usually away from the computer), create punch cards specifying the instructions, and submit them as jobs during scheduled mainframe access time (also referred to as *batch-processing*), sometimes travelling a long distance to reach the computing facility. The process was extremely time-consuming. A minute of audio might take several hours or more to compute, and turn-around times of several weeks were not uncommon. Furthermore, there was no way to know ahead of time whether the result would sound anything like what was intended! After a job was complete, the generated audio would be stored on computer tape and then be digital-to-analogue converted, usually by another computer. Only then could the composer actually hear the result. It would typically take many such iterations to complete a piece of music.[3]

In 1968, *MUSIC V* broke the mould by being the first computer music programming system to be implemented in *FORTRAN*, a high-level general-purpose programming language (often considered the first). This meant MUSIC V could be *ported* to any computer system that ran FORTRAN, which greatly helped both its widespread use in the computer music community and its further development. While MUSIC V was the last and most mature of the Max Mathews/Bell Labs synthesis languages of the era, it endures as possibly the single most influential computer music language. Direct descendants include *MUSIC 360* (for the IBM 360) and *MUSIC 11* (for the PDP-11) by Barry Vercoe and colleagues at MIT, and later *cmusic* by F. Richard Moore. These and other systems added much syntactic and logical flexibility, but at heart remained true to the principles of MUSIC-N languages: connection of unit generators, and the separate treatment of sound synthesis (orchestra) and musical organisation (score). Less obviously, MUSIC V also provided the model for many later computer music programming languages and environments.

The CARL System (or 'UNIX for music')
The 1970s and 80s witnessed sweeping revolutions to the world of computing. The *C* programming language, one of the most popular in use, was developed in 1972. The 70s were also a decade of maturation for the modern *operating system*, which includes *time-sharing* of central resources (e.g. CPU time and memory) by multiple users, the factoring of runtime functionalities between a privileged *kernel mode* versus a more protected *user mode*, as well as clear process boundaries that protect applications from each other. From the ashes of the titanic *Multics* operating system project arose the simpler and more practical *UNIX*, with support for multi-tasking of programs, multi-user, inter-process communication, and a sizeable collection of small programs that can be invoked and interconnected from a command line prompt. Eventually implemented in the C language, UNIX can be ported with relative ease to any new hardware platform for which there is a C compiler.

Building on the ideas championed by UNIX, F. Richard Moore, Gareth Loy and others at the Computer Audio Research Laboratory (CARL) at University of California at San Diego developed and distributed an open-source, portable system for signal processing and music synthesis, called the *CARL System* (Loy 1989; 2002). Unlike previous computer music systems, CARL was not a single piece of software, but a collection of small, command line programs that could send data to each other. The 'distributed' approach was modelled after UNIX and its collection of interconnectible programs, primarily for text-processing. As in UNIX, a CARL *process* (a running instance of a program) can send its output to another process via the *pipe* (|), except instead of text, CARL processes send and receive audio data (as sequences of floating point samples, called *floatsam*). For example, the command:

```
> wave -waveform sine -frequency 440Hz | spect
```

invokes the wave program, and generates a sine wave at 440Hz, which is then 'piped' (|) to the spect program, a spectrum analyser. In addition to audio data, CARL programs could send *side-channel* information, which allowed potentially global parameters (such as sample rate) to propagate through the system. Complex tasks could be scripted as sequences of commands. The CARL System was implemented in the C programming language, which ensured a large degree of portability between generations of hardware. Additionally, the CARL framework was straightforward to extend – one could implement a C program that adhered to the CARL *application programming interface* (or API) in terms of data input/output. The resulting program could then be added to the collection and be available for immediate use.

In a sense, CARL approached the idea of digital music synthesis from a *divide-and-conquer* perspective. Instead of a monolithic program, it provided a flat hierarchy of small software tools. The system attracted a wide range of composers and computer music researchers who used CARL to write music and contributed to its development. Gareth Loy implemented packages for FFT (Fast Fourier Transform) analysis, reverberation, spatialisation, and a music programming language named *Player*. Richard Moore contributed the *cmusic* programming language. Mark Dolson contributed programs for phase vocoding, pitch detection, sample-rate conversion, and more. Julius O. Smith developed a package for filter design and a general filter program. Over time, the CARL Software Distribution consisted of over one hundred programs. While the system was modular and flexible for many audio tasks, the architecture was not intended for realtime use. Perhaps mainly for this reason, the CARL System is no longer widely used in its entirety. However, thanks to the portability of C and to the fact CARL was open source, much of the implementation has made its way into countless other digital audio environments and classrooms.

Cmix, CLM and Csound

Around the same time, the popularity and portability of C gave rise to another unique programming system: Paul Lansky's *Cmix* (Pope 1993; Lansky 2006). Cmix wasn't directly descended from MUSIC-N languages; in fact it's not a programming language, but a C *library* of useful signal processing and sound manipulation routines, unified by a well-defined API. Lansky authored the initial implementation in the mid-1980s to flexibly mix sound files (hence the name Cmix) at arbitrary points. It was partly intended to alleviate the inflexibility and large turnaround time for synthesis via batch processing. Over time, many more signal processing directives and macros were added. With Cmix, programmers could incorporate sound processing functionalities into their own C programs for sound synthesis. Additionally, a score could be specified in the Cmix scoring language, called *MINC*.[4] MINC's syntax resembled that of C and proved to be one of the most powerful scoring tools of the era, due to its support for control structures (such as loops). Cmix is still distributed and widely used today, primarily in the form of *RTCmix* (the RT stands for realtime), an extension developed by Brad Garton and David Topper.

Common Lisp Music (or *CLM*) is a sound synthesis language written by Bill Schottstaedt at Stanford University in the late 1980s. CLM descends from the MUSIC-N family and employs a LisP-based syntax for defining the instruments and score and provides a collection of functions that create and manipulate sound. Due to the naturally recursive nature of LisP (which stands for List Processing), many hierarchical musical structures turned out to be straightforward to represent using code. A more recent (and very powerful) LisP-based programming language is *Nyquist*, authored by Roger Dannenberg (Dannenberg 1997). Both CLM and Nyquist are freely available.

Today, the most widely used direct descendant of MUSIC-N is *Csound*, originally authored by Barry Vercoe and colleagues at MIT Media Labs in the late 1980s (Boulanger 2000). It supports unit generators as *opcodes*, objects that generate or process audio. It embraces the instrument versus score paradigm: the instruments are defined in orchestra (*.orc*) files, with the score in. *sco* files. Furthermore, Csound supports the notion of separate audio and control rates. The *audio rate* (synonymous with *sample rate*) refers to the rate at which audio samples are processed through the system. On the other hand, *control rate* dictates how frequently *control signals* are calculated and propagated through the system. In other words, audio rate (abbreviated as *ar* in Csound) is associated with *sound*, whereas control rate (abbreviated as *kr*) deals with *signals that control sound* (i.e. changing the centre frequency of a resonant filter or the frequency of an oscillator). The audio rate is typically higher (for instance 44100 Hz for CD-quality audio) than the control rate, which usually is adjusted to be lower by at least an order of magnitude. The chief reason for this separation is computational efficiency. Audio must be computed sample-for-sample at the desired sample rate. However, for many synthesis tasks, it makes no perceptual difference if control is asserted at a lower rate, say of the order of 2000Hz. This notion of audio rate versus control rate is widely adopted across nearly all synthesis systems.

This first era of computer music programming pioneered how composers could interact with the digital computer to specify and generate music. Its mode of working was associated with the difficulties of early mainframes: offline programming, submitting batch jobs, waiting for audio to generate, and transferring to persistent media for playback or preservation. It paralleled developments in computers as well as general-purpose programming languages. We examined the earliest music languages in the MUSIC-N family as well as some direct descendants. It is worth noting that several of the languages discussed in this section have since been augmented with real-time capabilities. In addition to RTMix, Csound now also supports realtime audio.

The computer age (part II): realtime systems

This second era of computer programming for music partially overlaps with the first. The chief difference is that the mode of interaction moved from offline programming and batch processing to realtime sound synthesis systems, often controlled by external musical controllers. By the early 1980s, computers had become fast enough and small enough to allow workstation desktops to outperform the older, gargantuan mainframes. As personal computers began to proliferate, so did new programming tools and applications for music generation (Lyon 2002).

Graphical music programming: Max/MSP and Pure Data
We now arrive at one of the most popular computer music programming environments to this day: *Max* and later *Max/MSP* (Puckette 1991). Miller S. Puckette implemented the first version of Max (when it was called *Patcher*) at IRCAM in Paris in the mid-1980s as a programming environment for making interactive computer music. At this stage, the program did not generate or process audio samples; its primary purpose was to provide a graphical representation for routing and manipulating signals for controlling external sound synthesis workstations in realtime. Eventually, Max evolved at IRCAM to take advantage of DSP hardware on NeXT computers (as *Max/FTS*, FTS stands for 'faster than sound'), and was later released in 1990 as a commercial product by Opcode Systems as *Max/Opcode*. In 1996, Puckette released a completely redesigned and open source environment called *Pure Data*, or *PD* for short (Puckette 1996). At the time, Pure Data processed audio data whereas Max was primarily designed for control (MIDI). PD's audio signal processing capabilities then made their way into Max as a major add-on called *MSP* (MSP either stands for Max Signal Processing or for Miller S. Puckette), authored by Dave Zicarelli. *Cycling '74*, Zicarelli's company, distributes the current commercial version of *Max/MSP*.

The modern-day Max/MSP supports a graphical patching environment and a collection containing thousands of *objects*, ranging from signal generators, to filters, to operators, and user interface elements. Using the Max import API, third party developers can implement *external* objects as extensions to the environment. Despite its graphical approach, Max descends from MUSIC-V (in fact Max is named after the father of MUSIC-N, Max Mathews) and embodies a similarly modular approach to sound synthesis. Well-known uses of Max/MSP include Philippe Manoury's realisation of *Jupiter* (which in 1987, was among the first works to employ a score following algorithm to synchronise a human performer to live electronics, as well as being the test case for Puckette's work), Autechre's exploration of generative algorithms to create the recordings for their *Confield (2001)* album, and Radiohead's employment of Max/MSP in live performance. Cycling '74 themselves have a record company whose releases promote artists using the Max/MSP software. The Max community is extensive and the environment has been used in countless aspects of composition, performance and sound art.

Max offers two modes of operation. In *edit* mode, a user can create objects, represented by on-screen boxes containing the object type as well as any initial arguments. An important distinction is made between objects that generate or process audio and *control rate objects* (the presence of a '∼' at the end of the object name implies audio rate). The user can then interconnect objects by creating connections from the *outlets* of certain objects to the *inlets* of others. Depending on its type, an object may support a number of inlets, each of which is well defined in its interpretation of the incoming signal. Max also provides dozens of additional widgets, including message boxes, sliders, graphs, knobs, buttons, sequencers and meters. Events can be manually generated by a *bang* widget. All of these widgets can be connected to and from other objects. When Max is in *run* mode, the patch topology is fixed and cannot be modified, but the various on-screen widgets can be manipulated interactively. This highlights a wonderful duality: a Max *patch* is at once a program and (potentially) a user interface.

Max/MSP has been an extremely popular programming environment for realtime synthesis, particularly for building interactive performance systems. Controllers – both commodity (MIDI devices) and custom – as well as sensors (such as motion tracking) can be mapped to sound synthesis parameters using Max/MSP. The visual aspect of the environment lends itself well to monitoring and fine-tuning patches. Max/MSP can be used to render sequences or scores, though due to the lack of detailed timing constructs (the graphical paradigm is better at representing *what* than *when*), this can be less straightforward. PD, maintained as an open source project, is itself still under development and freely available for all modern

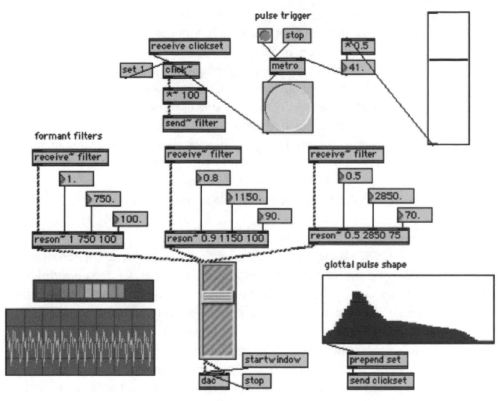

Figure 4.1 A simple Max/MSP patch which synthesises the vowel 'ahh'

operating systems. Additionally, the graphical patching paradigm has found its way into much modular synthesis software, including Native Instruments' *Reaktor*.

Programming libraries for sound synthesis

So far, we have discussed mostly stand-alone programming environments, each of which provides a specialised language syntax and semantics. In contrast to such languages or environments, a *library* provides a set of specialised functionalities for an existing, possibly more general-purpose language. For example, the *Synthesis Toolkit* (STK) is a collection of building blocks for realtime sound synthesis and physical modelling, for the $C++$ programming language (Cook and Scavone 1999). STK was authored by Perry Cook and Gary Scavone and released in the early 1990s. *JSyn*, released around the same time, is a collection of realtime sound synthesis objects for the *Java* programming language (Burk 1998). In each case, the library provides an API, with which a programmer can write synthesis programs in the host language (e.g. $C++$ and Java). For example, STK provides an object definition called Mandolin, which is a physical model for a plucked string instrument. It defines the data types that internally comprise such an object, as well as publicly accessible functionalities that can be invoked to control the Mandolin's parameters in realtime (e.g. frequency, pluck position, instrument body size, etc.). Using this definition, the programmer can create instances of Mandolin, control their characteristics via code, and generate audio from the Mandolin instances in realtime. While the host languages are not specifically designed for sound, these libraries allow the programmer to take advantage of language features and existing libraries (of which there is a huge variety for C++ and Java). This also allows integration with C++ and Java applications that desire realtime sound synthesis.

SuperCollider: the synthesis language redefined

SuperCollider is a text-based audio synthesis language and environment first developed around the early 1990s (McCartney 2002). It is a powerful *interpreted* programming language, so that new code can be run immediately, even being written while existing processes occur, and the implementation of the synthesis engine is highly optimised. It combines many of the key ideas in computer music language design while making some fundamental changes and additions. SuperCollider, like languages before it, supports the notion of unit generators for signal processing (audio and control). However, there is no longer a distinction between the orchestra (sound synthesis) and the score (musical events): both can be implemented in the same framework. This tighter integration leads to more expressive code, and the ability to couple and experiment with synthesis and musical ideas together with faster turnaround time. Furthermore, the language, which in parts resembles the Smalltalk and C programming languages, is *object-oriented* and provides a wide array of expressive programming constructs for sound synthesis and user interface programming. This makes SuperCollider suitable not only for implementing synthesis programs, but also for building large interactive *systems* for sound synthesis, algorithmic composition, and for audio research. SuperCollider has been used in Jem Finer's millennial thousand-year installation *LongPlayer*, Chris Jeffs' *Cylob Music System*, Nick Collins' *Infinite Length Pieces*, electroacoustic works by Scott Wilson, Joshua Parmenter and Ron Kuivila, and many other compositions, artworks and systems.[5]

At the time of this writing, there have been three major version changes in SuperCollider. The third and latest (often abbreviated to *SC3*) makes an explicit distinction between the language (front-end) and synthesis engine (back-end). These loosely coupled components communicate via *OpenSoundControl* (OSC), a standard for sending control messages for sound over a network. One immediate impact of this new architecture is that

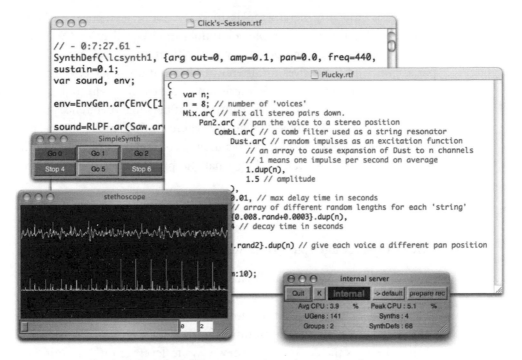

Figure 4.2 The SuperCollider programming environment in action

programmers can essentially use any front-end language, as long as it conforms to the protocol required by the synthesis server (called *scsynth* in SuperCollider). A second is that SuperCollider is inherently ready for network music.

Graphical versus text-based approaches

It is worthwhile to pause here and reflect on the differences between the graphical programming environments of Max/MSP and PD versus the text-based languages and libraries such as SuperCollider, Csound, and STK. The visual representation presents the dataflow directly, in a what-you-see-is-what-you-get sort of way. Text-based systems lack this representation and understanding of the syntax and semantics is required to make sense of the programs. However, many tasks, such as specifying complex logical behaviour, are more easily expressed in text-based code.

Ultimately it's important to keep in mind that most synthesis and musical tasks can be implemented in *any* of these languages. This is the idea of *universality*: two constructs (or languages) can be considered equivalent if we can emulate the behaviour of one using the other, and vice versa. However, certain types of tasks may be more easily specified in a particular language than in others. This brings us back to the idea of the programming language as a tool. In general, a tool is useful if it does at least one thing better than any other tool (for example, a hammer or a screwdriver). Computer music programming languages are by necessity more general, but differing paradigms lend themselves to different tasks (and no single environment 'does it best' in *every* aspect: it's important to choose the right tools for the tasks at hand). In the end, it's also a matter of personal preference – some like the directness of graphical languages whereas others prefer the feel and expressiveness of text-based code. It's often a combination of choosing the right tool for the task and finding what the programmer is comfortable working in.

The computer age (part III): new language explorations

With the growth of low-cost, high performance computers, the realtime and interactive music programming paradigms are more alive than ever and expanding with the continued invention and refinement of expressive interfaces. Alongside the continuing trend of explosive growth in computing power is the desire to find new ways to leverage programming for realtime interaction. If the second era of programming and music evolved from computers becoming commodities, then this third era is the result of programming itself becoming *pervasive*. With the ubiquity of hardware and the explosion of new high-level general-purpose programming tools (and people willing to use them), more composers and musicians are crafting not only software to create music, but also new software to *program* music.

As part of this new age of exploration, a recent movement has been taking shape. This is the rise of dynamic languages and consequently of using the act of programming itself as a musical instrument. This, in a way, can be seen as a subsidiary of realtime interaction, but with respect to programming music, this idea is fundamentally powerful. For the first time in history, we have commodity computing machines that can generate sound and music in realtime (and in abundance) from our program specifications. One of the areas investigated in our third age of programming and music is the possibility of changing the *program* itself in realtime – as it's running. Given the infinite expressiveness of programming languages, might we not leverage code to create music *on-the-fly*?

The idea of run-time modification of programs to make music (interchangeably called *live coding, on-the-fly programming, interactive programming*) is not an entirely new one.[6] As early as the beginning of the 1980s, researchers such as Ron Kuivila and groups like the Hub experimented with runtime modifiable music systems. The *Hierarchical Music Scoring Language* (HMSL) is a Forth-based language, authored by Larry Polansky, Phil

Figure 4.3 The ChucK programming language and environment

Burk, David Rosenboom and others in the 1980s, whose stack-based syntax encourages runtime programming. These are the forerunners of live coding (Collins *et al.* 2003). The fast computers of today enable an additional key component: realtime sound synthesis.

ChucK: a strongly timed and on-the-fly programming language

ChucK is one of the newest members to the audio synthesis programming language family, originated by the author of this chapter and Perry Cook (Wang and Cook 2003). ChucK is derived indirectly from the MUSIC-N paradigm with some key differences. First, the chuck operator ($=>$) is used to perform actions in a left-to-right way, including UGen connection. The language also establishes a strong correspondence between *time* and *sound* in that the programmer controls temporal flow (via special language syntax) to allow sound to be generated (this is referred to as *strongly timed*). Additionally, different *processes* can synchronise to each other according to the same notion of time, or to data. There is no separation of orchestra versus score, and control rate is programmatically determined as a consequence of manipulating time. In this sense, ChucK is the first realtime synthesis language to move away from the classic notion of control rate. The programming model lends itself to representing low-level synthesis processes as well as high-level musical representations, and the language makes it straightforward for learning sound synthesis and for rapidly prototyping compositions. In addition to realising score-driven synthesis, ChucK is also used as a primary teaching and compositional tool in the *Princeton Laptop Orchestra* (PLOrk), serving as the workbench for creating live performances (for solos, duets, quartets, and for the full ensemble of fifteen humans, fifteen laptops, and ninety audio channels).

Custom music programming software

An incredibly vibrant and wonderful aspect of the era is the proliferation of custom, 'home-brew' sound programming software. The explosion of new high-level, general-purpose programming platforms has enabled and

Figure 4.4 slub in action (photo by Renate Wieser)

encouraged programmers and composers to build systems very much tai-lored to their liking. Alex McLean describes live coding using the high-level scripting language *Perl* (McLean 2004), a technique he has utilised in club and gallery performances both solo and with the duo *slub*. Similar frame-works have been developed in *Python*, various dialects of Lisp, Forth, *Ruby*, and others. Some systems make sound while others visualise it. Many sys-tems send network message (in OpenSoundControl) to synthesis engines such as SuperCollider Server, PD, Max, and ChucK. In this way, musicians and composers can leverage the expressiveness of the front-end language to make music while gaining the functionalities of synthesis languages. Many descriptions of systems and ideas can be found through *TOPLAP* (which usually stands for Transnational Organisation for the Proliferation of Live Audio Programming), a collective of programmers, composers, and per-formers exploring live programming to create music.

This third era is promising because it enables and encourages new com-positional and performance possibilities not only to professional musicians, researchers and academics, but also to anyone willing to learn and explore programming and music. Also, the new dynamic environments for pro-gramming are changing how we approach more 'traditional' computer music composition – by providing more rapid experimentation and more immediate feedback. This era is young but growing rapidly and the possi-bilities are truly fascinating. Where will it take programming and music in the future?

Future directions

Lady Ada Lovelace foresaw the computing machine as a programming tool for creating precise, arbitrarily complex and 'scientific' music. What might we imagine about the ways music will be made decades and beyond from now?

Several themes and trends pervade the development of programming languages and systems for music. The movement towards increasingly more realtime, dynamic and networked programming of sound and music continues; it has been taking place in parallel with the proliferation and geometric growth of commodity computing resources until recent times. New trends are emerging. At the time of this writing in 2006, the focus in the design of commodity machines is shifting to distributed, multi-core processing units. We may soon have machines with hundreds (or many more) cores as part of a single computer. How might these potentially massive parallel architectures impact on the way we think about and program software (in everything from commercial data-processing to sound synthesis to musical performance)? What new programming paradigms will have to be invented to take advantage of these and other new computing technology such as quantum computers, and theoretical (for now) computing machines? Finally, an equally essential question: how can we better make use of the machines we have?

ARTISTS' STATEMENTS I

LAURIE SPIEGEL

From the earliest, I craved the arts, any of the arts, all of the arts. The feelings, thoughts and imaginings presented to me by other minds did not represent, reflect or resonate with my solitary subjective experience, nor did they provide the means I so urgently felt I needed of making life's moment-to-moment intensity more comfortable.

As a result I have always been involved in far too many things at once: writing, playing and composing music, making visual images and pursuing the externalisation of the evolving images and sounds that appear only on my imagination's retina, developing new tools for these tasks including sawing, soldering, coding for computers, and generally getting excited about ideas in many fields.

At every stage several threads intertwine, components not only of created work (sound, image and text), but of daily life (home, dogs, friends, beloved acoustic instruments, several sciences, electronic and mechanical tinkering . . .) and the pursuit of understanding. I have found myself almost always in overload, especially as a little goes a long way, any interesting idea tending to intersect with others to spin off into many more. As a teenager, a shy awkward 'girl nerd', I was seen playing guitar and banjo, taking woodworking shop, calligraphy and drafting classes, running little scientific experiments, drawing and sculpting, writing poems and fiction, doing science fair projects, inventing a phonetic alphabet, even winning a prize for advertising layout, and reading, reading, reading.

More recently, technology has furnished a means of interconnection for all the parts of this disparate array. Paradoxically, by specialising in music (always the least resistible of all my pursuits) I found that all the other domains that I thought I had traded off against it were drawn back in. Music does not exist in isolation any more than any individual, society or subject of study. Music touches upon everything else, from mathematics to philosophy to carpentry. Most important though, it touches our innermost selves.

I did not expect to become a composer. I just kept finding, when I went to my scores or record collection, that the music I was looking for and wanted to play was not there. So being a tinkerer prone to 'do it yourself', I would make myself some of whatever music I couldn't find. My computer music software, best known of which is my little program *Music Mouse*, is similar, made for my own use, and only ex post facto discovered to be wanted by others. Though I have made music 'on demand' and to others' specifications, such as for dance, theatre or film, I am primarily inner-directed and all of what I consider my best work is always made for my own needs. This is another wonderful paradox that perhaps only the arts manifest well, that by ignoring others and pleasing the self we are more able to please others more effectively.

Because much of what I have felt and seen in my mind and imagination is difficult to mash into conventional media, I have spent astronomical amounts of time on the design and creation of tools, mostly electronic and computer-based, to create what previously could not be made or to do so by methods not tried before. I love this work almost as much as the music itself. Each tool (instrument, medium, technique) is like a language, able to express some things inexpressible by others of its kind, and yet full of commonality with them. Each may severely limit the nature of one's creative output but in the cause of revealing with a clearer focus a unique delimited aesthetic domain. In this way an instrument is like a person, and each individual artist has similar uniqueness and communality with others.

This is why I have also worked hard to make it easier for more people to be able to express themselves in music and art by use of new technology. There should never be a minority category of 'creative artist' from which most people are excluded. All who wish to speak any language – sound, sight, speech – should have the opportunity to do so. And I have long hoped that the immediacy of electronics and the logic of computers will make this possible for far more people than ever before. This is important because the benefit of creative self-expression falls mostly to the maker, leaving to any audience only a secondary level of involvement, a vicarious self-expression through the artefacts that the creative process leaves behind it.

These attitudes have of course reduced my apparent output not only due to the time taken from music for toolmaking but because I too rarely write down or record the music I come up with, though ironically it means the world to me for someone to listen and hear what I've made.

YASUNAO TONE

The origin of the 'Wounded Man'yo-shu' pieces

It was five years ago, for the opening of the Yokohama Triennial, that I created a sound installation from Walter Benjamin's text titled 'Parasite/Noise'. An interviewer from the *Bijutsu-Techo*, a leading Japanese art magazine, asked me why I liked to obsess with language and text. I answered that it is not just language and text, but Chinese or Japanese text. Before the gramophone, as Kittler explained, there were only 'texts and scores, Europe had no other means for storing time'. Only the alphabet and its subsystem, staff notation, could preserve works, at least until mechanical reproductions were invented. In other words, Western music always coexisted with Western languages.

I have been working on creating music outside the European alphabetic/tonal system all along, since I started consciously using Chinese characters for a performance piece called *Voice and Phenomenon* in 1976. As you might suppose from the title, it was based on Derrida's texts. The piece resonates with Derrida's critique of alphabetical phoneticism as ethnocentrism. According to Derrida, the history of Western philosophy from Plato to Husserl is the history of complicity by logos and phonè based on the metaphysics of presence. That is why Western metaphysics has given a privilege to voice over writing *(écriture* in the Saussurian sense). *Voice and Phenomenon* was a seminal predecessor to other works such as *Molecular Music, Musica Iconologos* and *Musica Simulacra.* All these works are made of sound through many layers of conversion from Chinese characters. Other pieces are derivative of those pieces, by way of prepared CDR.

JOHN OSWALD

The term Electronic Music is used in an historical and mutually exclusive sense by both the electroacousmaticians, and the purveyors of the countless subgenres of Electronica (House, Techno, Jungle, etc.). However, electronification is now the dominant state in which virtually all forms of music exist. In the twentieth century electricity and music, gradually, through radio, recording, amplification, electrogeneration and processing, became an ubiquitous relationship to a degree which likely caused a decline in both the creation and perception of purely acoustic sounds intended as music, such as singing.

This attrition applies especially to music as a form of communication or social congress. Only the classical concert milieu remains acoustic, to a near militant degree, although the practice of classical music, in its dissemination, has been transformed by recording technology. When electricity arrives in a culture, musicians use it. Electricity has generally made music louder, more pervasive, and, globally, more homogenised. At the same time recordings have increased the available variety of music and personal playback devices have enabled private sound worlds devoid of immediate shared experience. Recording and broadcasting have spawned an increasingly homogeneous global music, even as the possibilities of electronic transformation of sounds have created an ever more multifaceted range of possibilities.

Perhaps as a reprieve to the long solitary hours I spend in the studio composing in an electronic environment of recordings, and re-recordings of recordings (of which a subset is plunderphonics), I have tended to eschew electricity when I play music as a sociable form. Like sex, music thrives on spontaneity, and there's nothing more sonically convivial than a group of musicians picking up things to pluck, blow into or bellow. I do look forward to someone showing up at one of these gatherings with a soniferous computelligent electrosonic device as sensitive, flexible, and quick-to-boot as these musicians who needn't plug in.

MATHIAS GMACHL (FARMER´S MANUAL)

physical reality, as modelled by many temporal, local theories, appears to be fundamentally linked to a zoo of oscillation processes. our senses synthesise these cycles into experiences, be it sonic events, phenomena of light, aware-ness of space, wireless communication, plain matter and much more. as indicated by the order given, the sonic poses a very accessible and rewarding way to explore wave phenomena, but this is not where it ends.

engineering activities have uncovered the electromagnetic within certain limits, or to particular purposes, although to a great extent in disregard or disinterest of secondary effects on physiology and consciousness. in other words, the medium is not neutral and on its own commences sending mes-sages of unintended content to unintended receivers.

indifferent music becomes sound as it identifies itself as operations on the organisation of weak processes, disregarding boundaries of occlusion. so that towards the end the authors become the audience and the audience stretches to the horizon, populated by machines infinitely rendering a stream of minute semantic lunacy.

what is left is the establishment of a musical use of a broader band of waves, both regarding frequency range and media.

a system regulating frequency, duration, event-clustering and arbitrarily more parameters is at least a musical system. in a stochastic system this means choice of probabilities, in a process-coupled system this means filling the system with life by choice of governing events.

i'm sorry i couldn't elaborate on a geometric perspective due to lack of time and misplacing the resonating compass.

ERDEM HELVACIOGLU

It has been nearly fifty years since we heard the first electronic music work by a Turkish composer. That was when Bulent Arel's piece *Music for String Quartet and Tape* was premiered. Looking back now, I am still amazed by the compositional virtuosity, talent and vision of the great pioneer, and the sheer beauty of this wonderful work. A monumental piece composed with very simple tools in an environment with political and economic problems, and where there was nearly no knowledge about international contemporary music. I wonder what Bulent Arel felt when the premiere took place: he must have been very proud!

It's now 2007, and today in Turkey, we have many opportunities, with the latest technology and well-equipped studios. We have a great number of talented people interested in music technology and young composers who want to create interesting electronic music, following the path of Arel.

I am one of those composers. My biggest aim is to contribute something meaningful and significant to this aural world. I hope my personal artistic statement stated here below, will be my guide in the forthcoming years: *'The crackle sound of a lo-fi record player and the pristine sound of a digital processor . . . the chaotic recording of a daily street life and the sterile studio sound . . . the sounds of traditional Turkish instruments and their contemporary versions . . . This musical and historical integration moulds the wide time span into one immediate moment, where the listener actually is: the present. And this is my music . . .'*

PAULINE OLIVEROS

As improvising agents, computers may push us or teach us about the mind and facilitate a quantum leap into unity of consciousness. Technology should provide tools for expanding the mind through deep listening. Music and especially improvised music is not a game of chess – improvisation, in particular free improvisation, could definitely represent another challenge to machine intelligence. It is not the silicon linearity of intensive calculation that makes improvisation wonderful. It is the non-linear carbon chaos, the unpredictable turns of chance permutation, the meatiness, the warmth, the simple, profound humanity of beings that brings presence and wonder to music.

I continue to work on my Expanded Instrument System (EIS) so that I may play with the developing intelligence of the machine. This enables me to explore improvisation beyond the boundaries of my own carbon-based physical system in collaboration with silicon-based systems. Note EIS takes any acoustic or electronic input and processes it with delays and algorithms that I devised. I use this system most often with my accordion. The system began in 1965 with my early electronic music such as *Bye Bye Butterfly* and *I of IV*.

CHRIS JEFFS

Why am I making electronic music instead of making tracks some other way? The answers are boring and obvious: I can make many sounds at once, I don't have to explain my ideas to someone else in order to hear them, and most importantly, I can potentially make strange, new, previously unheard sounds.

Object-oriented programming has led me to view pitches, rhythms and timbres as nothing more than sets of data to be manipulated. In my uber-sequencer, the *Cylob Music System*, a sound can be made up of a sequence of other sounds, and a sequence can be played as if it is a sound in itself, so the dividing line becomes blurred, because it's all just data; any distinction of these types is conceptual, and impacts on the constraints of the user.

As regards the electronic music-making scene, I feel that as access to electronic music has spread, so any sense of ambition or notion of quality has decreased, and I wish everyone to rediscover the feeling of novelty that, for example, greeted the first 'sample' records (remember that barking dog one, or much better, early Art of Noise?), instead of treading the same paths all the time. This might happen because too many people use the same sorts of software. These programs have largely reached a consensus on how things are done. It's really useful and important to me to make my own software, then, because I can aim to sound as different as possible from those who remain constrained by the interfaces they simply adopt. It is very time and energy consuming, but that feeds into the ambition, and I hope, into the quality.

RODRIGO SIGAL

Music technology is a flexible and ever-changing tool with which one can solve problems and set personal challenges. The possibilities for macro and micro control of structure have generated a specific discourse which we as composers are just beginning to develop. However, it is evident that there is a temptation for the electronic music composer to take refuge in technology at the expense of musical concept. For this reason, it is important to hold a self-critical perspective so that musical ideas may be understood in regards to their musical coherence as opposed to the complexities of the technology utilised to produce the sounds.

This perspective is especially relevant in Latin America, where the use of technology in concert music is a key factor in fundraising. This has led to short-term projects based mainly on the provision of technological infrastructure without much regard to solid artistic and educational concepts. I believe the future of electronic music in Mexico and other countries of the region resides in taking advantage of the democratisation of musical tools (as in the use of laptops and computer software, perhaps specifically open-source programs such as SuperCollider, PD, ChucK and CSound). It will make us independent of government grants and truer to our own creative directions. The studio, in electroacoustic composition, instead of being the main source of musical technology, will become a place for information, education and the sharing of ideas to better shape our artistic future.

MIRA CALIX

I was just a little miss when I first got a copy of OMD's *Dazzleships* on record. I used to listen to it in the dark and was completely transfixed by the sonar bleeps and the screwed up voice with numbers on *ABC*. I couldn't figure out how all these foreign sounds got onto the record – I had no idea but it completely absorbed and delighted me. I think I was hooked from that point onwards on all things a little odd and synthetic. I knew that what I was listening to weren't 'real' instruments, like I'd heard before, but I couldn't figure out what kind of devices were making these strange sounds. The first electronic instruments I really got my hands on were an MC202 and a TR606; I finally had a go at making my own strange sounds in the dark, and I haven't stopped.

As far as the future of electronics goes: I'm fairly easy to please, and as long as I can get my hands on a good string sound, muck up my own voice, and sample a couple of pebbles, I'll be happy (although a 120-piece orchestra and a Cray would be nice).

DENIS SMALLEY

The acousmatic

The whole point of acousmatic music, expressed in the meaning of the word 'acousmatic', is that there is nothing to watch, no observable activity to confirm how the sounds are made, and often no certainty about where the sounds originate. The implication is that we should perceive and respond to the sounds – the music – through listening alone. Acousmatic music is by definition an invisible sonic art, which invests in the liberty of an open sound world and in the imagination of the interpreting listener.

Visible music, a music produced by singers and instrumentalists, automatically carries a sense – the sense of its making. It is 'understood' because the means of production are understood, and there is an intimate liaison between means and sounding result: sound is the direct utterance of, or an extension of, the body and bodily expression. This evident human foundation ensures a basic understanding regardless of our sympathies for the particular genre or style of music that emerges. But with acousmatic music we have to search for an understanding in the relations and implications discovered within the musical context as it unfolds. Sometimes we will recognise, through sound alone, the tell-tale signs of human presence, of sounding materials, of the sounding world. . . . or we think we can; but sometimes we cannot.

Acousmatic experience is part of culture. We often glean information about our surroundings from hearing alone, deducing potential consequences from what we interpret. (Anticipating what might happen based on what we have already heard is also central to music listening.) But in navigating our way in daily life we are not that aware of hearing as an independent sensory channel because it is so tied up in a convergence of the aural, visual and kinaesthetic senses, all of which govern habitation and physical experience. When one sense alone cannot fully inform us, we call on other senses to help sort out discrepancies, so that we can arrive at a better understanding about what is going on.

It is a mistake to think that because acousmatic music is perceived via a single sense, that the other senses lie dormant. In our imagination what we hear crosses over into what we know of the world via the collaboration among the sense modes, even if these modes are not directly activated in order only to listen. For example, texture we know to be physical (touch), and visual, not just (or even primarily) aural; when we mentally take in the motion of sounds, we refer to our kinaesthetic experience and observation of motion – our experience of space. This is *spectral space* – a uniquely sonic version of space and spaciousness produced by occupancy of, and motion within, the range of audible frequencies. Articulating and exploring spectral space is inherent to acousmatic music, and is often aligned with the perspectival aspects of space – the experiences of proximity, distancing, approaching, opening out, closing in, emerging, disappearing. There is an affinity with environmental experience.

From sound alone I may constitute, in my imagination, the configurations of a scene or narrative, or a spatial climate; the visual and physical appearances of objects and textures; the motion of entities and shapes in spectral space. These may have a certain reality if I think I can identify possible sources or causes of sound, but they may equally be fantasy, a kind of 'vision' where the auditory sense calls on companion senses to participate in interpretation. This conjunction of imagined sensory phenomena may be captured in the idea of the 'acousmatic image'.

Acousmatic experience is more prevalent than many realise, and the development of technology has brought us new means of acousmatic experience. The telephone, in its masking of visual identity, concentrates our attention on the sound of the voice; it is remarkable what one can tell about the person on the other end of a phone line based on minimal phonemes of greeting: such timbral signatures can not only identify a particular person, but can also tell us about state of health or mind, via the manner of an utterance rather than what is actually uttered. This underlines our sensitivity to spectral detail and the subtleties of meaning carried by recognisable acousmatic sound-types.

Radio continues to be a robust acousmatic medium despite supposed competition from visual media. In our aural imagination we construct mental images of people, scenarios, and places, and programmes that explore mixes of sounds, music and voices might be regarded as a genre of acousmatic 'art'. With radio I am particularly interested in the spaces we associate with the sounds we hear; recorded sounds do not acoustically carry with them all their spatial attributes. Consider mono radio, which can technically carry depth perspective, but not panoramic breadth or spatial elevation. What we recognise are *source-bonded spaces* – the spatial zones and mental images produced by, or inferred from, a sounding source and its cause. Source-bonded spaces carry with them an image of the activity that produces them. In acousmatic music this is particularly important not only with sounds we recognise, but also with more ambiguous sounding contexts, which can take on attributes of known sonic behaviour.

Film absorbs acousmatic sound and music, and did so before electroacoustic music was developed. Acousmatic sound can be used to circumvent the physical frame of the screen, drawing attention to the fact that we rely on sound to gather spatial information. And acousmatic sound can also be used to create psychological ambience and states, as well as steer fluctuations in temporality. Acousmatic conventions have evolved in order to transcend the constraints of the silent visual image.

This brief sketch of acousmatic media (or in the case of film, a medium in which the acousmatic participates) serves to indicate that there are sets of expectations, or schemas, associated with acousmatic contexts. These are carried over into the comprehensive sound world of acousmatic music.

Many electroacoustic composers, and performers of electroacoustic music, are preoccupied by 'liveness', with rooting electroacoustic music in the continuing tradition of instrumental or vocal gesture, of 'visible music'. Instrumental performance and acousmatic sound have tried to collaborate since acousmatic music began, but the relationship between the visible and the invisible has not always been comfortable: the acousmatic offers adventure while the instrument constrains the musical 'language'; the acousmatic taps into mental schemas of which instrumental gesture and human sound-making are but a part. Too often, the basic convention of relying on limited types of live processing of instrumental sounds to form a parallel fabric, and to create a semblance of interaction between the seen and the heard, results in a very predictable music and an interactive play appreciated more by composer and performer than by the listener.

With new performance interfaces (many of which have a fleeting life), and with laptop performances, what purports to be 'live' is often, from the listener's point of view, too acousmatic, in that the relationship between what is witnessed visually and physically, and the music emitted, can be so covert that the presence of 'performers' is mystifying. I christened this phenomenon *live acousmatic performance* as long ago as 1992. If only primitive vestiges of performance articulation remain, composer and performer need to realise that the covertness of their acts requires some elaboration in order to justify the public nature of the event, possibly by creating a richer audiovisual context. Furthermore, a greater awareness of acousmatic schemas and the meanings carried by sonic configurations, might aid the creation of a music better adapted to acousmatic reception conditions. If in seemingly live, public events, sound and music are to take on acousmatic guises, the one requirement is that they should richly do so.

Today, the prevalence of acousmatic sound and acousmatic music listening means, generally, that the need for a live listening experience is less of a concern for the listener, who now accesses music and sound via CD, SACD, iPods and computers, listening in domestic settings or on the move. In a way, the liveness of music lies in its nowness – its happening at the moment of listening. Whether the sound is physically created at that moment, or is capable of being generated or assembled in the instant of reception, is of secondary concern.

It is often said that acousmatic music could better communicate if aided by visual images. While I recognise that something unfamiliar may initially be disquieting, I do not favour a visual add-on strategy, particularly bearing in mind the transmodal perceptual nature imbedded in aural perception itself, and the vast expressive range of the purely sonic acousmatic 'image'. There is no need to use visual images to direct the listening imagination, no need to serve out semiotic supplements that restrict the 'meaning' of the music, no need to hold the listener's hand. Not that I am against audiovisual arts, given a properly considered trans-sensory conception. Listeners need not be apprehensive about their personal aural imagination, or worry whether a particular interpretative response is expected.

The twenty-first century is an era where technologically mediated creativity offers an expanded awareness of the aural sense as a dominant, and highly valued channel for aesthetic communication. Acousmatic music, which embraces a mix of tendencies, offers us the richest realisation of this human need.

SEONG-AH SHIN

In 1990, when I was a freshman at the University of Korea, the department had a very small electronic music studio. It contained a NEC8081, an eight-bit computer that only ran Common Music, and a Roland 100M, an analogue synthesiser. Most students called the studio the 'ghost room' because of the strange sounds which emanated from that dark corner of the building. However, for me, it was the most interesting room in the department, with new sounds and fascinating equipment. It was not that easy to study electronic music; I still remember that reading the manuals, written in English, was like code-breaking.

I cannot even compare that studio with the quality of equipment and documentation we have now. I deeply appreciate the advances of technology in the recent years, but I also value the patience I learned through working with older equipment.

Now, I teach electronic music at my old school. No longer the ghost room, all the students are required to take the electronic music class and most of them enjoy it. I believe technology helps composers and students focus their musical imagination and express their emotions.

In my own work, I find and create sounds, allowing me the profound pleasure of living more than one life. I compose music in the present with sounds reaching into the past, guiding the future structure and substance of the sonic result. For me, this process of connection is composition, linking past, present and future – the inevitability of the musical experience transformed through technology and the paradoxical mirror of time.

CARSTEN NICOLAI A.K.A. NOTO/ALVA NOTO

I was mainly working as a visual artist when I made my first recordings in 1994–5; these originated from researching materials that would actually dematerialise. Without being aware of it at first, the sound experiments I did at that time were actually what I was looking for.

My main focus then was, and now still is primarily oriented towards the question of how time is perceived through sound. In the works under my pseudonym noto – that focused on the physicality of sound and its instantaneous effects – I did this very empirically by varying loop speeds and altering pitches to watch if and which emotional reactions I experienced. Also, I tried to find out more about other qualities of sound: the tracks were based on sine wave tones and avoided overtones, melody and musical orders, to rather establish structures that sprang from visual patterns or mathematical models. In experiments with ultra-high and ultra-low frequencies I pushed those explorations to physical and material limits.

But I was also interested in looking at the effects that occurred when visual structures are transformed into audible patterns and vice versa. In terms of synaesthetic perception I constructed some installations (*wellenwanne*, 2000/*telefunken*, 2000), where I documented sounds creating visible patterns. This was to demonstrate their hybrid value – to show and sensitise the viewer/listener for how those spheres intertwine. For my compositional work this has always been very important, as among other principles I used visual structures as a basis for tracks.

The notion to introduce all these experiments to a more musical approach came later when I did my first recordings under the name of alva noto. Here I tried to strip bare pop music standards to a minimum level of rhythmic structure and fathomed strategies to explore extreme poles in my collaborations with other artists: from micro-structure experiments to working with acoustic instruments.

In the context of the complete merging of our information system in the digital sphere – accompanied by the phenomena of acceleration, fragmentation and dispersion – I developed my own strategy to assess personal space. In my *transall series* I misread and transformed information, leading me to unusual results that challenge the rules of existing standards. You can listen to the rhythm of the code which by transformation reveals its sheer aesthetic.

My latest project *xerrox* engages with erroring and mutation. It observes the gradual transformations the sound undergoes by constant copying. The process of de- and recomposing of the musical source causes inherent errors and results in self-generated mutations that finally overcome the original and take over its essence. One of my key references for these experiments – and for many of my former works as well – was a text on artificial intelligence, Takashi Ikegami's article 'Active Mutations of Self-reproducing Networks, Machines and Tapes' (1996), which engages with the logic of self-regulation of cybernetic systems. He describes the emergence of new forms and patterns by mutation intrinsic to a system. Ever since, this has been very influential to me, and is as present in my early works based on loops, white noise and mathematical principles as it is in my current projects.

Over the years I have had the wish to combine all of those ideas into an overall project simultaneously, a work, which would bring visual elements, sound and space together. An attempt to do so is the installation *syn chron* (2005), which fuses an interplay of laser light projection and sound with a crystalline shaped, architectural form. It enables the visitor to get an holistic experience from interacting elements of time and space. In this sense it comes close to an ideally autonomous Gesamtkunstwerk, which could prospectively, as a consequence, allow me to disappear.

WARREN BURT

Contradictory thoughts on electronic music

'Electronics has changed everything in music.'
'Electronics has changed very little in music.'
'We have extended our bodies and our consciousness in ways undreamed of.'
'We are still dancing, singing monkeys.'
    (We were dancing, singing monkeys before we became jabbering apes.)

It's not a question of whether electronics. They're essential. But we shouldn't have an exaggerated idea of their importance.

I was studying Indian music. My teacher said, 'In Indian music, we say that you must sing the music before you can play it.' 'Like this?' I asked, doing my best vocal imitation of the first thirty seconds of Stockhausen's *Kontakte.* 'Precisely!' my delighted teacher said.

The biggest change electronics have made to music is sociological. It's certainly allowed the exploratory, inquiring side of classical music to survive the fossilisation of the orchestra . . . the interesting thinkers just went elsewhere . . . along with their machines.

I will allow that electronics has made some things faster and easier. For example, microtonality and works of extremely long duration. But people have been making microtonal music for centuries, and anyone who has ever heard a Hindu priest chanting the thousand names of the goddess knows that minimalism didn't begin in the 1960s.

'Electronics has removed the body from music.' Yet, the equipment is still operated by bodies, and bodies are listening to it, and even dancing to it. Is electronics any more of a conceptual extension of the body than, say, a clarinet?

Is there any music that's truly native to electronics? That couldn't exist without it? Maybe. Maybe a realtime algorithmic interactive piece with synthetic timbres is native to the medium. I don't think there's any way to do that without electronics. But I might be wrong.

MAX MATHEWS

The past and future of computer music

The year 2007 marks the fiftieth anniversary of the birth of music synthesis on a digital computer – an IBM 704 computer which filled a big Madison avenue showroom in New York City. At that time, I worked for the Bell Telephone Laboratories who rented time for me on the IBM for four 1957 dollars a minute. My job was studying new telephones with the computer. But, sound-is-sound, and if you can make speech on a computer you can also make music.

During this half-century the musical computer has changed from a huge expensive machine, affordable only by universities and research laboratories, to a laptop which almost anyone can afford. It took the IBM minutes to compute a second of music with limited timbres. Today's musical laptop is small enough to fit in an orchestra chair and can generate rich timbres in realtime, that is to say, it can be played live as any other traditional instrument.

A comparison of the IBM 704 to my current laptop is revealing:

ASPECT	IBM-704 (1957)	IBM-G41 (2005)	RATIO
CLOCK	1/10 MHZ	3 GHZ	30000
RAM	192K BYTES	1 G BYTES	5000
MEMORY	6 M BYTES (TAPE)	80 G BYTES (DISK)	10000
COST	$200/HR (RENT)	$2000 (BUY)	
SIZE	FULL ROOM	7 LB LAPTOP	

Computer technology no longer limits computer music. Now we can attack much more interesting problems than computer programs.

In the past I have often quoted the SAMPLING THEOREM which for music says: 'ANY SOUND the human ear can hear can be made from digital samples.' I still believe that beautiful as is a violin's tone, neither it nor any other musical instrument can make this claim. However, I have recently added a corollary to this theorem:

COROLLARY (MATHEWS-2006) For musical purposes, in the class ANY SOUND, almost all timbres are uninteresting, and many timbres are feeble or ugly. Moreover, there is a great temptation to try to strengthen weak timbres by turning up volume controls thus creating dangerously loud sounds. It is VERY HARD to create new timbres we hear as interesting, powerful and beautiful.

Instead of technology, new music is now limited by the limits of our understanding of the perception of music by the human ear and brain. What is it in music that we find interesting and beautiful? What sounds do we find dull and unpleasant? What is learned from the music in our lives? What is inherent in our genes? These questions are much more challenging and interesting than writing new computer programs. Progress will require much more research in musical psychoacoustics. Computers have already supplied new tools to carry out this research. New brain-scanning equipment is already showing us what parts of the human brain are activated by music.

But research itself does not lead directly to new music: only musicians and composers create new music. We also must provide new education for these musicians. I believe new courses with names such as Orchestration for Electronic Music and Ear Training for Electronic Musicians must and will soon be added to the composer's training.

Computers in the last fifty years have changed our lives in many many ways. But I believe this is only the crack in the door and in the next fifty years we will see great progress in our understanding of our musical selves. Computers will help us in our quest by synthesising and analysing a lush jungle of new timbres which our ears and brains will hear and judge, will accept and reject, will love and hate, and which we will learn to understand and use in our music.

PART II

Electronic music in practice

5 Interactivity and live computer music

SERGI JORDÀ

'When asked what musical instrument they play, few computer musicians respond spontaneously with "I play the computer." Why not?'(Wessel and Wright 2002). Actually, most computer music performers still seem shyly reluctant to consider the computer as a *regular* musical instrument, but nonetheless, the computer is finally reaching the point of feeling as much at home on stage as a saxophone or an electric guitar. This assimilation was boosted over the last ten years with the arrival of affordable machines powerful enough for realtime audio processing and of versatile audio software such as Max/MSP, Pure Data or SuperCollider, but live computer music is far from being a novelty; computer-based realtime music systems started in the late 1960s and early 1970s and non-digital live electronic music goes back as far as the nineteenth century.

An ambitious goal for any new instrument is the potential to create a *new kind of music.* In that sense, baroque music cannot be imagined without the advances of sixteenth- and seventeenth-century luthiers, rock could not exist without the electric guitar, and jazz or hip-hop, without the redefinitions of the saxophone and the turntable. This chapter explores the potential of computers as musical instruments and analyses what it is that makes them so especially different from previous instruments, unveiling the novel possibilities as well as the drawbacks they entail.

The computer as a sound-producing device

While acoustic instruments inhabit bounded sound spaces, especially constrained in terms of timbre, tessitura and physical mechanism, computers are theoretically capable of producing any audible sound, either from scratch (through sound synthesis techniques) or by sampling existing sounds and altering them further through processing. For many musicians, this ability to explore an infinite sonic universe, an aspect that will be explored in chapter 11, constitutes the first and most obvious advantage of the computer over traditional instruments. For our purposes, another essential distinction between the computer and acoustic instruments lies in their control mechanisms, i.e. in the way they are played.

In traditional instrumental playing, every nuance, every small control variation or modulation (e.g. a vibrato or a tremolo) has to be addressed physically by the performer (although this level of control is almost automatic and unconscious in a trained musician). In digital instruments, all parameters can indeed be varied without restriction, continuously or abruptly, but moreover, the performer no longer needs to control directly all these aspects of the production of sound, being able instead to direct and supervise the computer processes that control these details. A related automation mechanism is already present in several electric instruments; applying a mechanical vibrato by means of a Leslie speaker in a Hammond organ or of a variable-speed motor in a vibraphone is indeed much less demanding than keeping a wobbling finger on a violin string! In the case of digital instruments, these automation processes cease to be restricted to simple oscillations and can grow in number and complexity. As a result of the potential intricacy of the ongoing processes, which can be under the instrument's sole control or a responsibility shared by the instrument and the performer, performing music with 'intelligent devices' tends towards an *interactive* dialogue between instrument and instrumentalist.

Interaction

'Interaction' involves the existence of a mutual or reciprocal action or influence between two or more systems. Few of our daily activities do not involve some kind of interaction, as we humans constantly interact with other humans as well as with many artefacts. Driving a car or swinging on a rocking chair are two examples of interactive activities with mechanical devices, since they both involve a two-way communication channel or a feedback loop. Because human communication is the paradigmatic example of interactive communication, complex systems that sense and react to human behaviour through the detection of aspects such as direct physical manipulation, body movement, or changes in the human physiological or psychological states, are often called *interactive*, although it should be pointed out that when cognition is left out of the equation, reaction replaces interaction (Rafaeli 1988). In merely reactive systems, output messages are only related to the immediately previous input message, which makes these systems fully predictable. A light switch will remain a (reactive) light switch independently of the amount of sophisticated sensors it may hide.

Music, on the other hand, has always been a highly interactive activity. Musicians interact with their instrument, with other musicians, with dancers or with the audience, so from this perspective, the very idea of 'interactive music', a term often employed for referring to the music resulting from the dialogue between a musician and a computer, seems self-evident. Ironically enough, interactivity actually suffered due to technological advances attained in the nineteenth and twentieth centuries. Recorded music eliminated the feedback dialogue between the audience and the live musicians, turning music performance into a one-way communication. Later, as a result of multitrack recording, even the dialogue between different players was eliminated. We will here discover how, with their added 'intelligence', digital computers are finally prepared for paying technology's 'musical interaction debts'. We will learn how computer-based instruments can surpass the sound and note levels, flirt with composition and respond to performers in complex, not always entirely predictable ways, even acting not only as instruments, but almost as performers, composers or conductors (Chadabe 1984).

First steps in interactive computer music

In 1957 Max Mathews had programmed the first sounds ever generated by a digital computer, but computers were not yet ready for realtime, so groundbreaking approaches undertaken in the 1950s and 1960s had to remain in the analogue domain. In the late 1950s, the American inventor and composer Raymond Scott[1] constructed electromechanical musical sequencers and *instantaneous music composition performance machines* that could harmonise a melody or provide rhythm accompaniments in realtime (Chusid and Garland 1994). Scott, also a pioneer in approaching electronic music from a pop perspective, was an important influence for Robert Moog, who several years later would construct his popular voltage-controlled analogue synthesisers.

But not everyone could afford Moog's invention. In the mid-1960s, Gordon Mumma and David Berhman, two young American composers distinctly influenced by John Cage, started building analogue circuits capable of producing or processing sound in response to external acoustic stimuli, predating the Machine-Listening interactive systems that will be further discussed in chapter 10. In Mumma's composition *Hornpipe* (1967), an analogue device analyses and amplifies the resonances of the hall in which the performer is playing the French horn (Mumma 1975). Mumma can indeed be considered among the first composers who integrated electronic principles in the realtime operation of the musical structures of the compositions, an approach he termed as 'Cybersonic' and which he applied in many of his pieces.

By the late 1960s, computers still lacked the computing power needed for realtime synthesis (i.e. crunching several hundred thousand operations per second), but they were indeed able to receive and send lower bandwidth information from/to the real (analogue) world. They could receive and digitise voltages (coming from sliders, buttons, sensors, etc.) and they could also send voltages back. This is what Max Mathews achieved again in 1969 with the GROOVE synthesiser, in which he decided to connect a computer to a voltage-controlled analogue synthesiser for managing from the former any parameter of the latter. In his first experiments, Mathews adopted a player-piano approach, storing in the computer the sequence of pitches to be played, thus leaving for the performer the control of timbre, dynamics and of the overall tempo of the piece (Mathews 1991).

Although Mathews' chosen approach can be considered conservative, he had set the basis for a new type of musical interaction. By storing in the computer the instructions that were to be sent to the synthesiser, he showed that new digital instruments could have memory; and when an instrument is capable of knowing which note comes next, some extra knowledge may enable it to take decisions on the fly, even taking into account the performer's gestures. In this context, each note emitted or each action achieved by this hypothetical instrument could thus be the result of a combined decision made by both the player and the instrument. The *musical computer* thus becomes the *philosophical instrument* endowed with memory *and* with sensibility, described by Denis Diderot in the eighteenth century: 'The philosophical instrument is sensitive; it is at the same time the musician and the instrument . . . Imagine the Harpsichord having sensitivity and memory, and tell me if it would not play back by itself the airs that you have performed upon its keys. We are instruments endowed with sensibility and memory' (Diderot 1951, p. 880).

Interactive music: the computer as a semi-autonomous device

The composer and software programmer Laurie Spiegel worked with Max Mathews' GROOVE in the early 1970s and started developing interactive programs for it. In 1973 she coined the term *intelligent instruments* and in 1985 she developed *Music Mouse*, a musical software for the Macintosh, the Commodore Amiga and the Atari ST (Spiegel 1987). The program, which was played by moving the mouse through an onscreen grid, enabled non-experts to perform as if they were accomplished musicians, turning for the first time a computer into a musical instrument that anyone could play. Yet, *Music Mouse* was also a powerful instrument, suited not only for amateurs but also for professionals, as the recordings of Spiegel's compositions and improvisations performed with it testify.

Along with Spiegel, in the early 1970s several other musicians and researchers began to work from similar premises. Joel Chadabe had already started experimenting with automated and random-controlled Moog synthesisers in live performances in 1967. Ten years later, in his piece *Solo*, he connected two Theremin antennas to a Synclavier (one of the first commercially available digital synthesisers) and controlled though the antennas the tempo and the timbre of several simultaneous but independent sequences. Moving his hands in the air allowed him to 'conduct' an improvising orchestra. As a result of these experiments, he coined the term 'interactive composing'. Several years later, Chadabe would found the company Intelligent Music, which in 1986 released the programs *M* and *Jam Factory* (Zicarelli 1987), which together with the aforementioned *Music Mouse*, constituted the first commercial *interactive music* software.

Salvatore Martirano started building electronic music instruments in the mid-1960s at the University of Illinois. Finished in 1972, the *SalMar Construction* included 291 touch-sensitive switches, connected through a massive patch bay to a combinatorial logic unit, which could affect in real time four concurrently running programs that drove the four voices of a custom analogue synthesiser. The fact that the four processes ran in parallel, concurrently modifying parameters such as pitch, loudness, timbre and envelope, made it impossible to fully predict the system's behaviour. In Martirano's own words, 'performing with the system was too complex to analyze . . . Control was an illusion. But I was in the loop. I was trading swaps with the logic' (Walker *et al.* 1992).

By the mid-1970s small microcomputers such as the Kim-1 or the Intel 8008 started to be affordable, opening the ground to a new generation of musicians and experimentalists that started performing with computers with little means and outside of the more academic circles. The *League of Automatic Composers*, the first microcomputer and network band in history, formed in California's Bay Area by John Bischoff, Rich Gold, Jim Horton (later joined by Tim Perkis), constitutes a perfect example of this trend. Each member of the group owned a Kim-1 microcomputer with a sound output, and each one programmed his own computer with programs that were able to produce music by themselves, but also to interchange data with their colleagues' computers, thus creating a network of mutually *listening* computers. 'When the elements of the network are not connected the music sounds like three completely independent processes, but when they are interconnected the music seems to present a "mindlike" aspect' (Bischoff *et al.* 1978). Influenced by the *League* approach, other musicians such as the trombonist, composer and improviser George Lewis began to experiment with computer music improvisation, establishing duets between his trombone and an autonomous computer. This and related approaches, in which the computer behaves more as a performance partner than as an instrument, also known as *machine musicianship*, will be further discussed in chapter 10.

A great technological and democratic breakthrough took place in the mid-1980s, when the MIDI standardisation finally allowed a musician to effortlessly connect every synthesiser with every computer (International MIDI Association 1983; Loy 1985). The MIDI standard coincided with the definitive popularisation of microcomputers, initially 8-bit machines (e.g. Sinclair ZX81, Apple II, Commodore VIC20 or C64) and 16-bit since 1984, with the release of the Apple Macintosh soon to be followed by the Commodore Amiga and the Atari ST. The combination of MIDI with affordable microcomputers finally triggered the commercial music software market. Among the release of many musical applications, most of them MIDI sequencers, there was also room for more experimental and idiosyncratic programs that could fall into the 'interactive music' category, such as the aforementioned *Music Mouse*, *M*, *Jam Factory*, *upBeat* or the interactive sequencers developed by the company Dr. T, which were conceived both as studio and realtime interaction tools predating *Ableton Live* by fifteen years.[2]

The aforesaid applications depict different strategies towards the real-time creation of music using computers, but the flexibility and versatility offered by computers is better explored using a powerful programming language that allows the development of one's own personal ideas. Although computer music programming languages are studied in depth in chapter 4, we cannot omit here some of the software environments that since the late 1990s, and in combination with the increasing power of personal computers, have allowed the definitive bloom of realtime computer music. Certainly, easy-to-use data-flow graphical programming languages such as *Pure Data* (Puckette 1996) or *Max/MSP* (Puckette 2002) or customisable audio programming languages such as *SuperCollider* (McCartney 2002), which musically speaking allow almost anyone to do almost anything, are partly responsible for the popular and definitive acceptance of the laptop as a musical instrument.

Live computer music: what can be done?

In the sleeve notes of their 1989 CD, John Bischoff and Tim Perkis note that 'for us, composing a piece of music is like building a new instrument, an instrument whose behaviour makes up the performance. We act at once as performer, composer and instrument builder, in some ways working more like sculptors than traditional musicians' (Bischoff and Perkis 1989). It is hard to provide a structured vision that covers the multiplicity of all current interactive music possibilities. It seems clear, to start, that such systems permit creative approaches that are sometimes closer to music activities other than the ones we conventionally understand by 'playing an instrument'. As a counterpart to 'unlimited' power, the work of many live computer musicians encompasses a broad range of activities, often more related to composition and to instrument design and building, than to performance or musical practice.

In 1990, Jeff Pressing listed some of these possibilities with the help of traditional music-making metaphors. Practical examples and applications have swelled, but his list, 'playing a musical instrument, conducting an orchestra, playing together (ensemble) with a machine, acting as a one-man band' (Pressing 1990), is still quite pertinent today. For the interactive music pioneer Joel Chadabe, performing with these systems is like 'sailing a boat on a windy day and through stormy seas'. The performer is not in control of everything; some external, unpredictable forces, no matter what their real origin or strength are, affect the system, and the output is the result of this permanent struggle. Whether surprise and dialogue is encouraged through randomness, by ungraspable complexity or by the machine's embedded knowledge, independently of the degree of unpredictability they possess, at their best, these new instruments often shift the centre of the performer's attention from the lower-level details to the higher-level processes that produce these details. The musician performs control strategies instead of performing data and the instrument leans towards more intricate responses to performer stimuli. This situation tends to surpass the note to note and the 'one gesture–one acoustic event' playing paradigms present in all traditional instruments, thus allowing musicians to work at different musical levels and forcing them to take higher-level (i.e. more compositional) decisions on-the-fly (Jordà 2002).

The concept of 'note', the structural backbone of Western music, becomes an option rather than a necessity, now surrounded by (macrostructural) form on one side, and (microstructural) sound on the other. As a matter of fact, the inclusion of audio synthesis and processing capabilities into the aforementioned programming environments such as *Pure Data*, *Max/MSP* or *SuperCollider* since the late 1990s is undeniably the single most important occurrence in live computer music for the last two decades. At first glance, virtual or software synthesisers may not seem a radically new concept, but they exhibit essential differences from their hardware counterpart, the venerable keyboard synthesiser. They first provide unlimited scope for freedom of sonic expression, experimentation and imagination. More importantly, they finally allow the seamless integration of macrostructural and microstructural music creation strategies, a blend that does not come without problems:

> What kinds of interfaces to sound might we want for this model? What can we make? Will we be able to move our hands through the space around us, shaping the sounds as we listen, roughing them up here and smoothing them there, and pushing and pulling areas of sonic fabric up, down, toward and away, together and apart? What might be the variables with which we interact? In what dimensions might we move.   (Spiegel 2000)

Or as a second observer notes:

> Certain gestures can manipulate sound synthesis directly, while others articulate notelike events, while other actions direct the structural progress of the piece. Applying these concepts to computer realization gives rise to new possibilities that blur the boundaries separating event articulation and structural modification. A single articulation can elicit not just a note, but an entire structural block. Variations in the articulation could very well modify the timbre with which that structure is played, or could introduce slight variations on the structure itself or could modify which structure is elicited. The potential combinatorial space of complexity is quite large.
> (Tanaka 2000, p. 390)

Although the computer does effectively bridge the gap between musical thought and physical instrumental ability, the above quotations remind us that live music performance cannot be separated from control and gesture. Having focused on the output of musical computers, in the next section we shall turn to the input side, studying gestural controllers.

Gestural controllers

Acoustic instruments consist of an excitation source that can oscillate in different ways under the control of the performer(s), and a resonating system that couples the vibrations of the oscillator to the surrounding air. Where in most non-keyboard acoustic instruments, the separation between the control interface and the sound generating subsystems is fuzzy and unclear, digital musical instruments can always be easily divided into a gestural controller (or input device) that takes the control information from the performer(s), and a sound generator that plays the role of the excitation source. The controller component can typically be a simple computer mouse, a computer keyboard, a MIDI keyboard or a MIDI fader box, but with the use of sensors and appropriate analogue to digital converters, any control signal coming from the outside (i.e. the performer, but also the audience or the environment – as in the case of interactive installations) can be converted into control messages understandable by the digital system. Changes in motion, pressure, velocity, light, gravity, skin conductivity or muscle tension, almost anything, can now become a 'music controller'.

In 1919 the Russian physicist Lev Termen invented the Theremin, the first electronic musical instrument to be played without being touched (Theremin 1996). With its two metal antennas, around which the performer moves the hands controlling respectively pitch and loudness, it constitutes one of the earlier and more paradigmatic attempts of alternative musical control. It should be pointed out, however, that unlike new digital systems, in which any input parameter coming from the controller can be arbitrarily assigned to any sound or musical parameter, the Theremin is a *real* instrument; its sound is actually the direct result of the electromagnetic field variations caused by the proximity of the hands around the antennas. If acoustic instruments are built upon the laws of mechanics, the Theremin behaviour is determined by the laws of electromagnetism. Digital instruments, on their side, are only limited by the imagination and know how of their constructors: a substantial distinction with both positive and negative consequences.

The burgeoning of alternative music controllers started two decades ago with the advent of MIDI, which standardised the separation between input (control) and output (sound) electronic music devices. In an attempt to classify music controllers, Wanderley (2001) distinguishes between (a) instrument-like controllers, (b) extended controllers and (c) alternative controllers. In the first category, not only keyboards, but virtually all traditional instruments (such as saxophones, trumpets, guitars, violins, drums, xylophones or accordions) have been reconceived as MIDI controllers. Although their control capabilities are always reduced when compared to their acoustic ancestors, they offer as a counterpart the possibility to ride an expanded, unlimited sonic palette. The second group, *extended controllers*, includes traditional instruments (which sometimes can be even played 'unplugged'), which with the add-on of extra sensors afford additional playing nuances or techniques and thus supplementary sound or music control possibilities (Machover 1992). Although several extended controllers have been constructed to measure (e.g. for virtuosi such as Yo-Yo Ma or Wynton Marsalis) none of them is being played on a regular basis; none of them has managed to 'dethrone' their original instrumental role model.

The two aforementioned categories profit from known playing techniques and thus may address a potentially higher number of instrumentalists. Until recently, and with honourable exceptions like the quasi-epic work of Donald Buchla (Rich 1991), all commercially available controllers, mainly *midified* versions of traditional instruments, have remained mostly imitative and conservative. Yet traditional performance techniques may not constitute the best strategy to confront the new music-making paradigms discussed in the previous sections.

When it comes to the third category, the jumble of alternative controllers not easily includable in any previous grouping, it is difficult to provide a taxonomy that facilitates a quick overview. Joseph Paradiso, one of the main experts in sensing and field technologies for music controllers' design, classifies controllers according to how they are used or worn. Some of the categories he proposes are *batons*, *non-contact gesture sensing* (which includes Theremins, ultrasound, computer vision, etc.) and *wearables* (which includes gloves and biosignal detectors) (Paradiso 1997). Among this plethora of alternative controllers, the Radio Baton, a crossover between a conductor's baton and a percussion instrument, conceived again by Max Mathews in 1987 and based on detection principles analogous to that of the Theremin, is one of the more popular (Mathews 1991). As a sign of the growing interest in this field, the annual conference *New Interfaces for Musical Expression* (NIME), which started in 2001 as a fifteen-person workshop, now gathers annually more than two hundred researchers, luthiers and musicians from all over the world to share their knowledge and late-breaking work on new musical interface design. The yearly proceedings[3] constitute the ultimate and most up-to-date source of information on this topic. A more concise but well documented overview of non-imitative controllers that covers dozens of control surfaces, gloves, non-contact devices, wearable or bioelectrical devices can be found in Cutler, Robair and Bean (2000).

Even if the universe of gestural controllers may appear at first glance a quite exclusive club, it definitely is not. Analogue-to-MIDI interfaces designed for converting analogue input values into any type of MIDI message provide straightforward means for opening the computer to the external world, and allow the connection of up to sixteen or thirty-two suitable sensors. Cheaper (and slightly less straightforward) options are offered by easily programmable micro-controllers (such as the Basic Stamp), which permit constructing a custom analogue-to-MIDI interface for less than 50 Euros. Sensors for measuring all kind of physical parameters are also readily available and can be connected to any of these devices, enabling virtually any kind of physical gesture or external parameter to be tracked and digitised into a computer. Moreover, many cheap and widely available control devices meant for the general market, such as joysticks or graphic tablets, can become interesting music controllers. The joystick is a wonderful controller: it has two, three or more degrees of freedom and several buttons and triggers which allow assigning different parameter combinations. Data gloves were originally developed for virtual reality environments, and while professional models are still expensive, several cheap toy-like versions sporadically hit the market such as the *Mattel Power Glove* (1989) or the *P5Glove* (2003). Graphic tablets, which offer great resolution along the X–Y axes plus pressure and angle sensibility, have also proven application for music. To conclude, several software toolkits exist that provide unified, consistent and straightforward connection and mapping of these easily affordable input devices (joysticks, tablets, game pads, etc.) into the more popular programming environments (e.g. Steiner 2005). The stage is definitely set for experimentation with new controllers.

Music controllers can preserve traditional playing modes, permitting us to blow, strike, pluck, rub or bow our 'computers'; new traditionalists in turn, may prefer to continue clicking, double-clicking, typing, pointing, sliding, twirling or dragging and dropping them. The decision is up to everyone. With the appropriate sensors, new digital instruments can also be caressed, squeezed, kissed, licked, danced, hummed or sung. They can even disappear or dematerialise while responding to our movements, our muscle tension or our facial expressions.

With the flexibility offered by MIDI, any controller can certainly be combined with any sound- and music-producing device. Still, each choice is critical. As pointed out by Joel Ryan, improviser, leading researcher in the NIME field and technical director of the Dutch laboratory STEIM, 'a horizontal slider, a rotary knob, a sensor that measures the pressure under one finger, an accelerometer which can measure tilt and respond to rapid movements, a sonar or an infrared system that can detect the distance between two points, each have their idiosyncratic properties' (Ryan 1991). Any input device can become a good or a bad choice depending on the context, the parameter to control, or the performer who will be using it. Just as the automotive engineer chooses a steering wheel over left/right incrementing buttons, 'we should not hand a musician a butterfly net when a pitchfork is required' (Puckette and Settel 1993). The challenge remains how to integrate and transform this apparatus into coherently designed, meaningful musical experiences with emotional depth. It is in fact extremely hard to design highly sophisticated control interfaces without a profound prior knowledge of how the sound or music generators will proceed; a parallel design process will surely be more enriching than buying the ultimate controller for plugging into any custom software.

A fruitful example of this suggested 'holistic instrumental design approach' can be found in the work of composer/violinist Dan Trueman who for almost a decade has pursued the deconstruction and reinvention of the electronic violin. Trueman's research has not been limited to adding sensors to a violin bow or to the fingerboard; in search of the 'real' acoustic instrumental feel, he has even designed special spherical and hemispherical speakers that better simulate the complex sound-radiation patterns of acoustic instruments. His BoSSa, an array of spherical speakers which can be excited and played with a special sensor bow, constitutes the perfect integration of both research lines (Trueman and Cook 1999; Trueman 2006).

The future of digital musical instruments?

We have postulated that by themselves, controllers are not musical instruments. From the same perspective, the computer is too generic to be properly considered one; many musical instruments can be conceived based on a digital computer, each with completely different idiosyncrasies. In this context, a new standard digital instrument has yet to arrive. In effect, not only has no recent electronic instrument managed to reach the (limited) popularity of the Theremin or the Ondes Martenot, invented in 1919 and 1928 respectively; the latest instrument that may argue to have attained classic status, is not digital, not even electronic. Since it started being played in a radically unorthodox and unexpected manner in the early 1980s, thus becoming a *genuine* musical instrument, the turntable has developed its own musical culture, techniques and virtuosi (Shapiro 2002; Hansen 2002). The fact that so many digital turntable simulators already exist, some of them even quite successful commercially, gives us as many clues to the health of the turntable, as it does to the sterility of new instrument design.

New standards may not be essential for the creation of new music; perhaps even the concept of a *musical instrument* is just an old romantic burden that would be better left aside, but somehow it seems that some unrestrained potential is being eschewed in this lawless anything-goes territory. New digital instruments conceived holistically and not as a conglomerate of several interchangeable components are scarce; even worse, in most cases they are only performed by their creators. This situation complicates any progression in the field, both from the design and from the performance perspective. It is not only that electronic music controllers evolve so rapidly that it is rare for a musician to work long enough with one to develop virtuosic technique; it is that every new incarnation seems to come out of the blue. 'A growing number of researchers/composers/performers work with gestural controllers but to my astonishment I hardly see a consistent development of systematic thought on the interpretation of gesture into music, and the notion of musical feed-back into gesture' (Michel Waisvisz, from Wanderley and Battier 2000).

The Dutch improviser (and founder of the aforementioned STEIM lab) Michel Waisvisz, can be considered indeed as one of the very few new instruments virtuosi. Since the early 1980s, Waisvisz has been performing with his self-designed *Hands*, a pair of ergonomically shaped plates fitted with

Figure 5.1 Michel Waisvisz performs with The Hands (photo: Carla van Tijn)

sensors, potentiometers and switches, strapped under the hands of the performer, which are meant to be played in a sort of 'air accordion' manner.
Nicolas Collins, with his Trombone-propelled electronics, Laetitia Sonami
with the Lady's Gloves, or Atau Tanaka, who has turned a medical elec-
tromyograph designed for evaluating the physiological properties and the
activity of the muscles into an instrument of his own (Tanaka 2000), are
among the few professional performers who like Waisvisz, use new idiosyncratic devices as their main musical instruments.

Interfaces for multithreaded and shared control

'The exploration of post-digital sound spaces, and with it laptop performance, is a dialog conducted with mice, sliders, buttons and the metaphors
of business computing . . . Many post-digital composers would be hesitant
to freeze this dialogic property through the design and use of a hardware

controller' (Turner 2003). Sad but true? When the improviser and software developer Emile Tobenfeld was asked, in 1992, about the desirable features a software instrument for computer-assisted free improvisation should include, he listed: (i) precise control of the timbre; (ii) gestural control of previously composed musical processes; (iii) simultaneous control of multiple instrumental processes; (iv) the ability to start a process, and relinquish control of it, allowing the process to continue while other processes are started; (v) the ability to regain control of an ongoing process; (vi) visual feedback from the computer screen (Tobenfeld 1992). With these ideas in mind we could probably deduce that Turner is wrong in at least one point: it is not the mouse that is so appreciated, but the *monitoring screen* instead. Many laptopists favour indeed the use of MIDI fader boxes for easily controlling the sliders of their *Max/MSP* patches, and the availability of this type of commercial device has increased in parallel with the availability of realtime audio software.

However, most of the music controllers being developed do not pursue Tobenfeld's proposed multithreaded and shared control approach, prolonging the traditional instrument paradigm instead. Trying perhaps to exorcise forty years of tape music, researchers in the field of new musical interfaces tend to conceive new musical instruments highly inspired by traditional ones, most often designed to be 'worn' and played all the time, and offering continuous, synchronous and precise control over a few dimensions. An intimate, sensitive and not necessarily highly dimensional interface of this kind (i.e. more like a violin bow, a mouthpiece or a joystick, than like a piano) will be ideally suited for direct microcontrol (i.e. sound, timbre, articulation). However, for macrostructural, indirect or higher-level control, a non-wearable interface distributed in space and allowing intermittent access (i.e. more like a piano or a drum) should be undeniably preferred (Jordà 2005). Moreover, not many new instruments profit from the display capabilities of digital computers, whereas in the musical performance approach we are discussing, given that the performer tends to frequently delegate and shift control to the instrument, all affordable ways for monitoring processes and activities are especially welcome. Visual feedback becomes thus a significant asset for allowing this type of instrument to dynamically 'communicate' the states and the behaviours of their musical processes. Visual feedback could partially solve another relevant problem of laptop performance, such as the perception difficulties and the lack of understanding these types of performances provoke in the audience (Turner 2003), which could be synthesised as 'how could we readily distinguish an artist performing with powerful software like *SuperCollider* or *PD* from someone checking their e-mail whilst DJ-ing with *iTunes*?' (Collins 2003).

A promising line of research in tune with the aforementioned problems is the application of tangible interfaces to realtime music performance. Tangible User Interfaces (TUIs) combine control and representation within a physical artefact (Ullmer and Ishii 2001). In table-based tangible interfaces, digital information becomes graspable with the direct manipulation of simple objects which are available on a table surface. This is attained by combining augmented reality techniques that allow the tracking of control objects on the table surface, with visualisation techniques that convert the table into a flat screening surface. Not unlike the tables full of toys and sounding gadgets of many free music improvisers, a table with these characteristics favours multi-parametric and shared control, interaction and exploration and even multi-user collaboration. Moreover, the seamless integration of visual feedback and physical control, which eliminates the indirection component present in a conventional screen + pointer system, allows a more natural, intuitive and rich interaction.

In recent years, researchers have developed a variety of tabletop tangible musical controllers, such as *SmallFish, the Jam-O-Drum* (Blaine and Perkis 2000), the *Audiopad* (Patten *et al.* 2006), or the *reacTable* (Jordà *et al.* 2005). In the *reacTable* several musicians can share the control of the instrument by caressing, rotating and moving physical artefacts on a luminous table, constructing different audio topologies in a kind of tangible modular synthesiser or graspable flow-controlled programming language. According to its creators, the reacTable has been designed for installations and casual users as well as for professionals in concert, as it combines immediate and intuitive access in a relaxed and immersive way, with the flexibility and the power of digital sound design algorithms, resulting in endless improvement possibilities and mastership. This claim seems especially relevant if we consider the speed at which technology and fashion shift in our current twenty-first century. Proselytism will surely not be attained by promising ten years of sacrifice. If we aspire for a new instrument to be played by more than two people it will have to capture the musicians' imagination from the start. Which brings us to the next and final section of this chapter: where is the frontier between the 'serious' musical instrument and the 'sound toy'?

Control, virtuosity, intimacy and expressiveness

The instruments we are discussing inhabit a continuum that ranges from the *absolutely passive* conventional instrument (in which the performer is in charge of every smallest detail), to the *fully autonomous* (i.e. human independent) performing machine. They could offer indeed the possibility – the

CD player would constitute an extreme example – to be played by pushing a 'powerful' button that would execute a whole precomposed musical work. With a CD player one can faultlessly play music of extreme complexity with absolutely no effort or training. Satirical as it may sound, this tricky illusion is used indeed in many current interactive sound installations, which seeking to guarantee a complex or predefined musical output, do not give to their interactors more than a couple of bits to play with. We are not criticising here the successful commercial crossover of interactive musical entertainment into mainstream culture, which in the recent years has brought a proliferation of musical game experiences such as *Karaoke Revolution*, *Guitar Hero*, Toshio Iwai's *Electroplankton* for the Nintendo DS, or Sony's Eye Toy rhythm action games (Blaine 2006). Computer-aided interactive music systems can have many applications, each of them perfectly licit and with their own place in the market. However, when faked or useless interactivity happens to be the blot of most contemporary interactive arts, we have to be cautious in order not to trivialise musical creation. *Good* new instruments should learn from their traditional ancestors and not impose *their* music on the performers. A good instrument should not be allowed, for example, to produce *only* good music. A good instrument should also be able to produce 'terribly bad' music, either at the player's will or at the player's misuse.[4] Only if these conditions are sufficiently fulfilled, will an instrument allow its performers to *play* music and not only to *play with* music.

A related control shortage, albeit for opposed reasons, can also be found in the work of many laptop music performers who embrace a bottom-up compositional style favoured by the flexible exploration encouraged in environments such as *Max/MSP* or *Pure Data*. Multithreaded musical processes proliferate in which the responsibility is often left almost entirely to the computer; control is forgotten or delimited to scarce macro control; musical contrasts are sandpapered, the music's inertia augments and the concepts of 'instrument' and of 'performance dexterity' vanish.

It should thus be the luthier-performer's responsibility to establish a balance between different musical levels so that accuracy and fine control on chosen levels do not happen at the expense of leaving important processes unattended. Conscientious instrument designers will better profit out of new digital instruments' possibilities if they do not overlook the essential (albeit implicit and hidden) control features that have made acoustic instruments good enough to resist the acid test of time. We have repeatedly pointed out how interactive music systems emphasise the dialogue between the performer and the instrument, often producing unexpected results, be they non-linearity, randomness or ungraspable complexity. Are these features incompatible with the idea of absolute control, mastery and confidence popularly associated with virtuoso performance? We should not forget that non-linear behaviours are not exclusive to digital interactive music systems. They can be found, for example, in the vocalised and overblown tenor saxophone style or in the use of feedback in the electric guitar. Musicians explore and learn to control these additional degrees of freedom, producing the very intense kinetic performance styles upon which much free jazz and rock music is based. If non-linearity is at first intuitively seen as a source of potential lack of control, it can also mean higher-order and more powerful control. Distinct virtuosity paradigms definitely coexist: whereas the classical virtuoso, with her infinite precision and love for details, may appear closer to the goldsmith, the new digital instruments virtuoso, not unlike the jazz one, could be compared to the bullfighter for their abilities to deal with the unexpected. Confidence is definitely a rare quality in digital instruments (they are computers after all), but a performer needs to know and trust the instrument in order to be able to push it to the extremes and to experiment without fear. Only when a certain level of confidence is reached will performers feel a sense of intimacy with the instrument that will help them in finding their own voice and developing their expressiveness.

Interactive musical instruments can do more than merely transmit human expressiveness like passive channels. They can also be responsible for provoking and instigating in the performer new ideas or feelings to express. When these and related issues are fully understood, we shall hopefully discover computer-based instruments which will not sound as if they were always playing the same piece (although they will be also capable of playing one piece repeatedly, with infinite subtleties and variations, sounding always fresh and innovative). These instruments shall be flexible enough to permit full improvisation without any prior preparation and finally, versatile enough to possess their own defined identities which will even allow the development of personal styles among their performers.

Selected discography

Bahn, C. 2000. *The Rig: Solo Improvisations for Sensor Bass and Live Electronics.* Electronic Music Foundation, EMF CD 030

Behrman, D. 1977. *On the Other Ocean; Figure in a Clearing.* Lovely Music LO 141

Bischoff, J. and Perkis, T. 1989. *Artificial Horizon.* Artifact Recordings, AR102

Brown, C. 1996. *Duets.* Artifact Recordings, AR115

Casserley, L. 1999. *Labyrinths.* Sargasso SG28030

Chadabe, J. 1981. *Rhythms.* Lovely Music VR 1301

Fenn O'Berg 2004. *The Return of Fenn O'Berg.* Mego 54

FMOL Trio. 2002. *The Köln Concert.* Hazard Records 028

Fuzzybunny 2000. *Fuzzybunny.* Sonore

Le Caine, H. 1999. *Compositions & Demonstrations 1946–1974.* Electronic Music Foundation 15

Lewis, G. 1993. *Voyager*. Avant 014

M. I. M. E. O. (Music in Movement Electronic Orchestra) 1998. *Electric Chair +
Table*. Grob

Mumma, G. 2002. *Live Electronic Music*. Tzadik TZ 7074

Pair A'Dice 2001. *Near Vhana*. Ninth World Music 15

Parker, E. 1997. *Evan Parker's Electro-Acoustic Ensemble: Toward the Margins*. ECM
453514

Ryan, J. 1994. *Enfolded Strings Inial Mix*. Inial

Scott, R. 2000. *Manhattan Research, Inc.: New Plastic Sounds and Electronic
Abstractions*. Basta 90782

Spiegel, L. 1991. *Unseen Worlds*. Scarlet

— 2001. *Obsolete Systems*. Electronic Music Foundation EM119

The Hub 1989. *Computer Network Music*. Artifact 1002

V. A. 2000. *Clicks & Cuts*. Mille Plateaux 8079

6 Algorithmic composition

KARLHEINZ ESSL

Dedicated to Gottfried Michael Koenig for his 80th birthday

Although Algorithmic composition became popular with the rise of computers, algorithmic thinking is far older – it can be traced back to the ancient times of Pythagoras and the Jewish Kabbalah. It is a method of perceiving an abstract model behind the sensual surface, or in turn, of constructing such a model in order to create aesthetic works. Behind the various approaches there is one common denominator: a longing to create something infinite that exceeds the limited horizon of our individual knowledge. Seen in this light, algorithmic thinking and its application in the arts can become a way to gain experience and to overcome barriers that are either implicit in ourselves, or erected by our social environment.

In this article, I am focusing exclusively on the use of algorithms in the compositional process, leaving aside other approaches like the algorithmic simulation of musical styles, the computational modelling of music cognition and the application of artificial intelligence techniques (Cope 1996; Ebcioglu 1990).[1] My primary aim is to demonstrate how the algorithmic spirit has evolved through the centuries – from medieval music theory to the interactive realtime-generated computer music of today.

Algorithm

The term algorithm was phonetically derived from the name of the Arab mathematician Muhammad ibn Musa al-Khwarizmi (ninth century) who introduced Hindu–Arabic numerals and the concepts of algebra into European mathematics. An algorithm can be defined as a predetermined set of instructions for solving a specific problem in a limited number of steps. Algorithms can range from a mere succession of simple arithmetical operations to more complex combinations of procedures, utilising more involved constructions from computer science such as rule-based grammars, recursion and probabilistic inference.

Although the term stems from mathematics and natural sciences its application nowadays is widely used in the field of art production and composition, especially in the domains of media art and computer music. The

'Algorithmic Revolution' in the arts started as far back as the 1950s and has drastically changed not only the way in which art is produced, but also the function and self-conception of its creators.[2] With the help of algorithms, the composer is no longer a demiurge who controls every tiny detail of a composition through the power of his imagination. By utilising algorithmic methods such as automatisms, random operations, rule-based systems and autopoietic strategies, some artistic decisions are partly delegated to an external instance. This might be regarded as a weakness of the subjective autonomy. On the other hand, it enables one to gain new dimensions that expand investigation beyond a limited personal horizon. From this basis, algorithms can also be regarded as a powerful means to extend our experience – they might even develop into something that may be conceived as an 'inspiration machine'.

Within the field of algorithmic composition the algorithm constitutes an abstract model which defines and controls some or all structural aspects of the music. This model can also serve as a generator that is capable of producing the piece as a possible variant within a field of possibilities. The latter approach can be implemented as a computer program, but the underlying idea is much older. In 1787, Johann Wolfgang von Goethe wrote a letter to his friend Johann Gottfried von Herder in which he reported enthusiastically about a discovery that he made in the botanic garden of Palermo, Sicily:

> The primordial plant would be the most wonderful creation of the world, for which nature itself should envy me. With this model and the key that it contains, one could invent an infinite number of plants, ones that despite their imaginary existence could possibly be real, thus which are not solely literary and painterly shadows and illusions, but which possess an inner truth and necessity. This same principle would be applicable to every other aspect of life as well.
>
> (Goethe 1787)

Goethe's primordial plant does not exist in reality. It is an abstract model from which every plant – and even those which do not exist! – can be deduced. A concrete form (for example, a beech tree) can be described as a structural variant of the general 'tree' model. This concept is also applicable to music – a specific model that describes a compositional 'gestalt' would allow for the generation of thousands of different variants.

Due to its rule-based nature, every algorithm can be expressed as a computer program. However, the use of algorithms is not solely restricted to computers, as we will see in the following section where I will briefly outline the historical development of algorithmic strategies in music and literature.

History

Rule-based and semi-automatic compositional methods are not at all an invention of our modern era – one can trace these principles back to the very beginning of European polyphony in the Middle Ages. In *Musica enchiriadis* (*c.* 895), Hucbald of St Amande described a method for improvising a second voice to a given Gregorian chant by singing in parallel intervals such as fourths and fifths – a practice which was later described as Organum. Instructions like these were called *canon* (from the Greek word *kanon* = rule) and had their first bloom in the Franco-Flemish polyphony of the fifteenth century. The prevailing method was to write out a single voice part and to give instructions as to how additional voices could be derived from it.

A highly complex form of the so-called riddle canon written by Johann Sebastian Bach entitled *Verschiedene Canones über die ersten acht Fundamental-Noten vorheriger Arie von J. S. Bach* (Various canons on the first eight fundamental notes of the previous aria by J. S. Bach, BWV 1087) was discovered in 1974 – a single handwritten leaflet containing fourteen different canons based on the ground of Bach's *Goldberg Variations* (BWV 988). In this piece, Bach supplies a highly compressed code, but without the algorithm that expands the rudimentary notation into something resembling a score. As this work constitutes a musical riddle, the solution has to be found by the user, through combining the various subjects in different forms such as retrograde, inversion and the retrograde of the inversion, partly with changing temporal compression or augmentation. Reinhard Böß was able to discover all possible solutions – 269 movements providing seventy minutes of astonishing music (Böß 1996).

These predecessors demonstrate the rule-based aspects of algorithmic composition. More or less automatically they yield stunning musical results which can be seen as the unfolding of the inherent potential of the material supplied.

A promising extension was the employment of random decisions in order to create music which is not limited to a fixed appearance. The invention of musical dice games by composers like Johann Philipp Kirnberger, Maximilian Stadler and Joseph Haydn[3] enabled musical amateurs to generate numerous variants of dance pieces. One of those musical construction sets is attributed to Wolfgang Amadeus Mozart. In *Musikalisches Würfelspiel* (Musical dice game, KV Anh. 294d, 1787), eleven different versions of each bar of the minuet have been composed beforehand. These bars can be linked together in any combination. By throwing two dice[4] (the sum of which provides eleven numbers from 2 to 12), one can create numerous variations of the underlying metric and harmonic model (Prieberg 1960).

As an exemplar of the manifold techniques of algorithmically inspired music particularly investigated in the twentieth century, and to be discussed further later in this chapter, one sometimes overlooked composer shall be mentioned here. Combinatorics coupled with a severe refusal to express personal sentiment characterises Josef Matthias Hauer's late *Zwölftonspiele* (Twelve-tone games) which he composed from 1940 to 1959. By applying his 'Klangreihen' algorithm which automatically generates a sequence of twelve four-part chords from any twelve-tone row, Hauer obtains sonorous chord progressions which serve as a harmonic model for a piece. The act of composing is reduced to building figurations and arpeggios on this 'ground'. For this, Hauer often used well-known baroque models, as he was not interested in inventing music himself – he rather considered himself a medium that transformed cosmic vibrations into sound.

Algorithms that are based on combinatorics and permutations, however, have a much longer history and are deeply rooted in kabbalistic thinking as it is expressed in the book *Sefer Yetzirah* (Book of Creation). This school of thinking probably influenced the Catalan monk Ramon Lull (1235–1315): in *Ars Magna* (Great art, 1305) he describes a method of combining attributes that describe the properties of God. Like in Mozart's dice game, a fixed matrix, now filled with carefully selected words, contains the basic material. The permutation is carried out by a machine (called the 'Lullian Circle') which consists of several rotating paper discs inscribed with symbols that refer to the divine attributes. By rotating these discs numerous permutations of the basic attributes could be created, generating universal conclusions about God (Eco 1995).

In the seventeenth century, the German poet Georg Philipp Harsdörffer systematically transferred Lull's concept to linguistics and literature. An algorithm described in his book *Fünffacher Denckring der teutschen Sprache* (Five-fold thought ring of the German language, 1636) demonstrates how anyone can generate all existing and potential German words through the combination of basic syllables (Cramer 2005).

Using formalisms in order to challenge the writer's and reader's imagination is the core idea of *Oulipo* ('Ouvroir de littérature potentielle', which translates roughly as 'workshop of potential literature') – a group of mainly French writers and mathematicians founded in 1960 in Paris. One of its members was Georges Perec (1936–82), well-known for setting up a system of constraints which is used as a means of triggering ideas and inspiration, most notably in his masterpiece *La Vie mode d'emploi* (Life: a user's manual, 1978). By employing a magic square he created a complex system which generated a list of items, references or objects that each chapter should allude to. Perec was also interested in computers and their algorithms, which stimulated him to create the radio play *Die Maschine* (The machine) – here we can literally hear how a computer program analyses Goethe's famous poem *Wanderers Nachtlied* (Wanderer's night song, 1780), and how it later on generates bizarre variants by applying various text-transforming algorithms to this basic material (Perec and Klippert 1972).

Pioneers

After this condensed trip into the history of algorithmic thinking, I want to introduce a pioneer in this field who is nearly forgotten nowadays. The Ukrainian composer Joseph Schillinger (1895–1943) emigrated to the United States in 1928 where he became a highly influential teacher and theorist. With the *Schillinger System of Musical Composition* (published posthumously in 1946) he developed a method of musical composition based on mathematical processes and algorithms, long before composers like Xenakis and others. Many of his concepts have penetrated modern compositional practice, from Allen Forte's work on pitch-class sets, to Karlheinz Stockhausen's so-called 'Formant-Rhythmik' or Gottfried Michael Koenig's concept of periodicity as it is implemented in his algorithmic composition software *Projekt 1*.

In the preface of Schillinger's book, Henry Cowell wrote:

> The idea behind the Schillinger System is simple and inevitable: it undertakes the application of mathematical logic to all the materials of music and to their functions, so that the student may know the unifying principles behind these functions, may grasp the method of analyzing and synthesizing any musical materials that he may find anywhere or may discover for himself, and may perceive how to develop new materials as he feels the need for them. Thus the Schillinger System offers possibilities, not limitations; it is a positive, not a negative approach to the choice of musical materials. Because of the universality of the aesthetic concepts underlying it, the System applies equally to old and new styles in music and to 'popular' and 'serious' composition.

In a highly systematic way, Schillinger invented algorithms for generating or transforming melodies, rhythms and musical forms: techniques that can be considered as tools for artistic imagination. Moreover, he applied his concepts also to graphic design (Schillinger 1948, p. 419) and even to colours (p. 346).

In 1955, the first experiments with computer-generated music were conducted by the chemistry professor and trained composer Lejaren A. Hiller (1924–94) together with Leonard M. Isaacson at the University of Illinois. They applied probabilistic algorithms – that were used for the calculation of polymer configurations – to music. The composition process was carried out by a three-step approach: a 'generator' which often employs random operations supplies the basic material; a 'modifier' applies transformations on it; and finally a 'selector' filters out unwanted results by testing the output against a rule-based system (Hiller 1959).

In 1957, the first complete computer composition – the well-known *Illiac Suite* for string quartet in four movements – was created, calculated by the University of Illinois's ILLIACI (Illinois Automatic Computer). The output was transformed manually into musical notation and performed by human musicians. Each of the four movements was carried out as a particular musical 'experiment', based on random notes controlled by rules of sixteenth-century counterpoint, paradigms of twelve-tone music or probability operations such as Markov chains.[5]

In the late 1950s and early 1960s, Hiller's experiments finally led to the development of MUSICOMP, one of the first computer languages for computer-assisted composition which basically consists of a library of subroutines. Afterwards, he also collaborated with John Cage on the multimedia piece *HPSCHD* (to be discussed later) and expanded his score-generating algorithms by digital sound synthesis (Hiller 1981).

Serialism

The Second World War not only destroyed cities and landscapes in Europe but almost eradicated musical life. Composers like Schoenberg had to flee from the Nazis, leaving a vacuum which was hard to fill. After the war, young composers from different parts of Europe – Luigi Nono, Karlheinz Stockhausen, Pierre Boulez (to name only a few) – gathered together at the Darmstadt summer courses where they tried to reconnect to the musical avant-garde which had nearly been extinguished by the Hitler regime. Confronted with the situation of a 'tabula rasa' they strived towards a 'musica pura' by developing a new musical grammar free of historical or traditional references.

For this bold endeavour a starting point was found in the late works of the Austrian composer Anton Webern (1883–1945) who, to composers such as Stockhausen and Boulez, seemed to have extended the serial principles from the mere determination of pitches to other aspects of composition such as the organisation of time, timbre and dynamics. Although it is widely accepted nowadays that this was not entirely true of Webern (who was still rooted in the classic-romantic tradition which he compressed into highly expressive micro-gestures), this productive misconception served as a trigger of enormous influence, even until today.

In Darmstadt serialism, Schoenberg's dodecaphonic technique, which predetermines all pitch material, is extended to the other so-called 'parameters' of musical structure like duration, dynamics and timbre. The series becomes a unifying principle which can control every detail of a composition – it affects all aspects of a musical structure, comparable with the DNA of a biological cell.

What characterises a series? A set of values from a scale with equal steps which are arranged in a specific order. It is much more than a thematic invention as it was once considered by Schoenberg: the series serves as the basic organisational principle and the core algorithm for a whole composition.

Numerous variations of the primary row can be obtained by applying transformations such as transposition, inversion, retrograde, and permutation. In order to achieve this by mathematical operations, it is necessary to translate the elements of a tone row first into a numerical representation.

A twelve-tone row

Eb – D – A – Ab – G – F – E – C# – C – Bb – F – B

can be transformed into a sequence of numbers (where we define C as index 0):

3   2   9   8   7   6   4   1   0   10   5   11

By using this number list, we can easily apply a basic transformation algorithm such as transposition. If we want to transpose this row a fifth up, we just need to add the number 7 (fifth = 7 half-tone steps) to each element of the list:

10   9   16   15   14   13   11   8   7   17   12   18

and perform a [modulo 12] operation afterwards in order to map the result back into the range 0–11.

10   9   4   3   2   1   11   8   7   5   0   6

As the series is now represented as a list of numbers, we can employ mathematical algorithms in order to create variations from its primary form. If we consider the numbers as addresses, it is even possible to utilise a row as its own permutation program.

Each number in the series can be seen as being contained in an indexed slot.

series	10	9	4	3	2	1	11	8	7	5	0	6
index	0	1	2	3	4	5	6	7	8	9	10	11

If we now decide that each number of the series will represent an index, then we can derive a new series by looking up the number contained at that index. In this case, the number 10, which in the original series is in the first position, by becoming an index, points to 0, as that is the number contained in the tenth position of the original series. In this manner we arrive at the following permutation:

series 0 5 2 3 4 9 6 7 8 1 10 11

This result in turn can be used iteratively for generating further permutations, and so forth . . .

Furthermore, we can use the numbers of the series as pointers to values of another list, e.g. of dynamic values. Applying the transposed row from above onto an array of twelve dynamic values from *pppp* to *ffff*,

pppp	*ppp*	*pp*	*p*	*quasi p*	*mp*	*mf*	*quasi f*	*f*	*ff*	*fff*	*ffff*
0	1	2	3	4	5	6	7	8	9	10	11

would yield the following sequence of dynamics:

fff ff quasi p p pp ppp ffff f quasi f mp pppp mf

In his *Structure 1a*, Pierre Boulez extended this principle to the organisation of rhythmical values and articulations. In one single night in 1951, Boulez composed this piece for two pianos subtitled 'A la limite du pays fertile' (At the border of the fertile country), named after the watercolour painting *Monument im Fruchtland* (Monument in the fertile country, 1929) by Paul Klee. This picture shows an abstract composition of orthogonal shapes, a pattern which brings to mind a rural landscape seen from an airplane. Boulez referred to the title as a metaphor for an attempt to test the serial method by developing a strict algorithm which was designed to eliminate subjectivity and personal taste.

Structure 1a is entirely based on a twelve-tone row (in fact the same series we used earlier) which Boulez extracted from Olivier Messiaen's piano piece *Mode de valeurs et d'intensités*, a piece that Messiaen wrote while teaching at the Darmstadt summer course in 1949 where he was extending the serial principle to the organisation of rhythm and dynamics. As György Ligeti describes in his analysis of *Structure 1a* (Ligeti 1958), Boulez used all twelve transpositions of Messiaen's series in four different forms – original, retrograde, inversion and the retrograde of the inversion – represented as a matrix where the note names have been replaced by numbers (as shown in the example above). This representation allows the mapping of rhythmical values to numbers which were obtained from the original dodecaphonic series; by multiplying the numbers from a series with the basic rhythmical unit – the demisemiquaver – Boulez creates series of rhythmical durations.[6]

The same is done with the dynamics, as described earlier in this chapter, and also – partly – with articulations.

This automatic process is carried out by a simple mapping algorithm that generates independent series for pitch classes, durations and dynamics. By superimposition, the parameter series are combined into a linear musical structure which manifests itself as a monophonic melody. These 'melodies' are then woven together in a polyphonic sense, forming a fabric of piano sounds.[7]

It is important to understand that by composing a piece with strictly pre-determined material drawn from an automatism, many artistic decisions are replaced by an algorithm. Although highly ordered by predetermination, the result appears as statistical agglomeration of points in space and time.

These experiments were important to the development of algorithmic composition as they shifted compositional thinking into the domain of algorithms. Furthermore, they provided the conceptual basis for the first computer programs which generated musical structures, such as Gottfried Michael Koenig's *Projekt 1* (1963).

Stochastic music

The fact that the strict predetermination of serialism results in an incomprehensible auditory chaos was fiercely criticised by Iannis Xenakis in 'The Crisis of Serial Music':

> Linear polyphony is self-destructive in its current complexity. In reality, what one hears is a bunch of notes in various registers. The enormous complexity prevents one from following the tangled lines and its macroscopic effect is one of unreasonable and gratuitous dispersion of sounds over the whole sound spectrum. Consequently, there is a contradiction between the linear polyphonic system and the audible result, which is a surface, a mass. (Xenakis 1955)

Xenakis proposed a solution to this problem through the use of statistical methods in musical composition:

> In fact, since these linear combinations and their polyphonic superpositions are no longer workable, what will count will be the statistical average of isolated states of the components' transformations at any given moment . . . Hence, the notion of probability is introduced, which, by the way, implies combinatory calculus in this specific case. (Xenakis 1955)

Xenakis suggested replacing the deterministic causality of serialism with the more general concept of probabilistic logic which could contain the strict serial approach as a particular case.

What Xenakis calls 'stochastic music' is based on random operations within time-variable constraints. The principle of indeterminacy and the statistical organisation of mass structures can also be found in nature – 'natural events such as the collision of hail or rain with hard surfaces, or the song of cicadas in a summer field' (Xenakis 1961). This concept subsequently led to Granular Synthesis which later became a core aspect of Iannis Xenakis's graphical UPIC system, a computer-based machine dedicated to interactive composition.

Xenakis first applied this concept in the 1950s to generate scores for instrumental music, mostly large orchestral works which employ a lot of musicians. In his orchestral piece *Metastasis* (1953–4) for sixty-one players, the single instruments cannot be perceived as individual voices as they melt together into a collective sound field. The mass structures of this piece, however, are not calculated by statistical methods – here Xenakis uses graphical methods which later led him to formulate the architectural design for Le Corbusier's Philips Pavilion for the Brussels World's Fair in 1958 (Xenakis 1961). *Pithoprakta* (1955–6) was the first work which he composed employing statistical methods and was based on Maxwell-Boltzmann's kinetic theory of gases, simulating the Brownian motion of gas molecules ricocheting off each other.

Having used composition algorithms without the aid of computers since the 1950s, Xenakis' probabilistic concepts could finally be implemented as computer programs using the FORTRAN programming language, which was running on an IBM-7090 mainframe computer in Paris (Xenakis 1965). This led to a series of works entitled *ST-xxx* (where ST stands for stochastic) composed in 1962, which includes pieces for string quartet, various ensembles and orchestra. Xenakis first designed flow charts for the various subroutines which he afterwards translated into computer language.[8] The result of the calculation was printed as a score list which later had to be transformed into musical notation.

The use of the computer was a relief for it freed the composer from painstaking bookkeeping tasks and shifted his attention to the exploration of the unknown:

> Freed from tedious calculations, the composer is able to devote himself to the general problems that the new musical form poses and to explore the nooks and crannies of this form while modifying the values of the input data. For example, he may test all instrumental combinations from soloists

to chamber orchestras, to large orchestras. With the aid of electronic computers the composer becomes a sort of pilot: he presses the buttons, introduces coordinates, and supervises the controls of a cosmic vessel sailing in the space of sound, across sonic constellations and galaxies that he could formerly glimpse only as a distant dream.   (Xenakis 1965)

Field composition/aleatoric composition

The pointillistic fragmentation caused by early serialism was not observed solely by Xenakis, but also by the serial composers. However, this reflection did not lead to the abolition, but to the refinement of the original simplistic concept. By extending the determination of single elements to several parameter values at once, Stockhausen introduced the notion of a 'group' where the parameters do not constantly change, being maintained for a longer time. He also formulated higher-level parameters like 'density' which control qualitative musical attributes on a global level. This was exemplified in his *Gruppen* (1957–9) for three orchestral groups and was accompanied by a thorough theory of musical time, formulated in his excellent article ' . . .how time passes . . .' (Stockhausen 1957).

By this time, the former pointillistic serialism had mutated into so-called 'field composition' which provided methods for creating musical structures that were capable of building musical forms again. A 'field' creates a synthesis between serial determinism and chance composition, as the single element is defined within a global context which described a 'field of possibilities'.

Paradoxically, in order to gain more control over the musical structure it had become necessary to involve random principles. Unlike Xenakis, who employed stochastic methods like the Gaussian distribution or Markov chains, serial composers – namely Gottfried Michael Koenig – have replaced the serial permutation mechanism with a non-deterministic, but promising strategy – the use of aleatoric principles.[9]

Gottfried Michael Koenig used this method for the composition of his *Streichquartett 1959* for which he developed a powerful algorithm defining a flexible multi-level process which involves random operations. Starting from a 'supply' which comprises all values of a certain parameter – for instance a list of possible rhythmic values – he obtains a data field by randomly selecting from the supplied elements. By repeating those elements according to a group list (which is also calculated by chance operations), a repetition list is created which contains the elements of the selection in different weights. Finally, this repetition list is brought into a random order and represents the result which can – for instance – be translated into a rhythmical structure (Essl 1989):

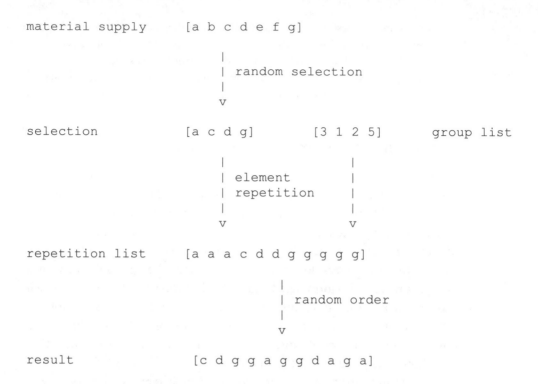

```
material supply      [a b c d e f g]

                          |
                          | random selection
                          |
                          v

selection            [a c d g]        [3 1 2 5]        group list

                          |                |
                          | element        |
                          | repetition     |
                          |                |
                          v                v

repetition list      [a a a c d d g g g g]

                              |
                              | random order
                              |
                              v

result               [c d g g a g g d a g a]
```

Although the entire work was composed by employing random decisions, it does not sound like arbitrary chance music thanks to the intelligence and skill that was put into the definition of the composition algorithm. However, at this time Koenig did not use a computer program – he had to do everything by hand (Essl 1989).

In 1963, Gottfried Michael Koenig began work on a composition[10] that was based on an algorithmic model which he implemented as a computer program – *Projekt 1* (PR1). Instead of rows, he assembled lists of parameter values, and in place of deterministic permutation algorithms he used random operations which select values for the four prototypic parameters of pitch, rhythm, dynamics, timbre. The random decisions were controlled by a group mechanism which determined its variety in time. Thus, Koenig was able to create transitions between regular and irregular events.[11] Moreover, he encoded the dialectic between determination and chance into an algorithm which could map various states between those antipodes (Koenig 1979).

> I had the idea of collating my experience with programmed music at the desk and in the electronic studio to form a model which would be able to produce a large number of variants of itself almost fully automatically. Faithful to the fundamentals of the nineteen-fifties, all the parameters involved were supposed to have at least one common characteristic; for this I chose the pair of terms, 'regular/irregular'. 'Regular' means here that a

selected parameter value is frequently repeated: this results in groups with
similar rhythms, octave registers or loudness, similar harmonic structure or
similar sonorities. The duration of such groups is different in all
parameters, resulting in over-lappings. – 'Irregularity' means that a selected
parameter value cannot be repeated until all or at least many values of this
parameter have had a turn. The choice of parameter values and group
quantities was left to chance, as was the question of the place a given
parameter should occupy in the range between regularity and irregularity.

(Koenig 1978)

PR1 in its original form was a computer program that did not allow
any user interaction. As an hermetic system that contained the algorithms
and also all necessary data (like a list of rhythmic values, a defined number
of dynamics and instruments) it would produce nearly infinite variants of
the same structural model which it output as a score list. This limitation,
however, was removed during the further development of the program and
by virtue of the fact that it was also used by other composers. Still, the degree
of determining the input data is limited: 'A composer using this program
only has to fix metronome tempi, rhythmic values and the length of the
composition: in other words, he only decides on the time framework of
the result, and this only roughly, because all details are generated by the
automatism of the program' (Koenig 1980).

The output of PR1 is a score list comprised of six columns: line number,
instrument, entry delay (ED), pitch, register, and dynamics. Each row defines
a musical event:[12]

#	Instr	ED	Pitch	Register	Dynamics
1	8	1/8	F	5	*mf*
2	8	1/8	D	4	*fff*
3	1	1/8	C#	6	*ff*
4	9	1/8	A# G#	3 4	*ppp*
5	3	1/8	G	6	*p*
6	6	1/8	F D	5 5	*f*
7	6	1/8	C#	3	*pp*
8	6	1/8	A#	3	*pp*
9	4	1/8	G# G	6 6	*pp*
10	5	0/0	F	4	*pp*
11	7	4/5	D C# B	5 5 5	*pp*
12	7	3/4	G# G F D C#	4 4 4 4 4	*pp*

In this example, one can clearly see that the rhythm of the beginning is very
regular, whereas the registers shift quite erratically.

The output as it is represented in the score table needs further refinement before it eventually becomes music, as the score list lacks some definitions – rhythm is only defined by entry delays (no rhythmic durations are supplied). Conglomerations of pitches such as in line 12 can be interpreted as straightforward chords, but might also be used to invent various modes of 'arpeggios'.

First, the score table has to be transcribed into an intermediate score ('particello') using traditional music notation. Then, after thorough analysis, the user might develop a specific strategy with which to interpret the aforementioned particello and to translate it into a composition which can be a piano piece, a string quartet or even an orchestral work. Gottfried Michael Koenig still uses *Projekt 1* nowadays. In 2005, he released a final version of his program that allows a more detailed specification of the input data.[13]

Chance

Whereas Xenakis and Koenig employ random operations within the context of an algorithmic model in order to gain control over the musical structure, John Cage uses chance decisions for achieving quite the contrary – creating music that is not defined by personal taste or individual dislikes. Instead of exploiting music for representing order systems or expressing subjective sentiments, the sounds are freed from meaning and historical connotations, free 'to come into their own' (Cage 1959).

In order to achieve this goal, Cage invented numerous algorithmic systems that employ chance operations (obtained from the Chinese oracle book 'I Ching' as well as from star atlases or by graphical methods) which he used for the selection and coordination of musical events. Despite the use of chance methods, the basic material of each piece was carefully chosen by Cage and shaped by his personal predilections. Organised in 'charts' (Pritchett 1993) elements were selected and combined by randomly controlled algorithms, with the aim of overcoming habitual modes and creating unpredictable results.

Cage's thinking is full of antagonisms and paradoxes – he adopts painstakingly elaborated control mechanism in order to lose control and to liberate music from the imperatives of human intervention. This, however, could only be achieved by algorithms that would abrogate the subjective intentions.

Cage had collaborated with Lejaren Hiller in the 1960s, who had written for him, amongst other software, a computer implementation of the 'I Ching'. Such a program enabled Cage to concentrate more heavily on the compositional outline of a piece and freed him from the time-consuming and unproductive task of tossing coins in consulting the 'I Ching'. They also collaborated on the gigantic multimedia spectacle *HPSCHD* (1967–9) which involved three sets of computer programs, one of them for composing the harpsichord part derived from Mozart's *Musical Dice Game* (Hiller 1981).

In the last decade of his life, John Cage also worked with Andrew Culver, who wrote computer programs according to Cage's instructions. This was especially helpful for mastering a work like *Music for...* (1984–7) which consists of numerous individual instrumental parts which have been generated by a computerised algorithm.

During the 1950s, while Cage was developing his concepts of chance composition and indeterminacy, he also created graphical 'tools' for musical composition. Instead of supplying a written score, a piece like *Fontana Mix* (1958) was delivered as '10 transparent sheets with points, 10 drawings having six differentiated curved lines, a graph (having 100 units horizontally, 20 vertically) and a straight line, the two last on transparent material' (Cage 1958). Together with the precise instructions, the performer can create any number of compositions.

The ingredients of the 'construction kit' have to be overlapped in random positions and placed over a page that contains six curved and intermingled lines. By measuring positions of intersecting lines, six parameter values which are needed to determine a single sound event are obtained. The choice of the parameters is free. 'Where possible technically this can be not only simple changes of time (starting, stopping) but also alterations of frequency, amplitude, use of filters and distribution of the sound in space' (Cage 1958).

Generative music

Cage's ideas of freeing the music from its social and historical bondage can be expanded to its primary obstacle – the temporal limitation. Music, whether it appears as a 'classical' composition, a traditional gamelan piece or a rock song, is defined by a beginning and an end, as opposed to natural sound phenomena like the rustling of leaves in the wind which can be regarded as an (infinite) stream of sound. Creating music that lasts forever without repeating itself became a concern of the pop artist Brian Eno, which he first realised in the sound environment *Music for Airports* (1978) for the 'Marine Air Terminal' of New York's LaGuardia Airport. This piece was created by simultaneously playing tape loops of different lengths resulting in an ever-changing, ambient-like sound texture of unpredictable combinations, an approach that was obviously inspired by some works of American

Minimalists like Steve Reich (*It's gonna rain*, 1965) and Terry Riley (*In C*, 1964). By employing a simple looping algorithm, Eno was able to create infinite soundscapes that are based only on a few basic elements. In 1990, his ideas were taken on by the software engineers Pete and Tim Cole for the development of KOAN – a commercial program for generative music in the style of Brian Eno's ambient music. With this software environment, one can define rhythmic models, harmonic progressions, selections of sounds and specify correlations and random variabilities. With such a set of rules an infinite sound stream is generated in realtime, as described by Eno: 'Ordinary music is like engineering, where everything's built according to a plan, and it's the same every time you play it. Generative music is more like gardening; you plant a seed, and it grows different every time you plant.'[14]

This statement contains an interesting accordance with Goethe's primordial plant (see above). Furthermore, Eno's ideas also relate to Erik Satie's 'furniture music' (1917) – background music which was originally played by live performers outside a concert situation. In the 1960s, this concept was rediscovered by John Cage and the American Minimalists. This finally led to the development of ambient music which is 'able to accommodate many levels of listening attention without enforcing one in particular; it must be as ignorable as it is interesting,' as described by Eno in the liner notes of *Music for Airports*.

Using generative composition algorithms on computers, music can be created in realtime by an autonomous and infinite automatic process. As this music has no beginning nor end, the distribution on a reproductive medium such as a compact disc seems highly inappropriate. This consideration led Maurice Methot and Hector LaPlante to the instantiation of 'The Algorithmic Stream'. Starting in 1997 as one of the earliest streaming audio systems on the Internet, this platform broadcasts non-repeating computer-generated sound and music live and in realtime as it is produced.[15]

One successor of this project is 'rand()%', an automated net radio station streaming realtime generative music. It serves as an independent platform for artists who can submit their own computer programs that create algorithmic music on-the-fly.[16]

Realtime

In the beginning of computer music, compositional algorithms were used 'out of time' (Xenakis 1971) for creating musical scores. In most of the pieces mentioned before – as for example those of Hiller, Xenakis, Koenig and Cage – a symbolic output in the form of a score list had to be translated into musical notation in order to be performed by musicians. However, over the last twenty years the permanent improvement of computer technology and the increase of processing speed has promoted the development of algorithmic composition environments which generate sound directly in realtime.

An important forerunner was the Institute for Sonology in Utrecht which was headed by Gottfried Michael Koenig between 1964 and 1986. Starting from compositional strategies that he had developed during the previous decade, a modular analogue studio based on the paradigm of voltage control was built. It consisted of independent hardware modules (such as oscillators, filter, envelop generators, logic circuits etc.) that could be connected with each other and the parameters of which were controlled by voltage. By creating a network of connected modules, one could implement an algorithm that produced sound in realtime.

The core of this system was a so-called 'variable function generator' – a programmable sequencer that stored a time-variant voltage function which could be read out at different speeds or scanned by a random mechanism. This function could likewise be used as a control and an audio signal, and was utilised by Koenig as the basic structural definition for an entire composition, functioning similarly to the series in serial music. This new technology enabled Koenig to compose electronic music through automatic processes, without the need of tape montage, as in the WDR studio in Cologne (Koenig 1986).

The structural paradigm of a modular analogue studio with independent units communicating by cable connections was later transferred into the domain of a computer language. This was the advent of Max[17] – a visual, object-oriented programming language, initially designed for interactive musical performance and which is also suitable for digital signal processing as well as realtime control.

Although Max had the potential to implement algorithmic music systems due to a core architecture which enabled realtime processing of data, it was lacking higher-level compositional tools. This led to the design of the *RTC-lib* (Real Time Composition Library for Max) – a software library for algorithmic composition – which I started together with Gerhard Eckel in 1992 and the development of which continues today.[18] Its software modules offer the possibility to experiment with a number of compositional techniques, such as serial procedures, permutations and controlled randomness. It comprises low-level objects for list processing and numerous random operations, but also high-level compositional tools like rhythm generators, harmony generators and envelope processors (Essl 1996).

The *RTC-lib* was utilised for the first time in *Lexikon-Sonate* (1992–2007) – an infinite interactive realtime composition environment that generates piano music in real time and plays it on a Yamaha Disklavier, reflecting the history of this genre from Johann Sebastian Bach to the avant-garde music of our times (Essl 1997). Originally conceived as an autonomous system acting on its own, it eventually developed into an instrument whose numerous compositional parameters can be controlled by attached MIDI fader boxes. This enables one to improvise highly complex piano music without even touching the keys of the instrument.

Recently, the realtime approach to algorithmic composition was expanded into the multi-user sound installation *Raumfaltung* (2003) where up to eight visitors could listen to eight different versions of the same piece at the same time – within a room installation by Beat Zoderer at the Kunst-museum Bonn, Ramón González-Arroyo and Gerhard Eckel set up an environment based on the LISTEN technology (Eckel 2003). This environment tracks the movements of listeners who are themselves equipped with headphones. The individual tracking information is evaluated by a computer system that generates control data for a granular synthesis program written in Max/MSP. It takes into account the current position of the visitor within the environment and also the relative positions of the listeners to each other. Using this information, an individual version of the composition is rendered for each person and broadcast to their headphones, creating a virtual auditory space that intermingles the spatial layout of Zoderer's installation (González-Arroyo 2003). In this piece, algorithmic compositional strategies have arrived at a state where music is not merely the reproduction of an artistic oeuvre; it has become an integral part of a multi-aesthetic environment that extends our perception into the realm of immersion.

Conclusion

Thanks to fast and affordable personal computers together with high-level software environments (such as CSound,[19] SuperCollider,[20] ChucK,[21] OpenMusic,[22] PD and Max/MSP), the development of compositional algorithms has become an integral part in the creation of electronic music. Nowadays, composers are no longer dependent on academic computer music studios with their specific aesthetics and production methods. This situation creates a new self-conception of a composer. Instead of delegating the computational work to an external programmer, one becomes an autonomous artistic individual who combines technical skills and artistic visions. By creating independent networks over the internet, communities are organising themselves which serve as think-tanks and pools for sharing ideas and code.

To me, algorithmic music generation in realtime seems the most challenging aspect. It enables the development of art forms where the generative concept of Goethe's primordial plant can be interactively controlled during its creation. Now the compositional process is taking place 'in time' again, as in musical improvisation, but depends on an algorithmic framework created beforehand. By this, 'instruments' can be constructed which connect to our body, creating a physical extension of our mind.

7 Live audiovisuals

AMY ALEXANDER AND NICK COLLINS

From festivals and dances, through opera, theatre and shadow play, from Wagner's *Gesamtkunstwerk* (total artwork), to cinema and virtual reality, the arts have often confronted the problems and potential of engaging many human senses (modalities) at once. Such multisensory (multimodal) entertainments are often underlined by strongly traditional narratives, yet linear storytelling is not necessarily the primary concern of some alternative artistic ventures. The degree to which any of these media allows for live performance varies, and this chapter will particularly treat the circumstance where the artistic output can be influenced during the course of performance itself, rather than being cast as a fixed product prior to presentation. A parallel chapter on music for broadcast media will analyse the opposing case, where the determination of a finished product, even if subject to a deadline, can be carried out free of realtime concert constraints. Yet there will necessarily be some overlap, and this chapter will in particular treat the case of some formative historical influences on contemporary live performers including the non-realtime work of abstract film visionaries such as Oskar Fischinger. We shall further broach some of the psychological and analytical perspectives on audiovisual work.

To give an immediate example of current concerns, one contemporary manifestation of realtime performance is exhibited by club VJs – video or visual jockeys. Whilst their profile in publicity billing and on-stage position has not matched historically to that of their foils, the club DJ (disc jockey), interest in VJ practice is very much on the ascendant in the arts (Spinrad 2005; Jaeger 2005). The typical VJ, if such an artist can be said to exist, will use dedicated software packages on a laptop computer, often mixed in realtime with prerecorded imagery on DVD and/or live video from a camera. The resulting imagery is centrally displayed by projector(s) in the performance environment. Frequently, analysis of the audio signal, tap tempo, or other control allows the synchronisation of visual events to music. It should be acknowledged, however, that these techniques are by no means universally performed; many VJs control all visuals manually.

A significant trend is the push towards a fuller integration of the senses, as shown by dedicated audiovisual performance groups whose protagonists are long-term collaborators from different backgrounds, or who themselves have developed skills across multiple modalities. Yet there has also been a strong historical counter-movement against over-integration by visual artists who want to emphasise the independence of moving visuals from audio, often considering moving visuals a form of music in their own right. There is a rich history behind this current enterprise which we shall endeavour to expose during this chapter. And whilst we might have introduced the club VJ in the previous paragraph, art is never limited to single functions or social settings. Performances unhindered by music club conventions can allow for a more focused style of live visual or audiovisual performance, an arena often dubbed live cinema. Nevertheless, both VJing and live cinema grow out of notions of expanded cinema, visual music and multimedia events. Indeed, whilst our survey will have to omit many theories concerning opera, film, media or virtual reality, the reader can anticipate the wide-ranging influences that must pervade practice which treats multiple senses. Visual and sonic arts have their own dense histories which have often cross-bred, one interface being their combination in audiovisual performance.

Colour organs and visual music

A futile attempt to tie up all the historical threads of audiovisual performance might lead us through landmarks in the history of theatre, the philosophical speculations of Ancient Greece or the ceremonies of pre-history. It is possibly safer to begin with a common source mentioned in all audiovisual histories, the colour organ (Moritz 1997, Peacock 1988), an invention that has been continually reinvented for about the last three hundred years. A colour organ is a device for the projection of areas of colour cued in a musical manner, often from a console similar to a musical instrument, most typically a keyboard. Even if based on an alternative control interface, the colour organ should at least allow the production of visual events over time; such interactive sequencing is analogous to the ordered revelation of music. It might be used in accompanying or complementing music, or in projecting novel visual work even independent of sound. Whilst early devices were fragile in their reactions, and had little control over the projected shapes, later devices in the twentieth century attempted to refine the quality and quantity of objects that could be presented. They also achieved a very different presence in terms of luminosity and quality of light to modern projectors.

Louis Bertrand Castel's first theoretical writing on the colour organ appeared in 1725, and acknowledges a debt to Athanasius Kircher's popularisation of the magic lantern (1646) and Isaac Newton's speculations aligning the spectrum to the diatonic scale (1704). Though he had intended only to write of the possibility of a *clavecin oculaire* (ocular harpsichord), a sceptical reaction prompted experiments in actually constructing the device. A small-scale prototype model was built by 1734, and whilst it is unlikely that he managed to construct any large-scale fully functioning colour organ (Peacock 1988), in principle his key-operated candle covers could reveal light through coloured paper filters under the control of an operator.

After Castel, in the second half of the nineteenth and first half of the twentieth century came a succession of inventions of functioning colour organs. Early examples include a contraption by D. D. Jameson (1844), Frederic Kastner's pyrophone (gas jets in tubes), Bainbridge Bishop's organ-top light projector (1877) and Alexander Wallace Rimington's Colour Organ (patented 1893).[1] The latter in particular was used in well-documented concert tours by its creator amid legions of self-publicity, a tactic followed by so many designer-performers, often claiming a spurious originality for their devices. With the field already established, that the score of Skryabin's *Prometheus* (completed 1910) has a part for light simply captures a spirit of the times, and perhaps spurred the creation of even more instruments (Peacock 1988).

Building on, and often contributing to, the tradition of colour organs is the genre of abstract filmmaking and visual performance known as visual music. Visual music filmmaking began in the early twentieth century, and continues to this day. Its earliest practitioners were largely abstract painters, already used to working with spatial rhythms in their static work, who then began working in film, thus introducing the element of time into their work. Although abstract filmmaking has not been universally considered by its practitioners as 'visual music', it's clearly been a recurrent theme. The earliest known text on abstract cinema, documenting possibly the first work in abstract filmmaking, was Bruno Corra's document, 'Abstract Cinema – Chromatic Music', published in 1912. Malcolm Le Grice points out:

> The title 'Chromatic Music' introduces a recurring tendency of artists
> concerned with abstract film to pursue a musical analogy for their work. It
> is difficult to think of music, certainly instrumental music, as ever having
> been other than essentially abstract, and considering that film like music is a
> time-based medium, it is not surprising that the analogy with music should
> be used, and that this analogy should continue to effect [*sic*] contemporary
> abstract film-makers.   (Le Grice 1977, p. 17)

Visual music takes as a central idea the strength of the visual forms on their own, rather than as subordinate or 'accompaniment' to musical sound. However, visual music films often have synchronous sound, and there are a range of approaches to the question of integrating sound and image – often even within the body of work of a given filmmaker. For example, the film

Radio Dynamics (1941), by probably the best-known abstract filmmaker, Oskar Fischinger, was intentionally made without sound; Fischinger's intent was to demonstrate that non-objective imagery could work on its own (Moritz 2004b). In fact, the film begins with a title slide that says, in large, handwritten letters, 'Please! *No Music* – Experiment in Color-Rhythm' (Fischinger 1942). In *Radio Dynamics*, as in most of Fischinger's films, the abstract forms create their own spatial and temporal rhythms. Fischinger had to make his silent film in secret, however, as he was at the time contracted by the Guggenheim Foundation to make a film synchronised to Bach's Brandenburg Concerto No. 3. Even here, the resulting contracted film, *Motion Painting*, was not synchronised to sound in the customary manner; rather than make the requested cel animation, Fischinger photographed a frame for each brush stroke of a multi-layered oil painting in progress. As William Moritz (2004b) has pointed out, 'his multi-layered style merely parallels the structure of the Bach music without any tight synchronization'. Despite this reluctance to regard his imagery as merely synchronised accompaniment to visuals, Fischinger did at other times intentionally synchronise sound and visuals. In his 1932 film, *Tönende Ornamente* (Ornament sound), the soundtrack was created by drawing directly onto the optical soundtrack. Fischinger saw this as the wave (literally) of the future for music composition, writing at the time: 'Now control of every fine gradation and nuance is granted to the music-painting artist, who bases everything exclusively on the primary fundamental of music, namely the wave – vibration or oscillation in and of itself. In the process, surface new perceptions that until now were overlooked and remain neglected' (Fischinger 1932).

In touch with currents in live performance, in 1926 Fischinger provided a multiple projector show which upstaged the Hungarian concert pianist Alexander Laszlo who had commissioned it; Laszlo responded by cutting Fischinger's films from his tour. In another show, *Vakuum*, as reported by the disgruntled Laszlo, Fischinger had seven projectors accompany a percussion group, the noise of the projectors almost overwhelming the musicians (Moritz 2004, p. 12). Fischinger also created and patented his own colour organ, the *Lumigraph*, in 1950 (Moritz 2004, p. 137). The Lumigraph was itself silent, though it could accompany music; it was performed live by manipulating a stretched elastic skin from behind, pushing portions of the skin into planes of coloured light that were projected just above the skin's normally unlit surface.

Although there is a well-known body of visual music work from the first half of the twentieth century, the practice continues to this day, both in filmmaking and live performance contexts. Some contemporary artists have taken to computer graphics and VJing, while abstract animation created using more traditional techniques continues as well.

The lineage of animation and live performance intertwines, as seen from the history of visual music and colour organ performance. Even if much early visual music was laboriously constructed, as a polished finished artwork for later presentation, its aesthetic is a precursor of many contemporary practices now possible in a live context. Just as technology has empowered the live production of electronic music that was once built outside of realtime, so technology has facilitated realtime visual performance. Again analogously to electronic music, the history of live visuals takes in the mechanical, electromechanical and analogue before the digital age.

Light shows

The 1960s brought psychedelia, social consciousness and communal activity. All these came together in visual performances known as light shows. Typically presented as visual accompaniment to rock concerts, these shows were generally performed by light show ensembles who were attached to particular venues and played with whatever bands appeared there. The visuals utilised various media, such as 16mm film clips, slides, transparencies, and coloured oils and liquids in clear dishes projected using an overhead projector. The media were displayed simultaneously to create the effect of superimposed layers, and they were manipulated live by the light show group: for example, the oils and liquids would be swirled in a dish; films might be looped or reversed, portions of the film frames might be masked by the performers' hands. Projections might be further modified by colour and strobe wheels rotated in front of the projection lenses. Some techniques were common to various light show ensembles, but individual ensembles also commonly developed techniques on their own. Since the group members were interacting live with one another and with the music being performed, group improvisation was an important element of light shows. David James writes of performances by one Los Angeles-based light show ensemble, Single Wing Turquoise Bird (SWTB):

> The most commonly invoked analogy to this group improvisation is the combined composition and performance situation of modern jazz, or indeed that of the Grateful Dead, and others of the bands whom they accompanied who had abandoned the regular repetitive structures of early rock 'n' roll for extended jams. The interaction among the projectionists themselves mirrored their responsiveness to the music, for rhythms, textures, and even graphic images were conjured out of their sensitivity to the bands' performances; sometimes the bands themselves would turn and face the screen and play to the images they saw, and indeed on several occasions the light show continued after the band had finished. At these

points, rather than the light show taking its direction from the music and
being subordinated to it, the whole ensemble was a fully reciprocal
collective audio-visual organism.   (James 2005, pp. 14–15)

Although light shows were best known as accompaniment to music at
rock concerts, SWTB went on to perform in other settings as well. The
ensemble had started out in early 1968 performing at LA's Shrine Exposition
Hall, accompanying bands such as the Velvet Underground, Pink Floyd
and The Grateful Dead. By late 1968, the abstract painter Sam Francis had
befriended the group as a patron; through Francis they came to perform at
art venues including museums and universities, as well as at studio spaces
such as Francis's studio and eventually the Cumberland Mountain Film
Co. loft above the Fox Venice Theater. At these post-Shrine performances,
SWTB performed as the 'headliner'. They still performed to music; the music
at most shows now consisted of preselected records and tapes, including
tapes the group had custom edited for their performances.[2] However at
some shows they performed with live musicians, and in some cases they
generated the sound themselves – for example by miking the outside street
sound and playing it amplified in the space, or by performing to the output
of a white noise generator.[3] Since they could now rehearse to the same
music or sound they would perform with, the ensemble were able to refine
and build more complex shows, whilst still collaboratively improvising in
performance (James 2005, p. 16). In that the ensemble had crossed over
from an accompaniment role in mainstream venues to headlining in art
venues, providing, as the group put it, 'instant cinema', SWTB's history can
be seen as a precursor to the transition some contemporary performers have
made from ambient VJing in clubs to live cinema performances.[4]

Light shows stand apart from most other historical forms of visual performance in that collaboration and improvisation between several performers was central to the form. Contemporary VJ and live cinema shows are
sometimes performed by 'crews' who project collaboratively; however, they
typically encompass significantly fewer performers, projections, and individual modes of performance than did light shows. With commonly half a
dozen and sometimes up to a dozen performers projecting simultaneously,
techniques parallel to those used in musical improvisation such as 'laying
in and out' were critical.[5] Whilst most known light show activity took place
in the UK and the US, light show groups are known to have existed in
several other countries throughout the world.[6] Although best known as a
phenomenon of the 1960s and 70s, there are still some 'psychedelic' light
shows in existence today. Further, the use of liquids has re-emerged at contemporary concerts and other events, largely as a reference or homage to
the light shows of the psychedelic era (Spinrad 2005).

From analogue video synthesisers to software

Realtime analogue video synthesisers, which were popular among video artists in the 1970s, are one bridge from the light show to the current day.[7] By processing analogue camera signals, or synthesising novel signals, they provided inspiring new tools, though the difficulty of their construction and associated price at first restricted their availability to special research institutions or studios. Video synths enabled realtime performance, but due to the size, expense and rarity of the equipment, were for the most part impractical for public performance. Even if used to create prerecorded works, much of the output resembles contemporary club or live cinema visuals.

From the 1960s into the 70s, video itself was becoming a medium of serious regard in art, through the efforts of such pioneers as Nam June Paik (who himself collaborated on an early video synth with Shuya Abe), or Woody and Steina Vasulka. Video was used for alternative presentations in galleries and by the late 1970s began to be part of visual display in some club settings.

Video synths could be entirely analogue, though analogue/digital hybrids (such as the Fairlight CVI from 1984) would later appear. Of particular interest in the history of electronic music was Laurie Spiegel's use of Max Mathews' *GROOVE* (Generated Realtime Output Operations on Voltage-controlled Equipment) hybrid system, a small computer controlling analogue equipment which just happened to include a video output. The *VAMPIRE* (Video And Music Program for Interactive Realtime Exploration/Experimentation) system developed by Spiegel from 1974 to 1979, was aptly named for the propensity of artists at Bell Labs to work during the early hours of the morning when the systems were not used for telecommunications research. It enabled her to write programs which closely controlled both audio and visuals as time-based signals (Spiegel 1998).

Digital computer technology was gradually to take over. Anticipating later visualisers, Atari released an Atari Video Music in 1978, even before the classic Atari 2600 games console, which could take in an audio signal and synthesise animated graphics onto home television screens.

By the 1980s, the cheapness of video tape had made bedroom production accessible to many artists. In the UK in particular, the scratch video movement saw cut-and-paste treatments of often political material for viewing in clubs. Meanwhile, the explosion in popular music video followed the 1981 launch of Music TeleVision. MTV dubbed their presenters 'video jockeys', a parallel definition to that claimed by a new generation of club performers.

The age of warehouse raves filled with Atari ST computers controlling sound was also the age of Amiga computers controlling video. Digital VJing was inevitable and irresistible; as has often been proved, digital technology makes experimentation very accessible to a wide base of artists, through the combination of power of processing[8] and relative cheapness of hardware. Nevertheless, many audiovisual practitioners remain aware of the rich history of the analogue domain, even if some are destined to reinvent or rediscover the concerns of earlier artists before the digital age.

There is a proliferation of hardware and software for audiovisual performance at the moment, and VJ gear has become as much a revenue stream for companies as DJ technology. Despite our provisos concerning the use of further equipment, from video cameras to video mixers to alternative controllers (just as standalone audio has explored), the entry set-up for many artists might be a software program on a laptop computer. Both commercial programs and freeware are available, and the usual continuums of customisation from limited proprietary interfaces to very flexible programming environments is evident. There are contrasts of visual-only generators (packages like Arkaos VJ or Motion Dive for example) and integrated environments for both audio and video signal networks (such as Max/MSP with Jitter or PD with GEM). Many programs support intercommunication with other software via MIDI or network protocols like OSC, enabling a user to blend their favoured visual and audio packages. Indeed, a general multimodal trend is evident in the audio field, as video support is becoming a standard in previously audio-only packages, from NRT media-composing software like Pro Tools or Logic, to live sequencers such as Ableton Live. Innovative projects, however, are often built using more customisable or self-built software, from Dave Griffiths' *fluxus*, a live coded 3D animation environment, to Andrew Sorenson's *Impromptu*, a performance programming environment for audio and graphics, both of which use the language Scheme.

No doubt fashions will change concerning artists' favoured audiovisual set-ups.[9] In the following we concentrate more on general principles and aesthetics independent of equipment.

Approaches to contemporary audiovisual performance

A point that's often missed is that contemporary audiovisual performance isn't just one type of artistic practice. There are various contexts in which such performance is taking place, and while there is substantial overlap, they often have different goals in mind.

In club VJing, the focus is often on ambient performance; although the VJ wants attention paid to her visuals, she also wants to provide an appropriate atmosphere for dancing and socialising, not to have audience members

Figure 7.1 VJ Olga Mink (Oxygen) (photo: Mark Trash)

focus solely on what's on the screen. This type of performance also tends to be very concerned with interpreting and integrating with the music played in the club. How tightly the VJ chooses to 'follow' the music is a matter of their preference and the influence of the audience, DJ and venue. The VJ often interprets the music by manually triggering, manipulating – and in some cases generating from scratch – animations, effects and video clips. Thus she improvises visuals with the music in much the same way as a jazz musician might improvise with an ensemble. The VJ may also choose to use hardware- or software-based automated sync features to directly 'visualise' the music to a greater or lesser degree. But whilst some software visualisers (like the iTunes energy tracking animations) might give the impression that automated visualisation is the central focus of mainstream audiovisual performance, VJ practice is usually far more varied and spontaneous. However, with VJing we more generally see a convergence of audio and visuals than with other contemporary modes of audiovisual performance.

A practice that's become increasingly familiar within electronic arts circles in recent years is that of 'live cinema'. Live cinema tends to make more use of a linear and/or narrative structure than does club VJing, and it is definitely less ambient. Audiences are often seated as though watching a concert or a movie. Frequently the audio and visuals are created by the same artists and developed together, and often the music is developed as subordinate to the visuals in reaction to club practice. In any case, there is little emphasis on visuals solely as an interpretation of audio.

It's worth noting here that live cinema and VJing have a good deal of overlap – just as visual music filmmaking practice has drawn both from the structures of music and experimental narrative film, live cinema practitioners often see their work as music as well as narrative. According to HC Gilje, from 242.pilots, one of the best-known live cinema ensembles:

> 242.pilots have been compared to free-jazz groups, operating on the outer fringes of experimental cinema. Using our individual video instruments the three of us respond to and interact with each other's images in a subtle and intuitive way. The images are layered, contrasted, merged and transformed in realtime combining with the improvised soundtrack into an audiovisual experience.
> (Gilje 2005)

However, Gilje also notes:

> People always look for some sort of story no matter how abstract and non-narrative the video is, and I find it interesting this dialogue between us and the audience in terms of creating meaning. Our improvisations are like taking a walk in some unknown landscape, and depending on the curiosity/attentiveness of each individual in the audience, they will all walk out of the space with their own unique experience.
> (Poole 2003)

Amongst audiovisual union groups, there is a great and healthy diversity of exploration, and some promising original takes on audiovisual performance itself are emerging, from the live audiovisual sampling cut and paste descendant from the scratch video circuit (EBN, Coldcut, Addictive TV) to audiovisual instrument models (chdh), a clash of narratives from a world of information (Farmer's Manual) or continual improvised renegotiation of mappings and audiovisual feedback (klipp av). Some groups are very adaptable to different contexts, where improvisation or preparation for specific shows allow them to attempt both VJ and live cinema sets on different nights. But touring acts working to be taken seriously within the art world often favour a live cinema setting, such as is exploited for expanded cinema style performances by groups like the Light Surgeons.

Both VJing and live cinema, while different in aim and drawing from various historical and contemporary influences, operate within a traditional performing arts context. A third, and lesser-known type of audiovisual performance practice operates within a performing arts context while also drawing from conceptual, performance art, and new media art practices. In the absence of a commonly agreed-upon name for this practice, we can refer to it here as 'conceptual audiovisual performance'. Examples of this type of practice include *WIMP*, by Victor Laskin and Alexei Shulgin, in which the visuals are composed entirely from elements of the Windows desktop of the performance computer; Sven Koenig's *ScrambledHackz*, in which audio and visuals are composed in realtime from familiar music video clips controlled by the performer's voice; *Movie Mincer* by Sergey Teterin, in which visuals are controlled by a hand-cranked, Soviet-era kitchen mincer; and Amy Alexander's *CyberSpaceLand* and *Extreme Whitespace*, two projects in which all the visuals are comprised of text, and the gestures of office work and gaming are exaggerated to become mechanisms of stage performance. These projects function to varying degrees as 'normal' VJ or live cinema projects; however, there is additional intentionality. Audiovisual performance itself is approached critically as part of the content; in addition, other topics, such as the role of software in contemporary culture, are also part of the subtext.

The psychology and analysis of AV

In this section of the chapter we consider some possible approaches to the theoretical analysis of audiovisual works. As a useful basis for such discussion we wish to draw the reader's attention to some issues in the cognition of such work for an observer. In spite of a clear separation of modalities so common in everyday parlance, we must go beyond the treatment of the modalities as separate entities, and consider their combination. In psychology, this is the area of crossmodal perception and multisensory integration, where the sense data input through different sense organs may interact at the neural level (Stein and Meredith 1993; Welch and Warren 1986).

There is some evidence to suggest that the prototypical state of a neonate (newborn baby), especially within the first three months of development, is a world of highly intertwined sense data, with extensive neural pathways for crossmodal information transfer (Harrison 2001). Such pathways are substantially pruned in the brain's natural early development, but some individuals (most likely determined by genetics) may retain more connections between modality-specific brain regions, giving rise to developmental synaesthesia. This condition is thus a lifelong, natural facet of existence for the synaesthete, whereby stimulus in one modality may automatically and involuntarily cause correlated activity in another representation. Whilst there are other possible cross-connections, directly relevant to our purposes is so-called 'coloured hearing', the projection of colours in response to sound, usually tones or spoken words.

It is inevitable in discussion of audiovisual art that the term synaesthesia intrudes, though its use in artistic practice has often not kept abreast of scientific investigation. As a neurological phenomenon, real synaesthesia is automatic and highly personal, thus providing no basis for generalisation to an audience any larger than the individual synaesthetic artist themselves. In terms of the prevalence of the condition, estimates vary widely, from one in twenty-three (for all kinds of synaesthetic experience) to one in a hundred (for a specific type, grapheme-colour) in the latest large-scale study at the time of writing (Simner *et al.* 2006), up to one in two thousand or one in twenty-five thousand (Baron-Cohen and Harrison 1997). Whilst some artists have been discussed as synaesthetes, many cases, including Skryabin's, have been debunked (Harrison 2001), and there remains some controversy as to the existence of any increased prevalence amongst artists or innate predilection of synaesthetes to artistic endeavour (Ramachandran 2001).

Aside from the pure developmental synaesthesia, there can exist associative, learnt synaesthesia (tending to be more voluntary and less intense), and also many confounding cases of simile, metaphor and linguistic convention (a blue Monday, red for rage, the ringing of the clarion sunset). What has been dubbed 'synaesthetic art' is really just art where the mapping between audio and visuals is held constant and is of an obviously high correlation. It is voluntarily embedded into a work by the artist. Such direct one-to-one mappings are not necessary, nor ubiquitous in art. Whilst certain novel techniques might favour injective mappings of this kind, such mappings can often become tiresome if overused.

The balance of power between the modalities is often a central aesthetical concern in artworks, and has implications in the analysis of work. Often, there is an inherent bias, perhaps from the perspective of who judges or creates a work, and the conventions of that art form. For instance, the music analyst's treatment of opera might remain overly locked to the score rather than the staging and narrative, or vice versa.

There is an often expressed prejudice both in science and culture in favour of visual information (Posner *et al.* 1976), ranking vision above the 'second sense' of hearing. Yet sound provides an environmental cue for fast-moving processes of much higher resolution than video, with a typical delay (to cortex) of five milliseconds, as opposed to thirty to fifty for visual information. Film and audiovisual art systematically exploit this; think of the punch sounds accompanying movie fights. 'Sound helps to imprint rapid visual sensations into memory' (Chion 1994, p. 122).[10]

However, from an analytic perspective, many authors have expressed reservations about assumptions of visual primacy (Lipsomb and Tolchinsky 2005; Cook 1998). Cook (1998) recognises that the typical situation of 'film music', where music is a subservient underscoring of the narrative action, is inverted in much multimedia practice to 'music film', the primary message in audition being supported by visuals. The latter is certainly the case in many instances of VJ practice, though again, we have noted that this factor may be inverted in live cinema back in favour of film – a tussle of the modalities indeed, often varying during the course of a show.

In practice, the combination of the two modalities may further empower both. But there are a number of strategies for the presentation of audition and vision, which may show varying degrees of object correlation and conflux of meaning (Chion 1994; Cook 1998). Even when a direct opposition of modalities is sought out, we have a tendency to impose our own alignments in making sense of the scene: 'Certain experimental videos and films demonstrate that synchresis can even work out of thin air – that is, with images and sounds that strictly speaking have nothing to do with each other, forming monstrous yet inevitable and irresistible agglomerations in our perception' (Chion 1994, p. 63). Our streaming capabilities in both visual and auditory modalities may only allow the simultaneous tracking of three to four objects at once; think of trying to follow the voices of a fugue, or individual birds in a flock. And when associations are clashed between modalities, the load on our attentional resources across many projector screens and loudspeakers can go beyond the level where we have a hope of following every event. This is demonstrated by Cage and Hiller's spectacle *HPSCHD* (first performed 1969); their solution to this overload of live harpsichord, tapes, slides and films was to have the audience wander round exploring rather than trying to take in everything at once.

The psychology of audiovisuals is under study at the present time, and naturally a complex problem. Studies may reveal dimensions in our attentional resources, the inherent crossmodal pathways, and the interaction of meaning. The artist and analyst must allow that our apprehension of multiple simultaneously presented modalities transforms the situation where either one is solo.

Conclusions

We hope that this chapter has demonstrated the divergent practices and given a flavour of the complex history of audiovisual performance. This rich field is populated by projects as diverse as Handel's *Music for the Royal Fireworks*, the multimedia theatrical spectacles of late nineteenth century Paris, Xenakis's Polytopes, Jean-Michel Jarre's laser light shows, and the raft of current experimenters in (often digital) audiovisual art.

The case of multiple modalities has always been a consideration in art, but has become extremely explicit in recent multimedia practice. We have seen how contemporary VJ and live cinema work is grounded in such facets as colour organs, visual music, light shows and analogue video synths. Whilst digital technology has empowered some novel aspects of live audiovisual activity, as well as making it highly accessible to producers and consumers, there is much to learn from historical approaches, and analogue experimental techniques and technologies are still evident and healthily represented in current praxis. Furthermore, many variations are to be expected in future art, from the foregrounding of conceptual and critical VJing, through new close unions of audio and visual artists, to novel narrative structures in live cinema work.

Again, it is not our place to prescribe that artworks should be predominantly audiovisual, with audio primary, or visualaudio, with visuals dominant, or indeed any precise blend of audio and visuals. Indeed, most new projects, where artists collaborate from the start from a crossmodal perspective, are seeking a better balance, a healthy coalition or competition between the two which may conceivably vary during the course of a show, or be subservient to some further unifying mathematical or conceptual principle. It is clear that audiovisual performance is now a mainstream within electronic music and provides a fertile ground for future work, especially if approached with an eye and an ear to its rich history and practice.

8 Network music

JULIAN ROHRHUBER

With the proliferation of transport infrastructure in sixteenth-century England, the term *network* appeared. From then on, its use spread to the most varied fields, so that today it occupies various significant nodes in our thinking – it has become a way to understand the world. *Network music* can be situated somewhere between such a conceptual and the more technical meaning of the term. It covers a broad range from collaborative composition environments to sound installations and improvised music ensembles. Within today's computer music, networks play an important role. Be it laptop ensembles that use the local ethernet to exchange hidden musical messages, composition tools for searching online sound databases, or shared environments for musical improvisation on the internet – the communicative and social aspects of music-making are reflected in the computer instrument. The history of the computer is closely linked with the history of telecommunication, so that it is not surprising that network music has been evolving together with computer music. Nevertheless, as we will see, network music goes beyond the technical needs of communication – it investigates the implications of networking in a much broader sense.

This chapter gives an introduction to basic aspects of this field, providing a background for understanding network pieces and giving inspiration for new developments. As far as possible, we try to include the cultural context that forms the background of contemporary network music pieces. The first two sections will cover the aspect of *transmission*, and the role of material and symbolic *mediation* within sound-based art. In the next section, we will first follow a brief history of the network paradigm in computer languages. Then, the reception of information theory within art will be discussed in order to understand the paradigm shift in the late 1960s that gave rise to the proliferation of the network idea. The last two sections cover *spatial and temporal structures* of computer music networks in more detail, to provide some insight into the rich possibilities of contemporary approaches.

Sound transfer

Sound in general, and voice and music in particular, have often played a key role in cultural techniques of transmission and knowledge exchange,

Figure 8.1 The Wilmington based Tel-musici Company, from the 18 December 1909 issue of *Telephony*[1]

as well as in the reflection about conversation and enquiry. On the one hand, sound is associated with the notion of *immediate connection* between phenomena, and the experience of being affected over distance. On the other, it forms a basis for the transmission of signs, and therefore listening is also related to an activity of *decoding*, to the extraction of meaning that is based on a convention or protocol. Thus the same sound can be perceived in two different ways: as a direct effect of a more or less remote sound source, or as a message encoded into the sound, and left to a listener's interpretation.

Of course, a sound wave itself can be transmitted through a wide range of materials and structures (such as water or electricity) and equally, it can be passed on in the form of signs such as text (e.g. a score or poetry). For instance, in 1909, in Wilmington, Delaware, a telephone exchange was combined with a music room, providing customers with live piano performance over the phone line (Fig. 8.1, cf. the Telharmonium). Since the invention of phonography and telephony, the means to encode, transmit and decode acoustic events have flourished, and have merged into other media infrastructures, such as film, or the internet. Most examples of network pieces, as we will see, relate in one way or the other to such transmission techniques.

The possibility of fast numerical operations on computers has brought the concept of *number* into a key position within almost all processes of transference. Numerical representation is a carrier for transmitting and reproducing sound, and at the same time it opens an extraordinarily wide field of translations and manipulations. In this role, the digital is both subject to confidence in its faultlessness and to doubts about its stainless fidelity. The development of media has been accompanied by an ambiguity between the fascination of identical reproduction, telepresence and remote access, and a distrust towards the authenticity of mediated effects.

As we will see, in the aesthetics of network music both the concept of *transparent telepresence* and the demonstration of the *opaque character of media* play a significant role.

Opacity and transparency

Over time, the need for transfer of information between geographically separated places has led to a multiplicity of media techniques, forming coexistent historical and functional layers of infrastructure. While normally those techniques 'simply function', artistic and scientific investigation is interested in appreciating their constraints and their cultural implications.[2] For network music the choice and combination of transmission media is in itself a considerable element, so that fields like the history of science, materials research, or other natural sciences become important reference points. Furthermore, due to the social relevance of communication, media techniques are always subject to power struggle and control. It is therefore common for network art to have its context in political theory or cultural anthropology: the often intricate combination of physical characteristics (e.g. due to physical properties of materials or processes) with the historical, social and aesthetic implications of media allows, and in a way, causes, the artist to be part of a broader cultural discourse.

A good example for an artwork that combines the physical with the cultural issues of transmission is *Firebirds* (2004) by Paul de Marinis. In this installation, recorded speeches by Joseph Stalin, Benito Mussolini, Franklin Roosevelt and Adolf Hitler are transmitted over gas pipes and played back by flames in bird cages, one after the other. The technique of using flames as loudspeakers can be traced back to the invention of the vacuum tube over a long series of 'orphaned technologies'.[3] While this piece investigates the translation between different sound-transmitting techniques (voice, microphone, mechanical engraving, electricity, loudspeaker, gas, flame), it does so not in isolation, but in its historical (the almost forgotten techniques of sound induction and the gas pipes being one of the first major urban networks) and political (e.g. the enclosed, delayed and channelled character of mediation and the collective space created by media) dimensions.

The distinction between the mediated and the medium is a significant part of artistic discourses in the twentieth century. While in traditional concert music, the contribution of the instrument to the artwork is usually well discerned, in music that goes beyond established sound production techniques this is often not the case. As a consequence, the investigation of transmission media themselves, as opposed to the idea of transparent transmission, has been of importance in many musical works. The *sounding object*, for instance, in David Tudor's *Rainforest* (1968), is not simply a transmitter, but its specific resonant behaviour in response to induced vibrations is essential to every realisation of the piece. The *sound event itself as an object*, on the other hand, is a central idea in *musique concrète*, being concerned with an aesthetic that derives from recordings, but erases all traces of their origin, locating the sound source in the loudspeaker itself.

But also a relatively simple and seemingly transparent *displacement* of sound into a new context is a way to investigate the field: Luc Ferrari's *music promenade* (1969), for instance, consists of an edited field recording of a promenade, played back in a concert room: 'musique concrète was a kind of abstractisation [*sic*] of sound – we didn't want to know its origin, its causality . . . Whereas here I wanted you to recognise causality – it was traffic noise it wasn't just to make music with but to say: this is traffic noise! (*Laughs*) Cage's influence, perhaps.'[4] Apart from its other political implications (Ferrari considers the piece 'a panorama of society'), this type of work demonstrates the fact that localities are not neutral, but are just as particular as the transmission and encoding media themselves.

Perhaps it is such an irreducible property of location (or *situatedness*) that is responsible for the fascination that accompanies the imagination of telepresence, or any kind of 'action at a distance'. Such an interest in unusual sonic spaces can be found in many network art pieces. Inspired by the spiritist Friedrich Jürgensen, who believed he could channel the voices of the dead via short-wave radio, the Swedish composer Carl Michael von Hausswolff built an installation, *Operations of Spirit Communication* (1998), that makes atmospheric electromagnetic fields and electric currents audible. Remote causation of yet another kind takes effect in Richard Teitelbaum's piece *Alpha Bean Lima Brain* (1971), transmitting brain waves via telephone from California to drive a pot of jumping beans in New York (Chadabe 1997). Generally, amongst the immediate precursors of network music, one can find many transmission-specific art forms that stage the situation of *telepresence* their infrastructures provide: *Radio-art*, for instance, uses the assemblage of diverse sources by a combinatoric switchboard, and stages the possibility of fakery, like Orson Welles' 1938 *War of the Worlds*.

Constructing a montage of previously unrelated sources, the *switchboard operator* is the simplest paradigm of a *network node*, the connection point of a network. Maybe the most far-reaching network music project of this type is *Radio Astronomy*, a live internet broadcast of the acoustic output of different scientific radio telescopes from Australia to Hawaii. Dependent on astronomers' target observations, atmospheric and technical conditions, the radio waves of different astronomical phenomena are combined in an automated composition, bringing cosmic noise into the context of a reading as musique concrète, glitch, or even as an indeterministic, contemporary reiteration of Kepler's harmonic music of the spheres.[5] While assembling the fragments of unimaginable distances and times, this piece also confronts the fascination of channelling with the intrusion of a third participant that is neither medium nor message, but their indistinguishability: noise.

Protocols and relations

So far we have discussed the transferences in the structured continuum between *displaced sound* and *sounding channel*. For networked computer music, not only processes based on transmission of sound energy are of interest, but also those of *symbolic* information, such as numbers or signs. Such a symbolic sign is special, because it can form a generic placeholder, standing in for something in respect to some interpretation.[6] As its meaning depends entirely on interpretation, it can be translated into other signs according to a set of rules, which makes it convenient as a way to transmit a message. There is a problem here though: both sides of the transfer must have had something in common already before they try to communicate. This common convention, the *protocol*, defines the basic rules according to which a message is interpreted.[7] Protocol, in this way, is nothing inherently different from a common language that forms a convention of how to interpret signs.

Be it simply that the participants are separate from each other, or that they improvise over a common musical basis: in a way, the whole point about transferring a message is that the receiver's context differs from the sender's context in some respect. Because the same sign may cause different interpretations, it becomes *itself* the branching point within a network of meaning. The sign thus generates divergent chains of causation: the exact same message could, for instance, be interpreted as a description of how to produce a sound algorithmically (e.g. as program code); it may also be measured data (e.g. recorded sound data), musical information (such as note values), or it can be interpreted as an abstract change within the receiver's current context (Fig. 8.2).

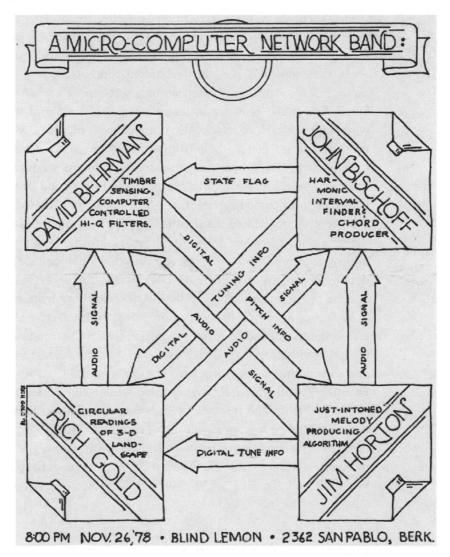

Figure 8.2 Flyer by Rich Gold for the network ensemble The League from 1978, showing the different types of musical data exchange.

While any computer program can be regarded as such a causal network, *message-oriented programming paradigms* are a good example for how context dependency can form an explicit foundational element of a computer language. In a *polymorphic* structure, the interpretation of a symbol, such as an operator, depends on its receiver, so that the same message may cause different chains of events. Alan Kay notes that it took him a long time to realise that one can invert the idea of a process that operates on objects (Kay 1993). This delegation of control from the *subject* to the *object* (both in the grammatical sense) means that the concept of an active power from the outside (process or declaration) that controls passive entities (data or description) is no longer valid. In a system in which there are only behaviours in response to messages, the structure of inclusion and control become inherently relative.

In the 1960s and 70s, such relational concepts became increasingly influential for computing, such as in *object-oriented programming* (e.g. Smalltalk), or the *actor model* (e.g. Planner). The attempt to model the world as a network of relations led to a concept in which each part of a program can act like a whole computer that interprets messages sent to it: 'The mental image was one of separate computers sending requests to other computers that had to be accepted and understood by the receivers before anything could happen' (Kay 1993). While in the 1950s, relationality was part of the modelling of individual concept formation, and the program mainly a tool for problem-solving, within the following twenty years the idea of programming became increasingly conversational (coinciding with the development of the early internet). Notions of symbiosis between programs and their writers (Licklider, Engelbart, Ashby) led to systems, such as *JOSS, LCC, Lisp,* or *Smalltalk,* that were more suited for interactive reasoning and for communicating ideas to other programmers. Today's network-oriented computer music languages, such as *SuperCollider, ChucK, Serpent or JSyn,* and also communication protocols like Open Sound Control (Wright and Freed 1997) and graphical programming systems like Pure Data and Max, are derived from and inspired by such concepts. These systems combine the concept of a program as a group of communicating individuals with a more conversational approach to code. In this way, they allow the network of human relations to include the algorithmic network of the program, and vice versa.

Formalism and information

A language, or a protocol, functions not only as a decoding mechanism. Being something that needs to be shared between participants, it is also a *description* of this mechanism, however generic. In other words, a protocol serves not only as the enforcement of a law, it is its explicit formulation. Just like for computer music as a whole, for many network music pieces, this explicit character has been a significant thematic element; and perhaps it is one of the interesting aspects of algorithmic music in general that description is not a mere means to reach a goal, but description and sound often are equally part of the artwork, exploring and structuring the complex field between the generic and the singular.

Even before 1920, artists had employed formal instructions to generate art: the Dadaists made the proposal that a painter could now order pictures by telephone and have them made by a cabinet-maker (Kaç 1992).

Duchamp's ready-mades were mostly the result of a formal instruction of actions, such as how to acquire an object from a department store.

It became central to *constructivist* and *formalist art* to embrace explicit convention as a way to construct independence from dominion by tradition. The idea of a universally valid artwork, existing beyond individual mani-festation in a collective space, was an important factor. Perhaps even more important was the conviction that art should be available for everybody: a formal description, provided to the public, makes the work reproducible and understandable, instead of hiding away its makings behind the doors of a genius. *Conceptual art* in the 1960s took a further step and established the instruction itself to be the art piece, its realisation becoming unimportant. By contrast, in the early forms of *telecommunication art*, the message is only transmitting the rules for the artwork. This is the case in Moholy-Nagy's telephone pictures from 1924 (see: Kaç 1992, pp. 47–57), which serve as an early antecedent of the 1969 exhibition *Art by telephone*, featuring works that were implemented by the curator after verbal instructions by the artists over telephone.

The notion of an objectivity of aesthetic qualities inspired *information aesthetics* in the 1950s to work on universal rules for the composition of art, which in turn became influential in *integral serialism* (Grant 2001). According to Abraham Moles, algorithmic mass reproduction and 'the annullation of the value of the original' (Moles 1984, p. 39) aids in overcoming exclusiv-ity and individual ownership as well as traditional conceptions of aesthetics. In a synthetic reversion of the analytical procedure, programs are written by the composer that create works from networks of relations derived by information theoretic considerations. In such a way, the algorithm is the implication of a whole distributed family of works, which all follow the same, explicit principle (this idea lives on in today's *generative art*). Moles describes the artistic expression, in reference to the *mathematical theory of communication* (Shannon 1948), as a message transmitted by an artist (*the transmitter*) to another individual (*the receiver*) over the systems of percep-tion (*the channel*) (Moles 1984, p. 13–18; see Fig. 8.3). In the cybernetic aesthetic theories of this time, objectivised concepts of information and the computational universality of the Turing Machine were expected to provide a starting point for a thorough understanding of the artistic domain, and for science and society in general.

The Other

The attempt to find a solid foundation for the arts by means of assumedly universal perceptual qualities, that was influential in this era, turned out to be problematic. Towards the 1960s, the paradigm of the artist as a sender of

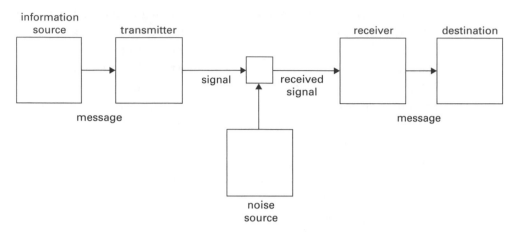

Figure 8.3 Adapted from Shannon's 'schematic diagram of a general communication system' (Shannon 1948)

information was increasingly questioned (Giannetti 2004) and the inclusion of the observer into the network of relations caused a paradigm shift within cybernetic aesthetics. This shift coincided with a change in the notion of the artwork that had already happened over the first half of the century. The question was not so much any more about the work as an autonomous (however reproducible) entity created by a gifted, introspective individual, but about how art comes about, or happens, in a collective process. As the observer became part of the work, media technologies became the subject of an art that started to critically investigate the power structures of mass distribution and intervened in the unidirectionality of transmission channels (Chandler and Neumark 2005).

Communication media, as well as the computer, inspired artistic games with formalist rules, the investigation of new conversational situations and the invention of objects that could be reconfigured by the audience. Alsleben and Passow (1960) understood their computer graphics as a visual *correspondence with the computer* (Giannetti 2004), and the fluxus *mail art* movement aimed at distributed authorship (Osthoff 2005). The artistic concern in such *conversational* and *participatory art* is not so much the expression of an existing intuition or dexterity, but the opening towards the unexpected. Under such circumstances, formal and algorithmic methods are a source of experimental exploration, their generic character aiming for new, and possibly unexpected, situations rather than for universal truths. In the form of an interactive, conversational relationship, the algorithm became an integral part of the art event (Drucker 2005).

In the 1970s, inspired by composers like Cage, Tudor and Wolff, the early network music scene in the San Francisco Bay Area used the first low-end microprocessors to implement sound algorithms and conversation rules. The *League of Automatic Composers* was an ensemble that declaredly consisted of composers and computers equally: 'the League is an organization that seeks to invent new members by means of its projects' (Brown and Bischoff 2002, 1.1). In this way, an active participation of the algorithm moved the composer into the position of an observer. Just in the same way as this turn of perspective opened up the social relations amongst the musicians, it also changed the role of the audience. Including the observer as an active participant into the system, the relational structure of a social and musical network cannot be based on an absolute reference system, but results in multiple points of observation: in a way, it has no single outside any more.[8]

The shift of interest to processes instead of products was evident in the exploration of the *immaterial* or *nonlocal* quality of artworks that exist only within a telecommunication network, within a conversational situation, between participants of a mail art exchange, or in the unpredictable character of a fluxus performance.[9] Over time, many projects have developed such concepts of *extended* or *hybrid networks*, converging with networked mobile games and opening a wide field for computer music: concerts and environments with audience participation, psychogeography and dérive, machine listening concerts, site-specific sonifications, gameboy and mobile phone orchestras, augmented environments, circuit bending, nomadic music instruments, participative seminars, massive multiplayer game networks, internet radio networks, ubiquitous computer music – these are only some of the multiplicity of fields that carry on the ideas of participation art and form the context for today's network music.

Topology

As we saw before, a number of networked computers is not inherently different from the graph of a single program. Since one program can contain multiple processes, just as several computers can participate in the same program, the underlying network implementation does not necessarily represent the factual interdependency of a situation: a network music piece might deliberately make this implementation structure the subject of discussion, but often, the resulting effective structure differs from its implementation.[10] Although a topology can thus be reduced to the logical structure of causal relations, due to the openness of music systems, it does matter how the algorithmic network is embedded in geographical, social and acoustic space. By creating connections where there were none before, and excluding influences which were relevant before, it intervenes in the causal milieu of an environment. In this sense, what is interesting here, is not so much something like a network of cables and hubs, but the variable and interlocated structure of causal topology.

Because a computer music network usually includes various active participants (people, processes) that are spread over space but are all potentially connected in the most unusual ways, causation becomes a really interesting issue both for audience and for the musicians (Rohrhuber and De Campo 2003). When confronted with behaviour of a certain complexity, it is often uncertain for an observer whether it is *random* (could as well be otherwise), *consequential* (due to a rule), or *intentional* (aiming at something). In such a way it may be a matter of perspective whether and how a given system 'works' or not. In systems for remote collaboration, for example, it is usually beneficial to make the interdependencies comprehensible and allow for a very structured delegation of control (Hajdu 2005; Barbosa 2006; Weinberg 2003), while for improvised network ensembles, this uncertainty of causation is often an integral part of the aesthetics. The fascination of self-regulating feedback networks, where causation is delocalised into an emergent pattern, is a common theme in cybernetics and music networks. Thus, since the early use of feedback in analogue synthesisers, the theory and aesthetics of dynamical systems has gained influence. Peter Blasser's electronic circuits, for instance, produce sound in an almost, but not entirely unpredictable way, which brings the musician once again into the position of an experimenter and listener. Such self-regulating systems have sometimes been treated as an authentic natural state, that is freed from the strict laws of formalism. In recent works, the indeterminacy of algorithms, as well as the power structure of implicit regulation, is contextualised more carefully (Arns 2004; Doruff 2006; Wieser and Rohrhuber 2006).

Letters and tandems

Within network music, as we have seen, there is a tendency to delocalise causation. At the same time though, there are always notions of *something*, that happens, or that is being changed (this notion is called *state*). Such states are *common* in two ways: information can be passed between the participants, or it can be accessed concurrently. Independent of a particular network infrastructure, distributed state can be modelled just as well as state can be passed around, within limitations. What seems more appropriate is rather an aesthetic decision: the metaphor of the postal system and its circulating letters is not without charm, just as the idea of a private shared space. The name of the early computer network ensemble *The Hub* (Fig. 8.4) originates from the interesting problem of how to share information

Figure 8.4 The network music ensemble The Hub, 1989 (top photo: Jim Block) and 2006 (bottom photo: Chianan Yen)

amongst participants of a networked music group. In this ensemble, the players each have their own musical rule systems, but use a common data space (the hub) to integrate their individual approaches.

A *shared object* (Fig. 8.5) is based on the idea of one *single state* that participates in more than one context, allowing several persons (or processes) to share one and the same causal milieu, which may be purely acoustic, but also visual or textual (Barbosa 2006). Noah Vawter's *WebSynths* (2004), for

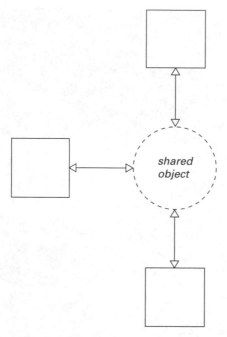

Figure 8.5 Shared object

instance, allowed online guests to remote control a selection 'of rare and boutique synthesisers', and to listen to the result via audio stream. Such a multiplayer or tandem instrument exists only in a single instance: in this way, *WebSynths* can also be seen as a slightly ironic comment on the exclusivity of analogue equipment, and the fact that sharing this equipment may mean cooperation, or even conversation. In such a way, a shared sound object can function as a hybrid form between *communication channel* and a *composition environment*. In *Auracle* (Neuhaus *et al.*), participants can use their voice to control a shared virtual acoustic space, which can result in a special kind of cross-cultural vocalisation when people from different language backgrounds join into musical conversation. In *KeyWorks* (Doruff) and in *PeerSynth* (Stelkens), the participants collaborate by manipulating shared graphical objects that represent sonic structures. *Quintet.net* (Hajdu), on the other hand, provides shared access to a musical score for collaborative composition, and in systems like *JITLib* (Rohrhuber) and *Co-Audicle* (Wang and Cook) the participants communicate with program text.

Somehow, as soon as state can be accessed by more than one person, the question of the *owner* appears out of thin air. Many archive music pieces play with the various implications of access, often entering a *plunderphonics* territory. Freeman's *N.A.G.*, for instance, assembles a collage of online soundfiles derived from keyword search, and Thomson and Craighead's

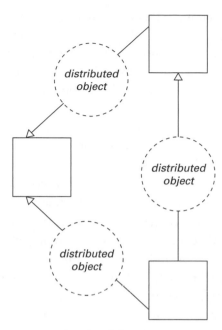

Figure 8.6 Distributed object

Unprepared Piano randomly downloads MIDI-files from the internet and plays back aleatoric recombinations on a player-piano. A playful comment on privacy issues is also The Hub's appropriation art piece *Borrowing and Stealing*. Here, elements of the musical score are accessible to all participants, leading to divergent modifications of the privately edited sound material. As soon as a new melody pattern comes into play, the collaborating players immediately use it as material, taking it apart, interpreting pitch as rhythm or rhythm as timbre and transforming it beyond recognisable connection to the original (Brown and Bischoff 2002).

Yet another piece by The Hub, named *boss*, consists of a virtual mixer that is only accessible to one band member at the time, who can use it to control everyone's output level. At any moment though, someone else may decide to take over control, leaving the former boss behind without control. This last example shows that, instead of concurrently changing a single object, one may also pass objects around like letters, being modified further and further, in each step changing the causal topology of the system. Such *distributed objects* exist in multiple concurrent versions at different locations (Fig. 8.6).

In networked *live coding* and collaborative composition, the participants send each other score or program text, which is applied in each local context to the composition, or the running sound, modified and sent on. Such *code chats* proliferate sound in form of its description over a network, as well as comments or other conversation, so that program text appears in a mixed, rather literary context, functioning not only as functional module, but more so as a form of public reasoning (Rohrhuber and De Campo 2003, 2005). Techniques from literary art, such as the surrealist *cadavre exquis* may thus be combined with formal languages, algorithmic composition becomes a conversational game, and the roles of senders, messages and receivers may swap positions. Sitting with their laptops in the audience space, the ensemble *powerbooks unplugged* consists of a cloud of distributed code, processes and messages, resulting in similarly delocalised clouds of microsonic pulses that find their way through the narrow band of laptop speakers. Here, various layers of distributed state come into play at the same time – small pieces of program text, comments on the current state of affairs and network messages causing sound events on different computers, almost completely dissolving the link between individual action and sound location.

In this example, the asynchronicity of the wireless network is part of the compositional strategy, merging the effect of acoustic spatial delay with the topology of network latency. Chris Chafe's works show that network latency can also be used directly for sound synthesis: constructing feedback loops over internet connections, *Network Harp* (2001) derives tones from network delay, so that the slower connections result in lower pitches than the fast ones. Just as other pecularities of transmission are part of the aesthetics of network music, the unavoidable latency in networks is an important issue. From a historical point of view, computation and telecommunication have many common aspects, the impossibility of a unified time being one of those with maybe the most immediate relevance for network music. While there are various schemes for arranging the situation in a way that network asynchronicity can be ignored, many systems, such as the above, decide to make the temporal incompleteness their foundation (see Chafe 2002; Barbosa 2006).

Sending a message always takes time, and in the mail coach era, the correspondence with the beloved often had to include intricate descriptions of one's own travel plans so that the next letter's destination could be determined. A common time was maybe the last notion of unified observation that persisted in science after having adopted an essentially relational view. While today, a century after the publication of the theory of special relativity, we can lean back and remark that 'there is no now without here',[11] telecommunication has never stopped struggling with synchronisation problems. The letter may well arrive at its destination, but while it is not only always late, even worse, time itself has meanwhile turned out to be a multiplicity. Looking back and planning ahead – perhaps we have no choice but to interact with slightly incoherent shared objects or to leave traces on chains of letters, engaged in negotiation, conversation and experiment.

Conclusion

Having discussed some of the history, the culture and techniques of network music, we hope to have provided an overview of some important aspects that are characteristic for this field. We have seen in what respect the two basic questions, *how to transmit*, and *how to form a network of relations*, play an important role. Further, questions of power-structure, rules, authorship and group-formation become important when the relation between artist and audience is redefined. In including the observer, the network paradigm becomes more complex, and brings up interesting problems of synchronicity and causation. Computer music networks form especially well suited environments for combining technical and cultural, formal and aesthetic aspects of networks, opening up a wide field for invention, intervention, and surprise.

9 Electronic music and the moving image

JULIO D'ESCRIVÁN

In the composer, [Tarkovsky] sought not the author of music, but the organiser of audio space of the film ... E. ARTEMIEV[1]

Washington, Virginia, USA, 1951; the Washington Obelisk; Lincoln Memorial. A strange low pulsing sound fills the air; it has a bell-like quality. You think you recognise the swelling of a tam-tam roll, but there is also a strange low pulsing sound which does not seem to match anything you have ever heard before. As you see a bright gigantic white disc overfly the Capitol, you recognise the familiar sound of some kind of aircraft. People stop and stare at the skies. A high-pitched bleep is heard momentarily as the disc flies overhead. Now both the pulse and the flying roar seem to modulate together varying in speed and timbral colour. People run and scream as the object prepares to land and the sound becomes more intense: a strong wind, static electricity, a motor sound; all fuse in and out of a pitch-bending tonal hum. The sound of a short servomechanism punctuates the landing. It has arrived!

Within *The Day The Earth Stood Still* (1951), the real and the imaginary become one through the magic of the soundtrack. As the film progresses, the leading musical themes are played by two Theremins. Thanks to their unfamiliarity to the listener, their characteristic gliding sound endows the music of the film with an otherworldly quality by visual association with UFO imagery. The soundtrack of the film contains, then, two main musical elements: the organisation of processed sounds to represent the noises of extraterrestrial elements and atmospheric moods, and the use of electronic instrumentation to imbue the orchestral film score with a futuristic sheen.

As a narrative accompaniment to familiar visuals, electronic and pre-recorded sounds colour our perception in a unique way, arguably beyond the possibilities of conventional instruments, when trying to affect our emotions. The omnipresent warnings of beeping mobile phones, pop-music ringtones and of course the sounds and music from video game consoles affirm that electronic music is not only functional, but almost mandatory. Electronic music has been influenced by the visual and in turn, the visual has been enriched by electronic music.

That musique concrète was born in the studios of the nascent French TV is a telling fact. It is in the context of media production environments in Paris, Cologne and Milan that electronic music began to be thoroughly investigated. In the rest of the world a similar relationship would rapidly become evident. The same technology that made the earliest 'talking films' possible also enabled much sound experimentation.

This chapter aims to examine some examples that will illustrate the fruitful relationship between moving images and electronic music. As well as looking into the incorporation of electronic instruments into the film orchestra, we will delve into the creative manipulation of recorded sound for film. We will also comment on the use of electronic music on TV and new media.

'Film music scoring' versus 'sound design'

While much has been written about the use of electronic instruments in film and television music (Chadabe 1999; Hayward 2004; Manning 2004; Wierzbicki 2005; Davis 2006), sound design has traditionally not been evaluated as music. This is interesting since one of the fruits of the electronic music genre has been precisely to open our ears to any sound being potentially musical. In the twenty-first century no serious contemporary music aficionado would deny this, yet evaluations of film music always seem to refer exclusively to the work of the music composer. I would argue that the sound designer is also a music composer and further, that the acousmatic compositional techniques of Pierre Schaeffer, Pierre Henry and later electroacoustic composers were prefigured by the experiments of directors and sound artists in film. In fact, it could be said that electroacoustic (as opposed to electronic) experimentation actually starts with filmmaking, perhaps even up to seventeen years before Schaeffer began formulating his musique concrète theories.

Schaeffer, being involved in broadcast media as an employee of the Office de Radiodiffusion Télévision Française (ORTF) in Paris, must have been exposed to the cinema and familiar with the 'blockbusters' of the time; their sonic experiments perhaps stimulated his natural curiosity towards the ways in which we listen. Although radio had broadcast 'canned music' since the 1920s (Fischer 1922) and even radio drama was making use of sound effects, it is arguably in cinema where they found their first home as the raw material for 'studio art'. Radio plays were read live and the sound effects artist would perform their door-closing, horse-galloping and so on with props. In cinema, however, 'off-line' performance was made possible. When the first of the 'talkies', *The Jazz Singer*, appeared in 1927, the magnetic tape recorder, which would enable extensive editing techniques, had not yet been invented, so film editing was really the only viable technology for assembling and mixing sounds. It is no coincidence that in John Cage's 'The Future of Music: Credo', written in 1937, we read this reference to the use of film sound machines to make music:

> The sound of a truck at 50 m.p.h. Static between the stations. Rain. We want to capture and control these sounds, to use them, not as sound effects, but as musical instruments. Every film studio has a library of 'sound effects' recorded on film. With a film phonograph it is now possible to control the amplitude and frequency of any one of these sounds and to give to it rhythms within or beyond the reach of anyone's imagination. Given four film phonographs, we can compose and perform a quartet for explosive motor, wind, heart beat, and landslide.   (Cage 1995, p. 3)

The aim of the film sound designer, typically, is to give credibility to the picture through the organisation and re-creation of sound. And sometimes their work seems closer to Cage's 'Credo' than to simply re-syncing production sound to visuals. Even though this may sometimes be transparent for the audience, their work is musical in so far as it involves the organisation of sound events and creative modes of listening. At once, familiar elements can be identified through a process of 'causal' and 'reduced' listening modes[2] (Schaeffer 1966; Chion 1990), but the meaning of these sounds, that which clearly indexes them to reality and should contextualise them, has been hijacked by the visuals; a sound which on reduced listening should represent something, by visual coincidence ends up representing something else. In this respect, the sound designer is in a position to arrange a relationship of coincidence or opposition between what is heard and what is seen.[3]

Composer and film-music theorist Michel Chion refers to the 'spontaneous and irresistible weld' of sounds to visuals as *synchresis* (synchronism + synthesis) (Chion 1994). Chion also explains how this relationship between visuals and sound 'is also a function of meaning, and is organised according to gestaltist laws and contextual determinations' (Chion 1994, p. 63). Synchresis, however, seems to refer to that fleeting moment in which sound and visual coincide for the viewer. It leaves open questions of longer-term form such as the overarching structure. It could be argued that helping establish these is part of the remit of the sound designer. In considering their work in the terms of Cage's 'Credo', this may aid grand-scale compositional coherence. The question that remains, then, is how to create this larger semantic context; perhaps techniques from electroacoustic music composition could be applied? As we've been implying, the sound designer already does something like this – I would argue that a more conscious compositional intent can be utilised. In this respect, a view such as Chion's idea that there is 'no soundtrack' (Chion 1994, p. 40), that the sounds of film have no real coherence separate from the image, might be taken. Yet radiophonic works already show us how easily implied images are evoked through sound.

The sound designer has practical experience of these issues, and one thing that they share with acousmatics is the sonic imagination that liberates sound from its original context. In choosing sound sources for syncing they tend to proceed in 'reverse', not by deducing a sound source but by inducing it from a given sound. In *Star Wars*, in order to give the robot R2D2 a friendly nature, Ben Burtt mixed robotic bleeps and buzzes with recordings of himself whistling. This helps humanise and give warmth to the robot, it endears it to us. Burtt imagined what R2D2 could sound like. In treating a fictional creation, he had no real sound source for this robot, so he induced from 'whistling' the humanness that he wished to bestow upon it, and the machineness he induced from various bleeps and servomechanism sounds. Burtt, as arguably all sound designers do, listened imaginatively in his search for useful sounds. It could not be termed causal listening, although this mode can be applied to the finished sound sync. It could not be termed reduced listening although this could also be applied to the sound effect. In view of this, maybe one could propose an additional mode of listening, that of 'imaginary listening'.

Electronic music and film

For those readers unfamiliar with film-music terminology I will briefly introduce two terms that will help us throughout this discussion. When music is perceived as belonging to the narrative space in which the film action takes place, it is called *diegetic*. An example of this would be the music from a radio which we can see onscreen. By contrast, *non-diegetic* music, also known as *incidental*, is that which the film composer has created for the accompaniment of the image and runs parallel to the actual narrative we can see.

In the late 1920s an age of sound experimentation was dawning. Thanks to the introduction of sound in film, most of the early sonic experiments were actually being carried out in film soundstages. In the relationship between electronic music[4] and film, two trends have become evident. One is the use of electronic sounds to portray the psychology of the characters, the 'inner space' as it were. The other is their use to portray futuristic elements, and aliens, or outer space.

In Rouben Mamoulian's *Jekyll and Hyde* (1932), the sounds that accompany the appearance of the psychotic Mr Hyde could easily be found in later musique concrète. Reverberation, close microphony, backwards sounds and even 'artificial sounds created by photographing light frequencies directly onto the soundtrack' (Hayward 2004)[5] were used for this film. More illustrations of character psychology are found in later films such as Alfred Hitchcock's *The Lost Weekend* (1945) through the use of the Theremin. Although this instrument had been used earlier in Max Steiner's *King Kong* (1933) and Franz Waxman's *Bride of Frankenstein* (1935), the first movie in which the Theremin is really used as a main soloistic timbre was *The Day the Earth Stood Still* (1951).[6] And it is here that it acquires a new association, that of outer space.

The 1950s spawned an interesting repertoire of sci-fi films. The use of electronic instruments and sonorities increased as the post-war world became fascinated with notions of the atom and outer space (Taylor 2001). In sci-fi films, electronic music was allowed to flow easily between diegetic and non-diegetic roles (Leydon 2004; Wierzbicki 2005). This is evident in Louis and Bebe Barron's music for *The Bells of Atlantis* (1952) and later *Forbidden Planet* (1956), where incidental music and sound effects are born out of the same haunting electric tones.

It is worth at this point to trace the artistic thinking that allowed this development to take place. In the late 1940s, Oskar Fischinger, an experimental filmmaker, was advising John Cage that 'there is a spirit . . . inside each of the objects of this world . . . all we need to do to liberate that spirit is to brush past the object, and to draw forth its sound' (Nicholls 2002). Fischinger himself would experiment with the synchrony of sound and film and with the direct 'painting of sound' on film. This encounter between Cage and Fischinger would prove important, as Cage later employed Louis and Bebe Barron to prepare the tape material for *Williams Mix* (1951–2). Perhaps the actual compositional scheme used for the preparation of its sonic material owes much to this meeting (Pritchett 1996). Cage's experiments with indeterminacy and 'noise' would also reinforce the Barrons' own unprejudiced creative attitude in their 'studio composition' methods. Arguably, this also makes them figurative heirs to Fischinger, whose ideas reverberate through them, back onto film. In fact one can just imagine the historic crossroads at which the Barrons found themselves, as their work for Cage also meant that they would come into contact with Morton Feldman, Earle Brown, Christian Wolff and David Tudor through the 'Project of Music for Magnetic Tape' (Manning 1985; Bernstein 2002). The Barrons' studio was operational from 1948 and their first electronic composition *Heavenly Menagerie* (1951) also predated the work of the more famous 'Stüdio für Electronische Musik' at *Nordwestdeutscher Rundfunk* in Cologne in October 1951 (Leydon 2004).

By the time the Barrons received the workprint of *Forbidden Planet*, before Christmas 1955 (Wierzbicki 2005), a mature compositional voice was already in place to reach beyond film-music conventions. Their score was truly novel for the time and even today sounds futuristic and intriguing. An example of this is found in their depiction of romantic love between the male and female lead. It is unusual in sound and style (Leydon 2004; Wierzbicki 2005), setting itself apart from any known cinematic cliché at the time with the use of electronics to convey emotional warmth. The music for *Forbidden Planet* is closer to the avant-garde than it is to the music of the Hollywood studio system. But perhaps one could speculate that the approach of the Barrons, who would let a circuit burn down just to be able to record it (Leydon 2004), is closer to modern day experimental electronica.[7]

Rather like the UFO from the opening scene of *The Day The Earth Stood Still*, in becoming associated with the mass media distribution of film, electronic music and studio composition landed upon our collective consciousness. Filmmakers, radio producers and other creators of media have taken advantage of this and in so doing have enabled electronic sound to become a powerful signifier of all the things that seem to lie beyond our grasp.

Disembodied electronica in film

The most likely precursor to 'disembodied' electric sound creation is drawn sound.[8] This is achieved by actually drawing with ink on the film's optical soundtrack. When talkies were introduced in the late 1920s, the technology to 'print sound' on film became available. If you physically held the film to the light you could see the waveform of the sound printed on it within its own sidetrack to the visuals. In fact, until quite recently, even though you could already record sound to 35mm magnetic tape ('mag'), which would then be synced when editing the film, in order to be projected with the film, sound had to be 'developed' just like the film picture. This practice was still in vogue in the early 1990s and has mostly died out now thanks to the spread of the Dolby digital audio formats.

Even though the avant-garde scoring approach espoused by the Barrons didn't become widespread, there are a few interesting examples to recall at this point. One would be the electronic music score for Kurt Maetzig's *Silent Star* (1960), an East German and Polish production where composer Andrezeij Markowski provides both acoustic and electronic music. The former only graces the opening and closing of the film; the rest of this story about a mission to Venus is completely scored with electronic music. Synthesised sounds were produced in the *Experimentalstudio* at Polish Radio, playing the alternating role of non-diegetic music and ambient sound effect. The versatility of the sounds is truly breathtaking, at times simulating the decoding of an alien message found in a rock from the Gobi Desert and at other times simulating a storm on Venus. Every device on the Kosmokrator spaceship has a sound but also an 'alter sound', as is illustrated when radio communications with the moon space station and with other cosmonauts are accompanied by incidental sounds. It is sometimes impossible to know if what you hear is an effect or an incidental musical commentary on the action. This in part is due to the fact that the sounds used seem to bear no evidence of human effort or corporeality. *Solaris* (1972), a sci-fi film by Andrei Tarkovsky, features an electronic score by Eduard Artemiev which focuses on the creation of ambient sequences that colour the psychology of the characters as well as representing the sonic atmosphere inside a space station orbiting the planet Solaris. In a theme reminiscent of *Forbidden Planet*'s 'monster from the Id', the fears and longings of the characters are made reality and pose all sorts of problems, driving the scientists to near madness. Even though in certain moments of the film, the F minor *Chorale Prelude* by J. S. Bach is used, traditional music with its gestural evidence of human action is less apt than the studio manipulations of sound to represent the world of the space station.

The approach to film music which we have discussed can further be explained by the imaginary listening mode proposed earlier; sonic representations of the unknown require speculation. In the tradition of illustrating mind processes through sound, in *Apocalypse Now* (1979), Walter Murch has the sound of a helicopter match the image of a ceiling fan. Through imaginary listening, the helicopter rotor is believable as a hyperreal ceiling fan and this tricks the audience into a false sense of confidence which is disrupted as the actual helicopters come on screen. Through creating possible imagined sounds, the sound designer can influence the audience's perception of the size or proximity of an object. They can add a layer of emotion that was previously lacking, create immaterial objects which the audience believes it is about to see and make the invisible believable by virtue of its sonic footprint.

In the 1970s sound designers became recognised in their own right, as seen in the work of Ben Burtt for *Star Wars* and later Walter Murch with his Oscar for the sound of *Apocalypse Now*. The term 'sound designer' as it is used today was actually coined by Burtt. Although his contributions remain firmly in the diegetic or narrative domain, the atmospheric overtones of his sound mixes help impregnate the film soundtrack with new meanings. A true virtuoso of imaginary listening, Burtt devised his now famous laser-gun sounds for *Star Wars* by recording a guy-wire from a radio tower in the Mojave desert. Having been out hiking in the Pocono mountains, his backpack got caught on one of these wires when walking under a tower and the 'twang' it made when released 'had an otherworldly sound to it'.[9] He immediately thought it was perfect for a laser-gun sound, and set about testing the guy-wires of many different radio towers until he found the best one. Burtt called himself a 'sound designer' on the strength of his involvement with film sound at all levels (recording, editing and mixing), but it could be argued that his contribution to the narrative through the creation of synthesised sound worlds is closer to electronic music than it is to foley-walking.[10]

Instrumental electronica in films

The use of electronic instruments in film scoring has, arguably, just extended the orchestral palette without making any real impact on the musical language itself. Film music in the tradition of *The Day the Earth Stood Still* is only quantitatively different from, say, *Clockwork Orange* (1971) with its all-electronic orchestration by Walter Carlos.[11] In these films, it is rather a question of how much of an 'orchestral' role is taken on by electronic instruments. We might agree with Cage's attitude to the Theremin as portrayed in the quotation in chapter 3.

After the initial use of electronic instruments as an addition to the film orchestra, the next important development was to use them as a substitute for the orchestra itself. From John Carpenter's soundtracks for his own films, to Hollywood blockbusters such as *Beverly Hills Cop* (1984) and its *Axel F* theme tune by Harold Faltermeyer, electronic instrumentation lends both a 'modern' sound, but also, conveniently saves the expense of performers' buyouts or royalties. With the introduction of MIDI instruments and computer sequencing, an arguable 'deregulation' of film music production ensued.[12] Advances in sampling instruments and the sampling of orchestral film clichés, such as can be found in many popular sound libraries today, have also contributed to the use of electronic scores. Most contemporary orchestral movie scores start at a computer sequencer. A fine recent excellent example of combining both electronica instrumentality and the disembodied sounds of the studio is in the soundtrack to the psychotic process that the character Max Cohen undergoes in the independent film π (1997) by Darren Aronofsky (composed by Clint Mansell). Here the electronic sound world illustrates the psychology of the character but also the technology that surrounds him and his scientific elaborations.

Electronic music on TV

Although Raymond Scott (1908–94) is far from being a well-known electronic music composer in the mass media, his name should rank among those of Schaeffer, Stockhausen *et al.* Although a neglected pioneer of electronic music, his 1946 patent disclosure for an 'orchestra machine' must surely be the first description of a sampling instrument. Equally concerned with composition and sound luthierie, Scott designed and built several new electronic instruments which he used for scoring his commercials and orchestrating his jingles, including the first sequencer (mid-50s), the *Clavivox* keyboard (1960), a rhythm machine called *Bandito the bongo artist* (1968) and an algorithmic composing machine without a music keyboard called the *Electronium* (late 50s). Scott was truly ahead of his time in using electronic instruments and sequencers for commercials. Perhaps he has been overlooked by many academics to this day on the grounds of being too involved with the commercial world. What he accomplished in compositional studio work in the late 1950s and 60s only became widespread practice in music for media by the mid-80s. Partly this is due to Scott wanting to protect the exclusive use of his inventions, confound his competitors, and so ensure his financial success. Just a provocative pause here . . . how much electroacoustic music would have been written since the 1940s if its survival had depended on audiences paying to listen to it? Or buying the recordings?[13]

As we have discussed earlier, electronic music had become strongly clichéd when used to accompany visuals, always illustrating psychotic states or alien beings. When incorporating electronica into commercials Scott helped widen the perceived emotional scope of electronic sounds. In 1960, in his commercial *Vicks: Medicated Cough Drops*, a straightforward jingle is entirely made of electronic sounds including a programmed rhythm track. The music here does not allude to any kind of altered state or outer-space imagery; the electronics make instrumental sounds that resemble a Hammond organ, except that the rhythm track is programmed and the sounds are sequenced by a machine which would eventually become the *Electronium* in the late 1960s. Scott nicknamed it the *Karloff*,[14] but one of his employees suggested it should be called the *Audimation* since it seemed to do for audio what cell animation did for pictures. The Vicks commercial was, according to Scott himself[15] (and nobody has claimed otherwise), the first commercial to use electronics. The ad executives from New York's famous Madison Avenue needed a distinctive sound, something that would be different and set the product apart. In the process they contributed to the history of electronic music by broadcasting the first electronic music made with a sequencer. Other electronic music commercials would follow, such as the 'lounge' styled *Lightworks*, the futuristic *Bendix 1: the Tomorrow People*, or the rhythmic piece made with bean shaking sounds for Nescafé. Scott also scored industrial films such as his *IBM MT/St The Paperwork Explosion*, as well as experimental films such as *Limbo: The Organized Mind* by puppeteer and animator Jim Henson.[16]

Music in advertising truly reaped the rewards, creative and financial, of Scott's contribution around the mid-80s when tracks could be easily produced in MIDI studios and overlayed with vocals and acoustic instruments on tape synchronised with 'SMPTE' timecode.[17] The advent of available consumer sampling instruments, such as the *S900* by AKAI, made it even easier to substitute live players for sampled versions of musical instruments. The workflow of creating music for commercials was still complicated though, as SMPTE had to be read off video tape and converted into MIDI in order to drive the sequencer (software or hardware). It was not until the widespread use of Apple's *QuickTime* video format in the late 1990s that issues of synchronisation ceased to be a problem for media composers. Computer software sequencers during this time began to allow QuickTime files to run concurrently with the music. It finally became possible to do on a desktop computer what Scott did in the late 1950s when using his *Videola* invention. He could compose music synchronised directly to film by controlling the transport of a remote machine from his keyboard, which projected film onto a small TV-like screen as he played and recorded his piano and electronic instruments.

One of the consequences of music for audiovisual pieces being created on desktop computers has been the increased use of electronic music to accompany moving images. Three aesthetic strands seem to have developed from this. Firstly, a 'natural' aesthetic: acoustic music is recorded, produced and edited on digital systems and a virtual performance of the piece is arranged and mixed to suit the visuals. Most acoustic film music is made like this. Secondly, a 'synthesis' aesthetic: music which owes its discourse to traditional musical forms but is made with electronic instruments. Works like *Blade Runner*, *Chariots of Fire*, Carlos's *Clockwork Orange* or Mansell's π fall into this category. Thirdly, an 'organised sound' (to paraphrase Varèse) aesthetic: music which is structured around *sound objects* and their development, without necessary reference to melody or harmony. Works like *Forbidden Planet* by the Barrons and *Silent Star* by Andrezeij Markowski are examples of this. In so far as *soundscapes* are created by sound designers without a 'one-to-one' relationship with the visuals, these also fall in this category as they illustrate the narrative musically. Examples of this are also found in Mansell's music for π, and in much of *Blade Runner*'s atmospheric sequences.

In the medium of commercials, the composer is nowadays expected to provide electroacoustic sound textures as necessary, either in addition to or as the unique element of the soundtrack. In this case, the formal issues of acousmatic music come into play with the added apparent contradiction of having to adapt to actual images, thus negating the initial acousmatic nature of the music. Initiated also by the work of Raymond Scott in the 1950s, and perhaps best illustrated by pieces such as *GMGM 1A*, part of his *Futurama* commercials for General Motors,[18] this trend has spread widely and is found almost continually in music for commercials. The term 'sound designer' is true here not only in the sense that Ben Burtt intended but also in the wider sense that we have been attributing to it throughout this chapter, namely that all sound, diegetic and non-diegetic, should be organised musically.

Electronic music and games

Electronic music and video games are natural partners. Video games reach their audience in a personalised and unique way, and in no small measure thanks to the sound and the music – both of which, if not electronic in source, will be electronic in processing, rendering and realtime arranging. The intention here is to recognise the importance of video games as a new form of media and to inform the reader on some of the basics of this fascinating field, without any claims to exhaustiveness.[19] We do not intend to provide here a comprehensive description of video games and their different types, but rather to discuss how they interact with electronic music and sound. There are also whole trends of electronica spawned from the aesthetics of game sound, forming another fast-growing area of musical interest.

Although there are a few early instances of using cathode ray tubes (CRT) for projecting games graphics, video games proper are those developed for raster video equipment such as TV sets or computer monitors and consoles that connect to them. And it is with the appearance of the latter that electronic sound began to be used. The first video game to include sound was named as a pun on the real-life game that inspired it. In 1972 'Pong', by Atari,[20] quickly became a mass phenomenon as young people across the US queued outside bars waiting for their turn to play the arcade version. The very naming of this game illustrated the dynamic relationship that would ensue between video games and electronic music: that music is firstly a means of aural feedback to the gamer, indicating his success or failure. And secondly, but not least important, it becomes a mood setter rendering the psychology of the game in sound.

The diegesis of games is in the progression through the game world, and here is where games offer a different challenge for electronic music composers from that encountered in other media: namely, that a composer must write music whose final structure will be determined by the gamer. There have been three main technological approaches for producing audio and music in games. Soundcard synths which can be played/controlled by the game via MIDI and pre-structured into tracks by using sequencer software; *redbook* audio which consists of streaming complete recorded tracks from a CD; and digital modules or *MODs* which are similar to redbook audio but closer to a sampling instrument.[21] Early games used electronic sounds programmed by the software designers working on them, but as the computing power of video games improved, the music made for them became more sophisticated.

Space Invaders (1978) by Toshihiro Nishikado[22] was the first game to have continuous music; it was available as an arcade game and later on such TV set-top boxes as the Mattel Intellivison console, and also had sound effects. The level of interactivity was quite low but nevertheless it was there: the tempo of the music accelerated as the player improved his score; a simple yet effective way of increasing tension and excitement throughout the game.

Early arcade games included simple fanfare tunes to announce the start and end of the game. In this sense the music was a branding tool. Some games also provided 'cut scenes' or interludes in which the players could watch a little audiovisual display intended as a reward for moving on to another level[23] (Collins 2004). Still to this day, interludes are inserted at points where it may be necessary to articulate the narrative or simply to give the computing engine the time to load the next sections of data required for the game to proceed (Wolf 2002). In games like *Myst* (1993) this is accomplished with sound effects and fade-outs when moving between 'ages'. As the game is itself so sedate, these pauses do not seem strange to the player and preserve the continuity of the game experience. In more recent games such as *Tomb Raider: Legend* (2006), video interludes are necessary for the story of the game to unfold and to give the player her next assignment within the game.

The music that was possible on the early games was very primitive in terms of sound generation, as the composer would at most be able to play one or two simultaneous voices. The music for *Space Invaders* gives a good idea of what this sounded like.[24] The quality of the sound was rather low, but as often happens, this very limitation eventually gave it a sort of 'cult' status. The use of 8-bit computing later became the inspiration for styles such as *clip-hop*, *micromusic* or *chiptunes* and other trends of *lo-fi* in electronica. Today, artists such as Bit Shifter, Bubblyfish, Random and Covox, who create their music using Nintendo *Gameboy* mini consoles or other hand-held or retro technologies, represent the creative dynamism of this trend. Today, synthesiser/sequencer/tracker programs, such as *nanoloop*[25] for the gameboy, potentially allow anybody to get into the video game-inspired music scene. In fact most 'flagship' sequencers now bring noise-adding, bit-downgrading plugins to achieve 'vintage' lo-fi sound.

In the early 1980s, *Defender* (1980) and *Donkey Kong* (1981) helped establish the sound we typically associate with video games. By the mid-80s the use of MIDI sequencers began to spread, as did FM synthesis (Frequency Modulation allowed more complex sounds to be produced with the same computing power; see chapter 11). The use of sound modules such as the *Roland MT32* allowed for fuller orchestration of MIDI soundtracks for video games. Nevertheless, the quality of the music often tended to be rather mechanical and 'gamey', although very catchy, as exemplified by the music for *Super Mario Brothers* (1985). In the 1990s, with the advent of the CD-ROM, full quality sound could be streamed during the game. This was good for quality but not so good for interactivity, as the more pre-recorded the music was, the fewer variations became possible. As the 90s progressed, the technology became capable of both streaming high-quality audio and providing for interactivity. In the early 2000s, games such as *Donkey Conga* combined interactivity and high quality sound.

Audio interactivity in some modern games can be viewed as an extension of algorithmic composition and generative music techniques (chapters 5 and 6 in particular deal more comprehensively with these subjects). In the context of games, this is often dubbed *adaptive* music: the musical structure is selected depending on the player's actions.[26] This interactive audio for games helps to endow characters with emotions, adding depth of sentiment to the playing experience (Eladhari *et al.* 2006). Abundant examples are found in recent games: *Legend of Zelda: Ocarina of Time* requires the player to interact by performing musical tasks; adaptive audio techniques have found their way into games such as *Lara Croft/Tomb Raider: Legend*,[27] signalling greater levels of musical interactivity in games.

The adaptive audio technique used in *Tomb Raider*, though not so effective in the 'chase' sequences, is very clear when Lara has to try and rescue some friends in an underground complex of tunnels. As she runs, jumps and hangs from every available handle in order to traverse the tunnels, the orchestral music offers an ever-changing rendition of its melodic elements. The music relies heavily on frequent changes of metre and slight changes of harmonic emphasis. The result is pleasing and exciting. As Lara's manoeuvres control new renderings of musical combinations, a potential for new forms that defy old compositional logics can be glimpsed.

From the compositional point of view the goal of creating game music which does not repeat but is continuous throughout the game is indeed a challenge, yet from an aesthetic point of view, the emphasis on repetition (Grodal 2003) is clearly a poietic element shared with many forms of electronica; as the rise and development of the latter has been parallel to that of video games, one cannot help but wonder whether an emphasis on hypnotic repetitiveness is indeed the result of a cross-fertilisation. The association between games and electronica was acknowledged 'officially' in 1995 when Sony released the game *WipEout* including tracks by *Orbital*, *Leftfield* and *Chemical Brothers*, and when they later installed a Playstation room at the Ministry of Sound club in London (Poole 2000).

Rather like algorithmic music itself, video-game music will continue to surprise us with increasing structural flexibility, high sound quality and the possibility for a set of rules to create many valid renditions from similar raw material. Other electronic and electroacoustic music trends should benefit from this as they take their cue from video games when adopting their road-tested multimedia techniques. Finally, the limitations of game sound are and will continue to provide aesthetic challenges which create virtue out of necessity; for instance, finding aesthetic beauty in the imperfection of lo-fi.

Future media?

Although it is not possible for reasons of space to go further into other trends, it is worth mentioning some new directions. An exciting area in electronica to watch for will be the interaction with video games and video game-like environments: as technologies for machine listening and algorithmic music develop, ever more subtle reactions to visuals can be planned by composers. As visual worlds become alive in synthesised 3D environments, so does the soundscape that accompanies them. This means that composers of music for media will now need to become more computer-literate than ever before; the new film orchestra will demand a healthy dose of programming.

As connection speeds increase, the 'live' interaction with the internet will require more creative ways of using sound and music to enhance the experience; innovative mappings between sound and vision (Collins and Olofsson 2006) will become enabled by greater literacy of software tools. Interactive cinema will ask for new musical responses and solutions from composers, probably in a way that is closer to video games; composing for film will increasingly make use of algorithmic techniques (Rohrhuber 2007). Generative techniques in both video and audio will probably become more popular in advertising and communication: 'master' messages may be re-cut on succesive deliveries, to continually present fresh perspectives for the same idea. Mobile telephony, now audiovisual, will continue to present new challenges for composers and sound designers; musical ideas will populate future portable media.

As we have seen, electronic music has become inseparable from the visual arts. In our urban and networked life we are surrounded by media which in turn are made alive by the sounds of electronic music. In film and TV, electronic music was born out of the technology that makes it possible for the image to move: this parentage ensures a fruitful relationship of which we have witnessed only the beginning. Sound design is becoming, increasingly, a more musical activity than previously thought. Electronic music instruments have found their 'desk' in the film orchestra. The Theremin has always enjoyed a presence in pop music, and perhaps looks to become a 'traditional' instrument. Synthesisers and samplers are more common than pianos in any music studio: they are also found in ensembles for almost every musical style one can think of.

Audiences who would not step into an acousmatic music concert are quite happy to enjoy the same electroacoustic sounds when they appear on screen in films such as *Bladerunner* or the *Terminator* series. Perhaps youngsters who have never heard Stravinsky's *Rite of Spring* (1913) are now ready to enjoy it, as Lara Croft has introduced them to polyrhythm and extended harmony; though they might demand that they interactively explore it, with a 3D animated orchestra and incidental visuals, such that it is never heard the same way twice.

10 Musical robots and listening machines

NICK COLLINS

Imagine being enraptured at the performance of a hotly tipped band, 'The Alan Turing Five', an epic fusion of thrash drumming, vocoded belting and virtuosic three-fingered guitar playing evoking a longing for a bygone age. Yet after the show, an ugly rumour spreads amongst the audience that even leads once-satisfied punters to demand their money back. All the personalities you observed on stage were really robot simulacra; no wonder they played so fast!

Is this tale so far-fetched? The work of the great French engineer Vaucanson was introduced in chapter 1 – a modern-day version of his 1738 flute-playing automaton has been designed by researchers at Waseda University, Japan. Their *Waseda Flutist Robot* aims to reproduce 'as realistically as possible, every single human organ involved in playing the flute' (Solis *et al.* 2006, p. 13). Although aspects of this project formulate an acoustical enquiry, the musical applications are not forsaken: the robot has performed duets with human flautists. Indeed, this is only one of a number of such robots produced since the 1980s, and a second musical robot will be featured later in this chapter. Robotics is a boom area of the current generation, particularly in Japan, and *androids* (humanoid robots) are even being given soft silicone skin and affective (emotional) responses. Media coverage of the 2006 International Next-Generation Robot Fair actively portrayed such uncannily realistic simulations, including the scarily lifelike *Repliee Q2*, an android interviewer.[1]

A cultural fascination with the machine existed far before the industrial revolution, though it has no doubt been intensified in the high-tech age. Automata can be traced to antiquity and the writings of Aristotle. In music, a fascinating history of machines and formalisms includes d'Arezzo's table lookup procedure for setting texts to melody (*c.* 1030), the first computational memory devices (thirteenth-century nine-thousand-hole carillons from the Netherlands), musical dice games (see chapter 6) and Ada Lovelace's prescient description of the application of the Analytical Engine to musical composition (Roads 1985, 1996; chapters 1 and 4). The fictional anticipations of artificial intelligence are also wide ranging, from the Golem myth and Shelley's Frankenstein's Monster to the introduction of the Czech term robot (from *robota*, to work) in Karel Capek's play *Rossum's Universal Robots* (1921). Indeed, robots, in the guise of the Man-Machine of Fritz

Lang's *Metropolis* (1927), appeared as a major preoccupation of Kraftwerk, not least associated with their *Man-Machine* album of 1978, and live theatrics with mechanical mannequins for performances of the song 'The Robots'. The current age sees a proliferation of cyborgs, robot orchestras and software composing machines.

There are further anticipations of autonomous creations in the virtual characters who populate computer games and computer-animated movies. In one entertaining trend, virtual bands have achieved chart success as the front for human musicians, the most recognised being the Gorillaz, but precedents exist from Alvin and the Chipmunks (1958) to the Japanese virtual idols, 3D animated pop singers with their own cult followings. Nevertheless, the backing musicians in such ventures have remained resolutely human: no one has yet exhibited a band of fully automated computerised musicians that can equal the scope of human musical activity. When we investigate the current musicianship of artificial musicians, they turn out to be far less skilled than their human counterparts, and this chapter shall reveal a few reasons why this is so.

Without wishing to denigrate the compositions, many historical performances in electronic music have been somewhat inflexible. Works for tape and soloist (like Javier Alvarez's *Papalotl* (1987) for piano and tape), whilst demonstrating great craft in the tape parts and great excitement when soloists can accommodate the demands, do enforce a certain rigidity out of keeping with conventional music-making; tape cannot yield an inch. A more pragmatic approach much used in current work is the live cueing of material by a human director. For instance, cues might be indicated from a MIDI keyboard, triggering complex processing mechanisms and event sequences. We shall later discuss accompaniment systems that seek to automate this playback further, given a known score. But electronic music must also be prepared to deal with improvised, spontaneous situations, and here the ability of machines to tread on an equal footing with humans is curtailed; there is no score for cueing or for more sophisticated accompaniment systems. We would like to take advantage of the many novel processing and generational capabilities that machines can offer, without compromising the sense of co-ordinated musical behaviour key to instrumental practice. The onus is upon the machines to be brought nearer to our musical practices, to instil a sense of what Robert Rowe terms *machine musicianship* (Rowe 2001).

Because such tasks quickly bring us to the fields of artificial intelligence and the cognition of music, the reader should not be too surprised to hear that they are unsolved problems. Engaging with music is a high-level cognitive task which stretches the resources of the brain.[2] The level of artificial intelligence achievable by engineering is hotly contested and debated by philosophers and scientists. Yet, we don't always have to seek substitutes for human brains and bodies; many fascinating new musical applications have been offshoots from the attempt, from the consequences of AI technology. Not all musical machines have to be androids, to act the same way and think somehow the same way as human beings, and many just exist as curious and fascinating software programs.

In treating such issues, authors have characterised their work in a variety of ways, as providing some form of interactive companionship (Thom 2003), self-reflexive music-making (Pachet 2003), as designing settings for novel improvisation (Lewis 1999), or as providing toolkits for machine musicianship (Rowe 1993, 2001) which might potentially support many varieties of performance situation. In this chapter we shall follow Robert Rowe in the use of the term *interactive music systems* to describe artificial non-human participants in musical discourse.[3] It is helpful to remember that all such systems are devised and built by humans, so even if their creators defer real-time interaction to their creations, these systems are not devoid of human spirit; they show exactly those assumptions that their makers have managed to program into them.

Four interactive improvisation systems

In order to reveal some of the principles at work in the practical construction of interactive music systems, four examples are discussed here. The selection is in no means meant to be definitive, but illustrative of the wider efforts of such creators as Robert Rowe (*Cypher*), Peter Beyl (*Oscar*), Belinda Thom, Jonathan Impett and others. Interest in this field is burgeoning, with the availability of realtime machine listening plugins for such environments as Max/MSP or SuperCollider, and organisations such as Live Algorithms for Music in the UK, or the artbots network in New York.

As suggested above, perhaps the greatest challenge in interaction terms is exemplified by systems built especially for co-improvisation with a human musician, from scratch. Improvisation is a ubiquitous practice in musical culture, providing an important sense of location in space and time for each performance essential to constant challenge and renewal for performers, and participation and communion for audiences (Bailey 1980). The four systems described here are unified by an ability to start from a blank slate in performance, and whilst this does not mean they are free of assumptions about what might happen, they should ideally allow immediate interaction. Yet they also demonstrate a variety of thinking on interactive systems. Whilst none of these four systems is available at the time of writing for public evaluation of their source code and interaction, they are all documented in videos, recordings, academic papers and most importantly of all, live concerts.

Voyager

George Lewis is an experienced improviser whose personal *Voyager* software (Chadabe 1997; Lewis 1999, 2000) tracks his trombone playing (through a pitch to MIDI convertor) and generates responses. The software was first written in Forth from 1986–8 and was subsequently extended through thousands of lines of code; it has been recently converted into a (large) Max/MSP patch. Voyager is a massive construction, devised to provide unanticipated responses and extremely abstract mappings through a 'state-based' parametrical rather than directly motif tracking approach to improvisational form (Lewis 1999, p. 105). States consist of such aspects as the current tuning system and melody-generating function for each of multiple voices. These states are cued by recent input parameter fields: Lewis calculates a set of statistics from the pitch-time distribution of input material, on a number of time-scales. The character of output can vary tremendously based on the emergent properties of the many simultaneously playing voices of the system, driving a MIDI synthesiser or Disklavier.

In a radio interview[4] Lewis described the system's multiplicity of outputs, the 'many different foregrounds vying for attention', how he had programmed 'rapid changes in timbre, multiple metres, multiple keys, multiple tonalities: there's a lot of information there.' The wilful independence of the software is part of his non-hierarchical improvisational aesthetic: 'I don't want to be in charge and I don't want anyone else to be in charge.' He contends that all interactive music systems must necessarily reflect the attitudes of their creators: 'Everyone's machine expresses their aesthetic view.' The Voyager system is a great exemplar of a highly subjective system, intimately expressing its programmer's personality, loaded with enough complexity to guarantee stimulating interactions.

The Continuator

In the last few years, François Pachet has demonstrated that many of the same processes that paid off well for David Cope's *Experiments in Musical Intelligence* algorithmic composition project can be directed to a responsive improvisation system. The *Continuator* (Pachet 2003) runs using a MIDI piano and a laptop, in a call-and-response fashion. Assumptions of style (outside the standard MIDI note representation) are not made; the system attempts to learn 'online' as it runs, constructing a special data structure from all the input material presented to it. Demonstrating a pattern matching process, a collection of chains of pitches is formed from input successions and adjacencies of notes. This allows varied responses to be made by reading back portions of this same data set; the Continuator searches for appropriate 'continuations' given any starting pitch or subsequence.

Pachet himself refers to the system as providing 'reflexive' rather than 'flexible' interactions, its chief role being that of a mirror through which the user confronts their own output, as analysed and echoed by the particular Markovian processes. What musical knowledge it has is implicit in the treatment of the input tokens in the Markovian deconstruction, so that it is fundamentally parasitic on the duration data passed to it. For the case of MIDI piano music, Pachet has constructed a relatively broad system, particularly for short-term pitch material, though one which has difficulty with longer-term structure and with more refined metrical frameworks and anticipation. For instance, there are discontinuities at the moment of handover between call and response observable in Pachet's demonstration videos. The system passed a musical Turing test (can you tell the computer from the human player?) for two expert listeners run by a radio station. Yet this is not so surprising since the output material maintains the same rates and densities as the input, as well as the same timbral base on a MIDI piano, and there was no substantial test of rhythmic (particularly synchronising) ability.

Acknowledging the Turing test for listeners as less indicative of the system's scope, Pachet is more interested in evaluating the effect of the system on its users, especially the investment of time that such a system can solicit. In particular he has explored the level of attention young children give who confront the system; its ability to respond without exact repetition captured their interest far more than simpler interaction modes (Addessi *et al.* 2004). This suggests that the continued interest of human musicians who engage with the machine, and the system's capacity to match a raising of skill level with appropriate further challenge, may form appropriate evaluatory criteria for interactive music systems. Is there any desire to follow up your work with a system? Would you play another concert with it, and invest more time practising with it?

William Hsu's system

A recent collaboration between the saxophonist John Butcher and the computer improviser William Hsu (Hsu 2005, 2006) recognises the importance of the timbral properties of Butcher's playing. Whilst also treating pitch and timing data, Hsu allows for the conveyance of musical information through timbral variation, for example during the course of a long-held note of stable pitch and loudness where the performer increases the perceptual roughness of the tone by embouchure control. The analysis front-end

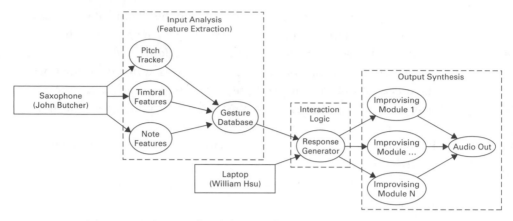

Figure 10.1 A schematic of Hsu's system

of his software records timbral fields including such parameters as noisiness, inharmonicity of partials, sharpness of attack, the presence of multiphonics, amplitude modulation (tremolo or flutter) and auditory roughness. This project is an example of the current trend towards founding systems on such audio analysis. The system does not necessarily extract 'notes' as such, but works upon implicit timbral streams, because in non-idiomatic improvisation discrete events are often rather ambiguous, and more continuous data representations are helpful for analysis and resynthesis.

Figure 10.1 gives an overview of processing and control in the system. The diagram is necessarily simplified, for it would be impossible to show all the interconnections of the programming. Further, important feedback loops from the system output to the most complex modules in the diagram, the human beings themselves (and between those participants), are not shown. Hsu's system is semi-autonomous, in that the human operator can step in to make high-level redirections (such as activating modules, setting parameter mappings, and linking modules), but the system may also operate on auto-pilot. In the latter mode, a set of compositional agents generates responses by transformations of material from a database of captured gestures; the transformed parameter data controls various timbrally rich synthesis models.

As timbre is an important element of Butcher's playing, the system is well attuned to the needs of the interaction, and indeed, was developed in close collaboration with the performer. Such partnerships are an important part of the design cycle between composer-programmers and acoustic musicians, exemplified in improvisation by the work of Joel Ryan with Evan Parker, or David Wessel and Roscoe Mitchell, amongst others. Hsu's system certainly makes possible novel interactions and timbral transformations that would not have been discovered without its construction and deployment.

Haile the Robotic Drummer

Many musical robots have been constructed in recent decades, including the *Wabot-2* score-reading and keyboard-playing robot (completed 1984) (Roads 1996), Godfried-Willem Raes' *Automatons*,[5] the New York-based *LEMUR* project (League of Electronic Musical Urban Robots),[6] MIT's *COG*,[7] which can engage in rudimentary drum tasks, and recently, the more accomplished *Haile the Robotic Drummer* from Georgia Tech, which shares a Native American Pow-Wow drum with a human partner (Weinberg and Driscoll 2006).

An important aspect of the Haile project is the actual physical embodiment of the robot,[8] which has a real (rather than computer-locked virtual) presence in the room, and produces sound through an acoustic instrument, the multi-player drum, rather than a loudspeaker. Weinberg and Driscoll (2006b) argue that this brings 'perceptual aspects of computer music into the world both visually and acoustically' whilst retaining the advantages of 'real-time analysis and response algorithms' which humans cannot calculate.

Haile can mechanically strike the drum up to fifteen times a second, whilst human percussionists are restricted to around 10Hz. The current model has a single arm, which can move across the surface of the drum to choose striking areas, and control the energy and timing of strikes with a modified solenoid-based piano-like action.

The creators of Haile have set up a number of different interactional modes, from simplistic imposition of a clock and a call-and-response structure, to more involved beat-tracking collaboration. In a short piece developed by the authors for the system, Haile plays in a trio with two human percussionists, listening to the aggregate rhythms on the drum, and responding to material via its analyses of activity.

Haile is prescient of future systems which may seek a human-like presence on stage, coupled to human-like perceptual and cognitive abilities. Whilst the extent to which human intelligence is dependent on our experience of the body remains an open issue in artificial intelligence, such physically grounded work is likely to provide fascinating insights into musical behaviours, and novel musical interactions.

Music understanding and machine representations

Because music-making can seem so natural at the time of playing, we often forget how many hours of practice lead up to such ability. By definition, we do not have conscious access to procedures we have automatised! Although basic musicianship is taken for granted, there are open questions concerning how to simulate similar abilities by machine, a product of the difficulty of introspecting on such procedures, and the general problem of translating cognitive tasks to computer formalisms. Whilst there is no restriction to follow the same biological mechanisms that underpin human musicianship (unless we should seek scientific models of these phenomena), knowledge of human auditory, motor and cognitive operations often influences research in this area. In many cases, humans provide the only 'existence proof' or 'proof of concept' we have of musical abilities which we are far from emulating well by machine.

Thus, work in this area can involve a fundamental interaction with the psychology of music (see chapter 12), and the composer-engineer is also a musician, acoustician, psychologist and auditory neuroscientist. Researchers at the MIT Media Lab named the simulation of human musical abilities *Machine Listening* though it has also been called *Music Understanding* or *Intelligent Signal Processing*, amongst other terms.

Modelling musical behaviour forces the formalisation of what has previously held many intuitive aspects. Yet there have been various historical attempts by music theoreticians to systematise counterpoint and the rules of harmony, and composers have engaged with formalisms particularly in the twentieth century (the archetypical example being serialism; see chapter 6). The field of *music representation* (Dannenberg 1993; Honing 1993) deals with how best to describe musical concepts within those general-purpose modelling tools ubiquitous in modern investigation – computers. Since we have to spell out in explicit detail everything we wish computers to do, we are forced to deal with music representation whenever we program.

An important aspect of music representation, which parallels a historical problem in artificial intelligence, is the clash of *symbolic* and *sub-symbolic*. Symbolic systems manipulate very explicit discrete entities, typically dealing with events like 'notes'; the MIDI specification provides an example of such a formalism. Sub-symbolic processes, typically continuous low-level audio signals, model 'the inarticulate aspects of musical activity' (Toiviainen 2000); examples might be the continuous sensor data from a joystick controller, or the stream of audio data from recording with a microphone. In this case, events are implicit, probabilistically implied but not demarcated precisely by the data.[9] The separation of symbolic and sub-symbolic became obvious in 1990s sequencer software, which combined audio and MIDI tracks; all users are aware of the difference between the types when editing these sorts of layers in their mixes.

In practice, we do tend to see a progression from low-level data-crunching to higher-level explicit symbolic object manipulation. There is a gain in abstraction as you move further from the audio signal, usually exemplified by a reduction in data rate, from sample frames to sound objects.[10] An important compromise is 'hybrid' systems (Camurri and Leman 1997) which combine both symbolic and sub-symbolic layers in a single system with multiple levels of representation. These layers may interact in complex ways, both bottom-up and top-down, the bottom being the low-level high sample rate data, and the top the high-level low sample rate data. Whilst some entirely MIDI-based systems can sidestep such issues, accepting the note representation de facto, all interactive music systems demand a choice of representation, even if their designers are not fully aware of the consequences of these issues.

An example of a hybrid system is Camurri and colleagues' own interactive multimedia system, for which their visual tracking *EyesWeb* software[11] is employed to follow dancers as well as musicians, demonstrating the combination of audio and visual signal-processing as well as higher-level compositional decisions. Of the four improvisation systems above, the Continuator is entirely symbolic, just using MIDI. Voyager uses a pitch-to-MIDI converter to quickly move from the audio signal to a more manageable MIDI representation. Hsu's system is very much founded on various low-level audio features, with some symbolic logic to control the routing and use of these signals. Haile also operates on audio, though there is necessarily some symbolic reasoning in order to schedule mechanical strikes of the drum; most audio-based systems which go beyond being fancy audio-processing effects are hybrid.

Machine listening techniques

An essential capability of systems that seek to interact with human musicians is to parse the flow of sound data in time and make good musical sense of it. A number of procedures for computationally extracting musical information from audio signals have been developed. This is an active area of current research, with an engineering literature too wide to cite anything but a few entry points here. Some representative tasks, varying in level from attributes of sound objects to more abstract musical constructs, are given in Table 10.1, along with some tutorial references for the interested reader who wishes to pursue this.

There are also symbolic versions of many of these tasks, such as for key-finding or beat-tracking on MIDI data (Roads 1996; Rowe 2001), which tend to be more easily solved. Though some authors have cast audio-based analysis solely as a front-end to the extraction of symbolic entities for symbolic algorithms, such a representation is not always available or suitable. Players can be forced to use MIDI-enabled instruments, or sensors will

Table 10.1 *Example machine listening tasks*

Technique	Description	Example tutorial reference
Onset detection	Isolate physical sound onset; segment, extract note objects	(Bello *et al.* 2004)
Pitch detection	Follow fundamental frequency (f0)	(Roads 1996; Gómez *et al.* 2003)
Timbral features	Characterisation of sounds	(Herrera-Boyer *et al.* 2003)
Harmony detection	Extract musical chords/key	(Gómez 2006)
Beat tracking	Follow metrical structure and predict temporal location	(Gouyon and Dixon 2005)
Melody extraction	Longer-scale isolation of a melodic phrase	(Gómez *et al.* 2003)
Polyphonic analysis	More involved transcription of multiple voices; multiple f0 estimation	(Klapuri 2004)

discretise data, even though this is sometimes incommensurate with the fine detail of expressive variations.

Pure audio signals provide many challenges. Human perception is active, in that high-level attention can mediate low-level detection, quickly involving complexities of human cognition in seemingly straightforward tasks. Furthermore, there are interdependencies between the tasks, which can even necessitate the co-estimation of features. Pitch detection might require onset detection to avoid registering a wild pitch estimate during the noisy initial transient of a note. Onsets might be detected by working backwards from the cue of a stable pitch, the beginning of vibrato or another timbral factor, or indeed, some combination of cues, learnt by familiarity with cultural and environmental mores. All this makes tasks that appear simple more complex, even before the additional difficulties of complex auditory scenes are raised. In polyphonic music, psychological factors of streaming and auditory scene analysis begin to rear their difficult heads (see chapter 12).

As applied to interactive music systems, these techniques can vary in their efficacy based on the challenges of different instrumental timbres, the room acoustics and close miking of instruments for isolation, and the players and musical styles themselves. Specialisation to particular situations is often necessary to avoid a high number of misdetections. This can require system designers to build their own variants of detectors for particular concert applications. Under the surface in Haile, the logic of the system rests upon some conventional audio-analysis abilities, fed from a built-in microphone in the drum, including Scheirer's audio beat tracker and onset/pitch and timbre detection for the limited case of the Pow-Wow drum.[12]

It should be pointed out that any advance in automatic music understanding by machine has multiple applications, not solely in concert systems, but in non-realtime processing of sound, in programs to support recording and compositional assistants, or to devise components of general music understanding tool kits. A recent area of substantial investigation is that of *music information retrieval* applications which can classify media files in a meaningful manner to the end-user based on audio analysis. High-profile applications have included *Shazam*, a music recognition tool via mobile phone used by clubbers to identify tracks, and commercial music prediction services from companies such as *Hit Song Science*, which chart the likely success of new recordings when compared to a large database of previous hits.

Anticipation and accompaniment

Music operates on multiple timescales, and we can look at extracting features associated with longer timespans, through statistics modelling changes in features or patterns of sound objects over time. It is also apparent that the human perception of time utilises prediction rather than reaction, no more so than in musical behaviours like synchronisation within ensembles; in order to play together, musicians must anticipate a future point of synchrony, because they would otherwise react too slowly to all perform in union.

There are non-human capabilities inherent in some tracking algorithms. To us, the perception of individual sound objects lags behind their presentation. Machines can respond more quickly in certain circumstances: imagine trying to hum along to a varying oscillator at a delay of twenty milliseconds, a facility some pitch-detection algorithms muster where the pitch period is sufficiently short. But a great advantage of human musicianship is preserved because we anticipate future events. The generation of an 'expectancy field' (a probability distribution for future events calculated from recent ones) allows a musician to stay locked within a collaborative performance, monitoring their own and other performers' playing and scheduling their own future actions.

Music understanding capabilities underlie performance systems that seek to follow musicians based on a known score. In such programs, past observations establish predictions about future context, checked against the database of expected events. The score tends to determine the bounds of interaction in advance, and some rehearsal training is often necessary to achieve a system capable of following the phrasing and nuance of a performer.

Automatic accompaniment has a twenty-five-year history, from the first attempts of Barry Vercoe and Roger Dannenberg in the early 1980s, to modern statistical inference systems developed at IRCAM and other institutions. The challenges include not only following the local position of the soloist in the score, and scheduling the appropriate accompaniment events, but coping with more substantial problems such as a missed repeat, player and tracking errors, or the sensitivity of the accompaniment to rubato, cadential phrasing and other conventions. One recent success in this field is the work of Chris Raphael (2001), an oboist and technologist whose *Music Plus One* system uses advanced statistical inference to reason about the matching of a known score to performance location. Raphael trains the machine accompanist in rehearsal in order to form a better predictive sensitivity between man and machine. Whilst he has applied this for many pieces from the classical repertoire, he has also collaborated with composers in exploring the new performance possibilities. My own *Concerto for Accompaniment* (2002) follows the example of Conlon Nancarrow's player-piano music[13] in seeking inhumanly fast passages, but synchronised via the accompaniment system to Chris's very human oboe part.

With scores settled in advance, the interaction is of a different kind from the improvisation systems described earlier. But score-following software may allow varying degrees of preparation of material, and formal structures can allow combinations of scored and improvised material. Score-following is a valuable component in a system designer's palette, and its achievements can help to inform other practices based on matching up musical material; how might an improvisation system recognise a context it has played with in the past?

Categorising and evaluating interactive music systems

Tied as they often are to specific and contrasting musical styles and situations, the great variety of interactive music systems somewhat defies a list of general properties. It can still be productive, however, to consider some descriptors, especially where these help to analyse the interaction effected by systems, and to point towards new regions of exploration. Robert Rowe (1993) has suggested three dimensions within which to classify systems:

1. *score-driven/performance-driven* – precomposed versus spontaneous
2. *transformative/generative/sequenced* – suggesting the treatment of musical material and processing, the 'composition techniques'
3. *instrument/player paradigms* – nature of the machine contribution, on a continuum from an extension of the human performance to an independent presence

To give some examples, a score-based, transformative, instrument-paradigm system might be exemplified by Stockhausen's *Mikrophonie I* (1964) for tam-tam, two microphones, two filters and six performers, or Boulez's *Anthèmes II* (1997) for violin with electronics. Meanwhile, Voyager is often taken as an exemplar of the player paradigm within Rowe's taxonomy, in that it seems wilful and independent, and might perhaps be dubbed (performance-driven, transformative/generative, player).

This taxonomy is certainly not the only one; for instance, Laurie Spiegel (1992) presents a useful list of properties for a continuous multidimensional description space. Rowe's three dimensions are criticised by Sergi Jordà (2005) for being too overtly oriented to MIDI and to Western instrumental traditions rather than multicultural notions of participation; he prefers the 'interactive instrument' and considers multi-user scenarios rather than single human–machine contexts. Another alternative formalism is the literature on agents in artificial intelligence, which can provide some useful characterisations (Collins 2006), though the definitions for agents themselves vary (d'Inverno and Luck 2001). For stronger conditions on agency all existing interactive music systems can fall short, for a failure to adequately probe their environment, decide upon new goals and learn from situations. This is not to say that some more complex aspects of agenthood have not been explored: Robert Rowe's Cypher can listen to its own output and self-criticise;[14] the Continuator is to some extent a learning machine. Yet all this goes to show how intimately the construction of advanced interactive music systems is related to capacities of artificial intelligence.

As well as descriptive taxonomies which can identify the space of possible systems, it is also productive to consider how to evaluate systems with respect to their performance on various dimensions. Three suggestions are:

1. Technical criteria related to tracking success or cognitive modelling
2. The reaction of an audience, (subjective) aesthetic criteria
3. The sense of interaction for the musicians who participate

The first involves engineering and scientific evaluation, usually tied to specific submodules for machine listening or algorithms for understanding and learning. The second takes in the qualitative artistic aims and their evaluation by populations of consumers, other artists and critics. The third is critical for the users of the system, that is, the musicians who interact with it; essential to new systems design, it may involve techniques from Human Computer Interaction. This question of evaluation has often been inadequately covered in existing reports (though see Addessi 2004; Collins 2006).

Conclusions

Building musical machines naturally leads one to want to place these machines in the same sorts of musical arena we frequent ourselves, to let them become active participants in musical culture. Certainly, machines tend to have novel abilities, though the degree to which they can comfortably integrate with existing musical practice remains an open question. For some creators, the fascination of such machines might extend to putting themselves out of business, though this is a nascent technology, and we do not need to cope with transhumanist conservatoires yet. Any fears that such investigations will make musicians obsolete are hardly well grounded;[15] the most interesting machines are built by humans, to interact with humans. It is the capabilities of the machine to empower new and rewarding interactions that deserves research.

We will accept an increasing flow of artificial-intelligence technology into our musical lives, just as such technology pervades other aspects of culture. We do not necessarily have to be frightened by the prospect of an invasion, but welcome the new possibilities for adventure. Many benign outcomes are plausible, including the prospect of musical companions who train with us as we develop our musical skills, systems that challenge us to improvise, adjusting their level as we improve, systems that accompany us in a respectful and sensitive manner. But I do retain a fond wish to see a new generation of interactive music systems which are themselves stars of the stage, alongside the human performers they interact with. Indeed, perhaps some creators will be happy to design and manage such stars, rather than push themselves into the limelight.

Returning to the opening paragraph of this chapter, would the formation of a band of such virtual, artificial and robotic musicians be at all desirable? Certainly, the creators of the machines could bask in some glory, but live music-making would now involve non-human agents. If the situation of human risk and participation is what fundamentally underlies music-making, to defer all actions to robots is to lose an essential part of our musical tradition. Whilst it seems inevitable that the technological development towards autonomous proficiency continues, as another mountain to climb, perhaps the more comfortable applications in performance will involve combining humans and robots on a concert stage as dual protagonists. Thus a more modest aim for the current era is to seek alternative ways of engaging musicians, and better ways to integrate electronic music's novel timbral and algorithmic processes with acoustic musicians.

ARTISTS' STATEMENTS II

KEVIN SAUNDERSON

Techno – the dance-driven sound that has been formed with the newest state-of-art electronic tech knowledge. By: Juan Atkins (The Originator), who was the first one to make it and give it a name, Derrick May (The Innovator), a protege of Juan Atkins, who made this music in 1983, and took it to a new level, with his creative edits and mixing style, music and rhythms (his sound being the first to receive recognition from the UK) and Kevin Saunderson (The Elevator), myself, who was friends with Derrick and Juan; I came into the picture in 1983.

Inspired by Juan and Derrick, I was led to make music that became big on the underground as well as releasing the huge hits *Big Fun* and *Good Life*. I also recorded my first Re-mix in early 1988 (for the Wee Papa Girl Rappers) which was the first remix of its kind, changing the face of the remix as we knew it then and how we hear it now.

Our sound together gave credibility to the music we created, which inspired many DJs, producers, artists, record companies and many more to jump on the boat. Yes, there were other bands making electronic music before us, the difference being we identified it, we played our music as DJs, we released our music on our own record labels, and our sound was much more unique, which caught on like the plague.

KANTA HORIO

I am working with electronics, which can have magical aspects. Electromagnetism can move various objects, and can convert between air pressure and electrical signals. I often create works which use kinetic movement driven by electromagnetism and pick up the sounds of this movement. In one such work, *Particle*, I created a board of controllable electromagnets on which I can place arrays of metallic clips – when they move, it causes sounds which I can pick up, amplify and process. But I don't know if my works could be called electronic music or not. I don't use synthesised or generated electronic sound, but I develop my works with actual sounds, utilising electronics.

Electronics also allow the division of sound and physical occurrence. For example, it is possible to make a piano sound without hammering the strings of a piano, only via electronics. We can make a sound we have never heard. But it seems like dividing taste from food. Do you want to drink beer which has a taste without any tactile substance?

For me, sounds can't be divided from physical occurrences.

http://kanta.but.jp

DONNA HEWITT

I am an Australian composer-performer working with voice, environmental and computer-processed sound. My compositional output includes works for live electronics, dance, theatre and video and much of it involves manipulating and processing voice and found sound to produce complex musical outcomes.

My interest in voice stems from my background as a professional popular-music singer, while my compositional work has been in the electroacoustic field and influenced strongly by the musique concrète school. As a vocalist, I enjoyed the immediacy of live performance and the direct engagement with an audience, while as a composer, I enjoyed the seemingly endless possibilities offered through the application of digital signal processing to sound. My compositional work was initially quite separate from my work as a popular-music performer and I have sought to blend aspects of these musical experiences into a distinctive creative practice. This has been achieved through the development of an alternate controller I designed, called the *eMic* (Extended Microphone Interface Controller). The eMic is based on a sensor-enhanced microphone stand and I use this in combination with AudioMulch and Pure Data software. The interface, which is intended to capture standard popular music microphone gestures, challenges the existing passive stereotype of the female singer (with their voice controlled by a male front-of-house mix engineer), in that it enables the performer to take charge of their own signal processing. The eMic project has helped me establish a unique creative space where I can comment on, and subvert, existing stereotypical male constructions of the female vocal performer.

ALEJANDRO VIÑAO

The future of technology in music

My views on the role and possible future of technology in music have varied considerably over the years. However, what has not changed is my belief that technology will play an increasingly central role in the future of music as art, regardless of the social aims and aesthetic direction that it may follow.

It would be easy to state that in the future most kinds of music will use the technology of our time: they more or less already do. However, it is relevant to make this statement because still today most European art music – however we may choose to define it – is produced using the technology of somebody else's time. Most art music is still written for string quartets, symphony orchestras, and instruments and instrumental combinations created in some time other than ours to fulfil the needs and vision of a different epoch. Even the microphone, this most fundamental and ubiquitous of musical instruments of the early twentieth century (yes, musical instrument) is still waiting to be acknowledged by the European serious music world. Not to mention the computer. This historical anomaly – a practice of rejecting the possibility of working with the technology of one's time – is luckily limited to the Western serious music community. The musics of most other cultures, from Indian to jazz, tango to rock, have incorporated or even pioneered technological changes.

Our serious music world has disowned one of its greatest traditions: that of being at the forefront of technological transformation in music. Far from inspiring change and invention like the composers of the past, most composers of the last sixty or seventy years have attempted to create the music of today with the technology of another time.

Let us leave this subject for the moment and consider the case of Electroacoustic Music over the last fifty years. This music too has been characterised by an approach that breaks with tradition. Where most musical evolutions or revolutions of the past have typically absorbed and included many, if not most, of the progressive features of the traditions they replaced, E.M. exceptionally attempted a clean break with the underlying fabric, the quintessential thread of serious music. In doing so, it denied itself the use of many if not most of the features that had until that point characterised Western music. During the post-war years E.M adopted this position with a militant conceptual fervour, a position that was emblematic of its uncompromisingly radical nature. E.M. was about sound objects, about the morphological evolution of sound in time. Its objects of manipulation ranged from environmental sounds, machine sounds and noise in all its variety and complexity to the oldest of all musical sound sources: the human voice. What E.M. was most definitely **not** about was the manipulations of notes. Structures and relationships that had underpinned music throughout much of the culturally relevant history were most emphatically denied. Melody, harmony, counterpoint and even rhythm (except when embodied in a sound object) were expunged from the compositional arsenal.

Over the decades these two streams in Western art music, E.M. and acoustic instrumental music, have shared in common a denial of fundamental aspects of our musical tradition. At the same time, this historical anomaly, this denial, has persisted throughout a period where the social relevance of Western serious music has consistently declined.

Both approaches are unique in our history. Both approaches have failed to project themselves in a socially significant way. Whereas E.M. – unlike purely acoustic music – has indeed managed to attract a small number of young people, its sphere of action remains limited to the 'initiated', or as the so called mainstream will have it, a small 'ghetto' within the already all too small ghetto of contemporary music. On the other hand, the purely instrumental acoustic 'scene', which failed to interact with the technology of its time, has rapidly lost its social grounding and now relies primarily on older generations for its audience; young people do not seem interested. It is poised above a demographic time-bomb.

The above characterisation may seem extreme, especially since the boundaries between electroacoustic and acoustic music appear to be breaking down. But much of the resulting music has not been too encouraging so far. And opportunism abounds. The state of affairs I have described has left us its weaknesses and blind spots. Those who use technology seem to lack the conceptual framework and technique to use all aspects of music when they compose, not just those embedded in the E.M. tradition. On the other hand, those who come from decades of technological denial do not seem to have the understanding of the syntactical and structural possibilities of the technology of our time. Furthermore, serious music is under enormous pressure to entertain. We are constantly reminded by our paymasters that a higher aspiration is pure indulgence.

I have no doubt that art music, with a large-scale narrative that has little to do with mere entertainment, will continue to exist and will eventually become socially relevant again. But I feel strongly that the conditions necessary for this to happen require that the two streams which I have discussed here (electroacoustic and purely acoustic) cease to exist as separate entities, and merge to form a single 'tradition'. In this new tradition the use of technology would not be an issue because its role in the creative process would be so well understood that it would be taken for granted.

BUBBLYFISH

In a former bank building in lower Manhattan one evening recently, I watched with about two hundred people as seven artists took the stage in succession, laying down some amazing music, each using some type of game hardware as their instrument. Despite the seeming restrictions, the diversity of musical styles was striking. This was just one of four nights of The Blip Festival 2006 and it was an absolute blast. Over thirty well-respected international 8-bit musicians and visual artists showed off their talents and electrified the audience.

8-bit or chiptune music refers to music created using video game platforms such as Amiga, Commodore 64, NES, and Gameboy. It grew largely out of the 'Demo Scene' of the 1990s and by 2001, music sequencers for use on the Gameboy were being developed, amongst them, nanoloop (http://www.nanoloop.com) and Little Sound DJ (http://www.littlesounddj.se)

The 8-bit scene is small but remarkably international with pockets in Sweden, Germany, the US, the UK, Poland, the Netherlands, Belgium, Switzerland, Austria, France, Italy, Spain, Brazil, Argentina, Australia, Japan and Russia. Individual artists communicate on the internet inviting overseas artists to play in their city. The styles vary from dance to videogame homage, noise, glitch, power-pop, electro and punk. Importantly, a number of artists are pioneering new styles that come more from the platform idiosyncrasies. 8-bit music has been slowly merging into popular music, and some mainstream artists like Beck and Malcolm McLaren have adapted 8-bit sounds into their music.

I started creating 8-bit music around 2002 when I picked up nanoloop, and was immediately drawn to the familiar, warm, lo-fi sound. My main interest was in exploring the unique sound and timbre of the Gameboy hardware, but I also liked the idea of repurposing the mass-produced game device to serve a personal artistic need.

Searching for more technical help, I soon found a growing and very international 8-bit music community on the internet. Perhaps because the instrument is so limited, each of these artists, forced to be creative, brings some quirk or stylistic flourish to the scene. For my own part, I try to bring a personal perspective to the instrument and to create music that could not be done in any other way. 8-bit music is growing rapidly. The most promising aspect seems to be that there remains an integral DIY spirit. As the genre moves more into the mainstream, this spirit ensures that innovation remains an important aspect of the scene.

BARRY TRUAX

Composers are generally concerned with real-world contexts solely in terms of dealing with performers, securing performances, recordings, commissions, etc. with their music sometimes composed specifically for those particular contexts. There are some notable exceptions where composers address extra-musical aspects of society, such as Rzewski's *Coming Together*, and often such works employ texts to make their subjects clear. But for the most part, extra-musical influences act as inspiration for music that is stylistically coherent with a body of other work. I think of this type of music as abstract in that it primarily deals with its own inner complexity.

Therefore, it is challenging to ask a composer to be concerned with something as complex as real-world acoustic environments, or soundscapes, and even more daunting to suggest that these could be the subject-matter of the composer's creative work. But this is exactly what R. Murray Schafer suggested nearly forty years ago in calling for the formation of the World Soundscape Project at Simon Fraser University. But then, why shouldn't composers take some responsibility for the acoustic well-being of society when they expect listeners to stretch their aural sensibilities that are daily being trampled on?

For many of us working in this tradition of acoustic ecology, the task is largely educational and interdisciplinary, filling gaps left by overly specialised professionals. Even more demanding has been the incorporation of environmental sound into our personal creative process in order to produce what I call soundscape composition. It involves listening to the world differently, being constantly aware of its outer complexity, and finding ways in which that complexity can inform what we compose. In a certain sense, these sounds use us as much as we use them, in that they direct every aspect of the composition. Most satisfying is the way in which soundscape composition offers to re-engage listeners with something they already understand, but often haven't thought much about. By heightening their experience of the all too familiar, or taking them on a voyage into imaginary or idealised soundscapes, I hope to revitalise the listener's connection to the real world, as well as my own.

Electroacoustic music compositional techniques provide a powerful range of expressive possibilities for addressing the imaginary world as well as the real one. The approach that I find most satisfying is where the work is grounded in a real-world context, whether it is a soundscape, a text, or an imaginary sound world. Current multi-channel loudspeaker diffusion techniques place the listener inside the spaces we create with the music, thereby encouraging a stronger engagement with the material. Works such as *Riverrun*, *Island*, and *The Shaman Ascending* attempt to do exactly that, with others involving live performers, such as *Androgyne, Mon Amour* or the opera *Powers of Two*, focusing on the relationship of the human performer to the virtual soundscape. Music has always addressed human needs and values, and I see no reason why current technology cannot continue that tradition and in fact enhance the artist's ability to engage with those issues.

Further information and musical excerpts are available at http://www.sfu.ca/~truax

LUKAS LIGETI (BURKINA ELECTRIC)

Burkina Electric is a music group and artist collective combining elements of the traditional music of Burkina Faso with contemporary electronica. The band members are Mai Lingani (vocals and dance, Burkina Faso), Wende K. Blass (guitar, Burkina Faso), As Hugues Zoko (dance, Burkina Faso/Côte d'Ivoire), Pyrolator Kurt Dahlke (electronic musical instruments and live video, Germany), and Lukas Ligeti (electronic instruments and drums, USA/Austria). All our work is created collaboratively. The music is very dance-oriented and uses traditional rhythms of the Mossi and other ethnic groups, as well as rhythms of our own creation based on these influences. We also use samples of traditional instruments, processed and/or detuned, and soundscapes recorded in Burkina. MIDI controllers such as Don Buchla's Lightning and Marimba Lumina are used.

We believe that Africa is an extremely fertile region for experiments with electronics, both for artistic and for research purposes. Concepts of mathematics are used in African art in very direct ways that are hugely different from the approaches in Europe or America. Music, dance and visuals are strongly linked, and we attempt to create live electronic performances which are different from the 'laptop aesthetic' in that physical motion of the performers is an essential component – the music is played as if we were playing instruments, but the instruments are new and have novel possibilities, and the approach to sound and interplay is based on the possibilities of computer technology. In a time when electronic music is making its first inroads in Africa, we attempt to find new and specifically African uses for electronics.

http://www.burkina-electric.com

CHRISTINA KUBISCH

The relationship with technology

Technology is something I love and hate at the same time. On one hand the absence of any kind of technology means silence (or an environment of natural sounds which we hear much clearer because of the general silence); on the other hand, you need technology to make art. An art that makes people sensitive to the wonderful structure of unknown sounds, noise, new acoustic worlds. People who listen a lot know much more about silence than people who hear sounds all day long without paying any attention to them.

The artists of the period of Romanticism talked so much about silence because the industrialisation of the nineteenth century made natural silence become more and more precious.

For me, silence and technology, electronic music and natural sounds are connected. All my work somehow is based on these apparent opposites. I try to integrate them instead of depicting them as a necessary choice between black or white. People who walk around in my installations based on magnetic induction in the open air, for example, listen much more to the 'real' sounds after having taken off their headphones. Do we remember the complex singing of a nightingale or do we pretend we know? Our acoustic memory is so much weaker than the visual one. So electronics and technology are the artistic tools for the hardhearing. And of course it should be fun and not politically correct. The music of the birds is often much crazier than any electronic music composition. Good for them. We still have to listen.

MURAT ERTEL

I used to stare at my grandmother's valve radio for hours watching the lights of the burning valves oozing from the front panel or I would take a closer look inside from the back panel . . . I really like machines and have a way to live together with them on friendly terms . . . my first group consisted of me manipulating that radio and a record player and two girls dancing and singing . . . I was around six . . .

I formed another group when I was in high school with a friend of mine . . . we were sharing the same Elka organ and were also using things like money boxes, radios and shaving machines . . . we recorded our first album on a cassette tape . . .

I really like acoustic instruments but I think I wouldn't have had such an enjoyable career without electronics . . .

With my latest group Baba Zula we use lots of effects and machines . . . we're proud of our Turkish 1980s rhythm machine collection, which we manipulate for their odd time rhythms . . . we never sell the effects we like . . . we don't like to sample other people's music so we sample ourselves . . .

The instrument I love to play most is an electric version of a Turkish saz . . . its origin dates back to the pre-Islamic days of the Turkish people in the steppes of Asia . . . now I can combine this history with the ocean of electronics . . . I really feel fresh and free because I know it was not done in the past . . .

We've been recording in Istanbul with the producer/remixer Mad Professor. He is also in love with the instrument and we're both looking forward to recording it together again . . . we always had a roots and electronics combination approach to Turkish music . . . when we met with the professor we felt the same was true for him for dub . . .

The most important thing I learned from the professor about electronics was never to trust your eyes but your ears. . . . . that's what I don't like about computers nowadays . . . you have to depend on your eyes way too much . . .

ADINA IZARRA

I believe electronic music, and particularly the use of the laptop computer in music has brought the composer down from the ivory tower. The demands of technology (contrary to those of written scores) have made us join forces and 'share', a word not very much known among acoustic composers in the twentieth century. This has surely taken us back into a renaissance mode of collaboration in art. It is a long while since I abandoned atonal music and arhythmic genres – acoustic or electronic, I hated MIDI and all the keyboard synths, the idea of doing electronics but having to play do, re, mi . . . completely put me off. I have always been close to cinema and video, but again it has been the laptop which has made them accessible for me.

A case in point is my recent piece *Toda mi vida Hos Ame* for vihuela which makes use of pitch following (using Max/MSP) and live video, both computational processes that in the 80s would have required considerable expense and equipment, and could certainly not be done in Caracas.

The laptop as an instrument is, no doubt, influencing musical aesthetics very much like the Mannheim orchestra did for early classical composers. This has also widely opened the doors for improvisation and algorithmic music to enter areas where they were not found before. There is now a true fusion of styles, from tonal to atonal, from popular to classical. The barriers are being torn down. Composers quickly need to re-format their way of thinking and working . . . otherwise they will miss all the fun!

CYBORK – MOSCOW LAPTOP CYBER ORCHESTRA

The Moscow Laptop Cyber Orchestra (http://cybork.theremin.ru) is an 'open source', improvised and highly integrated sonic environment, created by musicians, artists and programmers Andrey Smirnov, Lubov Pchelkina, Viktor Chernenko, Alexander Kulagin, Dmitry Savinov, Alexey Petrov, Dmitry Baikov, Dmitry Subochev, Artem Rukovichkin, Alexander Zenko and Eugeny Kuzmin as well as numerous collaborators and occasional partners.

It was founded in May 2006 at the Theremin Centre for Electroacoustic Music at Moscow State Conservatory (http://theremin.ru), an electroacoustic and interactive music lab.

Cybork is a large net of spatially separated mobile workstations, having local sound and integrated into a wi-fi network. It explores all sorts of interaction between players, algorithms, sensors, environments and audiences.

Although Cybork programs contain pre-composed and structured music, the core aesthetics is based on a Cyber-Jam idea – free improvised sessions, based on exploration of some predetermined common algorithms, where no other formal sonic, compositional or genre boundaries are fixed, no rules of acting are applied. There is only an entry point that triggers an adventurous search for a constantly changing identity evolving in common time and place, resulting in self-generative and self-organising sounding and visual textures ravelling and unravelling, fraying and renewing back, producing a rich palette of clippings, raw digits, dense overdriven noises, deep drones or skipping solos.

CyberJam sessions, taking place at the Theremin Center almost every Saturday, are free and open to any musician and artist interested in collaboration.

FRANCIS DHOMONT

For classicism

The view according to which the novelty of a work guarantees its quality is often expressed in electroacoustic music circles, and for some it is the only criterion of worthiness. I tend to believe that this evasive action, generally founded upon new technologies, is an error as dangerous – commensurately – as taking comfort in the certainties of the past. It is a conditioning of the modern consumer, born in the mid-twentieth century, surrounded by an industry of disposable goods; the apotheosis of which seems to be the fleeting lifespan of modern computer software. What can strictly be justified by technology and commerce, has contaminated the domain of thought and that of art. Today, invention is discredited if it holds no surprise and becomes recognised: it is then overlooked and dismissed as being academic. But then – when innovation is authentic and coherent – doesn't it rather participate of the foundations of a new classicism? And is it not, then, an aim also pursued validly within the multifaceted exploration of the contemporary music field?

Classical epochs constitute the successful outcome of periods of uncertainty and research, the maturity of an art; they are not generally reputed for their mediocrity. In the words of Valéry 'the essence of classicism is to come after', which does not mean stagnation. This is how music and the arts have proceeded since their beginnings, alternating a break with established practice (research and discard) with the affirmation of new theories (stability and classicism). Yet, the latter will also be considered obsolete (academic) and empty. Only the duration of stable periods is variable. The modal era has known long developments: the baroque and the classical of the eighteenth century have kept their time; the romantic has rushed its pace; the serial quickened its pulse; as the years go by, musical styles replace each other with increasing speed. In our times of overconsumption, we should not be surprised if novelty has a short lifespan and the notion of classicism is often confused by mistake with old-fashioned thought. Thus springs the eternal debate between academicism and the avant-garde.

The coherence of classicism does not imply a neglect of research, however; it does not require the continuous rejection of earlier findings either, the repetitive *tabula rasa*; it offers an enduring syntax which allows the musical signified to express itself thoroughly through the means of a signifier which ceases to be perpetually deferred into question. It is now time, perhaps, after a century of innovation, that electroacoustic composition should be concerned with implementing its technical advances, and cease to consider experimentation as an end in itself, and mere digital innovations as musically sufficient. There is a time for casting doubt upon and replacing old models, and a time for proving through strong works, the suitability of innovation. And I believe that the acousmatic modality, for its own part, is engaging in the initiation of this process.

Classicism is not to be feared, all true innovation arrives there one day or another. And it is perhaps in this way, that we will improve, if not solve, the issue of poor attendance at our concerts, through giving the audience the time to assimilate a repertoire founded upon mechanisms that will have become familiar, personal musical ideas expressed not in a vernacular tongue but in a common, recognised, intelligible one.

It is because of this, that I agree with François Bayle when he says:

> The role of the artists of our time is not any more to be in the avant-garde, which is a military term. The role of artists is, on the contrary, to be 'résistants' (wars have become civilian conflicts), to build over that which has been destroyed, to 'put in reverse' our relationship with the machines in order to re-encounter passion, spirituality.
>
> (F. Bayle, conférence Principes d'acousmatique. *Musique du XXe siècle*, Cologne, 23 June 2000)

DAVID BEHRMAN

I would rather write a few words about the present than be nostalgic about the past.

I'm still interested in work my friends Robert Ashley, Alvin Lucier, Gordon Mumma and I made and presented together during the time of the Sonic Arts Union in the 60s and 70s. There are other chapters in past decades that it might be good to touch on also – for instance, what it was like to be in California in the late 70s at the dawn of the 'microcomputer music' era. But I would rather focus on the unfolding possibilities of today.

(Once, in response to something I asked him about the past, John Cage said to me, 'I don't cultivate my memory.' I've thought of that remark often, taking it as a reminder that we should keep forging ahead with our newest projects.)

In two recent works, *Acoustica* (in which a computer music system makes no sounds of its own but only processes live acoustic sound) and *Long Throw* (made for the Merce Cunningham Dance Company, for violin, electric guitar, prepared piano and software for live processing), I've been pursuing two ideas that are on my mind these days. The first of these is that we want to find a location along the gamut from fixed score at one extreme to free improvisation at the other that is most fruitful and best suited to the particular music at hand. The second is that we should be able to find new ways to integrate sophisticated twenty-first-century electronic and computer technology with acoustic sound, whether it comes from our voices, the environment around us or the instruments, many of which are rich in cultural history, that have been handed down to us from past generations.

KEVIN BLECHDOM (KRISTIN ERICKSON)

It's a good idea to have a bad idea.
And every way of making music is possible.

I started making music with computers at the same time that laptop computers became powerful enough to do realtime DSP (digital signal processing). I jumped into Max/MSP (a graphical programming language for audio and video) and started performing live music with my laptop. My friend Blevin Blectum was working with portable samplers, and we played rhythmic, chaotic, funny music together. We did not synchronise our machines together with MIDI. We re-triggered and changed the tempos of the rhythmic phrases by hand and by ear during the show. Performing live consisted of constantly adjusting how the two streams of music were fitting together. Our set-up had rhythmic 'looseness' built in and we teetered between cohesion and chaos. Our band was called Blectum from Blechdom. We romped around San Francisco playing shows and overlapping our lives with the music. We laughed while we played because we could predict when and how the other person would change the sound as we pushed and transitioned through unexpected worlds, surprising ourselves along the way. We were playing live electronic music. We ran into resistance to what we were doing, and some of it may have been because we were two women using the technology as we intended. The messiest parts of our shows, the parts when we were most out of control, were our favourites. The experimental nature of the music was challenging, regardless of gender, but in combination with gender, we were an easy target for some critics. One could think the messiness was unintentional or the result of technical incompetence, when it was artistic decision. At the time, many artists were making tight, slick-sounding rhythmic electronic music. We were tired of 'that' sound and the elitist 'boys' club' surrounding it. We wanted to mess it up. We wanted to make music evolve.

My last solo album, *Eat My Heart Out*, contains mostly sounds generated with Quicktime General MIDI instruments. I am fascinated by standard MIDI files as a wonderful modern score format. This format has its quirks, but considering the large number of MIDI hobbyists and mobile phone ring-tone arrangers around the world uploading their own transcriptions of all the hits, new and old, it is mind-boggling. I really want to encourage software manufacturers not to give up on this format and to continue to support it, maybe even iron out some of the problem areas. If a new format is created, I hope it can be made backwards compatible with the already existing gigantic library of files. They are plentiful, diverse, and ripe for mangling, re-contextualising, and analysing. The information in these files is an excellent resource for researching patterns in musical structures, styles, melodies, chords, guitar solos, song structures, and sometimes lyrics. For instance, it could be a useful database if a predictive song-writing software were created.

Before General MIDI took over my life, I played music with Max/MSP. I designed a series of flexible sequencers (*Narctronic Processor* and *Klardiscopic Remedy*) to control digital synthesisers and samplers, including multi-metronome sequencers, sequencers with dynamic time windows that would slither around inside the sequence as it was playing, and multi-track sequencers with which you could tweak the timing differently for each track and then snap it back in place. I was interested in the shapes of the musical phrases instead of individual triggerings, combining the idea of envelopes and sequencers together in order to play with sounds in between continuous and discrete.

As for the future, I'll be excited to hear what I haven't yet heard. Music gets stuck in the thick mud of nostalgia and the general public apparently enjoys the taste of regurgitation. Music that is based on original and fresh ideas often overlooks the audience and the role that music plays in their everyday lives. The main limitation on music is a dimensional restriction due the linearity of time. Maybe we can find a way around that!

KARLHEINZ STOCKHAUSEN

The term **Electronic Music** which we used since 1953 was only related to *Art Music*, not to *Pop Music* produced with electroacoustic equipment.

Electronic Art Music will develop very much, after the consequences of the few compositions of the last fifty-three years are seriously studied and have become common knowledge.

Next to Electronic Music, vocal and instrumental music can only survive through soloists and relatively small groups, who specialise in performing new original works combining mechanical sounds with electronic sounds and developing the **timbres**, **dynamics** and **space movements**. These three parameters are still in their childhood.

What we really need are auditoriums which make the projection of music all around the listeners possible. The present fashion to add visual effects to almost all the music performed should diminish. Listening to music in the dark will become much more important in the future than today.

The main function of Art Music will be to make the souls of the listeners fly freely in the universes with infinite new surprises.

GEORGE E. LEWIS

On Creative Machines

The emergence of the computer as an integral part of new media practice has now placed interactivity at centre stage. In order to understand cultural production in the digital age, however, we must foreground the histories that bind interactivity with its dark-star counterpart, improvisation. In post-1950 Western experimentalism, improvisative presences and practices are repeatedly masked through the use of terms such as 'happening', 'action', 'intuition', and most recently, 'interactivity'. The need to exnominate improvisation here is due largely to its problematic social status, not only in the high-culture pan-European art practice that most theorists and researchers assume as a necessary cultural and historical foundation for all art production, but also in everyday constructions of morality and integrity that are active in many Eurologically imbued social spheres.

Nonetheless, a quarter-century of living with creative machines has shown me the centrality of improvisation to the practice of everyday life, and indeed, to our birthright as sentient beings. Improvisation, or the realtime analysis, generation, transformation, and exchange of meaning, is mediated by (among many factors) the body, history, temporality, space, memory, intention, material culture and diverse methodologies. As improvisers, we cast down our buckets where we are, as Booker T. Washington was wont to say, and it is at the point of the actualisation of desire that improvisation becomes far more than a subspecies of performance. Rather, improvisation's ubiquity becomes perhaps the primary modality through which the performative and the interactive are articulated. In such an environment, we can speak of a creative, interactive machine quite simply, as one that incorporates a dialogic imagination.

PART III

Analysis and synthesis

11 Computer generation and manipulation of sounds

STEFANIA SERAFIN

In 1963, an article entitled 'The Digital Computer as a Musical Instrument' appeared in the journal *Science*, in which Max Mathews, the father of computer music, declared the birth of computer-generated sound. For the first time, this article described the possibility of creating sounds by using computers, and explained how 'there are no theoretical limitations to the performance of the computer as a source of musical sounds, in contrast to the performance of ordinary instruments' (Mathews, 1963).

Sound synthesis can be defined as the production and manipulation of sounds using mathematical algorithms. A useful classification of sound synthesis techniques was proposed by Julius O. Smith (Smith 1991) who proposes four categories: processed recordings, abstract algorithms, spectral models and physical models. Synthesis techniques such as wavetable synthesis and granular synthesis belong, according to Smith, to the category of processed recordings. Considering these techniques as merely synthesis would contradict the idea that synthetic sounds are generated from scratch, while these techniques require some initial sonic material. Abstract algorithms include techniques such as amplitude, ring, frequency modulation and waveshaping. Spectral models simulate sounds as they are received and perceived by the ear, including techniques such as source-filter synthesis, additive synthesis, the phase vocoder and subtractive synthesis. Smith's last synthesis category involves physical models, which simulate the source of sound production. We shall consider all of these categories in this chapter.

The early days

The first experiments in computer generated sounds were performed in the early 1960s at Bell Labs. At the time, you could almost count the practitioners of computer music on one hand's fingers. Scientists and musicians certainly did not have our contemporary privilege of being able to synthesise complex sonic patterns in realtime on a personal laptop. At the origins of computer music, only high-end laboratories had the possibility to produce sounds by computer, and the generation of a few seconds of sounds usually took more than a day. To complicate the matter, decks of punch cards with recorded computer music scores had to be carried to the IBM building in Manhattan where the mainframe computer was located, as Mathews likes to recall during his talks on the birth of computer music. The mainframe computer converted the punch cards into a digital sound tape, which was later brought back to Bell Labs and played back through a digital to analogue converter.

These limitations and challenges certainly did not discourage the pioneers of the field. On the contrary, music software was starting to be developed, among which Music III and its descendants Music IV and V introduced the concept of a unit generator. A unit generator is a building block of a sound synthesis algorithm. Examples of unit generators are oscillators, filters, multipliers and adders, and amplitude envelope generators. Different complex sonic patterns and sound synthesis algorithms could be implemented by connecting different oscillators; see chapter 4 for more on this background to programming methods for computer music.

Among the computer music pioneers, Jean-Claude Risset, a French composer and scientist, began experimenting with synthetic sounds produced using *additive synthesis*. Additive synthesis is a synthesis technique derived from the Fourier theorem. Mathematically, the Fourier theorem states that a periodic function can be formulated as a sum of sine waves. When applied to computer music, the Fourier theorem can be interpreted as the possibility of creating any complex waveform by summing a set of sinusoidal components: this is the basic idea behind additive synthesis. In computer music, a sine wave is produced by an oscillator whose frequency, amplitude and phase can be varied.

In 1964, after reading Mathews' paper on the possibility of generating sounds by computers, Risset decided to visit Bell Labs, where he began to investigate the timbre of trumpets using analysis and synthesis techniques in Music IV. Risset discovered some important timbral properties of musical instruments, such as the fact that the attack is essential to recognise the sound of a trumpet. Moreover, by playing a piano sound backwards, he discovered that the spectral description of an instrument is not enough to recognise its timbre. He produced the first synthetic bell sounds using additive synthesis, by understanding the importance of the inharmonic spectra of such instruments and the role of their amplitude envelope. Thanks to these discoveries, Risset pioneered the combination of the disciplines of acoustics, sound synthesis and psychoacoustics, where the mathematical understanding of musical sounds and their reproduction by computers are tightly linked to the way such sounds are perceived by humans.

In 1968, after going back to France for a few years, Risset returned to Bell Labs and created a catalogue of computer-generated sounds, an important research contribution. In this catalogue, guidelines to synthesise different musical instruments using the notation of the Music V program were provided; particular focus was placed on bell and woodwind sounds. At the same time, Risset produced compositions using sound synthesis, such as the *Computer Suite from Little Boy*, motivated by the Hiroshima bombing. *Little Boy* explores instrumental simulation by additive synthesis, timbral mixing and auditory illusions impossible to generate using acoustical instruments. As an example, Risset used Shepard tones, which create an illusion of never-ending ascending or descending glissandi. The composition clearly shows Risset's interest on the influence of psychoacoustics on computer music, especially concerning the way the sonic structures affect the perception of the resulting sounds.

Another pioneer of computer music research who was strongly influenced by Max Mathews' 1963 paper was John Chowning. As a young graduate student, Chowning arrived at Stanford in 1962. As a composer, he had become interested in electronic music after having attended concerts in Paris, especially Pierre Boulez's Domaine Musicale series. When a colleague from Stanford handed him a copy of Mathews' paper, Chowning immediately arranged a trip to Bell Labs, to gain a deeper knowledge of the possibilities offered by sound synthesis. In particular, Chowning was intrigued by the sentence in the paper stating that a computer could give unlimited sonic possibilities, as opposed to traditional musical instruments. Going back to Stanford's newly established artificial intelligence lab, which later became the Center for Computer Research in Music and Acoustics (CCRMA), Chowning started to explore the musical potentials of computer-generated sounds.

While playing with combined oscillators, he discovered what is still nowadays the most successfully commercial sound synthesis technique: *frequency modulation*, commonly known as FM synthesis. The main idea behind frequency modulation is that when the frequency of an oscillator is modulated by another oscillator, a very complex spectrum appears. FM was particularly interesting at that time when computational cost was a real issue: thanks to FM, very complex and interesting sounds were produced using the mere combination of two nested sine waves. Chowning's discovery captured Yamaha's attention. The company bought the FM patent and in 1983 released the DX7, the most successful synthesiser in history. As a composer, Chowning naturally used FM in many of his pieces. For example, in *Turenas*, completed in 1972, FM synthesis is used to generate spectral transformations from harmonic to inharmonic spectra. Turenas is a four-channel composition, which uses spatialisation algorithms developed by Chowning himself. FM synthesis was also used by composer Paul Lansky in his first computer music piece, *Mild und Leise*, composed in 1973. It is interesting to notice how the Radiohead's *Idioteque*, from the album *Kid A* (2000), samples a snippet of this piece.[1]

In parallel to the development of new synthesis techniques, engineers and musicians were building new hardware synthesisers which could allow powerful sound manipulations and processing. In 1975, John Appleton produced the prototype for a self-contained digital synthesiser, in association with the New England Digital Corporation, commercially known as the Synclavier. The Synclavier had a bank of timbre generators, each providing a choice of up to twenty-four sinusoidal frequency components for each voice, depending on the version. Its on-board microcomputer had 128 kBytes of memory mainly used for sequencing.

In October 1977, CCRMA acquired the Systems Concepts Digital Synthesizer, commonly known as the Samson Box, named after its designer Peter Samson. The Samson Box, which resembled a big green refrigerator, provided 256 unit generators and 128 different modifiers such as filters, envelope generators or random number generators. Each modifier could be combined with delay units to produce reverberation effects. Moreover, the box provided four analogue-to-digital converters allowing four channels of sound output. All the synthesis techniques known at the time, such as additive, subtractive and FM synthesis were supported on the Samson Box. The box was a clear success, and much music was produced at the time. As an example, in 1980 Gareth Loy composed *Nekyia*, a four-channel composition combining recorded and synthesised sounds. Unfortunately this dedicated machine required special support, and lots of effort was put into software and hardware maintenance. Since developing new synthesis algorithms was far from straightforward in the Samson Box, the box became more a musical instrument rather than a research tool.

The events described till now have all taken place in the United States, predominantly at Bell Labs or at Stanford University. In 1970 Europe, and in particular France, started to become active in the field of computer-generated sounds, especially when composer Pierre Boulez was asked to become director of the *Institut de Recherche et Coordination Acoustique Musique* (IRCAM) in Paris. At the time of its creation, and for about a decade, IRCAM represented the main pole of research and development in computer music in Europe. Several composers and researchers such as Jean-Claude Risset, David Wessel and Tod Machover, to cite only a few, were invited to work in Paris to bring their expertise and contribute to the development of the centre.

The initial success of IRCAM was given both by the synergy of people working and by the possibilities offered by using powerful technology developed in-house such as the 4X digital synthesiser designed by Peppino

Di Giugno. Most of the synthesis techniques described in this chapter were developed or refined at IRCAM, especially at the origins of computer music and sound synthesis, when only few centres could afford powerful machines to create synthesised sounds. At the beginning of the 1990s, the development of personal computers facilitated the creation of several research centres around the United States and Europe. Nowadays computer music research and musical creation are spread across many different locations worldwide. In the following, the different synthesis techniques are analysed separately, together with their applications in musical creations.

Granular manipulation of sounds

In musical terms, a sound grain can be defined as a short sonic snippet of about ten to a hundred milliseconds, an elementary particle as opposed to a complex soundscape. By combining different grains over time, and by overlapping several grains at the same instant of time, interesting sonic effects can be produced. The synthesis technique in which different sound grains are combined is known as *granular synthesis*. One of the pioneers of the use of granular synthesis in computer music is Curtis Roads. Working together with his teacher Iannis Xenakis, he investigated the idea of composing with sound particles, an idea mainly inspired by the theory of the Nobel prizewinner Dennis Gabor, who claimed that all sounds can be considered as being made of elementary sound particles limited in time, frequency and amplitude.

In 1974 Roads wrote a computer program with Music V, implementing sound particle synthesis. A succession of such programs and techniques have been developed for his compositions in subsequent decades (Roads 1978; Roads 2001). His latest recorded collection of works is *Point Line Cloud* (2004); a point represents a grain, a line represents a set of points which create a musical tone, and a cloud is a connection of many grains played simultaneously.

Since its conception, many composers have utilised granular synthesis as a musically powerful technique to create and manipulate complex sonic universes using basic particles. Barry Truax has extensively researched granular synthesis, and produced in 1986 a realtime implementation using a digital signal processor controlled by a microcomputer, his PODX system, creating *Riverrun*. By 1987, Truax was using the technique of granulation to process sampled sounds as compositional material. In *The Wings of Nike* (1987) short sonic grains are preferred, while in pieces such as *Pacific* (1990) longer sequences of environmental sounds are sculpted. In each of these compositions, the granulated material is time stretched by various amounts and thereby produces a number of perceptual changes that seem to originate from within the sound.

A technique which is strongly related to granular synthesis is the so-called Fonction d'onde formantique (*FOF*), or formant wave function, developed at IRCAM in the early 1980s by Xavier Rodet, Yves Potard, and Jean-Baptiste Barrière. FOF is a technique used to synthesise vocal sounds by using short decaying sinusoidal bursts synchronously spaced over time. The resonant frequency of a FOF corresponds to one of the formants (that is, to one of the main resonances) of the vocal tract. By combining several FOFs together over time, and by having several FOFs played simultaneously, simulation of vocal sounds can be produced. In 1984, the FOF algorithm was used to synthesise Mozart's famous Queen of the Night aria, using a synthesiser called *Chant.* This demonstration was motivated by the need to create some convincing musical examples which utilised the Chant software, in order to show off its musical possibilities. A considerable amount of time was dedicated to carefully synthesising the aria, with an impressive result for that date. However, it is important to note that the team only tackled that section of the aria where vowels predominate, vowels being notoriously easier to synthesise than consonants.

Since the 1990s granular processes have been extensively used[2] by many composers for the wide musical possibilities they offer, and are readily available in many different software platforms. Curtis Roads' *Microsound* book (Roads 2001) provides an overview of many associated techniques and compositions.[3]

Sound modelling

Among the different synthesis techniques, sound modelling techniques have seen the greatest interest from acousticians, engineers, computer scientists and composers. While acousticians are interested in understanding how different musical instruments produce sound, engineers and computer scientists are interested in developing efficient yet accurate algorithms to simulate such sounds, and musicians and composers are interested in using modelling techniques to extend the sonic possibilities offered by traditional instruments.

Sound modelling techniques are commonly divided into *spectral models* and *physical models.* While spectral models simulate how a sound is perceived by the listener, physical models reproduce the source sound production mechanism. An advantage of spectral models is the availability of analysis techniques which allow the obtaining of control parameters for the models from recordings of real instruments. Such analysis techniques do not exist for physical models, so physical models usually also rely on spectral analysis techniques. Another important difference is the fact that physical simulations require a dedicated model for each instrument or sounding object reproduced, while spectral models have a unique representation which can then be adapted to different instruments.

It is essential to stress the distinction between the internal representation of a model (the mathematical model being employed to design it) and how it is seen from the outside (the external representation). Acousticians, engineers and computer scientists are concerned both about internal and external representation. On the other end, from the perspective of a musician, it is especially important that the external representation is understandable and usable. A model with few accessible control parameters can quickly become musically uninteresting, since very limited variations can be introduced. On the other side, a model with too many parameters or whose parameters are not understandable can easily become unusable and too complex. It is an additional challenge for the scientist, and especially for the interaction designer, to find the right trade-off between complexity and musical appeal.

Spectral modelling

Spectral modelling techniques are perhaps the most popular approach to sound synthesis. By using the Fourier transform, a sound is decomposed into its elementary sinusoidal components. Spectral modelling techniques are a derivation of previous research on additive synthesis as performed in the early years of computer music, together with phase vocoder techniques developed mainly for speech analysis and synthesis. Spectral modelling techniques allow several important sonic manipulations of original material, since every sound can be analysed, transformed in different ways and resynthesised. Common transformations include pitch shifting, time stretching and spectral morphing, the latter being a combination between spectra from different sounds to create hybrid instruments not existing in the real world. The different possibilities offered by spectral models have been for a long time very attractive to computer music composers.

Spectral modelling techniques facilitated the creation of so-called *spectral music*, music concerned with timbral structures obtained by Fourier-based analysis techniques. Originating in France in the 1970s, the 'spectral school' was nurtured by IRCAM, and included such figures as Gérard Grisey and Tristan Murail. Whilst it could include computer-based spectral

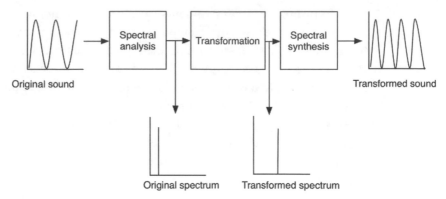

Figure 11.1 A simple analysis-transformation-synthesis representation based on spectral modelling

manipulation and transformation of sound, the computer was also used as an analysis tool, with compositions then developed as scored settings for performance by specially trained musicians, such as Grisey's *Partiels* (1975), for an ensemble of sixteen to eighteen musicians and based on an analysis of trombone harmonics. As another example, in 1980, Jonathan Harvey received an invitation from Pierre Boulez to work at IRCAM. During this time, Harvey composed *Mortuos Plango, Vivos Voco*, a tape piece that features extensive use of spectral manipulation techniques. Harvey was particularly interested in the technique of spectral morphing. In particular, Harvey merged the sound of the great tenor bell in Winchester cathedral with the sound of his son singing.

Figure 11.1 shows a block diagram of a simple spectral processing framework. In this example the analysis part is rather straightforward, since the input signal is a sine wave. The transformation applied to the sound is a change in frequency, obtained in the frequency domain after calculating the Fourier transform of the original sound.

Research in psychoacoustics has shown that noisy transient components of a sound (often in the attack portion of a sound) are especially important to identify a particular musical instrument, or to differentiate in sound quality between original and synthetically generated instruments. Since the transient portion of a sound is especially hard to synthesise using, for example, a sum of sinusoids, sometimes researchers prefer to use a sampled attack rather than a synthesised one. This obviously preserves the quality, but lacks the flexibility offered by richer sound synthesis. In the late 1980s, a technique called *sines plus noise* was developed by Xavier Serra as part of his Ph.D. dissertation at Stanford University (Serra 1989). In sines plus noise synthesis, a sound is decomposed into its sinusoidal components (partials) and residual (noise).

In the past decade different improvements to sines plus noise synthesis have been achieved, ranging from improved analysis techniques to better understanding of transients, to extracting features from the original sound such as the gender of the person speaking in the case of a voice, the amount of auditory roughness, the recognition of musical instruments by spectral analysis and so on. Serra's research group, the Music Technology Group of the Pompeu Fabra University,[4] is one of the new flourishing European computer music centres, and involved in technology transfer in collaboration with companies, as well as providing free open-source software implementations of much of their work. In some celebrated applications of the sines plus noise model, karaoke demonstrations have been made of live voice transformation where the singer can take on the voice of another (perhaps a famous singer), and through a collaboration with Yamaha, the singing voice synthesiser *Vocaloid*.

Linear predictive coding (LPC) can also be considered as a spectral modelling technique especially useful for voice analysis and synthesis. Originally developed for speech in the late 1960s and early 1970s, it is an example of the technology transfer that tends to occur between computer music and the larger research groups in telecommunications and speech. In LPC the main resonances of a voiced sound are represented in terms of a digital filter. By removing such resonances, the so-called residual part remains. By modifying the parameters of the filters, it is possible to obtain interesting sonic variations. LPC has been extensively used by composers such as Paul Lansky (famously, for *Idle Chatter* (1985)) and Charles Dodge. In his piece *Any Resemblance is Purely Coincidental* (1980), Dodge used a technique of source separation on a 1907 recording of Leoncavallo's aria 'Ridi Pagliacci' to separate Enrico Caruso's voice from the instrumental accompaniment. Dodge manipulated the voice using LPC, creating new contours and chorus effects.

As with granular synthesis, spectral manipulations of sounds are available in most software synthesisers and are extensively used by composers. Technology has reached a point in which sounds can be analysed and resynthesised in realtime.

Physical modelling

Sound synthesis by physical modelling is a class of synthesis techniques in which the source sound production mechanism is mathematically simulated. As opposed to spectral models, physical models do not consider the way the sound is perceived by the ear, but how it is produced by a vibrating object.

In 1961, Kelly and Lochbaum designed an algorithm to simulate the human vocal tract, considered as a connection of several cylinders with different lengths and widths. This algorithm was used to produce what is perhaps the first musical application of physical modelling synthesis. During a collaboration with Max Mathews, the physical model was used to simulate a human voice with a IBM 704 machine.[5] Arthur C. Clarke, visiting John Pierce at Bell Labs, heard this demo, and decided to use it in the movie *2001: A Space Odyssey*, where the HAL9000 computer slowly sings its first song 'Bicycle Built for Two'.

Concerning musical instruments different from the human voice, the first computer simulations by physical models were performed by Hiller and Ruiz in 1971, when a vibrating string was reproduced using numerical methods. To my knowledge such a simulated string was used only for scientific purposes, and no musical compositions were produced with it.

At the end of the 1970s, three acousticians named Michael McIntyre, Robert Schumacher and Jim Woodhouse wrote what is nowadays considered one of the landmark papers on physical modelling synthesis. In 'On the Oscillation of Musical Instruments', published in the *Journal of the Acoustical Society of America*, the three acousticians described mathematical simulations of three types of instruments: a violin, a clarinet and a flute. Such instruments can be considered as self-sustained oscillators, which means that the sound is produced as long as energy is provided to the system (by bowing or blowing). The paper describes how these three instruments have a very similar algorithmic structure, since they all have a linear element (the vibrating string for the violin or the tube for the flute and clarinet) which is excited by a non-linear element (the bow exciting the string or the player blowing inside the flute).

At approximately the same time Kevin Karplus and Alex Strong developed an algorithm to simulate sounds produced by plucked strings. They noticed that by feeding a circulating buffer with white noise, and adding a low-pass filter at one extremity of the buffer, as shown in Fig. 11.2, it is possible to simulate sonorities similar to those produced by a plucked string. Intuitively, the circulating buffer represents a vibrating string. The shorter the buffer, the higher the frequency of the string. The short noise burst of input simulates the energy imposed to a string at rest when it is put into vibration by plucking it, while the low-pass filter represents propagation losses along the string. This simulation is known nowadays as the Karplus–Strong algorithm. The main advantage of this algorithm is its low computational cost.

Julius Smith and David Jaffe extended this algorithm and analysed it from the physical modelling point of view. They improved the excitation and the filters, and added different effects which were not present in the original

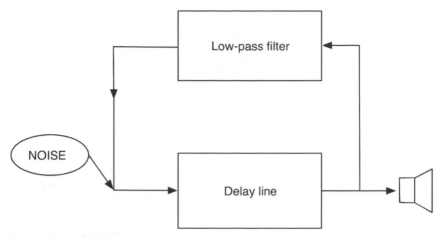

Figure 11.2 The Karplus–Strong algorithm

algorithm. The extended Karplus–Strong algorithm was used by David Jaffe in his piece *Silicon Valley Breakdown* (1982). Jaffe's work demonstrates a number of the compositional possibilities of physical models: the notes are often too fast for any human to play, including intricate time structures like sinusoidal tempo canons; the timbre of the simulated strings can be changed continuously, showing the potential for parameter variation in the model; and imaginary instruments impossible to realise in the real world can be explored, most notoriously, the conceit of plucking a string with the dimensions of the support wires of the Golden Gate Bridge. In 1990, Charlie Sullivan, as an undergraduate student at Princeton University, developed some extensions to the Karplus–Strong algorithm in order to simulate an electric guitar with distortion and feedback. This improved model was used by composer Paul Lansky in the piece *Things She Carried* (1997).

The extensions to the Karplus–Strong algorithm were part of Smith's development of the digital waveguide theory for physical models. Smith developed a solid physical modelling theory based on the principle of wave propagation in different media. Since then, using digital waveguides, several musical instruments have been simulated, and digital waveguides are the most popular synthesis technique by physical models. Digital waveguides were also licensed to Yamaha, who in 1994 released the *VL1*, a synthesiser based on physical modelling techniques. Unfortunately, the VL1 did not show the same commercial success as the DX7; this might have happened for several reasons. First of all, the synthesiser was rather expensive; second, it required practice in order to master the different controllers provided with it, such as the breath controller used as an input device to the woodwind physical models.

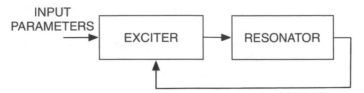

Figure 11.3 The exciter-resonator approach to physical modelling synthesis

An interesting aspect of physical modelling synthesis is the decomposition of a vibrating object into exciter and resonator, as shown in Fig. 11.3. Here, the exciter is intended as the source of energy imposed to the system, while the resonator is the object which produces sound. In Fig. 11.3, exciter and resonators are connected in a feedback loop – this is the case for self-sustained oscillators such as the violin, in which there is a continuous interaction between the bow and the string. In contrast, in percussion instruments the interaction between the player and the instrument is transient for each particular stroke, which means that the player interacts with the instrument for a finite amount of time, and then the instrument is left to resonate. The exciter–resonator approach is particularly interesting from a musical perspective, since unnatural exciters and resonators can be combined together, to create augmented virtual instruments.

Chris Chafe is a composer who has extensively used physical models and more specifically digital waveguides in his compositions. In the recent installation *Ping* (2001), developed by himself together with the digital artist Greg Niemeyer, the Karplus–Strong algorithm again stars. The name Ping derives from the Unix command which allows the probing of the distance to a target machine on a network. Chafe decided to sonify such connection time, by considering two locations as if connected by a vibrating string. When the two locations are close together and the network traffic is low, the frequency of the corresponding vibrating string is high. On the other end, when the two locations are far apart or there is a high network traffic between them, the frequency of the corresponding vibrating string is low. In an installation featured at the San Francisco Museum of Modern Art, visitors had the possibility to choose the different locations they wanted to 'ping', resulting in a sonification of the locations. In another attempt to create combinations of exciters and resonators impossible in the real world, Chafe created *Oxygen flute*. Oxygen flute is a growth chamber filled with bamboo and carbon dioxide analysers. In this installation, visitors can hear the exchange between their respiration and the respiration of the plants, and a flute physical model is activated by the breathing of the people inside.

A different approach to physical modelling synthesis is *modal synthesis*. Although for a long time very popular in engineering, its introduction to the computer music community is attributed to Jean-Marie Adrien around 1988. It can be stated that modal synthesis represents a hybrid between physical models and spectral models. A mode, in fact, represents a resonance of a vibrating system, and the modes of each object are a consequence of its physical structure. A synthesiser which implements exclusively modal synthesis is Modalys developed at IRCAM. In Modalys the user can choose different resonators and excite them with different inputs. In 1999, Hans Tutschku wrote *Eikasia*, an eight-channel electroacoustic composition, with Modalys. While in his previous work the composer had always used prerecorded sonic material manipulated in different ways, the goal of Eikasia was to achieve equivalent sonic complexity using physical models. The piece uses mostly circular and rectangular plates, whose spectra are tuned according to analysis data of low-frequency piano strings.

A third approach to physical modelling synthesis is represented by *mass-spring models*. In this method, each object is discretised as a finite connection of masses and springs. For example, when simulating a vibrating string a one-dimensional connection of masses and springs is required, while, when simulating a plate, masses and springs are placed in a two-dimensional configuration. Claude Cadoz and his team at the ACROE laboratory in Grenoble are among the pioneers, and developed a software package called Cordis-Anima. In this software, the user can combine different masses and springs to create simulations of existing musical instruments or hybrid objects. An example of a composition written using Cordis-Anima is *pico . . . Tera* (2001) by Claude Cadoz himself. The piece uses a single model with thousands of masses and several interacting objects; the five minutes of music in this piece are created by simply running such a model, without any external interaction or post-treatment.

The short history of physical modelling synthesis has shown some successful collaborations between composers and researchers, which have produced both a better understanding of physical modelling techniques and interesting musical compositions. Besides the examples described so far, a recent collaboration between composer Juraj Kojs and the author has produced a physical model of a rotating corrugated tube, together with the musical composition *Garden of the Dragon*, in which real and synthetic singing tubes interact. Singing tubes are musical toys, popular in the 1980s, which produce pleasant sonorities when whirled in the air. Such plastic tubes show regularly spaced corrugations in the inside; these corrugations are the reason for the pleasant sonorities produced by the tubes. The air in fact, travelling inside the tube, is perturbed by the corrugations, and the frequency of perturbation determines the fundamental frequency of the tubes. In *Garden of the Dragon*, the performers whirl singing tubes in the air, and such tubes interact in realtime with the virtual tubes simulated in software.

Yet sound synthesis by physical modelling is a technique which often seems more popular among researchers than composers. One of the common criticisms of this technique is the fact that it is pointless to use simulated musical instruments when the real counterparts have a much higher sonic quality. However, sound synthesis by physical models becomes musically interesting when sonorities which cannot be achieved with real instruments are produced. When the full potential of physical models is exploited, the composer is able to vary the size and shape of the virtual instruments, or create hybrid connections which are not present in reality.

Overall, physical modelling is much less exploited than other synthesis techniques. The main reason is the fact that fewer software packages which implement sound synthesis by physical modelling are present.[6] Moreover, physical modelling can also appear somehow frightening to some musicians, since they require a stronger knowledge of mathematics and physics. This last concern is, however, not always true, since composers using physical models can abstract from knowing how the model was implemented, and use it as a creative tool controlled by the same parameters as objects in the real world.

The present and the future

The availability of software and hardware technology at an affordable price has enormously expanded the quantity of compositions produced using sound synthesis, which is now part of the curricula and research efforts in many institutions worldwide. Programs like Max/MSP have radically changed the way composers and performers interpret the computer – from being a laborious tool which required lots of time to achieve even a very modest result, the computer has become another musical instrument with which composers and performers can interact in realtime. One aspect which is particularly interesting in the use of interactive sound synthesis programs is the possibility to create interactions between the real and virtual world. Such interactions can take different forms. As an example, augmented instruments use computers as an extension of the possibilities offered by traditional instruments, as discussed in chapter 5. Lately, augmented instruments have been designed as traditional instruments embedded with sensors. The aspect of the interaction between the human performer and computer-generated sounds is currently an important topic of research for interaction designers and composers.

In 2001, during a panel on the future of computer music research which took place in Barcelona, Xavier Serra claimed that sound synthesis is dead, since nowadays people are just reinventing the wheel, but no new algorithms such as FM synthesis have been invented during the past two decades. Perry Cook in his book *Real-sound Synthesis for Interactive Applications* (Cook 2002) presents a more optimistic view, claiming that the possibilities offered by sound synthesis are never-ending, since new algorithms and new physical phenomena will always be discovered, which can be applied to sonic simulations.

In a way both Serra and Cook are right. It is true that no new synthesis techniques have recently been invented. However, researchers are refining the existing algorithms to improve different aspects such as the analysis techniques or the creation of new sound effects, or they are developing novel software platforms. Moreover, composers are using the existing algorithms extensively to create art works. Successful traditional musical instruments have a history which spans centuries, and this is obviously not the case for virtual musical instruments. It is important to start thinking about issues such as repertoire and sustainability of virtual musical instruments. This will be possible only when new augmented instruments are designed to be used not only by the single musician who built them but by a larger audience.

Among the different sound synthesis techniques introduced in this chapter, research on spectral models is currently very active. Spectral analysis techniques are largely adopted in the field of music information retrieval, which show applications in query by humming, searching for music by similarities and many more. New hybrid synthesis techniques are also starting to appear, such as concatenative sound synthesis (Schwarz 2004), where a large database of sounds, segmented into units, is used as a starting point for producing complex sonic patterns. In the realm of sound modelling, researchers are starting to combine spectral and physical models, to be able to take the advantages of both techniques. This leads to the creation of so-called 'physically informed' techniques, in which the spectral data are driven by physical data. To achieve this goal, a better understanding of the relationship between the way a sound is produced and how it is perceived by the human ear is necessary. Hybrid spectral and physical models seem a promising approach which could limit criticisms of the physical modelling community, since the sound quality of physical modelled sound is often not appreciated by musicians and composers.

From the composers' point of view, however, the main goal in using synthesised sounds will probably always be the possibility to create sonorities which do not exist in the real world. As a researcher, I find it rewarding to see composers constantly interested in experimenting with new developments in sound synthesis; a better communication between scientists and composers should be established, since it is rarely the case that one single human being excels both as a researcher and as an artist.

12 The psychology of electronic music

PETRI TOIVIAINEN

Psychology provides an important base from which to understand music, and is very relevant for electronic music in particular, where psychological theories have even inspired new compositional explorations. Furthermore, in analysing and composing electronic music, traditional music theory is often not applicable. There is no conventional score available on which the analysis of the music could be based, for the music does not rest solely on certain standard notated pitch structures and rhythmic frameworks, but encompasses timbre, spatialisation and other general auditory parameters. An appreciation of the role of aural cognition is vital for a true engagement with this field, where any sounding object is fair game.

The purpose of this chapter is to provide an introduction to perceptual and cognitive processes of music that are fundamental for understanding electronic music. The chapter begins with a discussion of the neuroscientific basis of the auditory system. This is followed by a discussion of low-level phenomena of audition, including the localisation of sound sources, masking, auditory stream segregation and the perception of timbre. Next, the perception of pitch is tackled, with a discussion on its relation to alternative tunings. Finally, basic notions of rhythm perception are introduced. For each of these parts, electronic music examples illustrating the perceptual principles will be given. Any and all principles expounded in this chapter might be taken up and profitably investigated by electronic musicians.

The neuroscientific basis of audition

The auditory system can be partitioned into three processing stages (Pickles 1988; Moore 1997). These are the auditory periphery, the auditory pathway and the auditory cortex. The auditory periphery consists of the outer, middle and inner ear, the auditory pathway of the tracts connecting the ear and the auditory cortex, and the cortical level primarily of the temporal lobes at the left and right sides of the brain.

The ear transforms the mechanical energy of sound vibrations into nerve impulses. The *outer ear* consists of the pinna and the ear canal, whose function is to collect and amplify the energy of the sound and lead it to the tympanic membrane. The ear canal also acts as a closed tube resonator

[218]

and amplifies frequencies in the range of 2–5 kHz. The oscillations of the tympanic membrane are led to the inner ear via three bones (ossicles) of the middle ear, the malleus (hammer), incus (anvil) and stapes (stirrup). The vibrations of the ossicles enter the cochlea, a spiral structure of the inner ear, through the oval window.

The cochlea performs a transformation of the mechanical vibration into electrical impulses. This is carried out through the movement of the *basilar membrane*, which bends rows of hair cells beneath it. The bending of the hair cells gives rise to electric impulses that encode information about the periodicity and intensity of the sound.

Due to its mechanical properties, the basilar membrane acts as a frequency analyser. More specifically, the stiffness of the membrane varies along its length, causing the front end (base) of the membrane to resonate with higher frequencies, and its rear end (apex) with lower frequencies.

The *auditory pathway* leads neural impulses from the cochlea to the cortex. It also contains nuclei that carry out preliminary analysis of the sound signal with regard to, for instance, its intensity and spatial origin. The *cochlear nucleus* sharpens the frequency information contained in the neural signals. The *inferior colliculus* plays a role in sound source locating. The *thalamus* is considered as the 'gateway to cortex' and a 'gatekeeper of conscious experience' (Llinas *et al.* 1998); all neural information to the cortex passes through the thalamus.

The *auditory cortex* is one of the most folded parts of the brain. It is this part of the auditory system where identification and segregation of auditory objects occurs; memory-based sound processing also takes place in the cortex. Although the left and right cortices are mostly similar, some functional differences have been observed. In particular, the left hemisphere has been found to be dominant in rhythmic processing, whereas the right one is more relevant for pitch processing (Zatorre 2003).

There is still much unknown about the functioning of the cortex, but research in this area is active, and there will certainly be many implications of this research for musicians in the future. For instance, revealing the neural determinants of musical emotions is useful for understanding the elements of music that affect listeners' mood. Despite the present incomplete knowledge on the functioning of the brain, there have been several applications to use the activity on the cortex to produce music. In particular, brainwaves measured with electroencephalogram (EEG), have been used to control electronic synthesisers. Pioneers in this field include Richard Teitelbaum and David Rosenboom. For instance, in his work *In Tune* (1967), Teitelbaum combined amplified EEG signals with sounds of heartbeat and breath. In his composition *Ecology of the Skin* (1970), Rosenboom used ten live EEG performers to interactively generate immersive sonic environments.

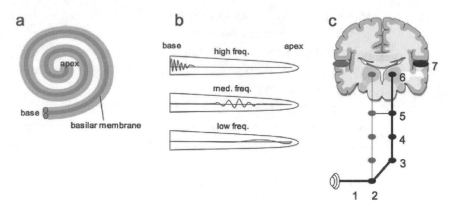

Figure 12.1 (a) Schematic presentation of the cochlea; (b) Excitation pattern of basilar membrane for high, medium, and low frequencies; (c) Auditory pathway; 1. Auditory nerve; 2. Cochlear nucleus; 3. Superior olive; 4. Lateral lemniscus; 5. Inferior colliculus; 6. Thalamus; 7. Auditory cortex

Several computational models of the auditory processing have been proposed and implemented as computer algorithms. For instance, the IPEM Toolbox (Leman, Lesaffre and Tanghe 2001) contains an implementation of models for pitch, sensory dissonance, onset detection, beat and metre, and timbre characteristics. Such models could have various applications as, for instance, artificial ears that could be used by composers to make perceptual analysis of their music. It must be noted, however, that a well-grounded theory of auditory processing only exists for the peripheral level, whereas models of the subsequent levels are much more speculative.

Localisation

Spatialisation has played an important role in electronic music throughout its history. Humans have a remarkable ability to localise sound sources accurately and rapidly. Sound localisation can be divided into three components: localisation of azimuth, elevation and distance. In what follows, each of these components is discussed in turn.

Localisation of azimuth refers to identifying the direction of the sound source on the horizontal plane. The two main cues used in this process are the *Interaural Time Difference* (ITD), and the *Interaural Level Difference* (ILD). The ITD is caused by the difference in the time it takes for the sound wave to reach the two ears. This is illustrated in Fig. 12.2a. The ILD, on the other hand, is caused by the fact that the ear that is more distant from the sound source receives less sound energy due to the head's shadow. This is demonstrated in Fig. 12.2b. To determine the azimuth, the auditory system uses both ITD and ILD information.

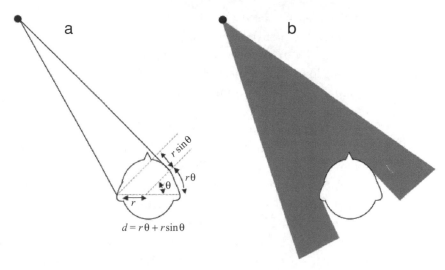

Figure 12.2 (a) Interaural Time Difference. The distance from the sound source (black circle) to the right ear is $d = r\theta + r\sin\theta$ longer than to the left ear, where r denotes the radius of the head and θ the azimuth of the sound source. (b) Interaural Level Difference. Head shadowing reduces the intensity of the sound arriving to the right ear

The *localisation of elevation* of a sound source is less accurate than that of azimuth. Still, we can easily tell whether the sound source is ahead, above or behind us. In this process, there are no binaural cues (ITD, ILD) to rely on; rather, the most important cues are related to the spectral shape of the perceived sound. In particular, the received sound spectrum is modified by reflections from the pinna that depend on elevation.

For *localisation of distance*, the loudness of a sound source is an evident cue, but cognitive knowledge about the quality of the particular sound has to be applied to utilise this cue. For instance, shouting from a long distance can have a higher perceived loudness than whispering from a short distance. A further cue is motion parallax, which refers to the fact that translational movement of the listener causes larger azimuth change for nearby objects than for distant ones. Further cues, sometimes used for musical purposes, are the loudness ratio between the direct and the reverberant sound (Zahorik 2002), and the brightness of timbre. More specifically, high intensity of reverberation gives an impression of a distant sound source. Furthermore, a dark (low-pass filtered) timbre may give an impression of a distant source, because high frequencies attenuate faster than low ones in the air.

One of the first electroacoustic compositions, Edgard Varèse's *Poème électronique*, was presented at the Brussels World's Fair in 1958. The audio part of this multimedia composition consisted of a three-track tape recording, each track of which was distributed dynamically to 425 speakers through an eleven-channel sound system with twenty amplifier channels. Karlheinz

Stockhausen has used spatial sound as an integral part of his work. He produced the first true quadraphonic composition for electronic sounds, *Kontakte* (1960). In this work, Stockhausen used a turntable system with a rotating loudspeaker mechanism, recording to four-channel tape via four microphones spaced around the table, creating an effect of sounds orbiting around the audience.

With methods of digital signal processing it is possible to spatialise sounds accurately by simulating the ITDs and ILDs as well as filtering and adding reverberation. John Chowning (1971) described techniques for the simulation of moving sound sources that are based on the Doppler effect as well as reverberation effects. The Doppler effect refers to the change of frequency caused by the movement of the sound source relative to the listener, and can be used compositionally to create an illusion of movement. Chowning's composition *Turenas* (1972) is a quadraphonic work based on these techniques. In the domain of digital signal processing, various techniques of sound spatialisation have been developed since and applied by composers of electroacoustic music. These include ambisonics, holophonics, wave-field synthesis, Dolby 5.1 Surround, and Digital Theater Systems (DTS) as well as binaural systems based on head-related transfer function (HRTF). Today's efficient computers and sound-processing software allow relatively easy experimentation with sound spatialisation effects. This issue is further discussed in chapter 13 of this book by Natasha Barrett.

Masking

Masking refers to a phenomenon whereby a signal with a low intensity (the maskee) is made inaudible by a stronger signal (the masker). There are two types of masking: simultaneous and temporal. In *simultaneous masking*, the strength of masking depends on the frequency content of the two signals. For instance, with pure tones, the masking effect is stronger the closer the frequency of the maskee is to that of the masker. Moreover, masking is stronger for frequencies above that of the masker than below. Simultaneous masking is caused by the overlap of excitation patterns on the basilar membrane. The range of frequencies within which masking occurs for a given frequency is referred to as the *critical bandwidth*. This bandwidth is about 90 Hz wide for sounds below 200 Hz, and increases to about 900 Hz for frequencies around 5000 Hz. The degree to which complex sounds mask other sounds, or are masked by other sounds, depends, in addition to their intensity, on their spectral content. For instance, a higher intensity difference is needed for a sinusoidal masker to mask a noise-like maskee than is needed for a noise-like masker to mask a sinusoidal maskee.

Temporal masking refers to the phenomenon whereby a soft tone is masked by a louder tone that occurs shortly before (post-masking) or after (pre-masking) the soft tone. For a constant difference in the intensities of the masker and the maskee, post-masking has been found to have a longer range than pre-masking. Typically, post-masking occurs within about 50–200 msec (milliseconds) after the removal of the masker, whereas the range of pre-masking is about one tenth of this (Zwislocki 1978). All three forms of masking are utilised in Perceptual Audio Coding, such as MP3, MiniDisk, and Ogg Vorbis.

The phenomenon of masking has a number of implications to compositional practice. For instance, a loud sound object in a composition may make weaker sound objects in nearby frequencies inaudible; assigning the sound objects different frequency ranges will diminish the effect of masking. For instance, a melodic line is often played in a higher register than the accompaniment to make it better audible. The implication of temporal masking is that the audibility of less loud parts of the musical material can be improved by placing them at different temporal locations than louder parts. Such techniques are applied by many musicians and mix engineers in their practice.

Auditory streaming

Our auditory system has a remarkable capacity to make sense of the sounds we receive from our environment. In particular, it can extract from the sound signals we receive meaningful chunks of information that correspond to real-world activities. For instance, in a room full of people talking to each other we can usually without any trouble concentrate on the speech of a single person. In other words, our perceptual system is capable of extracting meaningful *auditory streams* from the perceived sound signals. When listening to music, we also tend to hear the auditory information as a collection of streams, such as parts in counterpoint, melodic lines, inner voices, bass lines, and accompaniment.

The research on the formation of auditory streams has a long history. The founders of Gestalt psychology, such as Paul Ehrenfels (1890) and Max Wertheimer (1923), initially presented musical examples to support their notions. The main ideas of Gestalt psychology can be summarised into a few principles. The ones that are most relevant with regard to auditory streaming are the following:

Principle of proximity: objects that are close to each other tend to be grouped together

Principle of similarity: objects that share similar characteristics tend to be
   grouped together
Principle of good continuation: there is a preference for continuous forms
Principle of closure: objects that seem to form closed entities tend to be
   grouped together
Principle of common fate: objects that move together tend to be grouped
   together

In addition to the Gestalt psychologists, the problem of auditory streaming has been studied by researchers such as Hermann von Helmholtz, Carl
Stumpf, Jay Dowling, Diana Deutsch, Leon van Noorden, David Wessel and
Stephen McAdams. The most influential work in this field is the book *Auditory Scene Analysis* by Al Bregman (1990). In this book, Bregman presents
detailed accounts of various processes involved in auditory streaming, many
of which are based on the notions originally presented by the Gestalt psychologists. Bregman distinguishes between two main types of processes
that are involved in auditory streaming. These are sequential integration
and spectral integration.

Sequential integration refers to the putting together of events that follow
one another in time. Musical events can coalesce into a single stream if they
are sufficiently proximal in time and/or pitch. Moreover, the closer in time
two events are, the more proximal in pitch they have to be in order to be
integrated into a single stream. An example of this dependence is graphi-
cally depicted in Fig. 12.3a. The dependence between pitch and temporal
proximity in stream formation was quantified by van Noorden (1977), who
defined the temporal coherence and fission boundaries for auditory streaming. An example of auditory stream formation can be found, for instance, in
Andean pipe music where musicians play alternate notes that, due to their
pitch proximity, are perceived as a single stream. Sequential integration can
also be based on similarity in timbre or loudness, so for instance, if a musical
passage contains tones played by two instruments, these tend to be heard as
two separate streams.

Spectral integration refers to integrating components that occur at the
same time in different parts of the spectrum. There are a number of principles that govern this phenomenon. First, we tend to group frequency components by harmonicity. More specifically, components sharing the same
fundamental are likely to come from the same source, and are grouped
together. Second, we group frequency components by onset. This means
that frequency components that have proximal onset times are likely to
come from the same source, and are grouped together. Finally, we group
frequency components based on similarity of their temporal evolution.
For instance, spectral components sharing the same frequency modulation

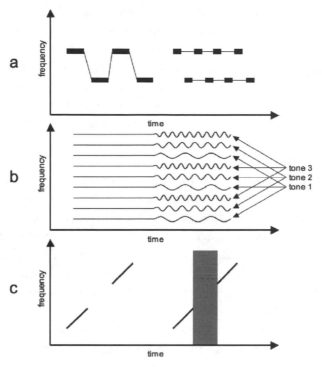

Figure 12.3 (a) Grouping by proximity. A slow sequence of tones with alternating frequencies (left) is perceived as a single stream; the same sequence played twice as fast is perceived as two separate streams; (b) Grouping by common fate. A collection of partials with no frequency modulation is perceived as a single tone (left); when frequency modulation is introduced, tones with similar FM pattern are grouped together, resulting in a percept of three separate tones (right); (c) Principle of 'old-plus-new heuristic'. Two frequency slides are perceived as separate tones (left); when a tone burst is played between the slides, they are perceived as a single tone

pattern (such as vibrato) are likely to come from the same source, and are grouped together (Cook 1999). An example of this phenomenon is shown in Fig. 12.3b. The last two principles are instances of the Gestalt principle of common fate.

A further principle involved in spectral integration is what Bregman refers to as the '*old-plus-new heuristic*'. This refers to perceptual continuation of an old sound at the presentation of a more complex sound. In other words, if part of a present sound can be interpreted as being a continuation of a previous sound, the auditory system tends to make this interpretation. An example of this principle is illustrated in Fig. 12.3c.

Perception of auditory streams plays a crucial role in the parsing of musical compositions. Based on the principles described above we hear, for instance, separate voices in a musical work. In much electronic music we cannot talk about melodic lines or even pitch, but the music still has temporal and spectral dimensions, to which the streaming principles apply.

As a result, in the total mass of sound we perceive layers that are independent from each other and that at some points fuse into a single percept.

Similarities based on timbre can be used to compose streams. On the other hand, introducing timbral differences within a sequential stream may add interest. This has been used, for instance in *Klangfarbenmelodien* by Schoenberg and Webern. In a melodic line, subsequent tones are played with different instruments. The rapid changes in timbre interfere with the smooth sequential integration, thus bringing interest to the music.

Very often a clear segregation of two streams in music is desired. To obtain this, one can, for instance, introduce differences between the spectral content of the two streams. A classical example of this is the singer's formant, a spectral bulge around the frequency of 3 kHz that helps the singer to be distinguished from the ensemble. Furthermore, the principle of common fate can be applied by introducing individual vibrato patterns to the streams. A further means is to add minor temporal deviations to otherwise simultaneous events. Even a slight asynchrony renders the two streams perceptually separate. Sound spatialisation provides a further means to separate streams: sound sources are segregated more easily when they are placed at different directions in the sound field than when they appear to come from the same direction.

Timbre perception

The timbre of sound is a complex phenomenon. There have been a number of studies aiming at extracting the most salient acoustic attributes affecting the perception of timbre (most aimed at studying monophonic instrument tone colour, rather than general sound objects). A widely used method is *similarity rating* (SR): subjects are asked to rate, on a given scale, the dissimilarity of all possible pairs in the set of stimuli. *Multidimensional scaling* (MDS) is then used to map the tones onto a low-dimensional space – frequently referred to as the timbre space. Most of these studies have found that a three-dimensional timbre space represents the dissimilarity ratings to a sufficient degree of precision (e.g. Grey 1977; McAdams *et al.* 1995). The first dimension in the MDS solution has been found to correlate with the *spectral centroid*, which corresponds to the perceived brightness of a tone. The second dimension in the MDS solution relates to the *attack time*, that is, the time it takes for the amplitude of the tone to reach the maximal value. As regards the third dimension, there is more discrepancy between the studies. It has been associated with spectral variation over time or spectral irregularity.

Most of the work on timbre has concentrated on single musical tones, that is, *monophonic timbre*, whereas the overall timbre of a musical piece, also referred to as the *polyphonic timbre*, has received less attention. Recently, however, there has been increased interest in the study of this phenomenon (Aucouturier 2006). Much of this work has been carried out in the field of Music Information Retrieval, where it has been found that various descriptors of polyphonic timbre can be leveraged, for instance, for the automatic classification of audio. A practical application of polyphonic timbre analysis is the Shazam query-by-example system for recognition of music via mobile phone. The system is based on a method of audio fingerprinting; relative positions of peaks in the spectrum of the audio query are located and converted into a fingerprint, which is then matched with the fingerprints of the pieces in the database.

A wider notion of timbre has played a vital role in electroacoustic music. For instance, the French composer Pierre Schaeffer (1910–95), the inventor of *musique concrète*, started from concrete sounds such as voices, noises, as well as sounds of prepared and conventional instruments, experimented with them, and abstracted them into musical compositions. Examples of such works by him are *Suite pour quatorze instruments* (1949), which is based on timbral transformations of orchestral instruments, and *Symphonie pour un homme seul* (1951), co-composed by Pierre Henry, which employed, among other things, the sounds of the human body. The composition *Atmosphères* (1961) by the Hungarian composer György Ligeti is a classic example of timbral composition. Written for a large orchestra, it abandons the concepts of melody, harmony and rhythm, while concentrating solely on the timbre of the sound produced. *Atmosphères* opens with a large cluster chord comprising every tone in the chromatic scale over a range of five octaves. Because of the pitch proximity of adjacent components in the cluster, the auditory systems cannot resolve every tone. Therefore, what is perceived is the timbre of the sound mass rather than a chord.

Advanced methods of digital signal processing allow operations on the microscopic level of sound structure, dubbed *microsound* by Curtis Roads (2001). Granular synthesis uses small pieces of sound, typically with a length between 1 and 50 msec, to build sound textures, or clouds. The first composer to use this technique was Iannis Xenakis in his compositions *Analogique A et B* (1958–9). Extended notions of timbre and sound materials are discussed in the next chapter in particular.

Pitch perception and alternative tunings

Pitch is a perceptual attribute of a tone that depends mainly on its frequency content. For complex harmonic tones, the perceived pitch is equal to the fundamental frequency of the complex tone, that is, the frequency of the first partial. For inharmonic tones, such as a bell tone, the perceived pitch may, however, be unclear. In fact, such tones often elicit a percept of several simultaneous pitches. Terhardt *et al.* (1982) proposed a model of *pitch salience* according to which this attribute depends on the degree of harmonicity of the tone, that is, the degree of coincidence of the subharmonics of the partials.

The *place theory* of pitch perception, originally suggested by George von Békésy (1963), states that the pitch percept can be explained by the locus of maximal vibration on the basilar membrane. The *rate theory* (Seebeck, 1843), on the other hand, states that the neural firing patterns encode the periodic structure of auditory stimuli. According to a commonly accepted view, both place and rate information are used by the auditory system to determine pitch, with rate information dominating for low frequencies and place information for high frequencies.

Traditionally, most music is comprised of a collection of discrete pitches, or *scales*, instead of a continuum of them. Furthermore, it is common that the scales repeat themselves after an octave, or a frequency ratio of two. Many studies have indicated that tones an octave apart are perceived as highly similar (Burns 1999) – a phenomenon referred to as *octave equivalence*. Conventionally, the number of pitches per octave has been between five and seven (Carterette and Kendall 1999). The repetition of pitch intervals after each octave is, however, dropped in some scales, such as the Bohlen–Pierce scale (see below). Moreover Iannis Xenakis uses non-octave scales in his works, such as *Tetora for string quartet* (1990), and discusses them in his writings on sieve structures (Xenakis 1992).

Scales are derived from *tuning systems*. In particular, a scale is a subset of a tuning system, often uneven in the sense that it consists of pitch intervals of varying sizes. There is a long tradition in the development of various tuning systems in Western culture, starting from Pythagoras (582–507 BC), who observed that consonant musical intervals produced by a vibrating string were associated with simple integer ratios of string length. In the Western world, the 12 Tone Equal Tempered tuning (or 12TET tuning) is the most prevalent nowadays. Although it is the most studied tuning system from both music-theoretical and perceptual points of view, it must be noted that it is not universally accepted.

The 12 Tone Equal Tempered tuning consists of intervals of equal size with a frequency ratio of $2^{1/12}$ between subsequent tones. It provides an approximation of tunings based on simple frequency ratios, while allowing for modulation between keys. It is possible to construct equally tempered scales beyond the 12TET tuning by using a frequency ratio of $2^{1/k}$, where k can be any integer. Many of these alternative tunings have been proposed to provide an approximation for a tuning based on simple frequency ratios. For instance, the 19TET tuning was used by the composer Guillaume Costeley as early as the sixteenth century. This tuning serves as an approximation for mean-tone temperament. The 22TET tuning, proposed by the nineteenth-century English scholar R. H. M. Bosanquet, provides an approximation of the five-limit just intonation, that is, a tuning consisting of frequency ratios that can be expressed with the primes 2, 3 and 5. Many composers, such as Charles Ives and Krzysztof Penderecki, have composed music using the 24TET tuning, consisting of half-semitone intervals. Higher-order equal temperaments that have been proposed include the 31TET, 53TET and 72TET tuning.

One great advantage of computers is the ease with which they allow exploration of alternative tuning systems. The 12TET tuning was originally adopted in order to allow flexible modulations between keys, for which the just intonations were not suitable. Today's computer technology allows the use of adaptive tunings, in which the just intonation is adapted to fit with the current key (see, e.g., Sethares 1994, 1999).

It is not necessary that an equally tempered tuning be based on the octave. Generally, one can design equally tempered tunings using a frequency ratio of $p^{1/k}$, where p can be any number. For instance, the Bohlen–Pierce tuning is a 13TET tuning based on a *tritave*, or a frequency ratio of $p=3$. This tuning can be seen as an approximation of a just intonation system based only on ratios of odd whole numbers, therefore being appropriate for timbres containing only odd harmonics. Composers who have utilised the Bohlen–Pierce scale in their works include Charles Carpenter (e.g., *Frog à la Pêche*, 1994), Juan Reyes (e.g., *ppP*, 1999–2000) and Richard Boulanger (e.g., *Solemn Song for Evening*, 1990).

Rhythm perception

The auditory system can accurately detect the temporal structure of the sounds it receives. In the shortest timescale, there are certain thresholds that are useful for electronic musicians. In binaural hearing, temporal differences as short as twenty microseconds can be detected. For monaural hearing, the threshold of simultaneity for clicks is about two milliseconds and for musical tones about twenty milliseconds. Echoes are discriminated if their temporal distance from the direct sound is at least fifty to sixty milliseconds.

Much music is organised so as to contain temporal periodicities that evoke a percept of regularly occurring *pulses*, or *beats*. The ability to infer beat and metre from music is one of the basic activities of musical cognition. It is a rapid process: after having heard only a short fraction of music, we are able to develop a sense of beat and tap our foot along with it. Even if the music is rhythmically complex, containing a range of different time values and probably syncopation, we are capable of inferring the different periodicities and synchronising to them.

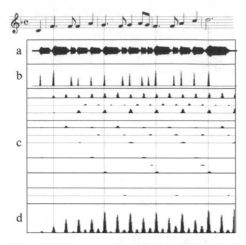

Figure 12.4 Response of a resonating oscillator bank to an excerpt from the Scottish folk melody 'Auld Lang Syne'. a) waveform; b) output of an onset detector; c) outputs of resonating oscillators; d) summed output of all oscillators. Notice the form of the summed output indicating a hierarchical structure of beat strengths.

A rhythmical sequence usually evokes a number of different pulse sensations, each of which has a different perceptual salience. The salience of a given pulse sensation depends on a number of factors related to the surface and structural properties of music. These factors include the frequency of tone onsets that coincide with the pulse (Palmer and Krumhansl 1990), and the *phenomenal accents* of these notes (Lerdahl and Jackendoff 1983). Phenomenal accents arise from changes in surface properties of music such as pitch, duration, loudness and timbre. For instance, a long note is usually perceived as more accented than a short one (Parncutt 1994).

A further factor that affects the salience of pulse sensation is the *pulse period*. According to a number of studies (Fraisse 1982; Parncutt 1994; van Noorden and Moelants 1999), the most salient pulse sensations have a period of approximately 600 msec, the region of greatest salience being between 400 and 900 msec. One should note that this range of periods corresponds roughly to the speed of some basic human activities such as heartbeat, locomotion, and infant sucking.

In much Western music, the perceived pulses are often hierarchically organised, and consist of at least two simultaneous levels, whose periods have an integer ratio. This gives rise to a percept of regularly alternating strong and weak beats, a phenomenon referred to as *metre* (Cooper and Meyer 1960; Lerdahl and Jackendoff 1983). In Western music, the ratio of the pulse lengths is usually limited to 1:2 (duple metre) and 1:3 (triple metre). It must be noted, however, that this kind of hierarchical organisation of pulses does not exist in all music. Examples of types of music that do not possess such metrical structure are found in Norwegian Hardanger fiddle music, Lappish *yoiks*, West African polyrhythmic percussion music and Eastern European *aksak* dance music. Electronic music allows the possibility to explore non-standard and alternative metrical structures which diverge from Western common practice to a wider sphere of human music-making, whilst still grounded in psychological percepts.

The perception of pulse and metre has been modelled computationally using a variety of different approaches (Gouyon and Dixon 2005; Collins 2006; also see chapter 10). Fig. 12.4 displays the response of a model of resonating oscillators to an excerpt of music. Whenever a note onset occurs, oscillators that are in synchrony with it are excited (Large and Kolen 1994; Toiviainen 1998).

Conclusion

This chapter has reviewed some of the important aspects of music perception and cognition that can be regarded as useful for gaining better understanding of the perception of electronic music. Although the different musical elements have been discussed separately, their interaction may also play a role in music perception, though this aspect has been less studied.

Most of the processes discussed in this chapter are relatively low-level ones. Higher-level aspects of cognition that are relevant include the perception of form and the effect of memory. In general, these processes are less well understood than the low-level ones. This is due to the increased effect of individual and cultural background on these processes and the consequent larger inter-individual variation.

Obviously, due to space limitations, many of these aspects have been described on a rather superficial level. To gain a better understanding of these processes, the interested reader is directed to works such as Deutsch (1999), Snyder (2000), and McAdams and Bigand (1993). Perceptual principles discussed in this chapter are intimately related to many issues that arise in other chapters of this companion.

Electronic music provides a range of devices for the production of sound and musical material that is far more extensive than that available with more traditional instruments. While these tools facilitate versatile expression of musical ideas, they also make it possible to produce musical material that exceeds the capacity of the human perceptual system. Therefore, for an electronic musician, being aware of the capabilities and limitations of human auditory processing is crucial for efficient communication of musical ideas and exploration of new grounds.

13 Trends in electroacoustic music

NATASHA BARRETT

The possibilities for sound manipulation, spatialisation and performance have given rise to a multidimensional approach to electroacoustic composition. Yet from whichever background we find ourselves, a number of trends following historical, sociological and technical developments can be uncovered. This chapter identifies these trends and their compositional and aesthetic circumstances, forming a springboard for a new composer to the genre. Although it is unrealistic to delve extensively into all that is relevant, I hope to encourage the reader to more deeply explore the issues raised through the references and discography. Without dwelling on the problems of terminology, let us accept for now the term 'electroacoustic music' as including all that is not purely acoustic music, based on instrumental models nor commercially orientated.

Where are we today?

The novelty of the early decades – of listening to strange sound emanating from loudspeakers – has passed. Trial and error has resulted in as many new approaches to materials and structure as has conceptualisation and intellectualisation. Yet if as composers we are to 'progress', and not 'recycle', we need to refine our art form and learn from those few works which have survived the past sixty years, as well as discover masterpieces from our current year. After all, music technology changes dramatically in less than a decade while musical aesthetics require reflection and development benefiting from longer historical periods. Too often do we hear new compositions from all environments where refinement and development in both technical approach and musical expression is stark – and would have benefited from a deeper insight into the repertoire.

In recent years, the popular versus high art divide in music has formed a topic of debate, predominantly driven by a social-economic underlay and a commonality of tools and sounds amongst diverse musical genres. As an electroacoustic composer and as a general electronic music consumer I see many music establishments – festivals, education institutions, funding bodies – attempting to collapse all electronic music genres into one enormous pool of equivalence. Although this approach is clearly useful in spreading genres across audiences it ignores two important differences:

(i) Sociological and economic differences attached to the creative process, determining the turn over of material, the importance of image and fashion in the final result and inevitably the intellectualisation and time involved.

(ii) Difference in demands on the listening process in terms of perception, cognition, the balance between emotional, intellectual and physical listening, and inevitably the duration over which listeners must actively engage and sustain the cognitive process.

Theoretically, a continuum between popular and high art genres may be possible, yet few works lie in the central part of this continuum and instead gravitate by either *poietic* (productive or formative) or *esthesic* (receptive or perceptive) constructs to each pole.

Sound for our ears: the conception of acousmatic music

The ability to record sound and compose music in a recorded format led to the most significant change in the creation, definition and perception of music. John Cage's early use of electronic means explored indeterminacy and the context of the live event, demanding a re-evaluation of the sound around us and of our definition of music. Yet the tape recorder offered much more. It allowed any sound to be used as compositional material, provided basic transformations and allowed identical replay. Most significantly, this way of working revealed new schemes for compositional organisation beginning with the sound itself. Yet in this aural compositional approach, non-aural based musical structuring might come into play at some point in the procedure.

The aesthetic differences between the *elektronische Musik* of the Cologne studio and the *musique concrète* of the Paris studio in the 1950s is well documented (Manning 1985, pp. 19–78). The former sound-world was concerned with purely electronic sources, the latter with acoustic sources of inherently complex spectra. Structurally, the former took advantage of electronics as a way to exercise precise control over the material such that detailed scores could be realised, and we can see a natural progression from the serialist techniques of the Viennese School. Stockhausen's works *Studie I & II* and Eimert's *Struktur 8* are representative examples. In contrast, musique concrète found inspiration from a rediscovery of sound via the recorded medium and an experimental aural approach. Early works from this period include Schaeffer's series of *Etudes* from 1947–8.

Musique concrète is commonly referred to as a music in which any sound can be used, but this is a misleading interpretation and I will later use the term 'concrete sound' to refer generally to recorded acoustic sources. The original compositional method began with what was *concrete* (sound) and the process was intended to result in *abstract* music. In musique concrète we are chiefly concerned with the way sound *functions* when detached from its visual and realtime original causation or a *perceptual* method of working. It is here that the objective term 'acousmatic' can be introduced. The term *acousmatic* derives from the Akousmatikoi, a group of Pythagoras' disciples who listened to his lectures from behind a veil. French theorist Jerôme Peignot later used Pythagoras' term to describe musique concrète's separation of sound from visual reference. Schaeffer used the term for musical description to assert that a visual link between the sound source and its origin was unnecessary. Under these criteria Schaeffer established a framework for compositional practice.

In 1952 he published a syntax for musique concrète in the treatise *Esquisse d'un solfège concrète*, which appeared as the last section of the book *A la recherche d'une musique concrète*. The treatise is divided into two main sections. The first consists of twenty-five definitions to describe the *objet sonore* (a sound event isolated from its original context). The second section describes how these definitions can be applied to create a language. This *solfège* underwent substantial work as Schaeffer continued to develop his ideas, culminating in the *Traité des objets musicaux* (1966). In this substantial text Schaeffer attempts to classify all sound-producing objects by dividing their characteristics into seven parameters: mass, dynamic, melodic profile, mass profile, grain, inflection and harmonic timbre. Schaeffer further describes how he viewed the listening process as consisting of four interrelated modes – the *Quatre Ecoutes*. These modes of listening are useful in understanding the development of electroacoustic music aesthetics since Schaeffer. The Quatre Ecoutes have undergone various adaptations in both French and English. Schaeffer's originals are:

Mode 1: *Ecouter* (information-gathering). This is where our attention is interested in the immediate identity of the sound.

Mode 2: *Ouïr* (to hear as passive reception). This is the lowest level in our auditory perception where we cannot help but *hear* the sound, but there is no intention to *listen* or interpret meaning. We exercise this listening mode every day in connection to background noise.

Mode 3: *Entendre* (responding to intrinsic properties of the sound). With this mode we ignore any meaning behind the causation and focus on purely spectral phenomena.

Mode 4: *Comprendre* (the coding of a musical language). Here sound is only the vehicle for the meaning. The practice of entendre is intended to lead to the emergence or structuring of a musical 'language'.

Modes 1 and 2 according to Schaeffer are spontaneous, universal and referred to as natural listening. Modes 3 and 4 are cultural – they require learning and cannot be regarded as universal. Schaeffer aimed to use the mode 3 approach to create a complex musical language ignoring referential aspects in the sound, proposing 'reduced listening' – where the listener concentrates only on the sound's inherent features. However, common experience tells us that it is nearly impossible to ignore referential information. Our perceptual mechanism has been biologically conditioned to explain causation and find meaning. Developing an entire musical language based on mode 3 listening is therefore unrealistic. But there are some exceptions. When working in the studio composers often experience reduced listening through intense repeated listening. With sufficient repetition within a composition, a normal listener may gain a similar experience. Steve Reich's tape work *Come Out* detailed later in this chapter approaches these criteria.

Michel Chion, who from 1970 worked as Schaeffer's assistant, prefers to explain three listening modes (Chion 1994, pp. 25–30). Chion's *Causal Listening* is where we listen to the sound in order to gather information (similar to Schaeffer's mode 1). *Semantic Listening* refers to a code or language that is needed to interpret the message (similar to Schaeffer's mode 4). *Reduced listening* is as Schaeffer explained. Chion therefore does not consider the act of *hearing* (the passive reception of Schaeffer's mode 2), only of *listening*.

Denis Smalley presents another variation by explaining greater cross-referencing between listening modes. Mode 1 perceptions may be culturally conditioned and therefore influence the syntax formed in mode 4 listening. In fact, one sound may be experienced as traversing *all* modes of listening depending on context. As Smalley clearly illustrates, if you mix a car sound into a surreal car-scape, mode 1 listening is most important. Whereas if you place the same sound in an acoustic instrument context, then its intrinsic – or mode 3 attributes – are more highly weighted within the complete context. Smalley suggests that our common listening experience is one of forming varyingly precise or vague mental connections to an idea of a source-sound, to a scenario, or to an idea of physical energy. In some shorter duration circumstances, when a sound is extremely abstract, the strength of referential images may be so vague that the ear is more attentive to a mode 3 listening state. Over longer durations, context will lead our perception through all modes of listening as new information is revealed.

In broader terms there are many ways to listen, and music is often designed specifically for these listening strategies. Religious music, political music, music intended for meditation and music intended to encourage other activities are common. For example, the allegory of political oppression in Trevor Wishart's *Red Bird: A Political Prisoner's Dream* (1978) clearly conditions the listener's approach. Pauline Oliveros's 'Deep Listening' suggests a multifaceted listening approach intended to evoke a heightened state of awareness.[1] *Muzak* plays on passive reception to encourage us in some other activity. The flip between passive and active reception finds its way into other types of music depending on the individual listener. Many listeners will flip between passive and active reception in response to lengthy minimalist structures, to overtly complex music or as a meditative act.

Schaeffer and his closer relations

Solfège of the sound object

In the *Esquisse d'un solfège concret* Schaeffer documented what he experienced during the working process from sound through to composition. This process began with the act of recording. Sound was then classified based on length and centre of interest without aesthetic or technical analysis. The next stage involved value judgements on complexity and how the ear may isolate aspects such as repetitive or thick sound complexes, or amplitude envelope morphologies prior to any sound processing or composition. Processing operations prior to composition are then discussed, based on how much the sound is altered from its original, and how much variation is applied to pitch, intensity or timbre. Finally Schaeffer discusses compositional processes such as the use of juxtaposition (montage), superimposition (mixing), instrumental sound and spatial issues connected to performance.[2] Schaeffer points towards the importance of perception yet separates sound processing from composition (a link that is now generally accepted as inseparable), but we can speculate that this separation possibly resulted from the era's labour-intensive tools. Likewise, spatial issues are seen primarily in a performance context, whereas our current technology allows the composer to embed spatial issues more deeply into composition.

The development of Schaeffer's theories and Spectromorphology

Spectromorphology, a term coined by Denis Smalley, is a concatenation of two words: *spectro* (spectra) and *morphology* (knowledge of shape). Typically, spectromorphology refers to the dynamic shaping of the sound-spectrum through time. Within spectromorphology Smalley embeds Schaeffer's theories while refining the perceptual approach. Smalley's aim was to present a comprehensive terminology for describing and analysing structural relations and behaviours *as experienced* in a multitude of Western musics and musical thinking, rather than outlining a methodology or to forge a new musical language. Some of the most important differences between Schaeffer's solfège and Smalley's spectromorphology concern this connection to the listening experience, and in doing so spectromorphology may also be used as an analytical method for many styles of Western instrumental music. In summarising Smalley's approach it is useful to first discuss *indicative fields* and *networks*. *Indicative* concerns the message in the sound, the link between human experience in a non-sounding world and musical perception. The indicative field can be regarded as beginning in Schaeffer's listening mode 1 and then spreading into mode 4 as the musical context develops. Nine indicative relationships are identified. Three are listed as archetypal and attached directly to our physical selves: *gesture*, *utterance* and *behaviour*, while the remaining six are: *energy*, *motion*, *object/substance*, *environment*, *vision* and *space*. Further, the idea of *surrogacy* is introduced concerning gesture and the supposed human presence behind the creation of the sound. It is however easy to find 'surrogacy' as pertinent to all the indicative relationships.[3]

Field refers to any one of the nine classes when regarded separately. *Network* is used to refer to an interdependent network of many fields surrounding a central field under focus. Smalley suggests that indicative fields cannot include 'compositional models based on scientific, mathematical, statistical or other theories, regardless of any universal validity', as these models cannot be understood without explanation. Here we may observe a difference between the concepts of Smalley, Xenakis and compositional techniques involving numerical data.

Delving into the sounding world fully embraces the original spectromorphology arguments. The main points of consideration are: the spectral typology (continuum between note and noise), morphology (temporal shaping archetypes), motion typology (motion analogies), motion style (the internal details of the motion typology) and spatial settings (acoustic analogies and pitch-space settings).[4]

Although spectromorphology is a descriptive tool based on aural perception, it has clearly influenced a great number of composers and compositions. Often a composer will use spectromorphological analysis techniques to clarify what has emerged from a compositional process, and then take the results of this analysis as a point of departure for further development.

In recent years, software that allows fine control over sound transformation has facilitated a greater exploration of motion morphology counterpoint, which the reader will hear by comparing early analogue techniques with later works employing computer tools. To draw from Smalley's own works, *Darkness After Time's Colours* (Smalley 1976) and *Valley Flow* (Smalley 1992) both strive for counterpoint rather than montage, yet the motion counterpoint in *Valley Flow* is clearer and more controlled in its musical purpose, particularly from 5′35–9′50.

Tape techniques and repetition

Compositional ideas stemming from the tape techniques of montage, mixing and looping have prevailed independently of the media and are common

in all forms of composition and music production. Schaeffer's first attention to repetition was in *Etude aux chemins de fer* (1948), composed almost
entirely from a succession of repeating sounds. The fact that the tape recorder
allowed identical replay was later exploited in Steve Reich's *Come Out* (1966).
In this work we hear a gradual abstraction process – where repetitive rhythmic organisation of text fragments emphasises phrase, rhythm and pitch
over semantic meaning, placing the listener in a Schaefferian mode 3 position. In Luc Ferrari's *Unheimlich Schön* (1971) the repetitive phrase is somewhat longer, and combined with an intense intimacy and clarity of closely
recorded text and breath sounds the listener may feel a simultaneous and
paradoxical need for listening with modes 1, 3 and 4.

Musical hierarchies constructed from repeated units of lengths ranging
from a few seconds to many minutes can be found in all musical genres in both western and non-western musical systems. Works as different
as Birtwistle's orchestral *Earth Dances* and Stockhausen's electroacoustic
Kontakte are constructed from complex synchronic relations between short
loops and cycles of greatly varying timescales. Yet the possibility of creating
exactly repeated loops and finely controlled microscopic changes in cyclic
constructions is unique to the use of tape or computer tools. In the following I focus on that which is perceptually relevant to exactly controlled
repetition and variation and therefore inaccessible to acoustic instrumental
performance.

Streaming effects and emergent information

A complex unit of sound created by micro-sound editing, sequencing, montage or transformation effects, or by selecting a single complex concrete
sound, may yield a seemingly random arrangement of amplitude and frequency variation when played through only once. Repetition of this unit
produces streaming effects revealing rhythm, pulse, phrase, complex syn-
copations and polyrhythms. The maximum possible duration of the unit
for the streaming effects to be audible is connected strongly to the type of
sound material, its complexity, and the attentiveness and skills of the listener,
often defying any rule base and requiring aural decisions. A composer may
control the emphasis of different emergent effects by changing the speed
of playback, timbre, relation between internal details, internal complexity,
duration, or by substituting or removing information. As the loop increases
in duration, or as the variation increases, the ear is less able to group similar
information and deduce the resulting streams. Thus the composer leads the
listener from a beat-driven experience to one where other aspects are more
immediate.

Over short listening durations we find a commonality between high art
and many popular electronic structures. The point of departure is found

when we look at simultaneous layers of information, development over longer durations, in the complexity of the syntax and ultimately the function of the music in relation to the listener and demands on the time span of attentive listening. To illustrate we can consider a seventeen-minute example interesting in its simplicity: François Bayle's *L'aventure du cri* from *L'expérience acoustique* (1970–2). As the music unfolds, three main layers consisting of slowly changing looped units, of greatly different duration and with varying degrees of surrogacy, weave in and out of focus. That which is set in counterpoint is unified by a common pulse, yet the listener needs to maintain attention throughout the work. In Luc Ferrari's *Les anecdotiques* (2001–2) we hear an alternative approach where the natural morphologies of spectrally and anecdotally complex sources are gently teased to subtly combine natural and studio edited repetitions, rhythms and cycles.

Voice and language in an acousmatic world

Language and utterance provide a rich set of source materials for composers, and their use far predates electronic media. Our voice is our primary expressive instrument. We all recognise vocal sources and it is nearly impossible to disentangle vocal and human associations. The voice is an indicator of complex emotional states as well as a carrier for communication. In a compositional context we may consider whether it is desirable to distance ourselves from the emotional content of the utterance to allow its musical role to be heard. If we consider Berio's *Sequenza III* (1966), analysis of the score reveals the compositional structure. Yet on experiencing a live performance the emotional energy and facial expressions of the live soprano may easily distract.

In Stockhausen's *Gesang der Jünglinge* (1956), Berio's *Thema (Omaggio a Joyce)* (1958) and *Visage* (1961) and in the works of Schaeffer and Henry we hear different approaches to the acousmatic voice. But these examples are isolated cases, rather than forming an aesthetic framework: *text-sound composition* began a clearer lineage (Hanson 1993). The term was first used by Lars-Gunnar Bodin and Bengt Emil Johnson, who from 1967–71 were active composers in *The Language Group* at Fylkingen, Stockholm. Text-sound composition began in acoustic performance as a way forward for modern poetry and literature in the late 1960s. Visuals, rhythm and implication were used instead of traditional metaphor. Sound itself, the method of sound production, and the connection to expressive utterance were more important than semantic meaning. Tape, and later computer resources, facilitated non-performable rhythm, 'pre-linguistic' utterances and the removal of semantic intelligibility. Once semantics are removed, the possibilities for non-linear forms increase, and parallel event streams become important.

Many composers also use longer text extracts either of their own recordings or from archival material – where the original semantic meaning, the delivery and possibly the identity of the speaker are important – and where tape or computer manipulation changes the semantic meaning in some way. Steve Reich's *Come Out* (1966) and Luc Ferrari's *Unheimlich Schön* (1971) have already been described above. In Paul Lansky's *Idle Chatter* (1985) we hear a texture designed to make it seem as if there are understandable words, but what results is rhythm and harmony created through processing the human voice using LPC (Linear Predictive Coding – a vocoder-type effect), granular synthesis and plucked string synthesis. Other techniques we hear are montage, often combined with sound transformations, creating a hybrid of transcontexts and surreal landscapes. Lars-Gunnar Bodin's *Cybo II* (1967) presents a short illustrative example. In *Vox 5* (1986) Trevor Wishart explores two compositional approaches to the voice: (i) Continuous transformations of vocal to non-vocal identities, making the source (voice) and the goal (other) clear, playing on symbolic connection; (ii) Vocal source transformations that hover in the centre point between source and goal such that dual meaning is found at a single point in realtime.[5]

Working in the extremes of sound: from sine tone to noise

Noise elements are clear throughout the electroacoustic repertoire. In one extreme we can hear Stockhausen's *Microphonie I* as containing significantly 'noisy' sound, yet the role of this noise is of low importance to the work's aesthetical and structural foundation. Noise may also result as a side-effect from some other sound transformation or compositional technique, or be the perceptual result of a spectral densification. We can also identify the use of noise as important to the compositional approach. Here are a few examples: to enhance temporal or spatial articulation, particularly within a microsound approach where shortening the sound grain creates a broader spectrum, such as in Road's *Volt Air* (2003); to mask, obscure and reveal layers in the composition, or temporarily distract the ear, such as in Ambrose Field's *One Hell of a Place to Lose a Cow* (2002); as inherent to environmental or natural materials, such as in Annette Vande Gorne's *Feu* (1986); to inject ambiguity in sound or spatial identity such as in Beatriz Ferreyra's *Vivencias* (2001); or to be explored for its intrinsic character, often set against sine tones and other repeated waveforms, such as in Elio Martusciello's *Hz – limits of the technology* (2000). Noise may also be used with intent in relation to its sociological implications. From a historical perspective, sociological noise elements in electronic music stem from the Japanese experimental music scene rooted in the punk movement and has very little to do with electroacoustic music. However, electroacoustic composers are also part of society, and if not drawing from punk history, convergent trends – particularly when based on a reaction against social, economic or political forces – will inevitably be found. Many will say that noise is 'annoyance', 'mess' and 'disturbance'. Others may say noise is beauty (as a reaction against stereotypes of beauty?), while many cultures associate noise with death, and in general noise as sound tending towards entropy (the 'end?'). How we perceive and approach noise changes continually – the historically shocking sounds of Russolo's *intonarumori* or noise machines are by today's standards tame.

Two recent, related trends are apparent. The first uses either a high percentage of coloured noise or broadband signals. Any sound without restriction may be used, but always significantly distorted in some way or behind the veil of a partly masking noise component obscuring referential sound information. With the problem of simultaneous counterpoint (due to masking effects) temporal ideas involving either microsound approaches, slowly changing masses or clear articulation necessarily predominate. The music is often intended to be played at a volume that pushes the listener to a state of sensation rather than conscious listening, and thus structural organisation is essentially of low importance. Often played over the threshold of pain the body begins to 'feel' rather than 'hear' the sound vibrations (particularly when bass frequencies are emphasised). Without ear protection the volume and density of sound may push the listener to a state of 'obliteration'. With ear protection the body will clearly feel the pressure waves, while appreciation of the 'obliteration effect' will remain conceptual. For an example the reader can delve into the experimental noise records of Japanese musician Masami Akita (Merzbow). The second trend stems from improvisation practice. Often using a variety of electronic sound-making devices or drawing from a wide realm of concrete sound, the sound worlds are generally more varied, as is the resulting improvised approach to structure. These two trends form the extremes of a continuum between which a vast amount of live electronic music exists from around the globe. For further discussion the reader is referred to other chapters in this companion.

Space

Spatial elements in acousmatic music are inherent to the art form, in composition and in the projection of music to the listener. Whether spatial information is bound up in the sound as composed, or whether spatial information is the result of the sound as played back in the listening space, sound and space are inseparable. As the perception of, and interaction with, our spatial world is vital to our every day it was inevitable that composers would find the need to draw spatial-structural functions into their music. Our current spatial aesthetics originate in three integrated sources: (i) conceptual visions, such as that of Varèse's interacting and colliding sound masses (Varèse 1971); (ii) specific recording and sound transformation techniques allowing the composer to capture and control spatial information within a controlled studio environment; (iii) solutions for taking a work from the studio *single listener* situation to a concert hall *many listener* situation.

In 1950, Schaeffer and Henry created a series of works using up to five tape signals routed to a four-channel speaker system. The speakers were arranged in a tetrahedral configuration, with Front Left and Right, Back, and Overhead. To facilitate distribution of the sound Schaeffer conceived a mechanism called the *potentiomètre d'espace* (1951) where a performer could control the spatial movement by hand as a performance action after the musical aspects of the composition were fixed. Cage's *Imaginary Landscape No. 4* (1951) used twelve radios, twenty-four performers and a conductor. At each radio, one performer controlled the frequency and the other controlled the volume. In the following year, *Williams Mix* (1952) for eight mono tapes was played through eight equally spaced loudspeakers surrounding the audience, and was the first work for eight-channel surround sound. Edgard Varèse's *Poème électronique* (1958), which was presented as part of a multimedia environment at the Philips Pavilion at the Brussels World's Fair, used three tracks distributed dynamically to 425 speakers via an eleven-channel sound system. In these historic examples the spatial element was an experiment in performance. The first true spatial composition conceived prior to the act of performance was Stockhausen's *Kontakte* (1960), consisting of a quadraphonic channel arrangement for front, left, right, and back speaker positions. In order to create the effect of sounds *orbiting* the audience, in the studio Stockhausen placed a loudspeaker on a rotating turntable surrounded by four microphones. In concert, the loudspeakers were placed in the same geometry as the microphones were previously. Thus the rotation effect is remarkable due to the recording capturing the real acoustic situation rather than attempting to synthesise the complexity of reality.

In the late 1950s François Bayle joined the GRM (Groupe de Recherches Musicales). Besides his music, Bayle has been the driving force behind two important technical developments influencing the aesthetics of acousmatic composition. The first is the development in 1974 of the *Acousmonium* – a loudspeaker orchestra for performing fixed works. The second is the support he gave to technological developments in sound transformation technology. The Acousmonium can be seen as an instrument for projecting the qualities of the music to a large audience – qualities otherwise only possibly understood by the single listener, situated in the perfect position, in the studio. Performance issues connected to sound diffusion may also be considered while composing, such that two mixes of the same work may be made: one version for diffusion performance, one version functioning in stereo or home listening situations.

Since its establishment, the concept of the loudspeaker orchestra as a performance instrument can be found worldwide. In France and Great Britain there are at least four large touring systems – the Acousmonium of GRM, the Gmebaphone of Institut International de Musique Electroacoustique de Bourges (IMEB), the Birmingham Electroacoustic Sound Theatre (BEAST) and the Motus-Acousmonium – of one of which most composers of electroacoustic music would have had first-hand experience. Contrary to what we sometimes read, the loudspeaker orchestra as a performance tool for acousmatic music is active and very much alive outside academia. Although the influence of the loudspeaker orchestra on compositional aesthetics is somewhat tenuous, it cannot be denied that on listening to a skilled spatialisation or sound diffusion performance the thrill of sound-space exploration is difficult to resist. Outside contemporary music circles spatialised sound is commonly encountered in most cinemas. However, this spatial information is normally for sound effects rather than for musical structure, and the possibilities for spatial interplay are often toned down so as not to distract from the film dialogue.

As multi-channel studio systems became more common, multi-channel composed formats were sometimes chosen. Technical solutions to spatial composition are numerous, involving sound recording techniques, transformation techniques, amplitude panning or more advanced sound-field recreation over multiple loudspeakers. Recent developments in holographic and three-dimensional sound projection will undoubtedly bear future implications on composition and performance. It is inappropriate here to argue the technical pros and cons of various methods and instead we shall see how spatial information may drive the compositional structure. In one area we find the use of space in electroacoustic works driven by the instrumental compositional tradition. In the other area we find spatial issues embedded in the acousmatic approach to sound. We shall now concentrate on the latter.

Space and composition

Spatial information is inseparable from sound identity, and can be investigated in a similar way to other aspects of sound. The spatial context is concerned with spatial situations (environments), spatial gestures (motions) and object-space connections. I here attempt to present a general picture by detailing four main compositional approaches to composed space (Barrett 2002) which can be summarised as:

(i) The illusion of a space or a spatial location of an object created by either spatial acoustic cues, image sizes, image motions or object relationships in terms of volume, frequency colouration or relative motion velocities. Spatial acoustic cues are connected to our understanding of room and environmental acoustics. Here we can include phantom imaging and information indicating the size, shape and materials of an enclosure. Image sizes, image motions or object relationships concern how objects within the space relate to the physical position of the listener and to each other. A simple example would be where a large image size results in a close, wide sound, while a point source may hover, at any chosen point in the stereo width, ambiguously close or far, depending on its relation to other sounding objects or to room acoustics. Similarly, a juxtaposition of sounds with different image sizes, volumes, spectral colour and motions will highlight their differences and define a composed spatial framework. The opening two minutes of my own work *Angels & Devils* (2002) illustrate how these techniques may unfold through the musical structure to set the spatial framework for the rest of the composition. Horacio Vaggione's technique of composing musical spaces by means of decorrelated audio channels (Vaggione 2001 and Roads 2005) explores the subtleties inherent to the illusion of space without delving into room acoustics or acoustical analogies, and can be heard in *Argon* (1998). Likewise, when the spatial resonance or material properties within the physical dimensions of a sounding object are captured by stereo or multi-microphone close-recording techniques, the results are heard in the context of the spatial illusion. Jonty Harrison's *Klang* (1982) clearly presents a compositional process beginning with this recording technique. Trevor Wishart lists a great number of example motions in the horizontal plane (Wishart 1996, chapter 10), but the reader should be aware that these are isolated from real natural spatial morphologies and from commonly experienced biological models involving social spatial interaction.

(ii) The allusion to a space or a spatial location of an object created by associating the sound with, or by placing the sound within, a space that is appropriate based on its identity.[6] By changing the sound allusion, the spatial landscape will likewise change. Allusion may involve an implicit awareness of the source bond demanding a spatial context, or remote spatial connotations derived from mass, density or non-aural models. Non-aural models are perhaps more important than currently assumed. Emmerson (1998) points out how sound in general evokes a sense of scene strongly related to our visual experience where 'the science of acoustics cannot any longer alone explain sound phenomena and requires psychological and ecological dimensions.'

(iii) The simulation and recreation of three-dimensional sound fields (with ambisonics or wavefield synthesis) results in spatial clarification by doing away with ambiguous phantom imaging and allows the direct transmission, without performance interpretation, of spatial information to the listener. Additional spatial compositional issues become apparent, such as increasing the possibility of spatial difference, allowing reality mimesis and increasing the number of simultaneously perceptually identifiable sounds. A few ambisonics compositions are available decoded for horizontal quadraphonic or 5.1 loudspeaker systems. My *Exploration Invisibilis* (2003) is one such example.

(iv) The effect of the listener's space is important to all public and private situations. Although I cannot here delve into the perceptual and aesthetic issues connected to the listener's space, we can briefly consider two examples where the performance room is inherently linked to the musical structure. Alvin Lucier, in *I am sitting in a room* (1970), used the acoustics of the recording/performing space as the essence of the composition. A chain of microphones, tape recorders, and loudspeakers were used to generate cumulative reiterations of a source text reading (Manning 1985, p. 199) such that feedback gradually obscured semantic meaning in preference for phrase, pitch and rhythm. Bill Fontana explores recontextualisation by transmitting live sound from one location to another, overlaying naturally occurring sound in the installation space. In *Sculpture with Resonators* (1972–5) microphones were placed inside objects such as large glass bottles, tubes and seashells. The objects were placed on the roof of a building, the natural sound environment being filtered through the resonance of the container, and the result played in the interior of the building. Fontana states, 'Most people use their visual perception to tune out and not pay attention to ambient sounds of a given space. By carefully placing naturally occurring environmental sounds in a space where they normally do not belong, this perceptual masking technique is defeated and people are confronted with sounds they cannot ignore' (Rudi 2005). Extreme separation in microphone placement effects a spatial re-composition, and not only spatial replay.

Sound diffusion: the final stage of composition?

Jonty Harrison summarises an approach to performance commonly accepted amongst acousmatic composers, but often misunderstood in other contexts. This approach regards sound diffusion as a continuation of the compositional process where the heritage of acousmatic composition is one of 'performing' in the studio. Therefore when performing the music to an audience it is 'appropriate that the same type of "physical" gestures that were used to shape material during the process of composition should be used again in performance to reinforce that shape in the audience's perception and to enhance further the articulation of the work's sonic fabric and structure' (Harrison 1999). This standpoint raises three issues. The first concerns the reality of diffusion automation and multi-track sources. Every performance space, every loudspeaker system and every audience bring their own differences to the totality of the space, and each performance needs to be tailored to function in each unique context – a tailoring less realistic with pre-programmed multi-channel sources. The second point concerns recent developments in the technology of sound field recreation where the spatial performance in the studio may be captured and then exactly recreated in the performance space. What effect does this have on composition and diffusion practice? The third point concerns the composer without access to a diffusion system. Does this mean that the composition is in some way less valid when heard in stereo at home, or when interpreted by someone else?[7]

Microsound

Analogue and later digital editing techniques have allowed the composer to control extremely short time durations and micro-sound details which have led to some characteristic aesthetic decisions. We can say that all music falls into the continuum between three timescales: micro (from the threshold of perception or microseconds up to short sounds), meso (a local rather than global timescale grouping information into durations measured in seconds) and macro (the entire work or the long term, subject to large differences in what each individual remembers) (Roads 2001, pp. 3–41).

Stochastic, algorithmic and numerical control of sound

Control over micro-sound details may result in a variety of sound types and approaches to temporal structure. We may hear continuous, smooth, spectrally simple tones, highly textured sound masses with large internal variation, continuous morphological change or sound identity abstracted through micro-sound decomposition. Since the mid-1990s these techniques have been readily available in low-cost granulation software running on home computers, such that they have infiltrated most sound and music creation. Here I focus on the use of micro-sound control as inherent to the compositional process.

Control over the micro-level connects to all temporal levels of structural organisation. As it is often unrealistic to control individual sound particles, some high level control is needed. A variety of solutions to this problem have been applied. Xenakis's approach drew from the statistical theories of physics, which enlarged the previously strict principle of causality and observed an evolution towards a stable state or a *stochos* (from where the word stochastic is derived). Embedded in this theory is a multi-scale approach to composition, where operations on one timescale generate structures that may be perceived on other timescales (Roads 2001, p. 331). In 1956 Xenakis completed the short study *Analogue B*. Sine tones were recorded on analogue tape, cut into hundreds of fragments and then laboriously spliced together. In this systematic and hand-controlled technique every sound could be understood as the assembly of a number of elementary particles (Roads 2001, p. 65; Xenakis 1971). In 1991 he began working on a programme called *GENDYN* (at the CEMAMu). *GENDYN* explores stochastic timbre constructed from waveform fragments controlled by probability procedures. The computer generates the sound and steers the compositional process as integrated entities, binding macro- and microstructures within one process. This is clearly heard in *S.709* (1994). I encourage the reader to explore the inventive legacy left by Xenakis through his other electronic and orchestral compositions. Xenakis's original interest in stochastic theories stemmed from what he saw as the crisis of serial music, discussed further in chapter 6. Many aspects of Curtis Roads' work – both as composer and researcher – have been embedded in the micro-sound aesthetic. In *Prototype* (Roads' first study in automated granular synthesis from 1975), fourteen interacting synthesis parameters described the global properties of a sound cloud filled with grains. As one parameter is varied other parameters linked to it also change. 'The connection between the parameters was not a simple linear scaling function, but rather a linkage between their degree of order or disorder' (Roads 2001, pp. 303–5). Since this time Roads has developed a number of synthesis techniques used by himself and others. The collection of compositions on *Point Line Cloud* (2003) presents a clear insight into Roads' aesthetic orientation.

Barry Truax, since the 1980s, emphasised a realtime stream-oriented approach to granulation implementation and the use of natural (acoustic) source sounds. Truax's connection to the soundscape aesthetic will be discussed later. Here we draw attention to lengthy time-stretching using granulation. To control granulation in realtime Truax developed the GSX and GSAMX systems. These allow the user to exercise different levels of control over grain parameters for realising planned structures or spontaneous improvisation. In *Riverrun* (1986) the listener will hear a temporal structure flavoured by the realtime aural approach.

If we regard micro-sound control as an aesthetic approach to the connectivity of material and structure, we see that high-level control algorithms are but one possibility. It is common for acousmatic composers to temporally connect material and structure using bottom-up manual arrangements of materials. Many of Horacio Vaggione's compositions are clearly illustrative, created by the manual placement and mixing of micro events. Through this labour-intensive approach we hear multi-scale relationships in parameters such as amplitude, duration, gesture, articulation and spatial imaging. *Argon* (1998) provides a clear example – 'Vaggione refuses to dissect music into sound objects on Schaefferian terms. Composition should not rely on juxtaposition, it should superimpose different processes into a sort of polyphony' (Risset 2005, p. 289).

In general terms we can see that the morphological archetypes and motion styles described earlier are likewise sculpted across micro, meso and macro timescales, relevant to sound transformation and as structural functions. Whether we perceive gesture or texture as dominant hinges on perceptual timescales and on the attention of the ear. On a micro timescale, attention to internal components of a gesture results in predominantly textural listening. Over a meso or macro scale the material will clarify larger contours and motion trajectories and gestural listening predominates. Whether the music is gesture- or texture-carried is thus guided by temporal unfolding, how extrinsic information may lead the ear, and inevitably whether the listener is new to the work and gradually gathering information, or whether a listening scheme has already been constructed.

Other types of high level control are also common. Non-audio numerical data describing, or extracted from, the natural world can be used as a template to create material or control musical structures. The mapping rules are particularly important, and if correctly chosen the musical results are *perceptually* understood as approximating to one of Smalley's indicative fields. For example, an avalanche model may create falling and cascading gestures implying both avalanche and more general second-order surrogacy. Likewise, spatial environmental data can be used for the more accurate control of the spatial distribution of sounds in the composition – strengthening the perception of *environment*, even when using sounds of vague connection to our real environment (Barrett 2000, pp. 20–3).

Connecting to the environment

Xenakis's early work *Concret PH* (1958) is assembled from a vast quantity of one-second extracts from a recording of burning embers and illustrates how some acoustic sound contains a naturally occurring statistical distribution of grains. Such properties are inherent to nearly all environmental sound, and most acousmatic composers have explored this feature in their music. Yet sound from the environment offers more. It is to this area we now turn.

Soundscape composition

Creative approaches to our sound environment show a great diversity in composed versus natural structures. Chris Watson, who works as a free-lance sound recordist, specialises in capturing wildlife sound environments that in our everyday we will rarely experience. Many listeners will have unknowingly heard his recordings in the soundtracks of well-known BBC nature documentaries. Since 1996 he has released his recordings on CD. In early productions such as *Outside the circle of fire* (1998) each track presents one sound recording. In later releases such as *Weather Report* (2003) some compositional rearrangement is employed. Unlike Luc Ferrari's approach, where it is clear that a variety of subtle approaches to composed forms and narratives are used – including using the microphone to 'search' for sounds specific to the composition in hand and forming a moving spatial perspective (particularly clear in *Presque rien No. 2* from 1977), Chris Watson's work up until now maintains a purity of documentation in its relative detachment from compositional intervention.

'Soundscape composition' is often used as a descriptive term, yet its meaning is vague. Hildegard Westerkamp explains that soundscape composition involves more than the mere use of environmental sound. She suggests that soundscape composition is not driven by the sound materials used in the work, but by 'deeper issues that had brought it into being: issues of environmental listening and active engagement with our soundscapes' (Westerkamp 2002). In this light, soundscape composition stems from the study of the interrelationship between sound, nature and society – or the stance of the composer listening to the world from an 'ecological' perspective. Westerkamp describes the approach more as a way of life than as a contained compositional aesthetic: 'the actual recorded materials are of course important, but the listening experiences while recording and while going about one's life are just as important and so always figure into the compositional process in some way.' With conscious listening and an awareness of our role as sound-makers, soundscape composition may be aimed at enhancing environmental listening, and is necessarily rooted in the themes of the sound environment. Westerkamp works with composed forms involving significant sound transformation and montage, experimental radio series blending soundscape documentary and commentary and 'soundwalks'. 'Soundwalks' are a way of actively participating in the soundscape through following a map – which can be interpreted as a score – where sound landmarks are identified. The participants are encouraged to make critical judgements about what they hear and even explore their own sound-making in conjunction with the environment. Truax supports Westerkamp's proposal, in that instead of listening being the end stage we can regard sound as mediating the relationship of the listener to the environment (Truax 1992, p. 377). Truax provides a list of specific trends in soundscape composition as developed at Simon Fraser University from the 1970s which may be summarised as approaches to material and approaches to structure (Truax 2002).

Landscape, the transformation of sound images and metaphor

Truax's all-encompassing perspective suggests a continuum from the real soundscape to the composed landscape where sound transformation, temporal structural rearrangement, sound images and metaphors gain importance.

Pierre Schaeffer's and Pierre Henry's early work *Symphonie pour un homme seul* (1949–50) relies to some extent on the listener recognising the source of the sound. This approach was afterwards rejected by Schaeffer. Later, Luc Ferrari embarked on a deeper investigation of the idea of landscape through careful sound selection and organisation. In *Presque rien No. 1* (1970) Ferrari takes a recording of activity on a beach lasting several hours and edits the material to twenty minutes. He does not attempt to change the scene, only intensify activity via careful microphone placements[8] and editing techniques. This approach Ferrari describes as *anecdotal*. He aimed to tell stories by bringing together extracts of reality while retaining the structural qualities of Schaeffer's musique concrète.

Trevor Wishart proposes an approach identifying three features of a landscape hinging on the extrinsic nature of sound: (i) the nature of the perceived acoustic space, (ii) the disposition of sound-objects within the space and (iii) the recognition of individual sound-objects. Wishart further suggests that the natural ambiguity of sound allows transformations impossible in the visual domain and the free manipulation of metaphor. This may involve a direct link from sound identification, or an indirect link from, for example, behaviour to connotation then to metaphor. Metaphor, myth and sound archetypes are not used for storytelling in a radiophonic or dramaturgical way, but as a way to unfold non-linear structures and relationships through time (Wishart 1986). When working in this way composers should be aware of whether everyday listeners form similar connections to the sound in its musical context. Likewise, as history proceeds, what is familiar also changes.

Jean-Claude Risset approaches the transformation of sound identity and sound archetypes by combining synthesised sound with acoustic sources from natural soundscapes. This approach takes advantage of the way acoustic sounds are constrained by their activation (hitting, scraping, blowing), and the way that synthesis is unlimited in its malleability yet restricted in the spectral and spatial morphological details characteristic of real-world sounds. With synthesis he creates a virtual world without a visible physical counterpart, while with acoustic sounds maintains a foothold in reality, effortlessly moving in and out of these worlds within the composition. Risset's acousmatic compositions *Sud* (1987) and *Elementa* (1998) along with Risset's own explanations (Risset 1996) provide useful insight.

Expansion from an instrumental aesthetic

Experimental sound art since the 1950s has harnessed both expensive technology and consumer electronics (see chapter 3). If, however, we study a compositional style that began with basic amplification we find an alternative path. In Stockhausen's *Mikrophonie I* (1964) close microphone techniques are used to capture sounds from a large tam-tam which you would not normally hear. Two performers follow a detailed composed score with directions to scrape, rub and hit a tam-tam while two additional performers amplify the sound with microphones. The way the microphones are used is just as important as the way the tam-tam is excited. The microphones are moved in varying 'rhythms' from the point of excitation, creating dynamics, changes in timbre and spatial information. Twenty years later, with the use of computers, it was clear that realtime modification within a concert or performance setting mainly concerned one or more of three compositional issues: the expansion of instrumental timbre, the expansion of non-instrumental acoustic sources in general and the adaptation of musical structures. Here I will focus on just one example: Boulez's *Répons* (original version from 1981, revisions up to 1988).

Répons is scored for conductor, orchestra, six soloists (cimbalom, xylophone/glockenspiel, vibraphone, harp, piano, piano/DX-7), 4X computer, Matrix-32 programmable patch bay and six loudspeakers. Its realtime technical solutions are embedded within the structure and concept of the work. Although what can now be achieved in realtime is more advanced than in the 1980s, similar motivations are found: to allow the subtlety in tempo that a fixed tape part takes away, to allow the composer to write for familiar instruments while creating a contrast with unfamiliar computer-generated or -transformed sound, to adapt musical structures as a performance action and to capture the spontaneity of public performance (see chapters 5 and 10). In *Répons* we find dialogues between the soloists and the ensemble, between soloists themselves, and between transformed and untransformed passages. Sound from the six soloists is transformed in the following ways: modulation of one instrument by another, frequency shifting, retardation and changes of phase to create rhythmic motifs, and spatialisation (Gerzso 1984, p. 22), and these processes are often integrated. The spatialisation aspect is particularly interesting due to its integration into the totality of the composition. The six soloists are positioned at the periphery of the concert hall, as are six loudspeakers. The instrumental ensemble is placed in the centre, and the audience surrounds the ensemble. Sound circulates from each of the six soloists among patterns of four speakers. The overall effect highlights the antiphonal relation between the central group and the soloists by making the audience aware of the spatial dimensions. The larger the amplitude, the faster the sound will appear to move (via technical solutions based on note attack-decay characteristics and a team of IRCAM technicians working off-stage). As soloists are independently amplified, a polyphony of spatialised gestures is produced – 'The overall impression for the listener is that of a single spectacular gesture slowly breaking up into several parts. Furthermore, as the overall amplitude decreases, the original impression of sounds moving rapidly around the hall is replaced by a sense of immobility' (Boulez 1988).

In connection to Boulez's *Répons*,[9] Gerzso (1984) writes, 'electronic writing is merely an extension of the traditional writing'. Likewise, many composers to have worked with electroacoustic music at IRCAM used 'electronic writing' as a way to develop or escape from modernism and post-modernism while staying within instrumental traditions. Spectral music – where the frequency components of a sound are used as a framework for structural relationships – has been used by Jonathan Harvey and Tristan Murail amongst others. Although orchestration of a sound spectrum will never result in close approximation of the analysed source (acoustic instruments themselves involve complex spectra and human performance factors can distort the timing), using the spectral and temporal relationship between these frequency components creates an alternative approach to hierarchical structure, helps blend acoustic and electroacoustic timbres (Harvey 2000) and is likewise useful within an acousmatic context. Harvey's tape composition *Mortuos Plango, Vivos Voco* (1980) is particularly successful in this respect due to the audibly clear separation of harmonics inherent to the bell sound source and the clarity of the simple spectrum of the boy soprano voice. Spectral music is however predominantly applied within an instrumental tradition.

Discussion

In this tour through electroacoustic composition and aesthetics I have mentioned only a few personal observations deduced as a freelance composer submerged within our rich world of sound. The body of the material is strictly historical. There is much I have by necessity needed to omit – the use of sampling and recontextualisation, the world of electroacoustic music involving acoustic instruments, live performance dealing with anything other than spatial issues, sound-art in the context of composition, algorithmic composition and my personal everyday encounter with electronica and electronic improvisation – to mention but a few areas. But what is common to all is that as listeners and composers we are submerged in an increasingly overwhelming sound world. Acoustic sounds no longer predominate our everyday. Did we today really discover or imagine something new in our own work, or did we unknowingly hear the same thing only yesterday in passing? Does it matter? Looking to historical models, theories and works may help us make sense of this world.

One of the traditional approaches for the electroacoustic composer is to descend into the barely audible, finding sources of sound and inspiration in uncovering that which exists but is not normally heard. This approach takes on new meaning as our world of music and sound increases in density, complexity and in literal and metaphorical masking. Perception is fundamental. Calculations, systems, theories, models and contemplation are simply irrelevant if they are not aligned with perception. Although outside the scope of this chapter, perception and cognition lie at the root of the theories and approaches here presented. In the CD booklet to *Etude* (1952) Stockhausen writes, 'Already upon hearing two synchronised layers, and even more so hearing three or four layers, I became increasingly pale and helpless: I had imagined something completely different!'

Discography: works cited

Barrett, N. 2000. *Utility of Space,* in *Isostasie.* IMED 0262

— 2003. *Exploratio Invisibilis* (5.1-decoding), in *Kraftfelt.* ACD 5037

— 2002. *Angels & Devils,* in *Sinus Seduction.* ACD 5018

Bayle, F. 1970–2. *L'aventure du cri,* in *L'expérience acoustique.* MGCB 5694

Bodin, L. 1967. *Cybo II,* in *The Pioneers: Five Text-Sound Artists.* PSCD 63

Boulez, P. 1984. *Répons,* in *Boulez: Répons.* LC0173

Cage, J. 1939. *Imaginary Landscape No. 1,* in *Credo in US.* Wergo 66512

— 1951. *Imaginary Landscape No. 4.* Hat Art CD 6179

— 1952. *Williams Mix,* in *John Cage 25-Year Retrospective Concert.* Wergo 145–4

Ferrari, L. 1970–86. *Presque riens 1–3,* in *Presque rien.* Musidisc 245172

— 1971. *Unheimlich Schön.* MKCD008 1993

— 2001–2. *Les anecdotiques.* SR207.

Ferreyra, B. 2001. *Vivencias.* Motus 302004

Field, A. 2003. *One Hell of a Place to Lose a Cow,* in *Cultures Electroniques 17,* LDC 278077/78

Harrison, J. 1982. *Klang*, in *Evidence matérielle*. IMED 0052

Harvey, J. 1980. *Mortuos Plango, Vivos Voco*, in *Computer Music Currents 5*, Wergo 114

Lansky, P. 1985. *Idle Chatter*. Bridge Records 9050

Lucier, A. 1970. *I am sitting in a room*. PhonCD L963.2

Martusciello, E. 2000. 'Hz – limits of the technology', in *Bowindo 01*. Bowindo 01

Reich, S. 1966. *Come Out*, on *Early Works*. Elektra 79169–2

Risset, J. 1987. *Sud*. INA 1003

— 1998. *Elementa*. INA 1019

Roads, C. 'Prototype' (extract on CD accompanying Roads 2001).

— 2003. *Volt Air*, in *Point Line Cloud*, ASP 3000

Schaeffer, P. 1947–8. 'Etudes', in *Pierre Schaeffer: L'oeuvre musicale*. EM155–3.

— and Henry, P. 1949–50. *Symphonie pour un homme seul*, in *Pierre Schaeffer: L'Oeuvre Musicale*. EM155–3.

Smalley, D. 1976. *Darkness After Time's Colours*, in *Impacts intérieurs*. IMED 9209

— 1992. *Valley Flow*, in *Impacts intérieurs*. IMED 9209

Stockhausen, K. 1964. *Mikrophonie I*. CD 9 Kürten: K. Stockhausen

— 1953–4. *Studie I & II*. CD 3 Kürten: K. Stockhausen

— 1960. *Kontakte*. Wergo 123

— 1956. *Gesang der Jünglinge*. CD 3 Kürten: K. Stockhausen

Truax, B. 1986. *Riverrun*, in *Digital Soundscapes*. CSR 8701

Watson, C. 1998. *Outside the circle of fire*. Touch TO:37

— 2003. *Weather Report*. Touch TO:47

Wishart, T. 1978. *Red Bird: A Political Prisoner's Dream*, in *Red Bird / Anticredos*. EM122

— 1986. *Vox 5*, in *The Vox Cycle*. OT 102

Vaggione, H. 1998. *Argon*, in *ICMC 2000 CD*, ICMC 2000 audio.

Vande Gorne, A. 1986. *Feu*, in *Tao*. IMED 9311

Varèse, E. 1949–54. *Deserts* in *Varèse – Complete Works*. Decca 00289 460 2082

— 1958. *Poème électronique*, in *Varèse – Complete Works*. Decca 00289 460 2082

Xenakis, I. 1994. *S.709*, in *Xenakis Electronic Music*. EM 102

— 1956. *Analogue B*, in *Iannis Xenakis: Music For Strings*. MO 198.

— 1958. *Concret PH*, in *Xenakis Electronic Music*. EM 102

Discography: supplementary listening

Adkins, M. 2005. *Silk to Steel*, in *Mondes inconnus*. IMED 0679

Alvarez, J. 2002. *Cactus géométries*, in *Cactus géométries; Offrande*. INA_E 5015

Bokanowski, M. 1983–4. *Tabou*. MKCD003 1992

Brummer, L. 2001. *Nyx*, in *Cultures Electroniques 15*, LDC 278074/75

Calon, C. 1985. *Portrait d'un visiteur*, in *Ligne de vie: récits électriques*. IMED 9001

Ceccarelli, L. *Hades*, in *Compendium International 2000 Bourges*. LCD 278 11 19/20

Dhomont, F. 1982. *Points de fuite*, in *Mouvances~Métaphores*. IMED 9107/08

Koonce, P. 1997. *Walkabout*, in *ICMC 1998 CD*. ICMC 1998 Audio

Lewis, A. 1997. *Cân*, on *CD 5 – Prix International Noroit – Léonce Petitot 1998.* NOR5 247982

Normandeau, R. 1999. *Clair de terre*, in *Clair de terre*. IMED 0157

Parmegiani, B. 2001. *La mémoire des sons*, in *La mémoire des sons* INA_C 2019

Parmerud, Å. *La vie mécanique*, in *Vol. 26: Compendium International 2004 Bourges*. LDC 2781133/34

— 1997. *Grains of Voices*. CAP 21579

Roy, S. 1994. *Crystal Music*, in *Kaleidos*. IMED 9630

Smalley, D. 2000–4. *Trilogy: Base Metals, Ringing Down the Sun, Resounding*. Not yet released

Tutschku, H. 1998. *Extrémités Lointaines*, in *Moment* IMED 9947

Westerkamp, H. 1981–1992. *Transformations*. IMED 9631

Notes

Introduction

1 There is a certain pressure to define and delimit electronic music, which we will sidestep. Electronic music has sometimes been technically differentiated from any music that might utilise electricity (in one sense, the brains of acoustic violinists use electricity!); for instance, the Wikipedia entry on electronic music founds its definition on the restriction of the IEEE standards body definition of 'electronic' (as referring to low-power components like transistors and integrated circuits). Whilst the main focus of our investigations in this book will refer to electronic circuits, and especially those modern-day hyper-miniaturised computer chips, we shall not refrain from discussing any electromagnetic and electromechanical technologies, especially where related to the history of electronic music, but also in contemporary work.

2 In one inspiring example of custom electrification and amplification, the ensemble Konono no.1 feature hand-built microphones salvaged from old car parts, and distorting sound systems incorporated into the essential fabric of their music (Congatronics, Crammed Discs).

3 In this book we will often emphasise such real-world examples, on one hand to support the ideas discussed, and on the other to serve as searchable topics for the Google/Wiki/YouTube/MySpace-friendly generation.

4 A large number of artists proudly declare that they bought the first or second Synclavier or Fairlight in the country . . .

5 This is especially true of the categorisation of electronica in the United States; elsewhere, it can connote a wider spirit of experimentation more readily.

6 At the time of writing, they both live in Germany, after all!

7 In another angle to such debate, fine artists who work with sound have entered into, well, not exactly competition, but correspondence and engagement with many of the same areas that musicians have explored. As we have discussed already, the music conservatoire education is not a necessary prerequisite for work in electronic music. It is often around the arena of electronic music where much of the sound art crossover takes place. Our own approach to this is pragmatic – everyone should learn about everyone else's work and background. It is now entirely normal practice that sound installations are cited as examples of work as well as tape pieces and live performances.

8 Further chronologies are provided in Cox and Warner (2004) and Shapiro (2000), or online, for example, http://eamusic.dartmouth.edu/~wowem/electronmedia/music/eamhistory.html

1 The origins of electronic music

1 This quotation has been cited by numerous musicologists over the years, including many of those listed in the bibliography.

2 First documented by Bartolome Ramos in 1482.

3 Recounted in Iamblichus (250–330 AD), *Life of Pythagoras*, chapter XXVIII: 'Organization Of The Pythagorean School'. Translated by Guthrie, K. S. in Fideler, D. (ed.) (1987) *The Pythagorean Sourcebook and Library*. Grand Rapids: Phanes Press.

4 For a good account of these questions in relation to electronic music, see Sethares (2005).

5 This piece was subsequently orchestrated by Beethoven for double woodwind (plus contrabassoon), four horns, six trumpets, three trombones, string section and large percussion section, including muskets and artillery alongside the usual timpani, drums and cymbals. The piece depicts a battle.

6 Franklin invented a *glass armonica*, in which revolving glass bowls pass through water and are then made to ring by gentle finger pressure on the rim.

7 The same book describes credit cards and shopping malls.

8 Had Cahill taken advantage of Lee De Forest's 'Audion' triode valve amplifier, invented in 1906, he could have achieved a reduction in size!

9 Buffet, *Musique d'aujourd'hui*, reprinted in the multi-volume work Slatkin, L. (ed.) (1971) *Les soirées de Paris*, vol. II. Geneva: Slatkin reprints, pp. 181–3.

10 The most celebrated example of a sound poem remains the *Ursonate* (1922–32) of Kurt Schwitters, a work which continues to influence contemporary sound poets such as Henri Chopin and Bob Cobbing.

11 Ball, H. (1927) 'Die Flucht aus der Zeit'. Reproduced in Elderfield, J. (ed.), Raimes, A.

(trans.) (1974) *Flight out of Time = A Oada Diary.* New York. The Viking Press, Inc. p. 70.

12 Specifically the Battle of Adrianopoli, 1912, in which Marinetti fought.

13 From Kostelanetz, R. (1970) *John Cage, An Anthology.* New York: Da Capo Press.

2 Electronic music and the studio

1 Gluck, B. 2006. Interview with the author. 19 November. Mr Gluck is one of the Executive Editors of the EMF, a web-based virtual museum documenting the history of electronic music.

2 Badagnani, D. 2006. E-mail correspondence with the author. 28 October. Mr Badagnani is the chief biographer for Halim El-Dabh.

3 Mathews, M. 2006. Interview with author. 8 September, San Francisco, CA. Max Mathews is one of the pioneers of computer music.

4 Hwang, S. 2006. E-mail correspondence with the author translated by Seong-Ah Shin. 9 October. Mr Hwang is the founder of the Korean Electro-acoustic Music Society.

5 Gluck, B. 2006. Interview with the author. 19 November.

6 Truax, B. 2006. Interview with the author. 4 December. Vancouver, BC. Mr Truax is an Associate Composer of the Canadian Music Centre and a founding member of the Canadian Electroacoustic Community.

7 Berg, P. 2006. Interview with the author. 20 September, Amsterdam, The Netherlands. Mr Berg teaches at the Institute of Sonology.

8 Dubois, R. 2006. Interview with the author. 6 October. New York, NY. Mr Dubois teaches interactive sound and video performance at Columbia's Computer Music Center and at the Interactive Telecommunications Program at New York University.

9 Oliveros, P. 2006. Instant messaging interview with the author. 11 September. Pauline Oliveros is the founder of Deep Listening.

10 Mathews, M. 2006. Interview with author. 8 September, San Francisco, CA.

11 Rai, T. 2006. E-mail correspondence with the author. 26 September. Mr Rai teaches computer music at the Kunitachi College of Music in Tokyo.

12 Mathews, M. 2006. Interview with author. 8 September, San Francisco, CA.

13 Wessel, D. 2006. Interview with the author. 26 September, Berkeley, CA. Mr Wessel is the director of CNMAT, the Center for New Music and Technology.

14 Sigal, R. 2006. Instant messaging interview with the author. 11 September. Mr Sigal is the director of CMAS, the Center for Music and Sonic Arts in Mexico.

15 Puckette, M. 2006. E-mail correspondence with the author. 26 September. Mr Puckette is the associate director of the Center for Research in Computing and the Arts.

16 Wessel, D. 2006. Interview with the author. 26 September, Berkeley, CA.

17 Sigal, R. Instant messaging interview with the author. 11 September.

18 Oliveros, P. 2006. Instant messaging interview with the author. 11 September.

19 Lippit, T. 2006. Interview with the author. 22 October, The Hague, Netherlands. Mr Lippit is a hardware developer at STEIM, the Studio for Electro-Instrumental Music.

20 Voudouris, D. 2006. E-mail correspondence with the author. 19 September. Mr Voudouris is the founder of UNYAZI, the first electronic music festival and symposium on the African continent in 2005.

21 Dubois, R. 2006. Interview with the author. 6 October. New York, NY.

22 Andrews, R. 2006. Interview with the author. 26 September, Berkeley CA. Mr Andrews is the Associate Director of the UC Berkeley Center for New Music.

23 Berg, P. 2006. Interview with the author. 20 September, Amsterdam, The Netherlands.

24 Oliveros, P. 2006. Instant messaging interview with the author. 11 September.

25 Berg, P. 2006. Interview with the author. 20 September, Amsterdam, The Netherlands.

26 Voudouris, D. 2006. E-mail correspondence with the author. 19 September.

27 Voudouris, D. 2006. E-mail correspondence with the author. 19 September.

28 Helmuth, M. 2006. E-mail correspondence with the author. 2 October. Dr Helmuth is the director of (ccm)2, the College-Conservatory of Music Center for Computer Music at the University of Cincinnati.

29 Sigal, R. Instant messaging interview with the author. 11 September.

30 Berg, P. 2006. Interview with the author. 20 September, Amsterdam, The Netherlands.

31 Chowning, J. 2006. Interview with the author. 3 September, Sausalito, CA. Mr Chowning was the director of CCRMA, the Center for Computer Research and Musical Acoustics at Stanford University.

32 Campion, E. 2006. Interview with the author. 26 September, Berkeley, CA. Dr Campion is Co-Director at CNMAT, the Center for New Music and Audio Technologies.

33 Chowning, J. 2006. Interview with the author. 3 September, Sausalito, CA.

34 Hwang, S. 2006. E-mail correspondence with the author translated by Seong-Ah Shin. 9 October.

35 Shin, S. E-mail correspondence with the author. 9 October. Dr Shin teaches at the Baekseok University as a full-time lecturer and Korea National University of Arts, Seoul City University, Chugye University for the Arts in Korea.
36 Helmuth, M. 2006. E-mail correspondence with the author. 2 October.
37 Mathews, M. 2006. Interview with author. 8 September, San Francisco, CA.
38 Garton, B. 2006. E-mail correspondence with the author. 19 September. Dr Garton serves as the Director of the Computer Music Center at Columbia University.
39 Barnhart, M. 2006. E-mail correspondence with the author. 12 December. Mr Barnhart teaches electronic music at Shawnee State University.
40 Dubois, R. 2006. Interview with the author. 6 October. New York, NY.

3 Live electronic music

1 Unanticipated problems arose as telephone usage surged: crosstalk between adjacent cables caused the high-voltage signals of the Telharmonium to interfere with telephone conversations. Cahill tried alternative strategies, such as installing the instrument in a concert hall and broadcasting its sounds using nascent radio technology, but by 1914 his company was bankrupt.
2 Although it is worth noting that Robert Moog got his start by designing and selling Theremin kits while still in high school.
3 In fact in 1930, German film director Walter Ruttman used film soundtrack to create *Wochende* ('Weekend') a collage of environmental sound generally accepted to be the first work of *recorded* electronic music.
4 Private conversation between John Cage and the author, February 1974.
5 Which included over the years John D. S. Adams, Nicolas Collins, Paul De Marinis, John Driscoll, Phil Edelstein, Linda Fisher, D'Arcy Philip Gray, Ralph Jones, Martin Kalve, Ron Kuivila, and Matt Rogalsky.
6 At Mills these included Kenneth Atchley, Ben Azarm, John Bischoff, Chris Brown, Laetitia de Compiegne, Scot Gresham-Lancaster, Frankie Mann, Tim Perkis, Brian Reinbolt and Mark Trayle; at Wesleyan University, Ron Kuivila and Nicolas Collins; at California Institute of The Arts, Rich Gold.
7 The concept of integrating the player's skin in the circuitry would later figure prominently in the Circuit Bending scene.
8 It should be noted that some of the essential concepts of interactive computer music can be traced back to the compositions of Christian Wolff from the 1960s, such as *For 1, 2 or 3 People*

(1960), in which acoustic players are asked to co-ordinate their playing by following rules very similar to the binary logical operations of computers.
9 This field was eventually institutionalised in the annual NIME (New Interfaces for Musical Expression) conferences, which began in 2001. See http://www.nime.org
10 'The Adventures of Grandmaster Flash on the Wheels of Steel', recorded in 1981 with The Furious Five, was the first record to feature these techniques, previously heard only in club settings.
11 I've yet to find a primary source for this possible urban legend. See:

> Will Hoover, 'CD generation spins LP revival; loyalty of fans helps vinyl recordings defy predictions of their demise', *Honolulu Advertiser*, 6 March 2000. http://the.honoluluadvertiser.com/2000/Mar/06/islandlife1.html
> Rajan Datar 'More Club. Club Class!', BBC News, *The Money Programme*, 8 March 2001. http://news.bbc.co.uk/1/hi/events/the_money_programme/1208710.
> 'DJ Interview: Jam Master Jay', *The Loop – Scratch Newsletter*, 1(1), August 2002. http://www.scratch.com/theloop/news/newsletter.html
> Virgil Moorefield (2001) 'From the Illusion of Reality to the Reality of Illusion: the Changing Role of the Producer in the Pop Recording Studio', Ph.D. dissertation, Department of Music, Princeton University. Chapter 3, pp. 11–12. http://www.virgilmoorefield.com/prodtext.html

12 In the 1990s German Electronica groups Oval and Microstoria rediscovered the CD glitch, and adopted it as a signature element in their music, which in turn influenced the emerging genres of 'Glitch' and 'Micro-house'.
13 http://www.windworld.com
14 See for example Reed Ghazala's web site at http://www.anti-theory.com
15 Personal e-mail correspondence, April 2005. Britain's particularly vibrant bending scene has roots in the popularity of toys as affordable, alternative noisemakers among improvising musicians, such as Steve Beresford, in the 1970s.
16 Personal e-mail correspondence, April 2005.

4 A history of programming and music

1 Let us dispel one notion at the outset. Many artists are content to work with computer software that is essentially designed for them, providing a certain rather rigid interface, but

one that can be quickly navigated after a short learning curve. There is no intention herein to disparage such creation – wonderful *breakcore* and *8-bit* pieces have been made with tracker programs, sequencers are a staple of electronic dance music (good and bad) and some electroacoustic composers craft fascinating works by essentially the manual use of a sound editor. But where the experimental composer wishes to face the responsibility of control over musical ideas, with novel nonlinear structures, customised interactions and nonstandard synthesis, they are often led to need the facility of programming.

2 http://sonic-arts.org/darreg/dar6.htm gives one contemporary report.

3 To those overly used to modern realtime interactive systems, the efforts of composers in the preparation of works without much feedback – Cage's months of tape splicing, Stockhausen's months of layering sine tones, or Babbitt's heroic fight with the RCA Mark II synthesiser – can seem awe-inspiring. Nevertheless, there are always new research directions to drive you through long projects of your own . . .

4 Which stands for 'MINC is not C!', an example of the type of computer humour we prefer to relegate to an endnote.

5 James McCartney's own example patches for SuperCollider are themselves often held up as fascinating compositions. The Aphex Twin track *Bucephalus Bouncing Ball* (1997) was alleged to have reworked (and extended) one such compositional demonstration . . .

6 For more background see the TOPLAP homepage at http://www.toplap.org

7 This photo was taken at the Changing Grammars symposium on live coding in 2005: http://swiki.hfbk-hamburg.de:8888/MusicTechnology/609

5 Interactivity and live computer music

1 Raymond Scott's music can mostly be heard in many Warner Brothers animated cartoons. The melodies he wrote in the 1930s, for his jazz Quintette, were used in more than one hundred classic *Bugs Bunny* and *Daffy Duck* animated features, often orchestrated or adapted by Warner's Looney Tunes musical director, Carl Stalling.

2 For more detailed information on interactive music software during the 1980s the reader can refer to Yavelow (1986).

3 Available online at http://www.nime.org

4 *Misuse* should not be interpreted here with ideological, moral or aesthetical connotations. What we suggest is that only when a performer is capable of relating unwanted results (effects)

with the actions taken (causes) will this performer be able to learn and effectively progress.

6 Algorithmic composition

1 These approaches are discussed thoroughly by Pearce *et al.* (2002) and Wooler *et al.* (2005).

2 'The revolution might almost be equated with an anthropological turning point because it introduces a further narcissistic insult (after Copernicus, Darwin, and Freud) – it wrests the initiative from nature and mankind and replaces it with an automatable inherent law of action. The illusion of sovereign action on the part of the individual and the romantic notion of anthropomorphic decidability are tempered as a result' (Weibel 2005, p. 1).

3 Johann Philipp Kirnberger, *Allezeit fertiger Polonoisen- und Menuettencomponist* (The always ready Polonaise and Menuet composer, 1757); Maximilian Stadler, *Table pour composer des menuets et des trios à l'infinie, avec deux dez à jouer, pour le forte-piano ou clavecin* (Tables from which one can toss off countless Menuets and Trios for the piano or cembalo, 1781); attributed to Joseph Haydn, *Gioco filarmonico o sia maniera facile per comporre un infinito numero de minuetti e trio anche senza sapere il contrapunto* (Musical game or easy method for composing an infinite number of Menuets and Trios, even without the knowledge of counterpoint, before 1790).

4 Random numbers achieved by throwing two dice are not equally distributed. The probability of getting the number 7 is six times higher than getting 2 or 11.

5 Markov chains are weighted chains of random number choices which can lead to the emergence of patterns and stable structures without fixing a specific route.

6 The arithmetical series of durations that was used by Boulez is characterised by its uneven proportions and the dominance of longer values. For the different time-based parameters (frequency, rhythmic durations, durations of formal sections), Stockhausen suggested the use of logarithmic scales where consecutive members of a series have the same proportional factor. Through this unifying organisational principle, non-related parameters like pitch, rhythm and form can be viewed as different manifestations of time in different temporal domains (micro-, meso- and macro-time) (Stockhausen 1957).

7 This is not achieved by an automatism; it is the result of compositional decisions (Ligeti 1958).

8 A flow chart and the entire FORTRAN code of the program 'Free Stochastic Music' can be found in Xenakis' book *Formalized Music* (1971), pp. 145–53.

9 This term was introduced by the physicist and information theorist Werner Meyer-Eppler who defines aleatoric processes as 'processes which have been fixed in their outline but the details of which are left to chance' (Meyer-Eppler 1955).

10 *Projekt 1 – Version 1* (1965–6) for small orchestra.

11 This was based on experiments in the electronic studio – a regular (= periodic) waveform would result in sound, whereas an irregular (= aperiodic) waveform produced noise.

12 Taken from Koenig (1997). The rhythmic values are shown as 'entry delays' (ED) which define the temporal distance between two adjacent rhythmical entry points.

13 Available on request from the author through his website http://www.koenigproject.nl

14 Quoted from Shachtman, N. 2001. 'New Eno Music Gets "Generative"', *Wired News*, 27 October 2001.

15 The Algorithmic Stream began in 1997 at Brown University and is today located at Emerson College. http://pages.emerson.edu/faculty/m/maurice˙methot/stream/newstream.html

16 http://www.r4nd.org

17 This started in 1986 at IRCAM, Paris, when Miller Puckette was designing a control language named 'Patcher' for the 4X machine – a digital sound-processing workstation developed by Giuseppe Di Giugno, initially for Pierre Boulez's live-electronic oeuvre *Répons* (1981). In the beginning, Max could only process MIDI data and was used to control external hardware like synthesisers, MIDI instruments or FX devices. This changed in 1990 with the development of the 'IRCAM Signal Processing Workstation' (ISPW) – a realtime sound processing unit comprised of a NeXT computer with a customised, highly-expensive sound card which was only affordable by computer music centres. As computers became fast enough to process audio without external hardware, PD (1996) and MSP (1997) were released – both are based on the original Max paradigm, but are capable of realtime synthesis and signal processing.

18 Available as Open Source for Mac OS and Windows XP and also for PD from http://www.essl.at/works/rtc.html

19 A programming language for sound synthesis by Barry Vercoe *et al.* (MIT 1984). http://www.csounds.com

20 A realtime audio synthesis programming language by James McCartney (1996). http://www.audiosynth.com

21 A strongly timed, concurrent, and on-the-fly audio programming language (2002). http://chuck.cs.princeton.edu

22 A visual programming language from IRCAM based on CommonLisp by Gérard Assayag *et al.* (1995). http://recherche.ircam.fr/equipes/repmus/OpenMusic

7 Live audiovisuals

1 See http://rhythmiclight.com/archives/timeline.html, or Peacock (1988).

2 These included works by Karlheinz Stockhausen, Pauline Oliveros and Morton Subotnick.

3 Personal communication with Michael Scroggins, e-mails to Amy Alexander, 1–5 October 2006.

4 They were not alone in this role. For example, Light Sound Dimension, a San Francisco-based ensemble, included both audio and visual elements: light show performers as well as electronic musicians comprised the ensemble, which rehearsed and performed together as an integrated unit. Light Sound Dimension made its first performance in early 1967 at the San Francisco Museum of Modern Art, and by 1968 had established their own theatre, the Light Sound Dimension Theater (Ham 2002, pp. 2–3).

5 As per note 2.

6 See for example 'The World's Largest List of Psychedelic Lightshows' http://www.angelfire.com/psy/liquid˙sound˙designs/LiquidSoundDesigns˙lightshows.html; and 'Pooter's Lightshow Index' http://www.pooterland.com/index2/lightshow˙menu/lightshows/lightshows.html

7 http://www.audiovisualizers.com/toolshak/vsynths.htm

8 Developments in visual computer technology have tended to lag a little behind audio, due to the increased processing load. Whilst at first sight the reader might believe the 44,100 samples a second of audio to be the greater challenge, if we imagine visual data processed as frames of size 640 by 480 RGBA pixels at a ballpark of twenty-five frames per second, the processing load is 30,720,000 floats per second, a factor of 697 times more!

9 An example of such fashion shifts is the move from the nato.0+55 extensions for Max/MSP under Mac OS 9 to Cycling 74's own Jitter package in more recent times.

10 A basic premise of much audiovisual performance is that extra stimulation in a further modality heightens audience's experiences. Commentators on audiovisual media have appreciated the 'added value' (Chion 1994) communicated by correlated information from stimulating two senses simultaneously. Indeed, in some cases, reaction time to stimuli in coincident modalities is faster than to either sense alone (Welch and Warren 1986).

8 Network music

1 http://earlyradiohistory.us/1909musi.htm

2 Bowker, G. and Star, S. (1996) *How things (actor-net)work: Classification, magic and the ubiquity of standards*, at http://epl.scu.edu:16080/~gbowker/actnet.html

3 DeMarinis, P. (2006) *Firebirds and Tongues of Fire*, at www.uiowa.edu/~iareview/mainpages/new/feb06/demarinis.html

4 Warburton, D. (1998) *Luc Ferrari, Interview by Dan Warburton*, at http://paristransatlantic.com/magazine/interviews/ferrari.html

5 Hyde, A. and Harger, H. (1998) *Radio Astronomy*, at http://www.radio-astronomy.net

6 Due to its relationality, Peirce's semiotics (theory of signs) provides a good model for reasoning about causality and programming in terms of sign processes (Peirce 1958; Andersen 2006). The notion that a symbol stands in for something else is equivalent to Shannon's concept of the message representing a *choice* in the receiver (Shannon 1948).

7 For a general discussion of transmission protocols see Holzmann (1990).

8 The absence of a unified system of truth doesn't mean, however, the absence of structure, and the experiment can't abdicate responsibility for the event. The paradigm rather shifts in another direction: the explicit intervention by rules, such as programs or instructions, is intended to formulate a problem, rather than a solution.

9 See Baumgärtel (2005) on the exhibition *Les Immatériaux* (1985), curated by Jean-François Lyotard.

10 A peer-to-peer network structure, for instance, may be used for a monopolistic control scheme and a central server for a pluralistic conversation.

11 De Campo, personal communication, 2006.

9 Electronic music and the moving image

1 Interview with Eduard Artemiev speaking of film director Andrei Tarkovsky and the music for *Solaris* (1972) (Egorova 1988).

2 A more extended discussion of Schaeffer's four listening modes is found in chapter 13.

3 A further refinement of this is found in Nicholas Cook's explanation of his models of multimedia: conformance, complementation and contest (Cook 1998, pp. 98–106).

4 Electronic music has traditionally incorporated the manipulation of sound recordings and this practice is implied throughout the discussion.

5 Although Davies (2006) states that the 'synthetic high and low frequencies' were actually drawn onto the soundtrack.

6 A more complete account of the use of the Theremin in film is contained in Hayward (2004); Wierbicki (2005).

7 It certainly makes them precursors to circuit bending.

8 By disembodied I mean that the sounds themselves don't necessarily bear a signature of direct human physical effort.

9 Burtt's own account in the audio commentary at 1:15:11 of *Star Wars IV*, from the Trilogy Limited Edition DVD set.

10 A technique named after Jack Foley, Hollywood sound effects pioneer who first recorded sound effects live and in sync while watching the film, to enrich the sound of early talkies.

11 Whose name today is Wendy Carlos.

12 There is a noticeable difference between having an orchestra booked for a three-hour recording session, including a fifteen-minute coffee break, under the careful eye of the musicians' union representative, and being able to make a similar sound with samplers and synths in the privacy of a home studio.

13 This comment is meant to be more thought-provoking than provocative. Academia can offer a safe haven to experimentalists who push the boundaries outside the commercial world and this benefits everyone in the end. However it is salutary to think that we are never that independent of our audience's taste or of contemporary musical trends. In any case, there is also such a thing as successful experimentalism, as the work of electronica artists such as Aphex Twin or Squarepusher demonstrates. Overall, we may even artificially separate academics, independent artists and commercial interests too much.

14 Scott had been developing it since 1948 (Blom and Winner 2000).

15 Track 23 from CD1 of *Manhattan Research Inc.: Raymond Scott*. Holland: BASTA Audio/Visuals.

16 The creator and producer of the children's TV programme *The Muppet Show*.

17 SMPTE stands for 'Society of Motion Picture and Television Engineers'; it is also a complex synthesised audio signal which is used in film/TV to identify a location by hours, minutes, seconds and frames.

18 In the *Manhattan Research Inc.* CDs mentioned above.

19 Given that video games are a very fast expanding industry, even by the time this book reaches the shelves anything billed as 'new' here may already seem slightly obsolete.

20 The first 'Tennis' graphic game was invented earlier in 1966 by Ralph Baer, in the US.

21 Tracker software, which is much like a sequencer program, can be found easily on the internet. Some of the earliest trackers were *Scream Tracker* or *Impulse*. If you search for MODs on the internet you will find many different applications for handling/sequencing this type of file. In any case, MIDI technology eventually took over as the favoured soundtrack creation tool.

22 Manufactured by Taito in Japan and distributed by Midway in the US.

23 Even though for those of us who owned an Intellivision console this may not be novel information, I would strongly refer the reader to Collins (2004): she presents a thorough account which is very worthwhile reading.

24 You can play an online version and listen to the hallmark accelerating tune at http://www.spaceinvaders.de/

25 Created by Oliver Wittchow, who to my knowledge was the first to make a full musical instrument out of the gameboy.

26 Thus, the algorithmic composition might be viewed as a secondary consequence of game world state.

27 These techniques have been widely utilised and were certainly not invented for the Lara Croft games, although recent media coverage would seem to suggest otherwise. Countless papers on adaptive music (and algorithmic composition) serve as a basis for it, in fact. See chapter 6 for examples of generative music and references. Such techniques have been around for a while in the music industry – as well as in academia – and, for example, featured in the Yamaha PSR series keyboards in the late 1980s, for which I was one of several music programmers at Yamaha R&D, London. To make 'styles', we would create the musical sections as 'cells' so that we had one or more introductions and endings, different transitions, breaks, and different accompaniments for verses, bridges and choruses. We also programmed different layers of orchestration that would only appear in response to the performer's musical activity. For instance, if they were playing a solo over the verse section and played many notes, very fast, brass sections would start to riff or string sections would appear. A specific site on adaptive audio in games can be found at http://www.iasig.org/aan

10 Musical robots and listening machines

1 The interested reader might follow up links to a blog of robot developments at http://techdigest.tv/robots or find further information on Repliee Q2 at http://www.androidscience.org

2 Indeed, this is a reason that there is much current research into the neuroscience of music, as an insight into brain activity.

3 In fact, the first reference to the term I have found is the Interactive Music System developed at CERL by Hebel, Scaletti and colleagues around 1981 (Chadabe 1997, p. 266).

4 http://www.studio360.org/show082104.html

5 http://logosfoundation.org/instrum_gwr/automatons.html

6 http://www.lemurbots.org

7 http://www.ai.mit.edu/projects/humanoid-robotics-group/cog

8 Paralleling contentions in the philosophy of artificial intelligence are issues of physical embodiment; many experimental systems are entirely virtual but for microphone input and speaker output. When this is accomplished well, it has the virtue of being non-invasive to traditional instrumental practice, such that acoustic musicians can quickly engage with a system. The disadvantage is a disquiet about the grounding in the real world; musical robotics, however, is a field of endeavour that is forced to confront the physical world outside standard computer interfaces.

9 Subsymbolic representations may prove very important for the modelling of non-expert listeners and indeed, the state of many musical situations even for experts (Scheirer 1996; Martin *et al.* 1998); for instance, in ambiguous harmony, or the difficulty of extracting inner voices.

10 This also implies some loss of information, however (Honing 1993). Whilst training and categorical perception tend to make certain sound objects jump out at us, we must be cautious about claiming that machines turn all audio into a perfect score-like representation (e.g. MIDI-style notes) as a necessary precursor to any further operation. An intelligent signal-processing device might operate entirely on low-level features and never deal with any discrete event formulation.

11 http://www.infomus.dist.unige.it/EywMain.html

12 So there are some flaws in the argument that the detection and anticipation of events is intimately tied to the physical substruct; for example, there is no tactile feedback or image of the body in beat tracking. Further, whilst the authors have attempted to fashion analysis routines for Haile based on theories of the perception of rhythm (the system remaining chiefly concerned with interaction in the rhythmic domain), these remain unproven and insufficient as regards human abilities. This is not to disparage the project; such undertakings

founded in cognitive science are extremely valuable approaches.

13 The reader unfamiliar with Nancarrow's wonderful contribution to music is encouraged to seek out the studies for player-piano, the culmination of fifty years of punching piano rolls by hand. These take advantage of mechanical pianos to explore territories beyond the limits of human performance, chronologically far in advance of later computer-based experiments.

14 Though this involves production rule mechanisms analogous to generate and test in algorithmic composition, and more advanced learning and critical mechanisms are open areas of research.

15 We are far from a time when machines might request membership of the Musicians' Union, though I heartily encourage any prospective system-builders to submit joke applications to the union for publicity purposes.

11 Computer generation and manipulation of sounds

1 http://www.music.princeton.edu/paul/radiohead.ml.html

2 Arguably to the point of overuse for certain basic granular techniques in much recent electroacoustic concert music!

3 Research is ongoing; in one recent development, the grains of sounds are analysed for their features and can be used to form large databases of sound material for compositional reuse. *Concatenative synthesis* (Schwarz 2004) is now a blossoming area of interest for researchers and composers, often bringing up issues of copyright anticipated by the manually constructed works of composers like Pierre Schaeffer or John Oswald.

4 http://www.iua.upf.edu/mtg/pages/home

5 Using results from recent research on speech sound by Gunnar Fant.

6 For example, unfortunately, both Modalys and Cordis-Anima have a rather limited number of users, which is probably due to the way the software packages can be obtained. Modalys needs to be purchased from IRCAM, while, at the time of writing, Cordis-Anima runs only on Silicon Graphics machines, and needs to be purchased from ACROE.

13 Trends in electroacoustic music

1 Oliveros, P. (last updated 2006). At http://www.deeplistening.org/pauline/

2 See Manning (1985), pp. 31–3 for a more detailed description in English.

3 The reader will find Smalley (1992) a useful elaboration.

4 The combination of two texts by Smalley (1986; 1997) provide the clearest description.

5 For further reading see Wishart (1996), pp. 239–315; Bosma (1996); Hettergott (1999).

6 In contrast to a spatial illusion which is normally revealed over shorter durations, the time it takes a listener to arrive at an understanding of a spatial allusion is tied to the sound type and the duration that is needed to reveal its identity.

7 To explore this answer I direct the reader to Francis Dhomont's article 'Acousmatic Update' (Dhomont 1995) which suggests that although the concert may be an impressive enlargement of an acousmatic work, the CD is an exact replica of the composer's (stereo) master, contrary to the reduction (recording) of an instrumental concert.

8 Ferrari, L. (1998) 'Luc Ferrari Interview by Dan Warburton', at http://www.paristransatlantic.com/magazine/interviews/ferrari.html

9 Gerzso (1984); Boulez (1988) are interesting reference texts which explain compositional and technical aspects of *Répons*.

References

Adams, J. (1997) 'Conversations with Jonathan Sheffer', in *Perceptual Processes: Minimalism and the Baroque.* New York: Eos Music, Inc.

Addessi, A. R., Pachet, F. and Caterina, R. (2004) 'Children Confronting an Interactive Musical System', in *Proceedings of the International Conference on Music Perception and Cognition,* Chicago

Allen, J. (2005) 'The Polarized Composer: Addressing the Conflict of Musical Upbringings of Today's Young Composers', *Proceedings of the Third Annual Spark Festival of Electronic Music and Art,* University of Minnesota

Andersen, P. B. (1997) *A Theory of Computer Semiotics.* New York, NY: Cambridge University Press

Arns, I. (2004) 'Read_me, run_me, execute_me. Code as Executable Text: SoftwareArt and its Focus on Program Code as Performative Text', at http://www.medienkunstnetz.de/themes/generative-tools/read_me/

Assche, C., Ranciere, J., and Diederichson, R. (2003) *Sonic Process.* Barcelona: Actar

Attali, J. (2004) 'Noise and Politics', in Cox and Warner

Aucouturier, J.-J. (2006) 'Ten Experiments on the Modelling of Polyphonic Timbre'. Ph.D. thesis, University of Paris 6, France, at http://www.jj-aucouturier. info/papers/PH–D2006.pdf

Bacon, F. (2006) *New Atlantis.* New York: Dodo Press

Bailey, C. (2004) 'An Interface for "Flat Music"', *Organised Sound* 9(3): 243–50.

Bailey, D. (1980) *Improvisation: Its Nature and Practice in Music.* Ashbourne, Derbyshire: Moorland Publishing Co. Ltd

Barbosa, Á. (2006) 'Computer-Supported Cooperative Work for Music Applications'. Ph.D. thesis, Universitat Pompeu Fabra, at http://www.mtg. upf.edu/publicacions.php

Baron-Cohen, S. and Harrison, J. (1997) *Synaesthesia: Classic and Contemporary Readings.* Oxford: Blackwell Publishers

Barrett, N. (2000) 'A Compositional Methodology Based on Data Extracted from Natural Phenomena', *Proceedings of the International Computer Music Conference*: 20–3

— (2002) 'Spatio-Musical Composition Strategies', *Organised Sound* 7(3): 313–23

Baudrillard, J. (1988) *The Ecstasy of Communication,* Schutze, B. and C. (trans.). New York: Semiotext(e)

Baumgärtel, T. (2005) 'Immaterial Material: Physicality, Corporality and Dematerialization in Telecommunication Artworks', in Chandler and Neumark, pp. 60–71

Bello, J. P., Daudet, L., Abdallah, S., Duxbury, C., Davies, M. and Sandler, S. B. (2004) 'A Tutorial on Onset Detection in Music Signals', *IEEE Transactions on Speech and Audio Processing*

Bernstein, D. W. (2002) 'Cage and High Modernism', in Nicholls, D. (ed.), *The Cambridge Companion to John Cage*. Cambridge: Cambridge University Press

Bischoff, J., Gold, R. and Horton, J. (1978) 'Music for an Interactive Network of Computers', *Computer Music Journal* 2(3): 24–9

Blaine, T. (2006) 'New Music for the Masses', *Adobe Design Center, Think Tank Online*, at http://www.adobe.com/designcenter/thinktank/ttap_music

— and Perkis, T. (2000) 'Jam-O-Drum, a Study in Interaction Design', *Proceedings of the ACM DIS 2000 Conference*. New York, NY: ACM Press

Blom, G. and Winner, J. (2000) 'Track Notes: Mining the Archives', in Chusid, I. (ed.), *Manhattan Research Inc.: Raymond Scott*. Holland: BASTA Audio/Visuals, pp. 119–21

Bosma, H. (1996) 'Authorship and Female Voices in Electrovocal Music', *Proceedings of the International Computer Music Conference*

Böß, R. (1996) *Verschiedene Canones . . . von J. S. Bach (BWV 1087)*. Munich: edition text + kritik

Boulanger, R. (ed.) (2000) *The Csound Book*. Cambridge, MA: MIT Press

Boulez, P. and Gerzso, A. (1988) 'Computers in Music', *Scientific American* 258(4)

Bregman, A. S. (1990) *Auditory Scene Analysis*. Cambridge, MA: MIT Press

Brown, C. and Bischoff, J. (2002) 'Indigenous to the Net: Early Network Music Bands in the San Francisco Bay Area, at http://crossfade.walkerart.org/brownbischoff

Burk, P. (1998) 'JSyn – a Real-Time Synthesis API for Java', *Proceedings of the International Computer Music Conference*

Burns, E. M. (1999) 'Intervals, Scales, and Tuning', in Deutsch (1999), pp. 215–64

Cadoz, C. (1979) 'Synthèse sonore par simulation des mécanismes vibratoires'. Thèse de troisième cycle. Grenoble: I. N. P.

Cage, J. (1959) 'History of Experimental Music in the United States', in *Silence*. London: Marion Boyars Publishers, 1978, pp. 67–75

— (1960) *Cartridge Music* (score). New York: Henmar Press

— (1960) *Fontana Mix. Material for tape music of that title . . .* New York: Henmar Press

— (1966) *Silence*. Cambridge, MA: MIT Press

— (1968) *Silence*. New York: Marion Boyars

— (1995) *Silence: Lectures and Writings*. London: Marion Boyars

— (2004) 'The Future of Music: Credo', in Cox and Warner

Camurri, A. and Leman, M. (1997) 'AI-based Music Signals Applications – a Hybrid Approach', in Roads, C., Pope, S. T., Piccialli, A. and De Poli, G. (eds.), *Musical Signal Processing*. Lisse, the Netherlands: Svets and Zeitlinger, pp. 349–81

Carterette, E. C. and Kendall, R. A. (1999) 'Comparative Music Perception and Cognition', in Deutsch (1999), pp. 725–92

Cascone, K. (2004) 'The Aesthetics of Failure: "Post-digital" Tendencies in Computer Music', in Cox and Warner, pp. 392–8

266 References

Chadabe, J. (1984) 'Interactive Composing: an Overview', *Computer Music Journal* 8(1): 22–8. Reprinted in Roads, C. (ed.), *The Music Machine*. Cambridge, MA: MIT Press
— (1997) *Electric Sound: The Past and Promise of Electronic Music.* Upper Saddle River, NJ: Prentice Hall
— (1999) 'Raymond Scott: Inventor and Composer', in Chusid, I. (ed.) CD booklet, *Manhattan Research Inc.: Raymond Scott.* Holland: BASTA Audio/Visuals, pp. 17–22
Chafe, *et al.* (2002) 'Physical Model Synthesis with Application to Internet Acoustics', in *International Conference on Acoustics, Speech and Signal Processing*, Orlando, FL, at http://www-ccrma.stanford.edu/~cc/soundwire/icassp02.pdf
Chandler, A. and Neumark, N. (eds.) (2005) *At a Distance: Precursors to Art and Activism on the Internet.* Cambridge, MA: MIT Press (Leonardo Books)
Chion, M. (1994) *Audio-vision: Sound on Screen.* New York: Columbia University Press. Original published 1990, translated by Gorbman, C.
Chowning, J. M. (1971) 'The Simulation of Moving Sound Sources', *Journal of the Audio Engineering Society* 19: 2–6
— (1973) 'The Synthesis of Complex Audio Spectra by Means of Frequency Modulation', *Journal of the Audio Engineering Society* 21(7): 526–34
Chusid, I. and Garland, D. (1994) 'Reckless Nights and Turkish Twilights: the Genius of Raymond Scott', *Naras Journal* 5(1): 69–79
Collins, K. (2004) *From Bits to Hits: Video Games Music Changes its Tune*, www.dullien-inc.com/collins/texts/bits2hits.pdf
Collins, N. (2003) 'Generative Music and Laptop Performance', *Contemporary Music Review* 22(4): 67–79
— (2006) 'Towards Autonomous Agents for Live Computer Music: Realtime Machine Listening and Interactive Music Systems'. Ph.D. thesis, University of Cambridge
— and Olofsson, F. (2006) 'klipp av: Live Algorithmic Splicing and Audiovisual Event Capture', *Computer Music Journal* 30(2): 8–18
— McLean A., Rohrhuber, J. and Ward, A. (2003) 'Live Coding in Laptop Performance', *Organised Sound* 8(3): 321–30
Cook, N. (1998) *Analysing Musical Multimedia.* Oxford: Oxford University Press
Cook, P. R. (ed.) (1999) *Music, Cognition, and Computerized Sound: An Introduction to Psychoacoustics.* Cambridge, MA: MIT Press
— and Scavone, G. (1999) 'The Synthesis Toolkit (STK)', *Proceedings of the International Computer Music Conference*
— (2002) *Real Sound Synthesis for Interactive Applications.* Wellesley, MA: AK Peters
Cooper, G. and Meyer, L. B. (1960) *The Rhythmic Structure of Music.* Chicago: University of Chicago Press
Cope, D. (1996) *Experiments in Musical Intelligence.* Madison, WI: A-R Editions
Cox, C. and Warner, D. (eds.) (2004) *Audio Culture: Readings in Modern Music.* New York: Continuum
Cramer, F. (2005) *Words Made Flesh. Codes, Culture, Imagination.* Rotterdam: Piet Zwart Institute

Cutler, M., Robair, G. and Bean (2000) 'OuterLimits', *Electronic Musician Magazine* (August 2000): 49–72

Dannenberg, R. (1993) 'Music Representation Issues, Techniques and Systems', *Computer Music Journal* 17(3): 20–30

— (1997) 'Machine Tongues XIX: Nyquist, a Language for Composition and Sound Synthesis', *Computer Music Journal* 21(3): 50–60

Davies, H. (2006) 'Drawn Sound' at http://www.grovemusic.com

Deutsch, D. (1999) *The Psychology of Music* (2nd edn). New York: Academic Press

Deutsch, H. A. (1976) *Synthesis: An Introduction to the History, Theory, and Practice of Electronic Music*. New York: Alfred Publishing Co

Dhomont, F. (1995) 'Acousmatic Update', *Contact!* 8(2): 49–54

Diderot, D. (1951) *Oeuvres*. Paris: La Pléiade, Gallimard

D'Inverno, Mark and Luck, Michael (2001) *Understanding Agent Systems*. Berlin: Springer-Verlag

Dornbusch, P. (2005) *The Music of CSIRAC – Australia's First Computer Music*. Melbourne: The Humanities, Common Ground Publishing

Doruff, S. (2006) 'The Translocal Event and the Polyrhythmic Diagram'. Ph.D. thesis, University of the Arts, London, at http://spresearch.waag.org/papers.html

Drucker, J. (2005) 'Interactive, Algorithmic, Networked: Aesthetics of New Media Art', in Chandler and Neumark, pp. 26–33

Ebcioglu, K. (1990) 'An Expert System for Harmonizing Chorales in the Style of J. S. Bach', *Journal of Logic Programming* 8(1): 145–85

Eckel, G. (2003) 'The LISTEN Vision', in *Beat Zoderer. Der doppelte Boden ist tiefer als man denkt*. Bonn: Kunstmuseum Bonn, pp. 96–7

Eco, U. (1995) *The Search for the Perfect Language*. Malden: Blackwell Publishing

Eladhari, M., Nieuwdorp, R. and Fridenfalk, M. (2006) 'The Soundtrack of Your Mind: Mind Music – Adaptive Audio for Game Characters', in *Proceedings of the 2006 ACM SIGCHI international Conference on Advances in Computer Entertainment Technology*. New York: ACM Press

El-Dabh, H. (2001) *Crossing Into the Electric Magnetic*. Lakewood, OH: Without Fear Recordings

Emmerson, S. (1998) 'Aural Landscape: Musical Space', *Organised Sound* 3(2): 135–40

Eno, B. (1978) *Music for Airports*, liner notes of the CD

Essl, K. (1989) 'Zufall und Notwendigkeit. Anmerkungen zu Gottfried Michael Koenigs Streichquartett 1959 vor dem Hintergrund seiner kompositionstheoretischen Untersuchungen', in Metzger, H.-K. (ed.), *Musik-Konzepte* 66. Munich: edition text + kritik, pp. 35–76

— (1996) 'Strukturgeneratoren. Algorithmische Musik in Echtzeit', in Höldrich, R. (ed.), *Beiträge zur Elektronischen Musik* 5. Graz: IEM, pp. 29–48

— (2000) 'Lexikon-Sonate. An Interactive Realtime Composition for Computer-controlled Piano', in Enders, B. and Stange-Elbe, J. (eds.), *Musik und Neue Technologie* 3. Osnabrück: Universitätsverlag Rasch, pp. 311–28

Filmer, P. (2004) 'Songtime: Sound Culture, Rhythm and Sociality', in *The Auditory Culture Reader (Sensory Formations)*. Gordonsville: Berg Publishers

Fischer, G. H. (1922) 'Concerning "Canned Music" Now Broadcasted' at http://earlyradiohistory.us/1922can.htm

Fischinger, O. (1932) 'Sounding Ornaments', in *The Fischinger Archive* www.oskarfischinger.org/Sounding.htm. First published in the *Deutsche allgemeine Zeitung*, 8 July 1932

— (1942) 'Radio Dynamics', in *Oskar Fischinger: Ten Films*. Los Angeles: Center for Visual Music DVD

Fraisse, P. (1982) 'Rhythm and Tempo', in Deutsch (1999), pp. 149–80

Gerzso, A. (1984) 'Reflexions on *Répons*', *Contemporary Music Review* 1(1): 23–34

Giannetti, C. (2004) 'Cybernetic Aesthetics and Communication', at http://www.medienkunstnetz.de/themes/aesthetics_of_the_digital/cybernetic_aesthetics/

Gilje, H. C. (2005) 'Within the Space of an Instant', *HC Gilje Texts*, at http://www.bek.no/~hc/texts.htm

Gluck, B. (2005) 'Conversation with Halim El-Dabh', *EMF Institute*, at http://emfinstitute.emf.org/articles/gluck.eldabh.html

Goethe, J. W. (1982) 'Letter to Herder: 17 May 1787', in Trunz, E. (ed.), *Italienische Reise* (= *Hamburger Ausgabe* 11) Munich: C. H. Beck, pp. 323–4

Gómez, E., Klapuri, A. and Meudic, B. (2003) 'Melody Description and Extraction in the Context of Music Content Processing', *Journal of New Music Research* 32(1): 23–40

Gómez, E. (2006) 'Tonal Description of Music Audio Signals'. Ph.D. thesis, Universitat Pompeu Fabra

González-Arroyo, R. (2003) 'Sound, Time, Form, and Movement in a Structured Space', in *Beat Zoderer. Der doppelte Boden ist tiefer als man denkt*, Bonn: Kunstmuseum Bonn, pp. 101–2

Goodman, N. (1979) 'Metaphor as Moonlighting', *Critical Inquiry* 6(1)

Gould, G. (2004) 'The Prospects of Recording', in Cox and Warner, pp. 115–26

Gouyon, F. and Dixon, S. (2005) 'A Review of Automatic Rhythm Description Systems', *Computer Music Journal* 29(1): 34–54

Grant, M. J. (2001) *Serial Music, Serial Aesthetics: Compositional Theory in Post-War Europe*. Cambridge: Cambridge University Press

Griffiths, P. (1979) *A Guide to Electronic Music*. London: Thames and Hudson

Grodal, T. (2003) 'Stories for Eye, Ear and Muscles: Video Games, Media and Embodied Experiences', in Wolf, M. J. P. and Perron, B. (eds.), *The Video Game Theory Reader*. London: Routledge

Guthrie, K. S. (trans.) and Fideler, D. (ed.) (1987) *The Pythagorean Sourcebook and Library*. Grand Rapids: Phanes Press

Hajdu, G. (2005) 'Quintet.net: An Environment for Composing and Performing Music on the Internet', *Leonardo* 38(1): 23–30

Ham, B. (2002) 'History', *Bill Ham Lights*. 24 January 2002: 1–4. http://billhamlights.com/history1.htm

Hansen, K. F. (2002) 'The Basics of Scratching', *Journal of New Music Research* 31(4): 357–67

Hanson, S. (1993) 'Text-sound Composition in the Sixties', in Hultberg, T. (ed.), *Literally Speaking: Sound Poetry & Text-sound Composition*. Sweden: Bo Ejeby Edition, pp. 23–9

Harrison, J. (1989) 'Denis Smalley, EMAS and (Electro-acoustic) Music', *Musical Times* 130: 1759

— (1998) 'Sound, Space, Sculpture: Some Thoughts on the 'What', 'How' and 'Why' of Sound Diffusion', *Organised Sound* 3(2): 117–27

— (1999) 'Diffusion: Theories and Practices, with Particular Reference to the BEAST System', *eContact!* 2(4), at http://cec.concordia.ca/econtact/Diffusion/index.htm

— (2001) *Synaesthesia: The Strangest Thing*. Oxford: Oxford University Press

Harvey, J. (2000) 'Spectralism', *Contemporary Music Review* 19(3): 11–14

Hayward, P. (2004) 'Sci-Fidelity: Music, Sound and Genre History', in Hayward, P. (ed.), *Off The Planet: Music, Sound and Science Fiction Cinema*. Eastleigh: John Libbey Publishing

Henkjan, H. (1993) 'Issues in the Representation of Time and Structure in Music', *Contemporary Music Review* 9: 221–39

Henriques, J. (2004) 'Sonic Dominance and the Reggae Sound System', in *The Auditory Culture Reader (Sensory Formations)*. Gordonsville: Berg Publishers

Herrera-Boyer, P., Peeters, G. and Dubnov, S. (2003) 'Automatic Classification of Musical Instrument Sounds', *Journal of New Music Research* 32(1): 3–21

Hettergott, A. (1999) 'Human Voice Treatment in Various Types of Electroacoustic Music', *Proceedings of the International Computer Music Conference*

Hiller, L. A. (1981) 'Composing with Computers: a Progress Report', *Computer Music Journal* 5(4), in Roads, C. (ed.) (1989), *The Music Machine*. Cambridge, MA: MIT Press, pp. 75–89

— and Isaacson, L. M. (1959) *Experimental Music: Composition with an Electronic Computer*. New York: McGraw-Hill

Holmes, T. (2002) *Electronic and Experimental Music*. New York: Routledge

Holzmann, G. J. (1990) 'Design And Validation Of Computer Protocols', Prentice Hall PTR, at http://spinroot.com/spin/Doc/Book91.html

Hornbostel, E. M. von (1925) 'Die Einheit der Sinne', *Melos (Zeitschrift für Musik)* 4: 290–7

Hsu, W. (2005) 'Using Timbre in a Computer-Based Improvisation System', in *Proceedings of the International Computer Music Conference*, Barcelona, pp. 777–80

— (2006) 'Managing Gesture and Timbre for Analysis and Instrument Control in an Interactive Environment', in *Proceedings of New Interfaces for Musical Expression (NIME)*, Paris

Inglis, S. (2002) 'Marcus Popp: Music as Software', *Sound on Sound* October 2002, at http://www.soundonsound.com/sos/Oct02/articles/oval.asp

International MIDI Association (1983) *MIDI Musical Instrument Digital Interface Specification 1.0*. North Hollywood: International MIDI Association

Jaeger, T. (2005) *Live Cinema Unravelled*. Self-published at http://www.vj-book.com

Jaffe, D. A. and Smith, J. O. (1983) 'Extensions of the Karplus-Strong Plucked String Algorithm', *Computer Music Journal* 7(2): 56–69

James, D. (2005) 'Expanded Cinema in Los Angeles: the Single Wing Turquoise Bird', *Millennium Film Journal* 43(44): 9–31

Johnson, S. (1999) *Interface Culture: How New Technology Transforms the Way We Create and Communicate*. Jackson: Perseus Book Group

Jordà, S. (2002) 'Improvising with Computers: a Personal Survey (1989–2001)', *Journal of New Music Research* 31(1): 1–10

— (2005) 'Digital Lutherie: Crafting Musical Computers for New Musics' Performance and Improvisation'. Ph.D. thesis, Universitat Pompeu Fabra

— Kaltenbrunner, M., Geiger, G. and Bencina, R. (2005) 'The reacTable', *Proceedings of the International Computer Music Conference*. San Francisco, CA: International Computer Music Association

Kaç, E. (1992) 'Aspects of the Aesthetics of Telecommunications', in *Siggraph Visual Proceedings*. New York: ACM, pp. 47–57

Kahn, D. (1999) *Noise, Water, Meat: A History of Sound in the Arts*. Cambridge, MA: MIT Press

Karplus, K. and Strong, A. (1983) 'Digital Synthesis of Plucked-string and Drum Timbres', *Computer Music Journal* 7(2): 43–55

Kay, A. C. (1993) *The Early History of Smalltalk*, at http://gagne.homedns.org/ ~tgagne/contrib/EarlyHistoryST.html

Klapuri, Anssi P. (2004) 'Automatic Music Transcription as We Know It Today', *Journal of New Music Research* 33(3): 269–82

Koenig, G. M. (1978) 'Kompositionsprozesse', in Fricke and Frobenius (ed.) (1993) *Gottfried Michael Koenig. Ästhetische Praxis. Texte zur Musik*, vol. III. Saarbrücken: Pfau Verlag, pp. 191–210 (English translation as 'Composition Processes', in *Computer Music Reports on an International Project*, Ottawa 1980)

— (1979) 'Projekt 1 – Modell und Wirklichkeit', in *Texte*, vol. III (1993), pp. 223–30

— (1986) 'Zu Funktionen', in *Texte*, vol. V (2002), p. 166

— (1997) 'PROJECT 1 Revisited. On the Analysis and Interpretation of PR1 Tables', in Jerry Tabor (ed.) (1999), *Otto Laske. Navigating New Musical Horizons*. Westpoint, CT, London: Greenwood Press

Kolb, T. (2002) 'Yamaha DX7 Synthesizer', at http://hem.passagen.se/ tkolb/art/synth/dx7_e.htm

Kostelanetz, R. (1970) *John Cage, An Anthology*. New York: Da Capo Press

Labelle, B. (2006) *Background Noise: Perspectives on Sound Art*. New York: Continuum

Lansky, P. (2006) 'CMIX Program Documentation', at http://music.princeton.edu/ winham/man/

Large, E. W. and Kolen, J. F. (1994) 'Resonance and the Perception of Musical Meter', *Connection Science* 6(2–3): 177–208

Le Grice, M. (1977) *Abstract Film and Beyond*. Cambridge, MA: MIT Press

Leman, M., Lesaffre, M. and Tanghe, K. (2000) *The IPEM Toolbox Manual*. University of Ghent, IPEM, Department of Musicology: IPEM

Lerdahl, F. and Jackendoff, R. (1983) *A Generative Theory of Tonal Music*. Cambridge, MA: MIT Press

Lewis, G. (1999) 'Interacting with Latter-day Musical Automata', *Contemporary Music Review* 18(3): 99–112

— (2000) 'Too Many Notes: Computers, Complexity and Culture in Voyager', *Leonardo Music Journal* 10: 33–9

Leydon, R. (2004) '*Forbidden Planet*: Effects and Affects in the Electro-avant-garde', in Hayward, P. (ed.), *Off The Planet: Music, Sound and Science Fiction Cinema*. Eastleigh: John Libbey Publishing, pp. 68–9

Ligeti, G. (1958) 'Pierre Boulez. Entscheidung und automatik in der Structure 1a', in Eimert (ed.) *Die Reihe* 4, Vienna: Universal Edition, pp. 38–63

Ligeti, L. (2006) 'The Burkina Electric Project . . . and Some Thoughts about Electronic Music in Africa', *Leonardo Electronic Almanac* 15(1)

Lipscomb, S. and Tolchinsky, D. (2005) 'The Role of Music Communication in Cinema', in Miell, D., MacDonald, R. and Hargreaves, D. (eds.), *Music Communication*. New York: Oxford University Press

Llinas, R., Ribary, U., Contreras, D. and Pedroarena, C. (1998) 'The Neuronal Basis for Consciousness', *Philosophical Transactions of The Royal Society: Biological Sciences* 353(1377): 1841–9

Loy, G. (1985) 'Musicians Make a Standard: the MIDI Phenomenon', *Computer Music Journal* 9(4): 8–26

— (1989) 'Composing with Computers – a Survey of Some Compositional Formalisms and Programming Languages for Music', in Mathews, M. and Pierce, J. (eds.), *Current Directions in Computer Music Research*. Cambridge, MA: MIT Press

— (2002) 'The CARL System: Premises, History, and Fate', *Computer Music Journal* 26(4): 52–60

Lucier, A. (1998) 'Origins of a Form: Acoustical Exploration, Science and Incessancy', *Leonardo Music Journal* 8(1): 5–11

Lyon, E. (2002) 'Dartmouth Symposium on the Future of Computer Music Software: a Panel Discussion', *Computer Music Journal* 26(4): 13–30

Mac Minute (2006) 'Nine Inch Nails Offers New Single in Garage Band Format', at http://www.macminute.com/2005/04/15/nin/

Machover, T. (1992) 'Hyperinstruments – a Composer's Approach to the Evolution of Intelligent Musical Instruments', in Jacobson, L. (ed.), *Cyberarts: Exploring Arts and Technology*. San Francisco: MillerFreeman Inc., pp. 67–76

Manning, P. (1985) *Electronic and Computer Music*. Oxford: Oxford University Press

— (2004) *Electronic and Computer Music*. Oxford: Oxford University Press

Martin, K. D., Scheirer, E. D. and Vercoe, B. L. (1998) 'Music Content Analysis through Models of Audition', in *ACM Workshop on Content Processing of Media for Multimedia Applications*, Bristol

Mathews, M. V. (1963) 'The Digital Computer as a Musical Instrument', *Science* 142(11): 553–7

— (1969) *The Technology of Computer Music*. Cambridge, MA: MIT Press

— (1991) 'The Radio Baton and the Conductor Program, or: Pitch, the Most Important and Least Expressive Part of Music', *Computer Music Journal* 15(4): 37–46

— Miller, J. E., Moore, F. R., Pierce, J. R. and Risset, J. C. (1969) *The Technology of Computer Music.* Cambridge, MA: MIT Press

Maur, K. von (1999) *The Sound of Painting: Music in Modern Art.* Munich: Prestel

McAdams, S. and Bigand, E. (1993) *Thinking in Sound: The Cognitive Psychology of Human Audition.* Oxford: Clarendon Press

McAdams, S., Winsberg, S., Donnadieu, S., De Soete, G. and Krimphoff, J. (1995) 'Perceptual Scaling of Synthesized Musical Timbres: Common Dimensions, Specificities, and Latent Subject Classes', *Psychological Research* 58: 177–92

McCartney, J. (2002) 'Rethinking the Computer Music Language: SuperCollider', *Computer Music Journal* 26(4): 61–8

McCartney, S. (1999) *Eniac.* New York: Walker Publishing Company

McLean, A. (2004) 'Hacking Perl in Nightclubs', at http://www.perl.com/pub/a/2004/08/31/livecode.html

Meyer-Eppler, W. (1955) 'Statistische und Psychologische Klangprobleme', in Eimert, H. (ed.), *die reihe* 1, Vienna: Universal Edition, pp. 22–9

Moles, A. A. (1984) *Kunst und Computer.* Ostfildern: DuMont Verlag

Moore, B. C. J. (1997) *An Introduction to the Psychology of Hearing.* New York: Academic Press

Moorer, J. A. (1979) 'The Use of Linear Prediction of Speech in Computer Music Applications', *Journal of the Audio Engineering Society* 27(3): 134–40

Moritz, W. (1997) 'The Dream of Color Music, and Machines that Made It Possible', *Animation World Magazine* 2(1). Available from http://www.centerforvisualmusic.org/Library.html

— (2004) *Optical Poetry: The Life and Work of Oskar Fischinger.* Bloomington: Indiana University Press

— (2004b) 'Oskar Fischinger Biography', at the William Moritz Archive, at http://www.iotacenter.org/program/publication/moritz/moritz32

Mumma, G. (1975) 'Live-Electronic Music', in Appleton, J. and Perera, R. (eds.), *The Development of Electronic Music.* Englewood Cliffs: Prentice Hall, pp. 286–335

Nakamura, K. (2006) 'Fieldnotes: Edirol R-09 Digital Recorder', at http://www.photoethnography.com/blog/archives/2006/06/fieldnotes_edir.html

Nexus6, Y. (1998) 'The Alternative Scene or Japanese Kotatsutop Computer Music', *Sound Arts* 11 (XEBEC SoundCulture Membership Magazine)

Nicholls, D. (2002) 'Cage and America', in Nicholls, D. (ed.), *The Cambridge Companion to John Cage.* Cambridge: Cambridge University Press

O'Brien, C. (2004) *Cinema's Conversion to Sound: Technology and Film Style in France and the U.S.* Bloomington: Indiana University Press

Oliveros, P. (1984) 'Tape Delay Techniques for Electronic Music Composition' (1969), in *Software For People.* Baltimore, MD: Smith Publications

Ostertag, B. (2001) 'Why Computer Music Sucks', *Resonance Magazine* 5(1)

Osthoff, S. (2005) 'From Mail Art to Telepresence: Communication at a Distance in the Works of Paulo Bruscky and Eduardo Kaç', in Chandler and Neumark, pp. 260–81

Pachet, F. (2003) 'The Continuator: Musical Interaction with Style', *Journal of New Music Research* 32(3): 333–41

Palmer, C. and Krumhansl, C. L. (1990) 'Mental Representations for Musical Meter', *Journal of Experimental Psychology: Human Perception and Performance* 16: 728–41

Paradiso, J. A. (1997) 'Electronic Music: New Ways to Play', *IEEE Spectrum* 34(12): 18–30

Parncutt, R. (1994) 'A Perceptual Model of Pulse Salience and Metrical Accent in Musical Rhythms', *Music Perception* 11: 409–64

Patten, J., Recht, B. and Ishii, H. (2006) 'Interaction Techniques for Musical Performance with Tabletop Tangible Interfaces', in *ACE 2006 Advances in Computer Entertainment*, Hollywood, CA

Peacock, K. (1988) 'Instruments to Perform Color-music: Two Centuries of Technological Experimentation', *Leonardo* 21(4): 397–406

Pearce, M., Meredith, D. and Wiggins, G. (2002) 'Motivations and Methodologies for Automation of the Compositional Process', *Musicae Scientiae* 6(2): 119–47

Peirce, C. S. (1894) 'What is a Sign?', in Peirce, C. S. (1931–58), *Collected Papers of Charles Sanders Peirce*. Cambridge, MA: Harvard University Press

Perec, G. and Klippert, W. (1972) *Die Maschine. Hörspiel*. Stuttgart: Reclam

Pickles, J. O. (1988) *An Introduction to the Physiology of Hearing*. London: Academic

Plomp, R. and Levelt, W. J. M. (1965) 'Tonal Consonance and Critical Bandwidth', *Journal of the Acoustical Society of America* 38: 548–60

Polansky, L. (2006) 'Panel on Electronic and Computer Music beyond Europe and North America', *International Computer Music Conference Program*, Tulane: Tulane University

Poole, J. (2003) '242.PILOTS', *Blog de JeanPoole: Some Words ++*, at http://www.octapod.org:8000/jeanpoole//archives/000428.html

Poole, S. (2000) *Trigger Happy: The Inner Life of Videogames*. London: Fourth Estate Limited

Pope, S. T. (1993) 'Machine Tongues XV: Three Packages for Software Sound Synthesis', *Computer Music Journal* 17(2): 25–54

Posner, M., Nissen, M. and Klein, R. (1976) 'Visual Dominance: an Information-processing Account of its Origins and Significance', *Psychological Review* 83(2): 157–71

Pressing, J. (1990) 'Cybernetic Issues in Interactive Performance Systems', *Computer Music Journal* 14(1): 12–25

Prieberg, F. K. (1960) *Musica ex machina: Über das Verhältnis von Musik und Technik*. Berlin: Ullstein, pp. 113–17

Pritchett, J. (1993) *The Music of John Cage*. Cambridge: Cambridge University Press

— (1996) '"Something Like a Hidden Glimmering": John Cage and Recorded Sound', *Contemporary Music Review* 15(1): 103–8

Puckette, M. (1991) 'Combining Event and Signal Processing in the MAX Graphical Programming Environment', *Computer Music Journal* 15(3): 68–77

— (1996) 'Pure Data', in *Proceedings of the International Computer Music Conference*. San Francisco, CA: International Computer Music Association, pp. 269–72

— (2002) 'Max at 17', *Computer Music Journal* 26(4): 31–43

— and Settel, Z. (1993) 'Non-obvious Roles for Electronics in Performance Enhancement', in *Proceedings of the 1993 International Computer Music Conference*. San Francisco, CA: International Computer Music Association, pp. 134–7

Rafaeli, S. (1988) 'Interactivity: from New Media to Communication', in Hawkins, R. P., Wieman, J. M. and Pingree, S. (eds.), *Advancing Communication Science: Merging Mass and Interpersonal Processes*. Newbury Park, CA: Sage, pp. 110–34

Ramachandran, V. S. and Hubbard, E. M. (2001) 'Synaesthesia – a Window into Perception, Thought and Language', *Journal of Consciousness Studies* 8: 3–34

Raphael, C. (2001) 'Synthesizing Musical Accompaniments with Bayesian Belief Networks', *Journal of New Music Research* 30(1): 59–67

Rich, R. (1991) 'Buchla Lightning MIDI Controller', *Electronic Musician* 7(10): 102–8

Risset, J. C. (1969) *An Introductory Catalogue of Computer Synthesised Sounds* (with sound examples on disc). Murray Hill, NJ: Bell Laboratories

— (1996) 'Real-world Sounds and Simulacra in My Computer Music', *Contemporary Music Review* 15(1): 29–47

— (2005) 'Horacia Vaggione: Towards a Syntax of Sound', *Contemporary Music Review* 24(4): 287–93

Roads, C. (1978) 'Granular Synthesis of Sound', *Computer Music Journal* 2(2): 61–2

— (1985) 'Research in Music and Artificial Intelligence', *Computing Surveys* 17(2): 163–90

— (1996) *The Computer Music Tutorial*. Cambridge, MA: MIT Press

— (2001) *Microsound*. Cambridge, MA: MIT Press

— (2005) 'The Art of Articulation: the Electroacoustic Music of Horacio Vaggione', *Contemporary Music Review* 24(4): 295–309

Rohrhuber, J. (2007) 'Artificial, Natural, Historical', in Deutsch, S., Power, D. and Sider, L. (eds.) *The Soundtrack*, vol. I. Bristol: Intellect Books

— and De Campo, A. (2004) 'Waiting and Uncertainty in Computer Music Networks', in *Proceedings of the 2004 International Computer Music Conference*, Miami

— De Campo, A. and Wieser, R. (2005) 'Algorithms Today – Notes on Language Design for Just in Time Programming', in *Proceedings of the 2005 International Computer Music Conference*, Barcelona

Rowe, R. (1993) *Interactive Music Systems*. Cambridge, MA: MIT Press

— (2001) 'The Aesthetics of Interactive Music Systems', *Contemporary Music Review* 18(3): 83–8

— (2001) *Machine Musicianship*. Cambridge, MA: MIT Press

Rudi, J. (2005) 'From a Musical Point of View, the World is Musical at Any Given Moment: an Interview with Bill Fontana', *Organised Sound* 10(2): 97–101

Russcol, H. (1972) *The Liberation of Sound: An Introduction to Electronic Music*. Saddle River, NJ: Prentice Hall

Ryan, J. (1991) 'Some Remarks on Musical Instrument Design at STEIM', *Contemporary Music Review* 6(1): 3–17

Salzman, E. (1974) *Twentieth-Century Music: An Introduction*. London: Prentice-Hall

Schaeffer, P. (1998) *L'Oeuvre Musicale.* New York: Electronic Music Foundation (liner notes)

Scheirer, E. D. (1996) 'Bregman's Chimerae: Music Perception as Auditory Scene Analysis', in *Proceedings of the International Conference on Music Perception and Cognition*, Montreal

Schillinger, J. (1946) *The Schillinger System of Musical Composition.* New York: Carl Fischer

— (1948) *The Mathematical Basis of the Arts.* New York: Philosophical Library

Schonfeld, V. (1972) 'From Piano to Electronics', *Music and Musicians* 20 (August)

Schwarz, D. (2004) 'Data-driven Concatenative Sound Synthesis'. Ph.D. thesis, Université Paris 6, http://recherche.ircam.fr/equipes/analyse-synthese/schwarz/

Seebeck, A. (1843) 'Über die Definition des Tones', *Annals of Physical Chemistry* 60: 449–81

Serra, X. (1989) 'A System for Sound Analysis/Transformation/Synthesis Based on a Deterministic Plus Stochastic Decomposition'. Ph.D. thesis, Department of Music, Stanford University

Sethares, W. A. (1994) 'Adaptive Tunings for Musical Scales', *Journal of the Acoustical Society of America* 96(1): 10–18

— (1999) *Tuning, Timbre, Spectrum, Scale.* London: Springer-Verlag. 2nd edn 2005

Shannon, C. E. (1948) 'A Mathematical Theory of Communication', *The Bell System Technical Journal* 27: 379–423

Shapiro, P. (2002) 'Deck Wreckers, the Turntable as Instrument', in R. Young (ed.), *Undercurrents, the Hidden Wiring of Modern Music.* London: The Wire – Continuum, pp. 163–76

Shimazu, T. (1994) 'The History of Electronic and Computer Music in Japan: Significant Composers and Their Works', *Leonardo Music Journal* 4: 102–6

Simner, J., Mulvenna, C., Sagiv, N., Tsankanikos, E., Witherby, S. A., Fraser, C., Scott, K. and Ward, J. (2006) 'Synaesthesia: the Prevalence of Atypical Cross-modal Experiences', *Perception* 35: 1024–33

Smalley, D. (1986) 'Spectro-morphology and Structuring Processes', in Emmerson, S. (ed.), *The Language of Electroacoustic Music.* London: Macmillan

— (1992) 'The Listening Imagination: Listening in the Electroacoustic Era', in Paynter, J. *et al.* (eds.), *Companion to Contemporary Musical Thought*, vol. I. London: Routledge

— (1997) 'Spectromorphology: Explaining Sound-shapes', *Organised Sound* 2(2): 107–26

Smith, J. O. (1991) 'Viewpoints on the History of Digital Synthesis', in *Proceedings of the 1991 International Computer Music Conference*, San Francisco: International Computer Music Association

Snyder, B. (2000) *Music and Memory.* Cambridge, MA: MIT Press

Solis, J., Chida, K., Taniguchi, K., Hashimoto, S. M., Suefuji, K. and Takanishi, A. (2006) 'The Waseda Flutist Robot', *Computer Music Journal* 30(4): 12–27

Spiegel, L. (1987) 'A Short History of Intelligent Instruments', *Computer Music Journal* 11(3): 7–9

— (1992) 'An Alternative to a Standard Taxonomy for Electronic and Computer
   Instruments', *Computer Music Journal* 16(3)

— (1998) 'Graphical GROOVE: Memorial for the VAMPIRE, a Visual Music
   System', *Organised Sound* 3(3): 187–91

— (2000) 'Music as Mirror of Mind', *Organised Sound* 4(3): 151–2

Spinrad, P. (2005) *The VJ Book*. Los Angeles: Feral House

Stein, B. E. and Meredith, M. A. (1993) *The Merging of the Senses*. Cambridge, MA:
   MIT Press

Steiner, H. C. (2005) '[hid] toolkit: a Unified Framework for Instrument Design', in
   International Conference on New Interfaces for Musical Expression (NIME05),
   Vancouver, BC, Canada, pp. 140–3

Stern, J. (2003) *The Audible Past*. Durham: Duke University Press

Stockhausen, K. (1957) '. . . wie die Zeit vergeht . . .', in Eimert (ed.), *die reihe* 3,
   pp. 13–42

— (2004) 'Electronic and Instrumental Music', in Cox and Warner

Strandh, S. (1979) *The History of the Machine*. New York: Dorset Press

Tanaka, A. (2000) 'Musical Performance Practice on Sensor-based Instruments', in
   Wanderley, M. and Battier, M. (eds.), *Trends in Gestural Control of Music*. Paris:
   IRCAM – Centre Pompidou

Taylor, T. (2001) *Strange Sounds*. London: Routledge

Terhardt, E., Stoll, G. and Seewann, M. (1982) 'Algorithm for Extraction of Pitch
   and Pitch Salience for Complex Tonal Signals', *Journal of the Acoustical Society of
   America* 71: 679–88

Theremin, L. S. (1996) 'The Design of a Musical Instrument Based on Cathode
   Relays', reprinted in *Leonardo Music Journal* 6: 49–50

Thom, B. (2003) 'Interactive Improvisational Music Companionship: a
   User-modeling Approach', *User Modeling and User-Adapted Interaction Journal*
   13(1–2): 133–77

Tobenfeld, E. (1992) 'A System for Computer Assisted Gestural Improvisation', in
   Proceedings of the 1992 International Computer Music Conference. San Francisco
   CA: International Computer Music Association, pp. 93–6

Toiviainen, P. (1998) 'An Interactive MIDI Accompanist', *Computer Music Journal*
   22(4): 63–75

— (2000) 'Symbolic AI versus Connectionism in Music Research', in Miranda, E.
   (ed.), *Readings in Music and Artificial Intelligence*. Amsterdam: Harwood
   Academic Publishers, pp. 47–68

Toop, D. (2004) 'The Generation Game: Experimental Music and Digital Culture',
   in Cox and Warner

Traub, P. (2005) 'Sounding the Net: Recent Sonic Works for the Internet and
   Computer Networks', *Contemporary Music Review* 24: 459–81

Truax, B. (1992) 'Electroacoustic Music and the Soundscape: the Inner and Outer
   World', in Paynter, J. *et al.* (eds.), *Companion to Contemporary Musical Thought*,
   vol. I. London: Routledge

— (2002) 'Genres and Techniques of Soundscape Composition as Developed at
   Simon Fraser University', *Organised Sound* 7(1): 5–14

Trueman, D. (2006) 'My Violin, My Laptop, Myself', *Chamber Music Magazine* (October 2006): 117–21

— and Cook, P. (1999) 'BoSSA: the Deconstructed Violin Reconstructed', in *Proceedings of the 1999 International Computer Music Conference*. San Francisco CA: International Computer Music Association

Turner, T. (2003) 'The Resonance of the Cubicle: Laptop Performance in Post-digital Musics', *Contemporary Music Review* 22(4): 81–92

Ullmer, B. and Ishii, H. (2001) 'Emerging Frameworks for Tangible User Interfaces', in Carnoll, J. M. (ed.), *Human Computer Interaction in the New Millenium*. Reading, MA: Addison-Wesley, pp. 579–601

Vaggione, H. (2001) 'Composing Musical Spaces by Means of Decorrelation of Audio Signals', *Addendum of the COST G-6 Conference on Digital Audio Effects*

Van Noorden, L. P. A. S. (1977) 'Minimum Differences of Level and Frequency for Perceptual Fission of Tone Sequences ABAB', *Journal of the Acoustical Society of America* 61: 1041–5

— and Moelants, D. (1999) 'Resonance in the Perception of Musical Pulse', *Journal of New Music Research* 28: 43–66

Varèse, E. (1971) 'The Liberation of Sound', in Boretz, B. and Cone, E. (eds.), *Perspectives on American Composers*. New York: Norton

von Békésy, G. (1963) 'Hearing Theories and Complex Sounds', *Journal of the Acoustical Society of America* 35(4): 588–601

von Ehrenfels, C. (1890) 'Über Gestaltqualitäten', *Vierteljahresschrift Wiss. Philos.* 14: 249–92

Walker, W., Hebel, K., Martirano, S. and Scarletti, C. (1992) 'Improvisation Builder: Improvisation as Conversation', in *Proceedings of the 1992 International Computer Music Conference*. San Francisco, CA: International Computer Music Association, pp. 190–3

Wanderley, M. M. (2001) 'Performer-Instrument Interaction: Applications to Gestural Control of Music'. Ph.D thesis. Paris: University Pierre et Marie Curie – Paris VI

Wang, G. and Cook, P. R. (2003) 'ChucK: a Concurrent, On-the-fly, Audio Programming Language', *Proceedings of the International Computer Music Conference*

Weibel, P. (2005) 'Die algorithmische Revolution. Zur Geschichte der interaktiven Kunst', in Weibel (ed.), *Die Algorithmische Revolution*. Karlsruhe: ZKM

Weinberg, G. (2003) 'Interconnected Musical Networks – Bringing Expression and Thoughtfulness to Collaborative Group Playing'. Ph.D. thesis, MIT, at http://www.media.mit.edu/hyperins/gil_weinberg_phdthesis.pdf

— and Driscoll, S. (2006) 'Towards Robotic Musicianship', *Computer Music Journal* 30(4): 28–45

— and Driscoll, S. (2006b) 'Robot–human Interaction with an Anthropomorphic Percussionist', in *Proceedings of The ACM Computer Human Interaction (CHI) Conference*

Welch, R. B. and Warren, D. H. (1986) 'Intersensory Interaction', in Boff, K. R.,
    Kaufman, L. and Thomas, J. P. (eds.), *Handbook of Perception and Human
    Performance*, vol. I, *Sensory Processes and Perception*. New York: John Wiley and
    Sons, pp. 25–36

Wertheimer, M. (1923) *Laws of Organization in Perceptual Forms*. [First published
    as *Untersuchungen zur Lehre von der Gestalt II*, in *Psychologische Forschung*, 4:
    301–50. Translation published in: Ellis, W. (1938), *A Source Book of Gestalt
    Psychology*. London: Routledge & Kegan Paul, pp. 71–88.] Available at
    http://psy.ed.asu.edu/%7Eclassics/Wertheimer/Forms/forms.htm

Wessel, D. and Wright, M. (2002) 'Problems and Prospects for Intimate Musical
    Control of Computers', *Computer Music Journal* 26(3): 11–22

Westerkamp, H. (2002) 'Linking Soundscape Composition and Acoustic Ecology',
    Organised Sound 7(1): 51–6

Wierzbicki, J. (2005) *Louis and Bebe Barron's Forbidden Planet, a Film Score Guide*.
    Lanham, MD: The Scarecrow Press, Inc

Wieser, R. and Rohrhuber, J. (2006) *The Invisible Hand*. Readme 100. Temporary
    Software Art Factory. Norderstedt: BoD

Wishart, T. (1986) 'Sound Symbols and Landscapes', in Emmerson, S. (ed.), *The
    Language of Electroacoustic Music*. London: Macmillan

— (1996) *On Sonic Art*. London: Routledge

Wooller, R., Brown, A., Diederich, J., Miranda, E. R. and Berry, R. (2005) 'A
    Framework for Comparison of Process in Algorithmic Music Systems',
    Proceedings of the Generative Arts Practice – A Creativity & Cognition Symposium,
    Sydney

Wright, M. and Freed, A. (1997) 'Open Sound Control: a New Protocol for
    Communicating with Sound Synthesizers', in *Proceedings of the 1997
    International Computer Music Conference*, at
    http://cnmat.cnmat.berkeley.edu/ICMC97/papers-
    html/OpenSoundControl.html

Xenakis, I. (1955) 'La crise de la musique sérielle', *Gravesano review* 1 (in: *Kéleütha.
    Ecrits*, L'Arche, Paris, 1994, pp. 40–2) – unpublished in English

— (1961) 'La musique stochastique: éléments sur les procédés probabilistes de
    composition musicale', *Revue d'Esthétique* 14 (4–5): 294–318 (English
    translation: *Formalized Music*, pp. 1–42)

— (1965) 'Freie stochastische Musik durch den Elektronenrechner', *Gravesano
    Review* 26 (English translation: *Formalized Music*, pp. 131–54)

— (1971) *Formalized Music*. Bloomington and London: Indiana University Press

— (1992) *Formalized Music: Thought and Mathematics in Music* (rev. edn).
    Stuyvesant, New York: Pendragon Press

Yavelow, C. (1986) 'MIDI and the Apple Macintosh', *Computer Music Journal* 10(3):
    11–47

Young, G. (1989) *The Sackbut Blues: Hugh Le Caine, Pioneer in Electronic Music*.
    Ottawa: National Museum of Science and Technology

Zahorik, P. (2002) 'Direct-to-reverberant Energy Ratio Sensitivity', *Journal of the
    Acoustical Society of America* 112(5): 2110–7

Zatorre, R. J. (2003) 'Neural Specializations for Tonal Processing', in Peretz, I. and
Zatorre, R. J. (eds.), *The Cognitive Neuroscience of Music*. New York: Oxford
University Press

Zicarelli, D. (1987) 'M and Jam Factory', *Computer Music Journal* 11(4): 13–29

Zwislocki, J. (1978) 'Masking: Experiments and Theoretical Aspects of
Simultaneous, Forward, Backward, and Central Masking', in Carterette, E. and
Friedman, M. (eds.), *Handbook of Perception*. New York: Academic Press,
pp. 283–336

Index

Cambridge Companions to Music

Topics

The Cambridge Companion to Ballet
Edited by Marion Kant

The Cambridge Companion to Blues and Gospel Music
Edited by Allan Moore

The Cambridge Companion to the Concerto
Edited by Simon P. Keefe

The Cambridge Companion to Conducting
Edited by José Antonio Bowen

The Cambridge Companion to Electronic Music
Edited by Nick Collins and Julio d'Escriván

The Cambridge Companion to Grand Opera
Edited by David Charlton

The Cambridge Companion to Jazz
Edited by Mervyn Cooke and David Horn

The Cambridge Companion to the Lied
Edited by James Parsons

The Cambridge Companion to the Musical
Edited by William Everett and Paul Laird

The Cambridge Companion to the Orchestra
Edited by Colin Lawson

The Cambridge Companion to Pop and Rock
Edited by Simon Frith, Will Straw and John Street

The Cambridge Companion to the String Quartet
Edited by Robin Stowell

The Cambridge Companion to Twentieth-Century Opera
Edited by Mervyn Cooke

Composers

The Cambridge Companion to Bach
Edited by John Butt

The Cambridge Companion to Bartók
Edited by Amanda Bayley

The Cambridge Companion to Beethoven
Edited by Glenn Stanley

The Cambridge Companion to Berg
Edited by Anthony Pople

The Cambridge Companion to Berlioz
Edited by Peter Bloom

The Cambridge Companion to Brahms
Edited by Michael Musgrave